India and Ceylon: Unity and Diversity

A SYMPOSIUM

edited by

PHILIP MASON

DIRECTOR
INSTITUTE OF RACE RELATIONS
LONDON

Published for the Institute of Race Relations

OXFORD UNIVERSITY PRESS

LONDON   NEW YORK   BOMBAY

1967

Oxford University Press, Ely House, London W. 1

GLASGOW NEW YORK TORONTO MELBOURNE WELLINGTON
CAPE TOWN SALISBURY IBADAN NAIROBI LUSAKA ADDIS ABABA
BOMBAY CALCUTTA MADRAS KARACHI LAHORE DACCA
KUALA LUMPUR HONG KONG TOKYO

Library of Congress Card Catalogue Number: 67-29174

Manufactured in the United States of America

Contents

87071

List of Maps and Tables

Note on maps

The maps in this volume are intended to remind the reader of the main political divisions in the Indian Union as they are now, and to show the approximate distribution of the linguistic families. The distribution of ex-untouchables is also shown. The main tribal areas can be seen in the linguistic map by the concentration of aboriginal languages and the Tibet/Mongolian languages. The smaller groups of tribes in the south referred to by Professor von Fürer-Haimendorf cannot be shown on a map of this size.

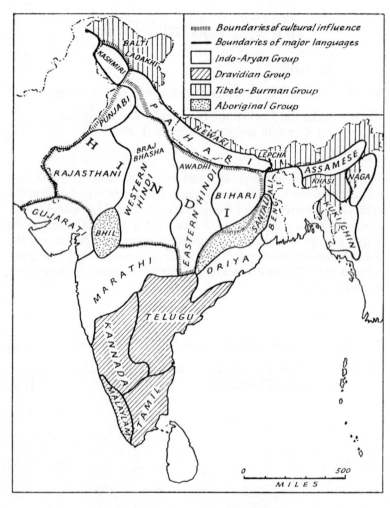

Map I: India and Ceylon, showing chief linguistic divisions

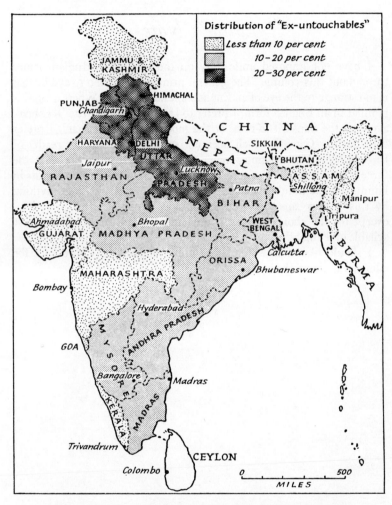

Map II: India and Ceylon, showing chief political divisions, together with density of ex-untouchables

Editor's Note

I have not imposed uniformity on the spelling of Indian names throughout this volume. The general principle has been to avoid what is too strange to the eye of an English-speaking reader. Where a word is familiar in an English form, I prefer to keep it. Thus I write 'Krishna', avoiding the Sanskrit 'Krsna' or the modern Hindi 'Kishan'. I prefer 'Chamar' to 'Camar', which does not represent sound to a reader of English. On this principle, many phonetic exactitudes are lost; the three consonants 't', 'd', and 'r' have to represent twelve consonants in Hindi. But the number of English-speaking readers who lose anything by this is very small. Vowels are usually pronounced as in Italian, except for the short 'a' (like 'u' in butter) which occurs in the first syllable of 'Panjab'.

I should like to take this opportunity of thanking Claire Pace for editorial work on these essays.

Philip Mason

I

Unity and Diversity: An Introductory Review

BY PHILIP MASON

Director, Institute of Race Relations, London

I: THE INTENTION OF THE SERIES

THIS book is part of a larger project which originated many years ago in the simple thought that it might be useful to compare the relations that have grown up in different parts of the world between different ethnic groups inhabiting the same state. It might—so the thought ran—be possible to analyse a number of widely different situations, to detect common factors in situations which resembled each other, and, among other things, perhaps to throw some light on the causes of the extreme rigidity of some attitudes in, say, South Africa and their greater flexibility in other areas such as Brazil, the Caribbean, and Spanish-speaking America.

To carry out this idea it was clearly necessary to initiate a number of studies, each of which would have as its primary object an analysis of one situation, or perhaps one group of similar situations, but each of which would constantly bear this wider comparison in mind. It is due to the generosity of the Ford Foundation that this has been possible and to the suggestion of officers of the Foundation that the Indian sub-continent and South-East Asia are included in this project as well as Latin America and the Caribbean. The first study on South-East Asia, by Guy Hunter, has already appeared.

In India, the problem was clearly very different from anything in South Africa and it might indeed be argued that it was inappropriate to regard diversities in the population of India as 'racial'. But it is one important hypothesis underlying these studies that there is a set of human relationships in which a sense of difference and a lack of communication are the dominant factors, and that the presence of a racial or biological distinction may sharpen, but does not fundamentally alter, the nature of the relationship. From this point of view, it was useful to include in the project a country in which the tensions have in the past usually been supposed to be primarily religious or social rather than racial.

It is true that, of the many diversities within India's vast population, several may be regarded as ethnic and some have a racial element. They are thought of as being connected with ancestry, but they are much more often spoken of in terms of function and social organization; the racial undertones, though they are there, are usually implied or subconscious. This in itself is interesting. Why? Again—differing from Africa or South America—these diversities are not the result of European exploitation. This is a country which was subject to a colonial power for longer than any of the new African states, but the share taken in the whole system of government by the colonized people was far higher; further, the cut with the former colonial power has been cleaner than was possible in the case of most African states, because the number of resident English was negligible. The relationship of Indians and Europeans is therefore marginal to an inquiry concerned with India today. In every way, then, India made a valuable addition to the series. Pakistan and Ceylon provide useful contrasts.

Two books on India have resulted from this project. They are of very different natures. Guy Wint, from his long experience of both China and India and after a visit made as part of this project, has written a wide-ranging but personal review of the problems of India and Pakistan as he sees them. The present book—*Unity and Diversity*—is a series of essays by leading scholars, each of whom considers one aspect of India's unity, together with one essay on Ceylon. The two books differ, not only because one is the product of one mind and the other of several—though with a surprisingly wide range of general agreement between them—but also because they take very different views of the future of the Indian Union. The group view, with which I am myself in sympathy, is in general optimistic; Guy Wint is much less hopeful.

The book is not a symposium in the literal sense. The writers have not met for general discussion nor even seen each other's work. But the questions they were asked were designed so that the replies should form a whole and I believe they do. I am particularly indebted for help in framing the questions to Professors Tinker, Morris-Jones, and Mayer.

II: THE FIVE AREAS OF DIVERSITY

Such a book as this calls for a review, for some endeavour to state the conclusions towards which the different authors point, and to indicate any degree of consensus that can be detected between them. It is a daunting task. It is in the first place not even easy to decide which essay to print first. Professor Srinivas' essay on Sanskritization is in a sense the key to the whole, because the concept runs through every discussion of caste or religion. Caste—both the links between caste-fellows and the revolt against Brahman dominance—plays its part in the region-alism of the South, in the struggle for linguistic states. Caste and its influence on politics is inseparable from discussion of the tribes, the untouchables, the influence of the educated. Caste is the centre—the most all-pervading, though not in my view the most important, factor in the whole situation. But should one begin at the centre? My instinct is to begin at the periphery and disentangle, so far as one can, some of the simpler problems. But there *is* nothing simple in so vast and complex a society as India's.

The questions asked of the contributors were about the unity and the diversity of India, but did not specify what was meant by 'India'. Are we thinking of Indian society or of the political framework of the Indian Union? Ultimately of both, but the distinction is, I think, important and it is clear that some of the discussion in the essays is concerned with Indian society and not with its embodiment in a single state. The distinction has to be asserted and as far as may be reconciled, but the subject of the book as a whole is not prophecy about the political future of the Indian Union. It is the diversities of Indian society, particularly those that resemble the cleavages associated with race, and how far they are likely to affect political stability and unity. My plan for this essay is to look in turn at the five main areas of diversity and then to consider how far they concern society and how far the State. The question of how far these diversities resemble those of race will be discussed in another book which will attempt to sum up the whole discussion.

Of the five main areas of diversity which may be dangerous for the Indian Union, the easiest to disentangle is religion. It has also played the most important part in the past, so that it may well spring to mind as the most threatening. Even after the split from Pakistan, there were still 50 million Muslims in India. It is with this, therefore, that we begin.

The second diversity, and the most immediately threatening, lies in language and region. Language constitutes a problem which in scale and intensity is unique to India; there are more than fifteen hundred languages spoken within the Union, of which fourteen may be called major languages, and there is no one language spoken by a majority of citizens; further, the main linguistic group in the North belongs to the Indo-European family, but the main Southern group to a quite different family, so that the whole construction of the forms in which thought is expressed is different in the South. With language go diversities in food, in custom, in dress—all that we usually mean by culture.

The third and fourth dangers are closely linked. There are tribal populations numbering about 30 million, of whom some are outside the money economy and all are outside Hinduism. And there is the most obvious manifestation of caste in the existence of 60 million ex-untouchables, the Harijans, whose separate status has been legally abolished, but who—like the American Negroes—are still cut off from their fellows, not only by prejudice but by centuries of poverty and ignorance. But caste is a divisive and all-pervasive influence in society, even for those who are not Harijans. It is also an influence in politics.

Finally, the fifth great element of disunity common to all developing countries is the division between the mass of the people and the educated middle-class leaders; this is far more sharp than in developed countries, not only because of poverty but because the middle classes are educated in the thought of an alien culture.

Clearly religion and education, the first and fifth of these causes of division and misunderstanding, have nothing to do with physical differences such as skin colour or hair formation. Both, however, result in manifestations which are sometimes startlingly similar to those produced by racial separation in South Africa—myths about what the other group do and desire, prejudices assumed to apply to every member of the group. But this is not the place for discussing this part of the subject. It is equally clear that language, caste, and tribalism are linked in people's minds with descent and with a whole set of quasi-racial beliefs. Popular mythology starts with an invasion of India by a race superior in every way—as companions of the gods, warriors, poets, and priests— who were distinguished by being taller and lighter-skinned than the dark, squat, primitives who were there before them. The descendants of the Aryans are supposed to be found in the higher castes and in the North; the descendants of the primitive aboriginals are, according to the mythology, more frequent in the South, in the lower castes, and in the tribes. It is a typical racial myth, oversimplified, overgeneralized, and ignoring inconvenient stretches of history such as the Indus and

Dravidian civilizations. In a more sophisticated form, it is the backbone of Nirad Chaudhuri's *The Continent of Circe*.

III: RELIGION: THE MUSLIMS

These then are the five great causes of anxiety—religion, linguistic region, the tribes, caste, the elites. On religion we need not spend long. Neither Parsis nor Christians are likely to keep the rulers of India awake at night; Buddhism is important only because it is the chosen escape-route of the former untouchables and will be discussed when we consider their case. The Sikhs have now obtained their own state and may be expected to be content with the part of a creative and energetic minority within the Union. Islam, by far the largest religious minority, remains, and is discussed in Dr. Spear's essay. It is the first stage of his argument that Islam in India has always contained two elements, the militant dogmatic Islam of the desert and a far more tolerant and indeed eclectic spirit which is peculiarly Indian.

This is a point that is worth stressing further because it throws light on caste, and on Hinduism as well as Islam. Akbar and Aurangzebe may stand as symbols of the two spirits—one militant and exclusive, the other tolerant and eclectic—but it was not only in government and among rulers that both are to be found. Persian sufism took a new shade of colour in India; poets and religious teachers—Ramanand and Kabir —tried to combine the best and condemn the worst in Hinduism and Islam alike. At the courts of Oudh and Hyderabad there grew up aesthetic standards in painting, in poetry, in love, and in food, which drew on the courtly traditions of Rajputana as well as Persia. Urdu poets used Hindi syntax as the cement in which they set Persian and Arabic phrases; the demotic language, Hindustani, drew on the classical languages, Persian, Arabic, and Sanskrit, and words derived from all three were used in almost every sentence by town-dwellers across the whole of the Gangetic plain. Muslims borrowed caste from Hindus; Hindus took purdah from Muslims, Sunnis and Hindus joined in celebrating the great festival at which Shi'as commemorate the deaths of Husain and Hasan at Karbala. But the fierce intolerant spirit never died; it triumphed—as Dr. Spear points out—with Aurangzebe's defeat of Dara Shikoh; in the fifty troubled years before Partition, it was fed by the fear of being defeated in the examination halls and at the ballot-box and flared with a steadily increasing intensity. It divided Indian Muslims into the conformists and the militants.

Partition presented a crisis to every Indian Muslim. For the educated, the rich, the mobile, the choice was clear-cut enough—India or

Pakistan? For the scattered peasants of the Eastern districts of Uttar
Pradesh or Bihar, it was not so easy; a long journey—through territory
which the traveller, by the very fact of moving, had himself declared
hostile—might well seem more dangerous than staying. And his assets—
hereditary rights as a tenant perhaps—were not easily realized. He had
little choice, and yet, by staying, he took an unconscious decision; he
had elected without knowing it to be conformist in a Hindu country.
Today he has even less opportunity for choice; the militants have gone,
the Muslims are too scattered for effective action. One strand only of
Islam in India remains—the conformist.

A momentary chance, however, may come for any minority; in his
study of Aligarh district, Paul Brass[1] has shown how overconfidence and
a split in the ranks of the Congress gave conservative Muslims the
opportunity to organize an improbable but victorious coalition with ex-
untouchables and disgruntled Congressmen. This kind of opening will
sometimes occur, but in general it is for individual opportunities of
advancement—not triumphs as an organized community—that Muslims
must hope. They are too weak to affect foreign policy; peace with
Pakistan is what they need—and know that they need—if they are to
survive. They are not a threat to the Indian Union in the sense that
they would side with a hostile power or even hope for secession. Their
existence is used as an excuse for not making peace, on the grounds that
a settlement over Kashmir would produce an attack on Muslims, but
this seems unlikely if the administration were determined that it should
not happen. They might, however, become—like the Harijans—a
threat, in the sense in which the Negro is a threat to the United States;
an underprivileged and discontented element is always an impediment
to health. For the Muslims, as for all the minorities, the question is
whether the Hindu majority can overcome its age-old clannishness
sufficiently to give them fair treatment.

IV: LANGUAGE, REGION, AND POLITICS

Linguistic and regional separatism constitutes a threat of quite a different kind. It is sometimes argued that regions may split off from the
Union and become separate sovereign states, or alternatively that
regional forces will be so strong as to paralyse the centre. In this volume,
Professor Morris-Jones deals specifically with language and region,
while Professors Tinker and Bottomore discuss the same problem from
slightly different angles. It is impossible to discuss this danger without

---

[1] P. Brass, *Factional Politics in an Indian State: The Congress Party in Uttar Pradesh*,
Berkerly, University of California Press, 1965.

also referring to the work of Selig Harrison[2] who, in a masterly survey, has dwelt on the dangers of separatism as even more formidable than what he calls caste lobbies.[3] It seems to me that, in his analysis of three elections in the delta area of what is now Andhra State, Harrison has proved without question that linguistic separatism has a strong emotional appeal, and that this can be translated into votes when it is backed by a party organization and the influence of a dominant landowning caste with a tradition of local influence. This was the recipe for the success of the Communists in the four delta districts of Andhra in 1951; their party organization was strong and made a separate Andhra State the first plank in their platform; they secured the backing of the overwhelming majority of the Kammas, a caste of landowners and rich peasants who dominate these four districts. But Professor Harrison has not, it seems to me, attached enough importance to the results of the election of 1955, when the new state was in being and there was much less demand for further separation. This time the Congress took fright and seriously addressed its whole resources to the delta; it was successful in exploiting differences among the Kammas. The Congress won sixty-three seats (twenty-four of their successful candidates being Kammas) against nine Communist seats of whom one was a Kamma. In 1951, the Communists had twenty-five seats (fourteen Kammas) to the Congress ten (three Kammas).[4]

Professor Harrison, of course, had not the advantage of seeing Paul Brass's study of factional politics in Uttar Pradesh. This suggests a pattern of democratic ebb and flow somewhat different from the alternation of two parties to which Anglo-Saxons are accustomed. The Congress leaders, being overwhelmingly strong in a district, become over-confident and are split by personal faction, whereupon other elements—such as the Muslims and Harijans in Aligarh—combine with Congress dissidents to defeat the main ranks of the Congress. But on this the Congress High Command intervenes and at the next election is usually able to recover lost ground by the immense weight of its organization and by adroit use of local circumstance, in which caste loyalties play a part. This is a situation which in varying forms recurs in Brass's analysis, and the fortunes of the Communists in the Andhra delta fall neatly into the same pattern.[5]

---

[2] S. S. Harrison, *India: The Most Dangerous Decades*, Princeton, N.J., Princeton University Press and Oxford University Press, 1960.

[3] Both Harrison's argument and Brass's are summarized by Professor Bottomore.

[4] Harrison, op. cit.

[5] If this implies too broad a generalization, the fault is mine; Brass is careful not to universalize what he has found.

Harrison of course recognizes that the appeal of separatism is greatly reduced once the linguistic state is achieved. None the less, he stresses the necessity for any ambitious politician of an appeal to parochial issues at the district and state level and argues that the central Government will always be weakened by the need to win seats on narrow grounds of local interest, often directly at variance with the party's policy at the centre. But this is surely in no way peculiar to India. It is not unknown even in the United States. And I call to mind an exceptionally clear statement of this widespread aspect of politics which occurs in a monograph about a tribe in Northern Nigeria.[6] Bohannan describes the difficulties of a leader among the Tiv who, having been acknowledged leader of one group, tries to add a second to his following. The first group resent anything he does for the second; the second expect him to favour the first. He must persuade the second that he is their leader as well, but it is fatal to lose his grip on the first, on which the whole structure depends. The principle is expressed in primitive terms, but to some extent is applicable to all political organizations and particularly to federations or semi-federal organizations. It emphasizes that need for flexibility and readiness to compromise, to balance different interests, which constitutes the grammar of political success, but it also surely implies the need for steadily widening horizons. And it seems to more than one observer that, in the last few years, Indian leaders have shown just these qualities. Kamraj Nadar came to power in Madras as the leader of a revolt against Brahman domination which, not surprisingly, was allied with particularist forces whose slogans was 'Tamilnad for the Tamils'; his electoral appeal was to forces which were repugnant to Nehru and the Central Government, who, as Harrison says 'looked the other way and hoped for the best'. Yet even before the death of Nehru he emerged as a unifying force and he has twice been the architect of a smooth change of power at the centre.

This suggests the hypothesis that two kinds of ebb and flow are to be expected. The first is represented by the sequence: (i) Congress

---

[6] P. Bohannan, *Justice and Judgment among the Tiv*, London, Oxford University Press for the International African Institute, 1957. Bohannan writes [X has been a leader of a group A as against B and aspires to lead group I (which includes A and B)]:

'Depending on his character and the frequency with which he has appeared as a leader of I, X may have considerable influence in B, even as opposed to A, but that influence is regarded with suspicion and jealousy by all members of B, who are convinced that X is bound to favour A at their expense. Equally, in affairs between A and B, A will regard as wholly unjustifiable any favouring of B at their expense. If, however, X loses influence in A by favouring B, he automatically ceases to be of importance in B, while to a certain extent X's position in I as a whole depends on how he treats B at other times. The effective juggling of these factors is the practical art of Tiv politics.'

dominance; (ii) Congress *hubris* and faction; (iii) a successful coalition of hostile elements; (iv) a Congress resurgence. The second moves—as among the Tiv—from (i) a stress on particular parochial interests, which enables a leader to establish his base in popular support, to (ii) a damping down of particularism as the leader moves on to the next stage of his career and seeks a wider support; (iii) in the next stage his younger, local successor is likely to invoke against him the forces he has relinquished. Perhaps he will have roused a genie too strong to be forced back into the bottle. But the risk is surely inseparable from a system of politics in which there are free elections by adult suffrage.

Professor Morris-Jones is far from underestimating the emotional importance of language, which he describes as 'more precisely discriminating than either colour or race'. He stresses the uniqueness of India's difficulties, but suggests that they must be 'lived with', not seen as 'problems to which solutions can be found'. And he finds evidence that this kind of attitude is spreading. It is sobering to consider alongside this guarded optimism the history of Ceylon. Dr. Arasaratnam describes the ten years immediately after Independence, during which a minority educated in the English language and Western modes of thought was successful in persuading the majority that 'communalism' was dirty politics and that nationalism should be secular and territorial, claiming the loyalty of all citizens of the State—which meant all resident in the island. But this was foreign to Asian tradition—to which the territorial nation is new and the language or kinship group familiar—and by the mid-1950s, the only kind of politics that could win at the polls was an appeal to the immediate advantages which a linguistic and religious majority of 70 per cent of the population could obtain at the expense of the rest. The worst force of this aggressive and intolerant nationalism may perhaps now have spent itself; the majority begins to be divided and once again faction may prove to be the opportunity of the minorities. But the reality of the danger for India is underlined. It is significant that this is just the kind of danger that Guy Hunter fears in South-East Asia.

V: CASTE, THE TRIBES, AND SANSKRITIZATION

Caste and the tribes must be dealt with together. Indeed, as this essay has already suggested, it is not easy to separate caste from any aspect of Indian life. It has not been possible to talk about politics without some discussion of caste; even to define the tribes involves mention of caste. They can most easily be described in negative terms, outside caste, in the sense that they are the people who have never been included in the unfinished, 3,000-year-old process of Sanskritization—not even in the sense in which the untouchables were included, at least by being formally excluded. Sanskritization is a process that seems to be without parallel in the world today; a culture spread by conquest, fed by a developing tradition of religious literature (as was Judaism), has not only persisted but continued to spread, surviving the tramplings of many conquests. It is still spreading, as Professor Srinivas points out; lower castes and some of those outside caste are adopting Sanskritic practices just as these begin to be abandoned by the higher castes, under the influence of modern education and 'Westernization'. Owing to the agglomerating undogmatic nature of Hinduism, it is a social rather than a religious process. The animist who becomes a Hindu need abandon little of his ideas about the soul or the infinite, just as those who abandon the ritual practices of Hinduism retain many of its habits of thought. But its effect on Harijans and on the tribes is not identical. While the Harijans were the servants of those who kept the traditions— were a part of the culture in much the same way as the Southern slave was a part of American culture—the tribes were outside it, much as the American Indians were. They were outside and ignored, except to be exploited or dispossessed; they were not 'kept in their place' on the assumption that they wanted to rise above it. Yet, over the centuries, at irregular intervals, erosion continued; here a group was driven back farther into the hills or the jungle, here the last speakers of an aboriginal tongue were surrounded by the Sanskritic culture, dispossessed of their land, and forced to become a caste, usually but not always at the bottom of the scale.

No one who reads the essays in this book can doubt the extreme complexity of Indian society; it cannot be explained in any lucid system in terms of a single principle or range of principles without simplification that distorts. But it can be simplified on one level provided one remembers there is another level beyond. The classical conception of caste as the four *varnas* or orders—priests; warrior-rulers; traders; peasants, artisans and servants who perform clean tasks—is a simplification of this kind. It is unreal, in the sense that there is no unity between, say, *Kshatriyas* or warriors from different parts of the continent, and because groups previously reckoned in the fourth grade as *sudras* are constantly thrusting their way upward and seeking and sometimes obtaining recognition, at least locally, in the higher orders, particularly the second. The reality lies in the thousands of endogamous groups known as *jatis*, which are theoretically subsumed under the *varna* headings. But there is no end here to the complexity, because within the *jati* marriage must be outside the *gotra* or clan and also, at least in Northern India, outside the village. The four orders or *varnas* exclude the Harijans or untouchables as well as the tribals.

On this system, which is seen to be complex even when stated in the most oversimplified terms, there are working a number of opposed forces. But it is almost always misleading to see these forces as sharply opposed; a dilemma of which one horn or the other must be accepted, an argument beginning 'Now of two things one . . .', are alien to Indian thought and institutions. It is better to think of opposed principles between which lies a spectrum of difference. Spatial metaphors are sometimes as misleading in describing society as they are in theology; the thought of an 'axis' between poles seems to me quite misleading. But it is clear that the two processes of Sanskritization and Westernization are both at work, that they are often opposed but sometimes in alliance, that here one prevails and here another, here there is revolt against one and here against the other.

Professor Srinivas' essay emphasizes the need for synthesis between the two principles, and indeed this has been a theme for fine minds from Raja Ram Mohan Roy to Gandhi; but the opposition between the two must not be forgotten. The brilliant scornful flippancy of Macaulay's minute on education is out of keeping with the intellectual climate of today, but it remains true that the two systems of thought involved different views of causation, and social customs that were mutually repulsive; that Europeans should kill and eat cows and use paper after defaecation were habits horrible to a Brahman, just as child-marriage and burning widows were to a Victorian Englishman.

Dennis Dalton has drawn attention to the acuteness of the conflict between cultures under the British and adds that by the time Mahatma Gandhi came of age 'the sense of purpose conceived to meet the cultural challenge of the West had to come to dominate Indian political and social thought . . .' As Professor Srinivas says, nationalism—a Western concept—was expressed in a Hindu idiom, trays of *arati* being waved before garlanded *satyagrahis*. But it is not merely an idiom; the conflict and synthesis between Sanskrit and Western concepts of social organization invade every aspect of life. Old relationships based on tradition and kinship give way to new, based on contract and competition; one group, traditionally despised, adopts child-marriage to prove how Sanskritized it is becoming, just as another, traditionally respected, repudiates it in the belief that mature parents will breed strong children, perhaps with some sense that it implies disrespect for the individual, more probably with a general feeling that it is 'not modern'. Modern communications spread both sets of ideas. Thus this first shifting and changing spectrum between Western and Sanskrit values cannot be isolated, but leads at once to others concerning individual and group relationships.

The second of these spectra—which result from looking at society from different angles, in different lights, and with different lenses—lies between two principles within the caste system. Professor Srinivas speaks of Hinduism as 'a loose confederation of innumerable cults, the connecting threads of which are found in Sanskritization' and of caste as 'a series of local systems of interacting *jatis* linked in an all-India framework by means of the idea of *varna*'. There are opposing forces within the idea and the system of caste, however it is looked at, because it is at the same time inclusive and exclusive, a system of mutual help and a way of keeping privileges for the group. But there is a more radical opposition than this, arising in part from the first spectrum.

To modern Western eyes, there is something basically unjust about caste, which restricts opportunity, occupation, choice in marriage, on the sole—and irrelevant—ground of birth. Yet at the root of Western political thought lies that long discussion of the meaning and nature of justice in which Plato concludes that justice lies in each person in a state minding his own business.[7] Indeed, the inquiry leads Plato to propose the deliberate invention of a caste-system, similar to the traditional Indian concept of *varna*, but with three classes only instead of four—rulers, warriors, and the mass of artisans and peasants; further, he would support this by a fiction, that there is gold in the composition of the rulers or guardians, silver in the warriors, copper and iron only in the common folk. And the city would perish when guarded by iron or copper.[8] What Plato called justice, or each man doing his proper duty in the State, is very similar to the *varnashramadharma* in which Gandhi (as Dennis Dalton tells us) continued till his life's end to preach belief, the main difference being that the latter is the virtue of doing one's duty not in the State but in society. This virtue of keeping due place and performing one's allotted function is the theme, too, of the *Bhagavad Gita*.

And surely for centuries it has been the basic assumption of every community of men, even the most primitive food-gatherers, that labour and functions must be divided and allotted to certain individuals and

[7] Plato, *The Republic*, Vol. IV, 433.
[8] Op. cit., Vol. III, 415.

classes. The task of politics has been to settle how the allocation should be done, but until the eighteenth century Europeans in general—in spite of occasional egalitarian revolts—were as confident as were Indians that this allotment by roles was just, though they might not, with Plato, regard it as the definition of justice. Even Plato would have permitted the occasional promotion of a child from the base to the precious metals; in medieval Europe an artisan's son might become a priest and rise to high place, and in Tudor England mobility was becoming much more common. In India the rigidity was more extreme, the theory more formulated, but the principle, until the Age of Reason and the proclamation of equality, was accepted both in India and in Europe. The change from a fixed hierarchical system to one of mobility and egalitarian theory came to India not over six hundred years, as in Europe, but in little more than half a century; it is not surprising that Gandhi had to go through the series of reformulations described by Dalton and that he continued to preach *varnashramadharma* while actively fighting the exclusiveness of the actual caste-groups, even arguing that it was a duty to go outside the *varnas* and marry a Harijan. His inconsistencies are due to his attempts to reconcile a basic conflict of principle in the social system; the caste system preserved a stable *society* (though seldom for long a stable *state*) for thousands of years, but between individuals it was by modern standards profoundly unjust.

This conflict within the basic idea of caste suggests that it cannot be compared with, say, child-marriage or purdah, institutions which find no educated defenders and seem unlikely to survive for long in a society in which secular education is widespread. Caste is out of date; no one will defend it, but it has, in fact, been socially useful for so long that the memory will persist. It will be whittled at and eroded; what is known in India as interdining will increase rapidly between castes on a similar level; even marriage between castes will become less infrequent, but surely for long it will still be rare. But this is not to say that caste will be the dominant influence in politics and national life that has sometimes been suggested. The overwhelming consensus of opinion among the writers in this book is that in politics caste will often play a part, but it will usually be one factor among many, and only rarely the decisive factor.

VI: CASTE, POLITICS, AND SOCIAL CHANGE

Brass relates the case of one constituency in Meerut district, in which the Jats actually outnumbered all other castes put together, being 60 per cent of the voters. It is, he says, the only case of its kind in Uttar

Pradesh. But in the election of 1962 a Jat candidate standing on the official Congress ticket lost to an independent Rajput candidate. This was because there were seven Jat candidates, so that the Jat vote was split, while the other castes united to vote for the one candidate who was not a Jat. It is true that in Meerut District, where the Jats are the largest community after the Chamars (who are landless labourers and Harijans) and the Muslims, the dominant figure when Brass wrote was a Jat Congressman. But he had to rely on alliance with a number of other castes—Tyagis, Gujars, Ahirs, agricultural castes who are neither Brahman, Rajput, nor Bania.[9] His strength lies, says Brass, 'in a certain egalitarianism'. In general in this district 'the success or failure of individual Congress candidates depends more upon the ability of the candidate to win support from a number of castes than on his ability to win support from his caste-fellows alone'.

In the present volume Bottomore quotes other findings which support this view, while Mayer in Madhya Pradesh found that a dominant Rajput group could only retain power by forming a Rajput core to a much wider group including other castes. Caste may be of paramount importance in municipal politics in one or two wards, but at constituency level the importance of caste varies, but is 'rarely paramount'. In fact, so long as 'caste' means '*jati*', an actual endogamous group, it is bound to mean a small world (as Bailey points out),[10] limited to a group of villages within a day's journey, not too far away for a daughter to come home to see her mother.[11] 'The traditional caste', Bailey writes, 'is not an effective means of getting votes, nor can it function as a pressure group. To be effective, such a group has to change its aims and change its form; it has, in fact, to become a caste association.'

But caste associations, though they may sometimes have slightly improved the ritual or social status of a group, have been little used politically and alliances between castes with different names but of similar status have so far proved brittle. And both caste associations and caste alliances are likely to be even more brittle in future; when the

[9] They are Sudras, in fact, though Jats are right at the head of this order and it seems strange to class them as Sudras. They formed the backbone of the Sikh armies and the Sikh state; the Sikhs in the British Indian Army were mostly Jat Sikhs, and Hindu Jats were also recruited.

[10] F. G. Bailey, *Politics and Social Change*, Berkeley, University of California Press, 1963; McKim Marriott (Ed.), *Village India: Studies in the Little Community*, Chicago, Chicago University Press, 1955.

[11] As Oscar Lewis and McKim Marriott point out (Lewis, *Village Life in Northern India*, Illinois, 1958; and Marriott, op. cit.), the network of villages in the North-West of Uttar Pradesh which are linked by marriage may be as many as 400. But at least a dozen *jatis* will be involved and it does not alter Bailey's point. The known caste world is small.

politician appeals to a village, he can promise a tank or a well; when he appeals to the local caste brotherhood, the endogamous group who know each other, he can speak of improving their status—but they are scattered over many villages, and it is no use talking about a well; as soon as he widens his constituency, he is faced with the difficulty of the Tiv politicians. The material interests common to a group of castes above the village level are seldom important; a politician can hardly base his platform on higher ritual status for Jats, Gujars, and Ahirs, because in this field they are in competition with each other. But he can base his appeal on the price of grain or fertilizer, and then—still thinking of the North-Western end of Uttar Pradesh—he may also get support from other peasant groups such as Kurmis and Muraos, as well as from owners of land, Rajputs and Rohilla Muslims.

Further, to base his appeal openly on caste is not only against the law[12] but against the prevailing tone of what it is suitable to say in public life. He will be far better advised to weave a network of personal influence and leverage, in which no doubt his kinsfolk and caste-fellows —people belonging to the same *baradari* or brotherhood—will take part, but in which he may well be opposed by someone who belongs to the same order in the ranking of *varna* or even by someone from another district with the same caste-name. It will be comparable to the network of old friendships at school and university in a Conservative Cabinet in Britain; no one will be appointed *because* he is an Old Etonian and indeed X may be appointed because he is *not*, but it may happen that when the appointments have been made rather a large number of Old Etonians gather round the table.

These essays, then, seem to suggest that caste within the *varnas* is likely to be one factor in politics among several, far more in evidence at the village level than at the constituency, more at the constituency than at the state, more at the state than at national level, while even at the constituency and district levels it will be effective mainly through a network of personal influence. Among the university-educated, it is now unfashionable to emphasize caste differences; it is rural, old-fashioned, backward. But at the lower levels of education caste will surely long persist, not only as a habit of thought but as a divisive factor, in marriage if nowhere else.

Even forty years ago it was apparent that in Indian society different scales of reference were used in different situations. A Brahman or Rajput might be a messenger in a government office, while a Kurmi, a

[12] Bailey, op. cit. Indian Constitution, Articles 15 and 16.

Sudra, one of the peasant castes, might be chairman of the district board, and a Kayasth—the caste of clerks and letter-writers, also Sudras—might be a pleader, a high government official or a Member of the Legislative Assembly. There were times when the Brahman, in spite of his high ritual status, would defer—indeed behave obsequiously —to the chairman, but he could not take food or water from him and there were occasions when—poor though he was—he would look down on this rich and powerful man.

Such occasions are today multiplied. It is one of the suggestions that emerges from these studies that in a developed and healthy society there will be an increasing number of scales of reference by which social status is judged in different situations and that, the more of these there are, the greater likelihood there is of social stability; the injustices suffered under one scale of reference cancel out those under another. The insufferable wrong arises when there is one scale only which overrides all else and cannot be changed; when, for example, the most brilliant writer, the most sensitive artist, remains socially at the bottom of the scale because of the colour of his skin. In India, the number of scales of reference is increasing; wealth, education, political power, international sophistication: all are more and more used not as alternative but as additional indicators of prestige in different situations. They have come to join caste, knowledge of the sacred Scriptures, ownership of land, ability to reconcile disputants—the traditional means of winning esteem.

VII: THE HARIJANS

Caste, then, within the four *varnas*, is likely to be of diminishing importance as a social as well as a political force. But one cannot be so sure about the ex-untouchables.

There is a revealing story told by Harold Isaacs[13] of a boy from one of the Harijan castes who left his village with a scholarship, made good at college, established himself in a profession and achieved some success and local fame—and then, for the first time, came back to the village where his parents had been glad to accept the unwanted remnants of food from higher-caste houses. His success was recognized. He was asked to take tea at the house of one of the leading men of the village— which means no doubt in the central courtyard round which the house was built. He was pleased and impressed—until, as he left, he met the caste-fellow who had brought the vessels from which he had drunk, and who had come to take them away afterwards so that they should not pollute the person of a twice-born.

[13] H. Isaacs, *India's Ex-Untouchables*, New York, John Day, 1964.

Comparison with the American Negro is implicit throughout Harold Isaacs's book; in the old relationship, the Harijan, like the Negro, was part of the society, but outside it; he dared not enter the quarter where the Brahmans lived, he must get out of the way when a twice-born approached, he must use terms of respect when speaking to him, must nor wear sandals, and so on. Like the Southern Negro, he was, until this century, a conformist, outwardly accepting these signs of subordination. He was the landless labourer, the scavenger, the skinner of dead cattle, virtually a serf, dependent economically and socially. Like the Negro, he begins to be tired of his humiliation—but, as with the Negro, there are different kinds of reaction. Some Harijans continue to hope for nothing more than Sanskritization; some Chamars (skinners and leather-workers), for instance, busy themselves making sure that none of their community eat beef, allow widows to remarry, or accept food from Bhangis (who are removers of night-soil, and even lower down in the scale). These Sanskritizing Chamars are like the Uncle Toms, who accept white values and try to be respectable. But others, like the Black Muslims, reject the values of the groups who have exploited them and adopt a new religion, in this case Buddhism, by which they hope to escape from the degrading net in which they are caught. Some revive or invent myths about their origin, usually from ancient Rajput heroes—like the Black Jews of Harlem or the *Ras Tafaris* of Jamaica. All—again like the American Negro in most Northern States—have now some legal protection against discrimination.

But while a law may be signed by the President overnight, ignorance and poverty cannot be overcome even in a generation. Opposition to Harijan advancement is less violent than in Mississippi, but it comes from the same segment of the community, those in the lowest ranks of the more privileged section who feel that at least they, are 'white' or 'within the *varnas*'. And, in both cases, a government that wishes to atone for past discrimination has to be careful; it must balance the pace of emancipation for the excluded carefully against the resentment of those just inside the society—the poor whites and the *sudras*. India has gone much further than the United States in benevolent discrimination, but special scholarships and reserved seats in the legislature carry the inherent difficulty that they cannot be used without proclaiming the status they are meant to end. 'It sometimes *is* a useful thing to be an orphan boy'—and just as Negro doctors and lawyers have not always wanted an end to their monopoly of a segregated professional practice and a captive clientele, some Harijans see the advantage of their special privileges. Indeed, there are stories from several sources of twice-born boys pretending to be Harijans for the sake of the scholarship—though I have seen no reported case of success, and one wonders how long pride would permit the pretence to be kept up. As long ago as 1955 Kathleen Gough[14] reported quite startling changes in the position of the untouchables in one Tanjore village, more marked than those recorded in Agra by Lynch in this volume; André Béteille[15] has dealt at greater length with the social and economic changes taking place in Tanjore. But whatever legal and political improvement is achieved, social esteem is likely to lag behind political, and economic may be last in the procession.

It is the Harijans who have been hit more sharply than anyone by the changes in society, which, at least in their immediate effect, are not wholly to their advantage. The old structure was rigidly stratified—and therefore abhorrent to the modern West—but it was a way of existence. The Harijans in the village were not free; they were virtually serfs. They had to work for the landowner of the dominant class who was their *jajman* or patron, and for very little reward. But the relationship, which was hereditary, did operate on both parties; if the patron exploited, he also protected. Wages were often as little as Rs.2 every six months with cloth and grain as well; if there was no hope of social improvement, there was some security. Like the Southern slaves, the Chamars were unprepared for freedom. They were not trained in its ways. As *jajmani*—hereditary patronage—gives way to a cash nexus, to competition and contract, insecurity grows more rapidly than social esteem—and real advance is for a very few. Lynch's account of the Chamars of Agra shows how they brought into the wards of the city the caste institutions of the village, and their caste committees and officials gave them some degree of protection and coherence; they were perhaps less helpless than the town labourers of England in the early days of the Industrial Revolution or than the former slaves in Northern cities. But their poverty is even more crushing. Legal emancipation does not bring a job.

There are 60 million Harijans—rather more now— in a population of 500 million—one in eight—a proportion that might count in votes if they were sufficiently united to make it count. But they are divided into Sanskritizers and Buddhists, into lower castes and lower still; the interests of the villagers are not those of the townsmen, they are split by region and language. Ambedkar is dead; they have no leader of their

[14] K. Gough, in Marriott (Ed.), *Village India.*
[15] A. Béteille, *Caste, Class and Power: Changing Patterns of Stratification in a Tanjore Village*, Berkeley, California University Press, 1965.

own of national standing, nor even a champion from within the *varnas*—a Gandhi, a Shaftesbury or Wilberforce.

Food and population are the two menacing question-marks that hang over India; if answers are not found soon, it is surely among the Harijans that the symptoms of social disease will begin to show. It is here, among a people released from legal and social bondage but deprived of security, admitted to education but to social esteem or to a means of livelihood, that one would expect to find movements like Chartism, Ras Tafarism or Nihilism. So far, the Harijans have usually seen the Congress, in the tradition of Gandhi, as their protector and patron against groups farther to the right; the machinery of reserved seats has provided a ladder for the ambitious leader, who has usually thought it an advantage to secure the party ticket—that is, the party nomination. But this can hardly continue indefinitely if there are no economic gains to show. The Communists have so far been successful only where they have had the backing of dominant landowning or rich peasant castes; the Harijans are a natural target for them, but they may find it difficult to shepherd the dominant caste and the Harijans into the same pen. If Congress fails and they turn neither to the Communists nor to movements of unsophisticated protest, the melancholy conclusion must be that malnutrition combined with centuries of hopelessness have destroyed the energy to revolt.[16]

VIII: THE TRIBES

The tribes are left for discussion until after the Harijans, because the fate of so many of them has been to become castes, usually at the bottom of the scale. A preliminary point made by Professor von Fürer-Haimendorf has first to be emphasized; the tribes are not going to melt into the rest of the population and disappear as a result of intermarriage and education. The enduring force of the caste system will see to it that they persist as endogamous groups. For most of the tribal groups of aborigines scattered in the geographically less accessible parts of Southern and Central India, it is surely likely that they will become more and more like a caste-group.

An excellent example are the Konds of Orissa, of whom I first read in the reports of British administrators in the 1830s and 1840s, when tentative[17] moves were being made to prevent their sacrificing human

---

[16] In writing about caste and village India I have used personal experience as well as the books specifically referred to, and also G. M. Carstairs, *The Twice-Born: A Study of a Community of High-Caste Hindus*, London, Hogarth Press, 1957.

[17] Tentative at headquarters, but more decisive on the spot.

victims to ensure fertility and rain. There can be no doubt that they
were then tribal groups, animists, outside the pale of Hinduism. 'The
Konds today', Bailey writes, 'say that they are Hindus like everyone
else, but they make a sharp distinction between themselves and the
Oriyas who live in their midst.'[18] He underlines what has happened by
speaking of Baderi as virtually 'a one-caste village', 70 per cent of the
inhabitants being Konds. Clearly it is impossible to draw a clear line
between caste and tribe; what was a tribe is becoming a caste and the
most one can hope is that the Konds will keep their language and something of their culture. Perhaps, like the Mohawks who left New York
State for Canada and now come back to New York for work on the
high skyscrapers, those aboriginals who have lost their tribal lands will
find special niches of their own in national life; they are beginning to
move into politics; their new leaders are not traditional chiefs but those
who can express themselves in political terms, and there are seats
reserved for them. They are really a detachable part of the problem of
the untouchables; like the Harijans, they are landless, ignorant,
unorganized.

But they are likely to be subject to less prejudice. It is one of the
paradoxes of Indian society that the caste element in Hinduism was
once their ally. There were no crusades by Hindu rajas to convert the
aboriginals; there was no Hindu gospel to which they could be converted and—as Professor von Fürer-Haimendorf points out—caste
rapidly became strong enough to keep out the fear of intermarriage,
which has been so strong an element in racial hostility. Caste Hinduism
left them alone; on the whole, the British left them alone. It was their
good fortune that among British officials there was a fairly constant
supply of eccentric originals who liked nothing better than working
among the tribes. The Congress criticized the British because they
failed to develop the tribal areas and perhaps it was in part to vindicate
this criticism that the new secular State felt it had to develop and
interfere. If it proves a true judgement that caste will persist in Indian
society generally for some generations, as an element in thought, in
habit of mind and in custom governing marriage, then the ex-tribesmen
are likely to remain a separate group from the main stream, but in many
ways more like the American Indian than the American Negro. They
are less of a threat, they are more remote, they have not been associated
with degrading occupations. But with this difference: much that has
been said of the Harijans applies to the Adibasis (tribals) who have no

[18] F. G. Bailey, *Tribe, Caste and Nation*, Manchester, Manchester University Press,
1960.

land; they may cling a little longer to the skirts of Congress, but if Congress shows them no benefits they are likely—in default of some heroic national figure who could attract a following throughout India from Harijans and Adibasis alike—to turn to Communism or some unsophisticated form of violent protest.

For the North-East Frontier Agency, Professor von Fürer-Haimendorf sees hope; an enlightened policy aims at bringing economic opportunity with a minimum of cultural disturbance. Most encouraging of all is his mention of a proposed special cadre of officers who would spend their whole life among tribal people. It is to be hoped that this cadre would operate not only in N.E.F.A. but in all scheduled areas; that is, broadly, wherever tribal lands remain, and that in all such areas the N.E.F.A. policy will spread.

There remain Nagaland and the Mizos (who used to be called the Lushai.) It seems impossible to dissent from Professor von Fürer-Haimendorf's view that the detailed rights and wrongs of the tragic rebellions of these peoples cannot be disentangled while the country is closed and the records inaccessible. Indeed, the whole truth may never be known. If Nehru's five principles (set out by Professor von Fürer-Haimendorf at the end of his essay) had been fully applied from the start, if the policy now followed in N.E.F.A. had been implemented here, too, perhaps the rebellions might have been avoided. One must also agree that basically the weakness lies in the stages between planning and execution; the intention in Delhi may be excellent, but the minor officials who carry it out are, no doubt, far too often authoritarian in manner and habit of thought; the tradition of extreme authoritarianism in officials goes back at least to the Maurya Empire, was in no way relaxed under the Mughals and only slightly and superficially modified under the British. Officials who are Hindus are liable to be contemptuous of tribals and are frequently so strongly urban in background that to be stationed in a remote area is regarded as a punishment. The degree of autonomy now offered is as far as any Indian government can be expected to go—at any rate since the Chinese incursion—and it is hard to reach any conclusion except that the Nagas should now regard it as the best they can expect and try to make it work. It may not be easy, while the memories of war and of the atrocities that always accompany war are fresh. But this is what ought to be done.

There are those who suggest that India should offer some kind of international guarantee to respect the autonomy she has offered. This would be felt as an affront to Indian pride; it would present all the usual difficulties of inspection and enforcement. Breaches would be hard to prove, because they would often be matters more of spirit and of manner than of legal act. It would be difficult to persuade a guaranteeing power to spend its diplomatic resources on enforcing compliance, and to the extent that diplomacy was used Indian resentment would increase. The ultimate hope for the Nagas is in Indian goodwill and at the highest level this does exist. To protect the Nagas against a high-handed political agent or a brutal platoon-commander, the best agency is publicity.

The first steps that seem desirable are that the Nagas should accept autonomy within the Indian Union and that India should admit foreign correspondents; the next step would be a delicate and gradual rehabilitation plan—and here some international help might be effective. Of all countries, Britain is the worst placed to help in this, because it hurts India's pride that the Nagas—who were startlingly loyal to the British during the Japanese occupation—should be provoked into full rebellion by the rule of enlightened, secular, independent India. To this independent observer it appears that any diplomatic initiative regarding what India believes to be essentially an internal affair must be international and should be conducted with the utmost delicacy and discretion.

IX: THE LEADERS AND THE MASSES

Two essays in this volume are concerned with the elites, the ruling and dominant groups who make or influence policy and who lead thought. There were three questions about these groups which needed answers if the book was in any way to fulfil its purpose. The first, with which Dr. Béteille was asked to deal, concerned the composition of these groups; to answer it would tell us a good deal about the changes taking place in Indian society. The second—addressed to Professor Bottomore—was how far the leading groups could be regarded as a unifying force. The third, implicit in both the others and indeed in most of the questions asked, was how far the leaders communicate with the masses.

There are certain preliminary points which must be emphasized because they are so obvious that they are easy to overlook. Quantitatively, the proportion of the masses to the leading groups is much higher in India than in the developed countries and qualitatively the gap is greater; less than 30 per cent of the population are literate and only 0.2 per cent go to college. Further, the system of education is not indigenous; even when the mother-tongue is used, the concept of education as well as much of the subject-matter is derived from an alien culture. Having emphasized these points, we can go on to accept Dr. Béteille's answer to the question put to him; it is much easier for a

which in its turn embodied Mughal features; it was essentially an authoritarian system by which in its heyday all executive power had centred in the district officer. The old system, which began to be re-moulded during the 1920s when District Board chairmen were first elected instead of being appointed by the Government, could only work because the district officer, in whom everything centred, was respon-sible to one central authority only and was left a very free hand. His staff in their turn were responsible to him alone; the aims of Govern-ment were not ambitious. Today, with a far more complicated set of administrative tasks, the district officer is the centre of a web of agencies to whom he can no longer give direct orders; his task is infinitely more subtle and difficult in itself and he is at every turn aware of politicians with factional interests whose constituencies, state and central, will cover his district.

There may, in a typical Uttar Pradesh district, be ten Assembly seats and two parliamentary. Thus there are twelve sitting Members—apart from prospective Members—whom it is dangerous to offend, not only for the district officer himself but for all his staff. The means by which offence may be avenged are numerous; there is the parliamentary ques-tion, which is tiresome, but there are far more serious means open, of which the most common is a complaint—in a criminal court or to a Minister on the right side—put forward, of course, by someone with no visible connexion with the initiator, of high-handedness, of improper favours, of some bias, if not of corruption or embezzlement. However far from the truth the allegation may be, the official attacked will be subject to suspicion and anxiety and it will be long before he is cleared. There is no longer any danger of officials ignoring politicians and being aloof; there is a real danger of their being too much enmeshed in the democratic machine.

It is possible, I believe, to conclude that the gap between masses and elite is, in fact, much more apparent than real. It is bridged by the politi-cal machine and—ignoble though the means of operating that machine may often be—the political and administrative elites are kept con-tinuously aware of the masses. From the village committee, or *pan-chayat*, to the parliamentary constituency, the means to power is by a mesh of personal support and popular backing; the official can no more dare to be indifferent to opinion than can the politician. The means of enforcing the sanction will be complex and often unsavoury; a charge of embezzlement may register a change in political power at some point in the web of faction and indicate that it is now safe to bring the charge, rather than that the accused has, in fact, done anything improper. But votes must be won and personal support kept. The response may be lethargic, the machinery elaborate, but there is a consciousness of the whole running through the entire system. Where that is so, the intellectuals, too, are brought in. Some may lose themselves in verbal spider's webs, as they do everywhere, but those who wish to be effective in the nation's life must have some touch of political awareness. But we are talking about the link between society and the State, which is the centre of our subject and its most elusive aspect.

X: SOCIETY AND THE STATE

It is not the purpose of this book to endeavour to foretell the political future of India. Its first aim—quite ambitious enough—is to consider how far Indian society is divided by fissions which are liable to disturb the State, and which have any affinity with the racial alignments we find elsewhere. The distinction between society and the State is vital. There are plenty of dangers which affect both and they have strong quasi-racial elements, but the overwhelming impression conveyed to me by the essays in this book is that the tough network of fibres binding Indian *society* into a whole will continue to hold. The divisive forces which simulate racial barriers are in retreat. There is a cultural inheritance of immense profundity; an Indian sociologist (as Professor Bottomore points out) considers it necessary to know Sanskrit and to be steeped in the Vedas and the Shastras, while it is not usually assumed that his European counterpart need be acquainted with the writings of St. Augustine or St. Thomas Aquinas. To this common culture I believe one of the central themes is *dharma*, which is often translated as 'religious duty', but carries with it also a sense of what must necessarily come into being. The *varnashramadharma*, which we have discussed, carrying out one's appointed function, is an essential part of *dharma*. It is an idea of what is fitting that has made India a stable society for thousands of years; it is still strong. Add to this the complexity of personal relations in a society traditionally linked by marriage in so wide a network that no one thinks of his village as a self-contained unit. Oscar Lewis has emphasized the ramifications of marriage links and contrasted the sophistication of outlook regarding other villages in Northern India with the isolation of a Mexican village.[19]

But while the village may be linked by marriage with four hundred others, the man in the village, the individual, is part of an extended

[19] O. Lewis, in Marriott (Ed.), *Village India.*

family related to a score of others in other villages and at the same time he is part of a village community, which although stratified has common interests, a common *panchayat*, a political life in which bitter factions will cut across caste and family and put a man in touch, as economic relations will, too, with those above and below him in the hierarchy. Several writers have made the point that in a closed society stratified by occupation—such as a traditional Indian village—the individuals are linked by *many* strands of relationship—feudal, ritual, economic. Those at the bottom of the scale plough for their patron as well as making his shoes and acting as beater when he goes shooting. He—ideally at least— gives them grain and cloth, protects them against others of his own rank, lends them something when a daughter is married. But in a modern society the strands are usually single. You buy a newspaper from the man at the corner of the street and that is an end of it. In India the mill-hand of Ahmednagar or Kanpur is no doubt in a much more single-stranded relationship with his employer than anyone in a village, but most people live in villages and even in towns the old many-stranded relationship persists surprisingly often.

This many-strandedness of relationships and consciousness of other communities may well contribute to the ease with which Indian thought understands the idea of unity in diversity, of an organic relationship between part and whole. We have seen how the setting up of a linguistic state has taken the sting out of regional separatism; the regional state is diverse within a unity. Indeed, the very qualities in Indian thought which have most repelled and irritated the Western mind, from Lord Macaulay to E. M. Forster, may have helped to hold Indian society together—the refusal to accept either horn of a dilemma, the evasion of harsh dichotomies, the readiness to acclaim as fact whatever is thought to be fitting.[20]

This suggests the likelihood of continued compromise in society, of social evolution by the development of new ties, while old become less important. And, as Paul Brass has very perceptively written, 'political institutions modernize society while society traditionalizes institutions'. In politics, too, the choice between extremes has so far been refused and the chosen leader at the centre continues to be the one whom the largest number do not find it intolerable to follow. This brings us to the machinery for linking society and the State, of which the driving engine is, of course, the Congress Party.

It is the strength of the Congress Party that it mirrors the paradoxes

[20] *'Decuit ergo factum est'*; the idea is not confined to India.

and complexities of Hindu society. Here, too, there is continual compromise and the reconciling of utterly opposed elements. Who in 1947
would have supposed that, once it had lost the stimulus of the struggle
for independence, one party could have kept its hold on millowners,
trade unionists, and untouchables? Yet this has in general been achieved,
by the exercise of a suppleness, a tolerance, a readiness to compromise,
that recalls the ability of Hinduism to include Shri Vaishnava Brahmans
and Gurkhas, the principle of non-violence, and the ritual slaughter of
goats at Dasehra. Both Hinduism and the Congress include elements in
thought which are highly individualist, indeed anarchic, and institutions which appear designed to suppress the individual.[21] In Indian
politics, the leader and his immediate followers recall the *guru* and his
chelas,[22] while the outer circle look to their leader as *jajman*—the
patron, protector and dispenser of favours. The Congress, like Hinduism, is eclectic and empirical, a loose confederation of many groups
and interests, protean in its readiness to tolerate the irreconcilable, and
yet so far always able to produce a core of energy at the centre that can
quell too violent an indiscipline at the level of the district.

One can write nothing of India without immediately perceiving that the
reverse is also true. If compromise and tolerance are keys to Hinduism
and to the Congress, implacable personal hostilities provide the driving
force to the party; indeed, at some levels, the hostilities seem the one
constant factor in politics. And India's readiness to placate produces
discordant results. Permissiveness over entry to universities and over
granting degrees has lowered university standards and produced a body
of dissatisfied and undisciplined students, liable to break into riot and
disorder at the least opportunity. These are realities which lie behind
the generalizations. It is characteristic that at the time of writing one of
the principal critics of Congress in the 'saintly' tradition has joined
hands with the Congress appeal to rioting students to go to famine areas
in Bihar.

Despite these contradictions, society has strong stable elements and a
machine is in being which links society with the State. It is a political
machine which bears many resemblances to the society out of which it
grows and this is a source of strength. But the recipe for a stable society
may not be the recipe for a stable state. Something different may be
required at a moment of crisis—and crisis is close. Over all India today
hover the spectres of food and population. China and Pakistan may well

[21] D. Dalton, *The Indian Idea of Anarchism*, Oxford, Clarendon Press, 1966.
[22] P. Brass, *Factional Politics in an Indian State*.

be unifying forces rather than a genuine threat; in any case to discuss them further is outside my present purpose. But food and population are terrifyingly near; the wrapper of Selig Harrison's book mentions a population of 500 million by 1971, but already, in 1966, that figure is said to have been reached. The qualities which make for unity in a stable society are not those needed to deal with so grim an apparition. Not suppleness and compromise are called for, but decisive action. It is famine, not the internal tensions of society, that is the enemy. If famine is not defeated, then each of these tensions—and particularly those concerned with region and the Harijans—may widen to a gaping crevasse.

II

The Position of the Muslims, Before and After Partition

BY PERCIVAL SPEAR

Lecturer in History, University of Cambridge and Fellow of Selwyn College

BEFORE Partition in 1947 the Muslim community in India stood in the ratio of one to four of the whole population, too small to dominate the country or insist on partnership, and too large to be shrugged off as a conventional minority. More important still, the Muslims as a whole had come to consider themselves, not so much as an Indian minority with special rights, but as a separate community with a distinct civilization. This was not always so, either in the high noon of empire or in the dark days of eclipse. It should be our first task to discover how this came about.

At the outset two common misconceptions should be noted. The first is the notion of Islam in India as a monolithic entity with one faith or creed, one race, and one political expression. Readers of the late M. A. Jinnah's pre-partition speeches[1] and much concurrent propaganda might well be pardoned for indulging this fallacy. Nothing could be further from the truth. The Islamic faith, in fact, was brought into India at various times and places by different groups and in different forms. It has proliferated into a great variety of sects and groups, many of which are important today.[2] The harbingers of Islam were of varied racial origin, and they brought with them far more than the Prophet's faith. The political expression of Islam has been almost as varied as its theological. The second part of this misconception is to suppose that Islam is the only significant thing about Indian Muslims. The different racial elements which brought in Islam coloured their religion with

[1] M. Jinnah, *Speeches and Writings* (2 vols.), Lahore, 1947.
[2] See M. T. Titus, *Islam in India*, London, Oxford University Press, 1930.

tribal or national characteristics. Turkish Islam was very different from Arabic Islam and Afghan Islam different again. Further, Muslims were influenced by their cultural surroundings. In particular Persian culture from abroad and Hindu ideas from within India have modified and variegated the Islamic complex. Indian Islam is a necklace of racial, cultural, and political pearls strung on the thread of religion. One cannot appreciate the necklace merely by studying the thread.

We should next note that the term minority is really a misnomer before the partition of India. The word implies helplessness; a minority must normally take what a majority chooses to give it. But the Muslims, after their early days, were a minority only in a numerical sense. For long periods of time they were able to impose their will on the Hindu majority and by the time of their political and social depression in the nineteenth century they were too numerous to receive the conventional minority treatment. It could be said that it was the attempt to do this which turned them into separatists. During the Mughal period they took the centre of the Indian stage, leaving little room in the wings for others. European travellers, while conceding that Hindus were to Muslims in the ratio of eight or nine to one, considered the Hindus rather as 'pagans', bound, like the rustic inhabitants of the Roman empire, by outworn superstitions. Presumably they would all eventually have become Muslims as the Roman pagans became Christians. A few rajas were excepted, but these were so closely linked with the Mughal Government as to appear in European eyes like Roman client princes clinging to ancestral cults. The great temples of the south were, of course, little known to these observers. India was a Muslim empire with a rustic majority still adhering to a variety of cults. Before, therefore, evaluating the position of Muslims in contemporary India, it is necessary to consider the circumstances of the formation of the Muslim body, its nature and its component parts.

The first Muslims appeared in India within a few years of the Prophet's death in A.D. 632. There was nothing unnatural in this, since Islam grew on Arabian soil and Arabs have historically been traders and seafarers. From the fourteenth century something of the same process was repeated in Indonesia with Muslim traders carrying Islam across the seas from Gujarat and Southern Arabia. The view that Muslim dominance inevitably follows Muslim contact or infiltration is rebutted in this case by the fact that the contact occurred in Malabar or the modern state of Kerala, still a Hindu majority area. There has, in fact, always been an important cultural element in the spread of Islam, and this has been more effective where less force was used. The seventh-century Muslim contact with Malabar was commercial and peaceful. The agents were Arab traders who had long carried on the Graeco-Roman tradition of direct participation in the Malabar spice trade. The contact continued peacefully for centuries and gradually built up the Mappilah or Moplah community of mixed blood, in modern times noted for its smouldering fanaticism. When the Portuguese arrived at the close of the fifteenth century these traders were allies of the Zamorin of Calicut. There were legends of one of these princes' conversion to Islam and suggestions have been made of Islamic influence on the development of Hindu thought and religion in south India.[3]

But not all Arabs were peaceful. The soldier-imperialist appeared in the person of Muhammed-bin-Kasim, the young general of the Damascus caliph, who conquered Sindh in A.D. 712. But he was soon recalled to an early death; Sindh was a cul-de-sac for the invasion of India and remained an isolated Muslim kingdom, nominally subject to the Ommayyad and Abbasid caliphs. The militant phase of the impact of Islam on India really begins with the advent of the Turks from Central Asia. Newly converted and as yet little touched by Persian or Graeco-Arab culture these tribes reinforced their natural militancy with the zeal of the convert. It was they who were responsible both for the conquest of India and for the aggressive reputation of Islam therein. They came like the waves of a rising tide, until the waters of aggression lapped at the temple of Madurai. The first was that of Mahmud of Ghazni in the early eleventh century, whose raids and sacks like that of the holy city of Mathura and the temple of Somnath gave Islam its reputation for iconoclasm and ferocity. His lasting achievement was a legend of horror and the conquest of the Panjab.[4] The next wave came at the end of the twelfth century, to engulf the whole of northern India within a few years. Riding this wave arose the Sultanate of Delhi which extended to Gujarat at the end of the century and then flooded the Deccan to reach briefly the extreme south in the early fourteenth century.

Ghaznavids, Ghorids, Slaves, Khiljis, and Tughlaks between them threw a Muslim political mantle over the greater part of India in about three centuries. They repelled the still wilder Mongols of Ghenghiz Khan and his successors and then, under stress of internal divisions and the hammer-blow of Taimur's invasion in 1398, dissolved into a

---

[3] I. H. Qureshi, *The Muslim Community of the Indo-Pakistan Subcontinent*, The Hague, Mouton, 1962, for Malabar and the general formation of the Muslim community.

[4] See M. Nazim, *Life and Times of Sultan Mahmud of Ghazni*, Cambridge, 1931.

number of warring factions. During the next century they were reinforced by Afghan chiefs, no less warlike but wilder and less politically
stable than they had become. The Mughals who followed provided
only a fresh infusion of much the same Turkish stock. These groups
between them achieved political supremacy, but they did not make the
Muslim community in India. They were a minority, not only within
India, but within the Muslim community itself. Their function was to
make possible the formation of that community by providing suitable
conditions for the mixture of races and the propagation of the faith. The
formation of the bulk of the Muslim community was a voluntary act
on the part of the converts.

We may agree that the Muslim community, apart from the traders
in the south, began with the marching Turkish chiefs, their followers
and hangers-on. Their numbers were augmented by local intermarriage,
often with Hindu captives. This was, however, but the beginning.
There was next forcible conversion in times of war or acute stress. This
known process occurred as late as 1921 in Malabar, but it was exceptional and occasional. Much of its prominence in the Muslim histories
derives from the fact that the authors were often *maulanas* or lawyer-
theologians who gloried in sending infidels to hell with their pens or
converting them at the point of their literary swords. While the element
of stress and force cannot be ignored, the fact remains that it does not
account for the community as a whole. The next category is that of
individual conversion of which there has always been a trickle and
rarely more than a trickle. Some of these were conversions of interest,
as we may suspect when we find former Hindus with Muslim names
holding high offices of state. But others were of conviction and no
doubt many were a mixture of both.

These recruits would not have formed a sizeable community but for
the addition of the next two groups who gave the body both its numbers
and its Indian character. In addition to intermarriage with non-
Muslims (usually in a superior-inferior relationship) there were clan or
group conversions and there were mass conversions. In different parts
of India, but specially in the Panjab and north-west India, clan groups
of varying distinction elected to go over to Islam in a body. So we have
Muslim Rajputs, Muslim Jats, the humbler Gujars and bodies like the
Meos on the borders of Rajasthan. These people, as it were, entered
in by the front gate, marching with colours flying as an act of collective
choice. They also went in on their own terms, taking their tribal customs with them. To this day many Muslim Rajputs, while respecting
the outward ritual and dogma of Islam, observe their tribal customs

within social life. The second addition may be described as mass conversions. There were groups of low-caste Hindus who opted for Islam as a way out of some of their Hindu disabilities. Such are scattered through Uttar Pradesh and Bihar in northern India, becoming prominent in the 1940s owing to their vulnerability to Hindu reprisals for Muslim attacks elsewhere. The Mumins are one such group; Kabir belonged to a weaver group who had opted for Islam in the fifteenth century. Somewhere between the group and individual conversion classes must be placed the mercantile communities of Gujarat and neighbouring western India. The Bohras and the Khojas[5] are amongst these formed partly by immigration and partly by missionary activity. By far the largest example of mass conversion occurred in East Bengal, now East Pakistan. Here, in the course of the thirteenth and fourteenth centuries, a whole countryside turned to Islam. It is thought that the decaying Buddhism of the Pala dynasty in Bengal had been superimposed on their rustic animism, that the substitution of the Brahminical Sena Kings for the Palas had meant a lowering of status and caste restriction, and that the Muslim conquest of Bengal with its casteless religion offered a welcome avenue of social escape. They also carried their customs with them, so that it could be said that the Islamization of India (so far as it went) also involved the Hinduization of Indian Islam.

The Indian Muslims were then of highly divergent origin, but in blood they were mainly Indian. Socially they tended to classify according to their previous standing. The conquering Turks, Afghans, and Persians formed the aristocracy, being reinforced by the well-born among the Indian converts. The Bengali peasants kept their status, as did the merchants of western India, the artisans and the craftsmen. What is more important to observe is that the intellectual influences were not all foreign. There was the Arabic influence stemming from the Koran and its theology. There was the Turkish influence, seen chiefly in action and administration, the purveyance of other men's ideas, and there was the all-pervading Persian influence, providing a language, a literature, a code of manners, of taste and of elegance. If the mental make-up of Indian Islam had stopped there, it would indeed have been a foreign exotic, doomed to separation or destruction. But what needs to be emphasized in addition is the Indian intellectual contribution as well as the social and customary. Of the social penetration there is no doubt. What Arab, for example, would have approved of the celebration of the Hindu *Holi* and *Diwali* festivals as occurred

5 Titus, op. cit., pp. 97 and 101.

regularly in the Mughal court from Akbar's day to the imperial collapse? Intellectual influences were more subtle and less easy to identify. They can be broadly classified as a tendency to mysticism, a tendency to reverence the creature as well as the Creator, and a tendency to tolerance. Mystical elements in India found a link and a response in Persian thought; the *sufis* from Persia provided a bridge between Indian and Islamic thought and practice. Their centres like that of Salim Shah Chishti at Ajmir were places of resort and of pilgrimage, their methods were peaceful; their appeal, unlike that of the *maulvis* with their denunciation of infidels and reliance on fear, was to the heart. In the interplay of Persian and Indian mysticism, Indian Islam found its soul. It was the Muslim weaver-poet Kabir who proclaimed that the same God reigned in mosque and temple.[6] Along with mysticism went the tendency to reverence and worship created 'beings and things' as well as the Creator. Highly unorthodox as it is, this trait constantly creeps into all sections of Indian Islam. But a further consequence of this interchange has been the Indian Muslim tradition of tolerance. After the early angry exchanges and acts of ferocity, the Muslims, influenced by their Indian environment, settled down to live and let live. In pre-Mughal Bengal, in fifteenth-century Deccan, and in Gujarat there were remarkable cases of cultural syncretism. All over India there was a general acceptance of the principle of 'live and let live', and only occasionally, in times of storm and stress, did fanaticism replace mutual respect. Muslim and Hindu kings are generally found to have Hindu and Muslim troops respectively in their armies.

It was in the three hundred years up to 1500 that the Muslims in India became a community with specific characteristics rather than a collection of individuals or groups. There was in this community an element of separateness or uniqueness, the Islamic heritage; there was also an element of identity, of oneness with the country. An Indian Muslim was now a very different person to the Muslim of Persia, Arabia, or the Turkish lands. He was proud of his heritage and had every intention of cherishing it. This feeling was no doubt encouraged by the Muslim possession of the sceptre which, with the advent of the Mughal empire, was to become the empire of all India. It perhaps reached its peak in the time of Akbar and in the early seventeenth century. Akbar gave the idea political expression with his policy of toleration, of intermarriage, and of taking the Rajput chiefs into partnership. Islam was to be the state religion in a comprehensive Indian

[6] See Aziz Ahmad, *Studies in Islamic Culture in the Indian Environment*, Oxford, 1964, Part II, Ch. IV; S. M. Ikram, *Cultural Heritage of Pakistan*, Karachi, 1953, pp. 70–78.

state. His later imperial cult was a device, not for undermining Islam or Hinduism, but for giving the imperial office an aura of divinity. His great-grandson Dara Shikoh sought to reconcile, through Sufism, Vedantic ideas of identity with the Muslim doctrine of creation.[7]

From that time the rival concept of Indian Islam, that of separateness, began to gain ground. Dara Shikoh's defeat by Aurangzebe was its symbol and Aurangzeb's reign its political expression. He conceived the empire, not as an Indian state with Muslims as rulers and Islam as the state religion, but as an Islamic state, a part of the *Dar-ul Islam* which happened to contain a majority of non-Muslims, and of which he was the benevolent ruler. Hence the reimposition of the *jizya* and the breach with some Rajput princes. This process continued, but it was not, so far as I can see, inevitable. Its acceleration was connected with another factor, that of the political decline of Indian Islam. The successors of Aurangzeb repealed the tax and sought Hindu co-operation, but they were too much concerned with the problem of survival to work out, much less to implement, a consistent policy. If Bahadur Shah had succeeded fifteen or twenty years earlier, he might possibly have restored the Indian Mughal empire. As it was, the crash of the empire in the mid-eighteenth century, and the failure of its Muslim successors to contain or beat back Maratha and British advances, had a stunning and unnerving effect on the whole community. In the north virtual tribalism and adventurism replaced the imperial idea; only in the extreme south did Haidar Ali and Tipu Sultan revive for a time the Muslim military reputation, while Nizam Ali of Hyderabad maintained an uncertain and precarious hold in the Deccan.

Indian Islam had been remarkable for its identification with India without ceasing to be Islamic. But it had also leant upon and prided itself on its political dominion. The religion of adventure had become the creed of empire. Now this prop was rudely knocked away; as the eighteenth century closed it seemed clear that there was no hope of revival. The roles of *maulvi* and emperor were reversed; it was the *ulema* who preached Islamic dominion while the last emperors (Akbar II, Bahadur Shah II) became religious preceptors. Indian Islam faced a crisis of confidence within itself and as to its future.

At this juncture the British completed their hegemony of India up to the Sutlej in 1818, advancing to the Indus and beyond with the Afghan and Sikh wars by 1850. The immediate effect was to depress the community still further. The British were not hostile to them. Though they widely described them as proud, perfidious, and licentious, these

[7] K. R. Qauungo, *Dara Shikoh* (2nd ed.), Calcutta, 1952.

epithets were balanced by others applied to the Hindus and an overall condemnation of the 'abominations of heathenism'. The British found more common ground with the Muslim than the Hindu aristocrat. Apart from the mutual love of sport, there was a common love of bravery and martial exploits, of conviviality and good living. Wellesley insisted that *nawabs* should be treated as gentlemen even while taking their kingdoms away from them. The Muslims might have continued to have enjoyed a twilight prestige and even a modest revival if the British had continued to employ them, as Warren Hastings did, as subordinate officers or agents. But the anglicizing policy of Cornwallis swept them away; only Ali Ibrahim Khan, the 'incorruptible judge' of Banaras, was left undisturbed. Their official position was reduced to that of legal assessors on Muslim law in the British courts. From virtual monopoly of high office[8] the old official classes failed to retain even the modest share which they received in the Hindu and Sikh régimes. And when responsible (though still subordinate) posts began again to be opened to Indians from the 1830s, a fresh obstacle arose. The use of Persian as the language of higher governmental and legal business was abolished in favour of English. Tradition-bound Muslims held back from learning English, while enterprising Hindu Brahmins and Kayasths stepped in. Muslims became the victims of a self-imposed boycott, without office, without the *izzat* or prestige which went with it, and without prospects. Dalhousie's annexations in the 1850s, culminating with Muslim Oudh in 1856, restricted their field of employment in their surviving subordinate states. Then came the final blow, the Mutiny of 1857. Though not its originators, they became the scapegoats. The Mughal emperor at Delhi was made a figurehead of the rebellion for lack of any others, thus identifying Islam with rebellion in British eyes. Further, the apparent sudden collapse of the British stirred atavistic political ambitions and activated agrarian grievances. Not much was heard of the cry 'Islam in danger', but a good deal of the cry 'Restore Muslim rule and eject the infidel'. An abiding sense of identity can be noted in the fact that in those months of stress Muslims were far more hostile to the infidel European from overseas than to the infidel Hindu at their doorstep. Great pains were taken in Delhi to restrain Muslim fanatics from provoking Hindus; even some Sikhs co-operated with the Muslims.[9] From this time until about 1870 the

---

[8] They continued to enjoy subordinate local office, but this was no solace to the former aristocratic bureaucrats.

[9] P. Spear, *Twilight of the Mughals*, Cambridge, Cambridge University Press, 1951, Ch. 10.

Muslims were in disgrace with the British; they were not only bereft of office and influence, but were regarded as both past and potential rebels. Demands to hang the last Mughal emperor and raze the great mosque of Delhi made in the heat of the moment were rejected, but the suspicion and fear that had inspired them continued to be expressed in official disdain and aloofness.

Indian Islam, in its secular and political aspect, had then reached its lowest ebb. It might have been supposed that a body thus bruised and battered by fortune would lose hope and decline. Its very identity with India might have promoted some sort of merger with Hinduism. Instead, Indian Muslims steadily increased in numbers and began to revive in spirit. The one to eight or ten ratio of Muslims to the whole population reported from the sixteenth to the early nineteenth centuries became a one to four ratio by the time of Partition in 1947.[10] The explanation of this surprising development is to be found in the new emphasis on the 'separateness' concept of Indian Islam and the impetus given to it by the political collapse. Some would trace the beginning of this movement to the work of Sheikh Ahmad Sirhindi,[11] in opposition to the syncretism of Abu'l Fazl in Akbar's reign. Certainly the movement had begun by the time of Aurangzeb, but so far it was one of withdrawal from Hindu contacts, not from the secular world itself. The next step was taken by Shah Waliullah of Delhi (1703–62).[12] He not only continued Sirhindi's work of intellectual distinction but began the process of withdrawal from the Imperial Court to the congregation of all Muslims. As political troubles thickened, his first instinct was to call in secular Muslim help to withstand the Marathas. When this failed, he began to preach a reliance upon God rather than upon the emperor, a return to the first principles of Islam from the panoply of empire, to the congregation of Islam from the diplomacy of princes. This movement took time to grow and was perhaps hardly known in the upper ranks of Muslim society outside Delhi in the late eighteenth century. But the deepening clouds of Muslim fortune drove more and more people in upon themselves. The movement took various forms. There were the activists who thought in terms of the Houses of War and Peace, and of *jehad* or holy war. Their leader was Sayyid Ahmad

---

[10] Census of 1941. A partial reason for the disparity between the early and the later quoted ratios may be ignorance on the part of early observers of the mass Muslim population in East Bengal (now Pakistan). But when this is allowed for, it seems certain there was a steady increase in the Muslim ratio. For this the most likely reason is a regular stream of conversion from the 'underprivileged' Hindu classes to Islam.

[11] Qureshi, op. cit., p. 150–9.

[12] Ahmad, op. cit., p. 201–9.

of Bareilly, who, first stirred in Delhi, was inspired by his residence with the Wahabis of Arabia to wage a holy war against the Sikhs in which he met his death in 1831. The 'Wahabi' movement with its headquarters at Patna was long a matter of concern to the Government and the Patna conspiracy case was one of its outcrops. Its adherents, such as the Maulvi of Fyzabad, naturally regarded the Mutiny as a heaven-sent opportunity to fight for the faith. Then there were the peaceful movements for renewal.[13] One of these was that of Haji Shariatullah, whose followers in Bengal were known as Faraizis and engaged in agrarian as well as religious agitation. Another was that of Maulvi Karamat Ali of Jaunpur, who for forty years carried on a campaign of renewal in eastern Bengal directed from a flotilla of boats which moved to and fro on the intricate river system.

All these movements had three features in common, a turning away from courts to the people, from politics to theology, and an emphasis on separateness. Islam was unique and Indian Islam must be purged of all Hindu accretions. Their implications were divisive, intolerant, and separatist. But they provided the Muslim masses with a reason for their existence, with a solace for their privations, and with a new sense of self-respect. What they did not do was to touch the upper, ex-official, landed and ruling classes. Neither did they meet the new challenge from the West, because the people they influenced had not yet been seriously affected by it.

It was these omissions in the popular movements that Sayyid Ahmad Khan, of Mughal traditions and in British government service, set out to repair in the years after the Mutiny. He started, as it were, from the secular end, the political plight of the Muslims after that catastrophe. But his remedy was not withdrawal into primitive Islam or reconciliation with Hinduism. He had to deal with not only a resentful infidel government and an increasingly confident Hindu society, but also an intellectual and moral challenge from the West, now in its most self-confident and aggressive mood. His remedy was reconciliation with the West through the study of science, the use of reason and a flexible attitude to social reform. Indian Muslims, he maintained, had much to learn from the West without committing any treason to Islam. With its help the Indian Muslims could become a modernized and self-reliant body which could hold its own with the alien government and resist the octopus-like embrace of Hinduism. Thus under his inspiration there was a movement for renewal and separation in the

---

[13] Ikram, op. cit., 181-3.

upper as well as the lower ranks of Muslim society. The difference lay in the fact that while the popular leaders harked back to the past, to the national Islam of the seventh century, Sayyid Ahmad looked outwards and forwards to a modernized Islam borrowing what was needed from the West to make it a viable and challenging way of life in the modern world. For controversies on the meaning of the obligation of Holy War or the relevance of the ban on idolatry to gramophone records he substituted the study of science and the promotion of Western education. It was significant that one of his school entitled his apologetic work *The Spirit of Islam.*[14]

The influence of both groups is visible during the next ninety years, though we should remember that, until the last few years, the efforts of both parties were confined to activist minorities. On the popular side we can note the Deoband Centre for Islamic Studies, which, though opposed to partition until the end, actively and effectively promoted Muslim separateness. There was the heretical Ahmadiya sect of the Panjab, whose missionary efforts had the same effect. More spectacular was the Khilafat movement of the Ali brothers, during and after the First World War. Appealing to the masses in the name of Islam, they campaigned for the Turkish caliphate and sent a pitiful caravan of the faithful to the Muslim land of Afghanistan. Their alliance with Congress during Gandhi's non-co-operation movement of 1920-2 was a *mariage de convenance* which broke down as soon as Ataturk abolished the caliphate. Then their essential mass appeal and Islamic separativeness asserted itself; and the Hindu character of Congress tactics provided a convenient target. Many of the same leaders began to promote anti-Hindu feeling in the name of Islamic separatism and were behind the increasing tally of communal riots. When Jinnah later raised the flag of Islam in danger it was these people who waved it and carried it through the villages.

On the other side the first overt act to be noticed was the creative one of the foundation of the Aligarh Muslim College (later University) in 1875, by Sayyid Ahmad Khan. This became the centre of Muslim modernist thought, as Deoband was of traditional, though the Sayyid never interfered with the college mosque and its teaching. It poured out a stream of young men who took their places in the government services and the public life of the country. Western education ceased to be regarded as a gateway to infidelity; the example of Aligarh was followed by degrees all over India. In this way the Muslim Westernized class grew up which, small though it was, contained men of great ability

[14] Sayyid Ameer Ali, b. 1849.

who carried the main burden of Pakistan in its early years. The second turning point was the Sayyid's attitude to the Indian National Congress founded in 1885. For a time there was doubt and an interesting correspondence exists between him and the pro-Congress Badr-uddin Tayabji on the subject.[15] Sayyid Ahmad Khan decided against Muslim participation and his reason was significant. The Congress aimed at democracy; democracy meant majority rule and the majority were Hindus. Self-government therefore meant Hindu *raj* and this was not to be thought of. This was the separatist principle in its modernist garb and in a political setting. The Sayyid used all his influence to prevent Muslim support of the Congress and he largely succeeded.

From this attitude stemmed directly the foundation of the Muslim League in 1906 as soon as the first sign of the Morley-Minto reforms appeared on the horizon, with the accompanying demand for safeguards in the new Constitution. Significantly again, it was the English principal of Aligarh who acted as go-between for Mohsin-ul-Mulk and his friends with the Government.[16] Each further instalment following each Congress-Government clash was greeted with further and successful demands in the form of separate communal electorates and constituencies and communal quotas in the services. When Congress leaders like Gokhale or Bannerjea protested their political secularism, these Muslims pointed to the attitude of other leaders like B. G. Tilak and Lala Rajpat Rai. Their suspicions only seemed to be confirmed when Gandhi, proclaimed a *mahatma* and preaching non-violence, captured the Hindu masses for the Congress by giving it a Hindu dress. The Congress, these people came to think, was only Hinduism at the ballot-box.

By 1930 it was clear where this mood of radicalism was moving. By then the intellectual leadership of the Sayyid and his followers had been replaced by the more dynamic doctrines of the poet Muhammed Iqbal.[17] No less definite than the Sayyid in separation from Hinduism, he was also highly critical of Western 'materialism'. But his criticism was selective, aimed more at the spirit of its institutions than its products or its sciences. The essential burden of his message was a new confidence in the inner strength of Islam. He was not so much a pruner

[15] Husain B. Tayabji, *Life of Badr-uddin Tayabji*, Bombay, 1952. See also forthcoming *History of Freedom Movement*, Calcutta, Firma K.L. Mukhopadhayaya, Vol. II, chapter by Dr. A. Seal.

[16] Mr. W. A. J. Archbold. See Syed R. Wasti, *Lord Minto and the Indian National Movement 1905-1910*, Oxford, Clarendon Press, 1964, pp. 61-66.

[17] 1876-1938. See his *Reconstruction of Religious Thought in Islam*, Oxford, Clarendon Press, 1934; and *Secrets of the Self* (trans. R. A. Nicholson), London, Macmillan, 1920.

of decayed boughs as a planter of new seed. His work amounted to a spiritual declaration of independence of the new Islam against the new West as well as the old India. From this stage it was but a step for Choudhri Rahmat Ali to coin the word 'Pakistan' and a stride for Muhammad Ali[18] Jinnah to turn it into a political programme. Congress leaders may have helped the process by errors of judgement, but it is difficult to see how the logic of events could have been deflected in the long run by differing sets of circumstances.

Thus the thread of separateness developed into a thick rope of what proved to be irresistible strength. In this rope there were still the two strands of separation in the name of traditional Islam—a 'back to the Koran' or an 'Islam in danger' movement—and a separation in the name of a forward-looking Islam, ready to exploit the knowledge of the West and to adjust customary society to modern conditions. The inherent inconsistencies and dilemmas involved in this dichotomy are something which the new Muslim society of Pakistan has had to face and are outside the scope of this essay. But what of the complementary thread of identity or comprehension, so strong until the middle of the seventeenth century? And how was it that the urge to separation only swept Indian Islam to become a national movement by the end of the Second World War? We have first to remember that between the two activist groups advocating separation and political assimilation lay the great inert majority of Indian Muslims. And just as the separatists were divided into traditionalists and progressives, advocating a common political goal but with by no means common objectives in view, the passive majority contained both the traditionalist peasant and the satisfied man of property and profession. The peasant at the plough, the artisan at his trade, the comfortable landlord, and the rising lawyer or teacher had no wish to uproot themselves so long as their way of life or their material interest and prospects did not appear to be threatened. This passive contentment explains why the Muslim majority areas like the Panjab and Eastern Bengal were the last to join in the Pakistan movement. The spearhead of the movement came from the Muslim minority areas like the former United Provinces, where Muslims dwelling in the shadow of prospective Hindu favour were more susceptible to doubts and fears. It could be said that Pakistan was achieved by the efforts of minorities who could only expect to lose by it.

The advocates of identification came also from both the traditionalists and the modernists. Among the former were the Deoband theologians, and the organization *Jamiat-ul-Ulema*. Maulvi Maududi, now a

---

[18] 1876–1948. See H. Bolitho, *Jinnah*, London, John Murray, 1954.

leader of orthodox and traditionalist opinion in Pakistan, opposed the Pakistan idea until the last moment. These people, though hostile to the British, considered that Islam was sufficiently safeguarded, and that with similar arrangements in independent India they could continue to live peacefully and piously. The whole of Indian Islam should not be sacrificed for a part. The modernists believed that the Islamic way of life was viable in any liberal modern state. British India had become one of these and independent India might be considered likely to continue on the same lines. Muslim minority areas should rely on the countervailing influence of the majority areas. Politically Muslims would gain more by co-operation with the Indian Congress than by either opposition or actual separation. This school of thought had distinguished representatives of all departments of public life. In politics there were the Panjabi leaders Sir Fazli-Husain, Sir Sikandar Hayat Khan, and Sir Khizr Hayat Khan Tiwana; the Bengali leaders Fazl-ul Huq and H. S. Suhrawardy, and Dr. M. A. Ansari in the Congress: in administration there were men like Sir Mirza Ismail and Sir Akbar Hydari: in education Dr. Zakir Husain and Professors Sir Shafaat Ahmad Khan and Muhammed Habib. Above all, as a meeting-point of traditional and progressive, Islamic and Indian, was Maulana Kalam Azad. Jinnah himself belonged to this group until his breach with the Congress over the terms of the Nehru Report of 1928.

For all their distinction these men could not hold the bulk of their own class, much less the masses, when the crisis came. They were rich in ability and experience; they may be said to have been the officer corps of an army which marched in the opposite direction. They had in fact, everything except a dynamic which could have convinced them and their class of their call to leadership and which could have charmed the masses into following them. Islamic idealism had passed from the logic of the followers of Ahmad Khan to the poetic mesmerism of Iqbal. Muslims in his vision were to conquer their environment and shape the future by struggle, while the moderates could only maintain a dead-level of bureaucratic expertise. The wine of Muslim nationalism in a Hindu goblet was a diluted, pallid drink, while the potion of independence, if heady, was exciting. At the level of the masses there was no answer to the Khilafat movement and its successors, with their memories of glory, their notions of grandeur and their evocation of deep feeling with the cry of 'Islam in danger!'

Various reasons can be advanced for this election by the majority for separation. M. A. Jinnah himself can be regarded as betraying the Muslim nationalists, first by breaking with the Congress in 1928 on the issue of separate electorates for Muslims, and then by his appeal to mass Muslim prejudice and hysteria after his rebuff by Congress on the coalition issue in 1937. To the lost leader could be added the lost mystique of secular democracy. Here the traitor was Gandhi, who may be said to have nationalized the Congress by Hinduizing it. A joint nationalism depended on the building up of a supracommunal secular national consciousness; Gandhi's Congress, on the other hand (as did the Khilafatists on their side), emphasized the communal aspects of nationalism in order to gain the ear of the villagers. It did not signify that Gandhi's creed was gentle and peaceful; its broad effect in Muslim eyes was to turn the independence movement into an expression of Hinduism. *Swaraj* means 'our own government';[19] it was as divisive a phrase in its own way as was *Sinn Fein* ('ourselves alone') in early-twentieth-century Ireland. Behind these popular and religious feelings which affected the common man came the power struggle, which affected the leaders. The feelings and fears of the many were the fuel for the torches of ambition of the few. It was this combination of circumstances which hastened the slower train of political logic to produce the mass upheaval of separation. The fears and ambitions of the leaders were stimulated by a new ideology, and these found in the masses a ready-made reservoir of power. Outside influences, both world-wide and Hindu, stirred these forces so that the leaders could make use of them. For a long time the issue was one of 'either-or', and some believe that Jinnah never intended it to go further than this. But, as so often has happened in history at the crucial moment, the lower took charge of the higher. Jinnah called on the people for support in his vendetta against Congress and it was the people who carried him to Pakistan.

The Muslims who were left in India at partition and the subsequent migrations numbered about 35 millions, those who left being about 65 millions. Now they are thought to be about 50 millions, as they have shared in the general Indian population explosion. Beneath the inner tensions and public fears of pre-partition India the Muslims as a whole had enjoyed substantially the same degree of security as the Hindus, and reasonable opportunities for development. They had their share of public appointments in the services under a quota system, and if they felt hindered by some Congress provincial ministries they enjoyed governmental support for development plans in their majority provinces like the Panjab. In general they were a poor community, but could hardly be called an exploited one. They had a minor share in

[19] It also had religious overtones, as signifying 'the heaven of India'.

modern industry, mainly confined to cotton mills in western India. But in the same region they had important commercial groups, as also existed in Bengal. Education, from its focus at Aligarh, was steadily spreading to add to the small Muslim middle class.

At partition the official class largely, though not entirely, disappeared. The cultivators of the East Panjab and some in West Bengal migrated to their respective wings of Pakistan. But there were still left agricultural pockets all over North and Western India and in Hyderabad. The Mumins, the one-time weaver converts from Hinduism, were an example of these. In general the urban artisan class east and south of Delhi remained, though reduced in Delhi itself by riot and migration. But even where they were still numerous, as in Agra, they were overawed by the knowledge that authority was now in Hindu hands. The professional and commercial classes remained in large measure, though there was a considerable 'skimming off' from both classes, especially from Uttar Pradesh and Bihar. Many families were divided, one branch migrating and the other electing to stay. Indian Islam was not left a bleeding trunk of cultivators and small traders, bereft of its professional and intellectual head. The head had been scarred, not severed. Politics, for Muslims as Muslims, was virtually dead, for there was clearly no room in India for a Muslim League advocating Pakistan. Such politics consisted largely of public meetings called to affirm loyalty to the new Government, or to disavow successive actions by Pakistan, as in Kashmir for instance, which further strained Indo-Pakistan relations.

In public life as a whole, however, Muslim leaders experienced even a certain enlargement. Congress was the dominant power, other groups in the early years virtually existing by its grace. Those Muslims who had been loyal Congressmen as Muslim nationalists (and they were considerable in number, though few by percentage) found themselves cherished and often promoted by a Government anxious to prove to the world that it was secular and non-communal. Thus Maulana Kalam Azad was Minister of Education and a confidant of Mr. Nehru; Asaf Ali became successively Ambassador to the United States and Governor of Orissa. Nor was this tendency a mere passing phase. At the moment of writing Dr. Zakir Husain is Vice-President of the Republic itself, while the Minister of Education and the Mayor of Delhi, to mention but a few examples, are Muslims. In law they retain their traditional customs, social reform being confined to Hindus. The time may come when Pakistan, with its social legislation, will be ahead of the Indian Muslims.

Outwardly, the observable change is not very great.[20] Muslims have disappeared from the East Panjab, it is true. There village mosques decay and minarets are broken. In former semi-Muslim cities like Delhi and Lucknow the Muslims though still numbered by thousands are subordinate in function and unassuming to the eye. But elsewhere the mosques are frequented and the monuments maintained though the absence of headwear makes Muslims less easy to identify. The theological centre at Deoband and the educational one at Aligarh are still maintained, though at the latter there is an infusion of Hindu elements. One sees little overt sign in the north of any government desire to depress the status of Muslims any more than that of Christians. In the south, where the Muslims have been a relatively small minority without ruling status for over 150 years, affairs go on much as before. Muslims there have no civil war or dominion to look back to, no holocaust to dread in the future.

If this is the visible state of the Muslim community, how are we to assess its inner life or soul in the New India? The first impression is one of shock, a shock which has perhaps not even yet fully worn off in the north. The events of 1947 overtook that part of the community which was least antagonistic to Hinduism, that part of it, in fact, who believed in identifying themselves with the country as well as in maintaining a separate existence. It is true that many had not the means to uproot themselves had they wished to do so; it is also true that many could have done so had they wished it strongly enough. Many of the self-conscious classes deliberately chose to remain, believing this to be a right they owned to a patrimony they would not give up. At the height of the crisis some exhorted their friends to stand by their poorer brethren in the name of this right and faced division of family as well as country in its cause. The shock of the massacres to these coexisters was therefore all the greater and one could not but detect in many conversations the queries, 'How could it have happened in the first place?' and 'Will it happen again?' Such people find it difficult to take a friendly view of Hindu society, though they know they have to live side by side with it. They remain in it, but not of it.

Arising out of the shock is a continuing sense of insecurity. For this the Government, at any rate in recent years and by responsible Muslims, has not been held to blame. It is high policy to avoid communal clashes; when they have occurred recently it is acknowledged that

[20] For the remaining section the author has relied on personal observation and conversations during a visit to India in 1965.

action has been prompt. The Muslim minority's fears concern the activist Hindu groups—the Hindu Mahasabha with its orthodox cultural overtones, its political expression the Jan Sangha, and its youthful spearhead the R.S.S.S.[21] This activism could easily run into militancy, as was shown in the recent Panjab and Delhi disturbances over the Panjab *suba* question.[22] If Hindus can fight Sikhs and other Hindus, argues the thoughtful Muslim, why not on occasion the Muslims? This fear has been sharpened by the apparent growth of extremist sentiment and influence, especially in the Ganges valley and Central India. Its existence was one of the ostensible reasons for Nehru's refusal to contemplate a Kashmir settlement involving concessions. The absence of communal clashes during the recent Pakistan war was a governmental triumph and a great relief to Indian Muslims. But the absence of any real *détente* and the rebuilding of tension must cause those fears to remain.

The sense of insecurity is also connected with Pakistan relations. The continuing controversy between India and Pakistan has been a grave embarrassment to the Indian Muslims. The contention that India is really an intolerant Hindu state is fed in the Pakistan Press by highly coloured accounts of any incident affecting Muslims reported from India. It is difficult to authenticate them, but it may be supposed that many reports coming through the regular news agencies are substantially true. But it is impossible to deny that they are exaggerated and highly coloured in presentation. A reading of the Pakistan Press a few years ago suggested that India was full of Hindu-Muslim conflicts. This constant hostile publicity, this blowing up of the minor into the major, could not be more embarrassing for the Indian Muslims, especially in the North. It provides just the handle needed by Hindu extremists for casting doubt on Muslim good faith and suggesting their disloyalty and sedition. A credited connexion with Pakistan is the Indian Muslims' nightmare.

Informed Muslim opinion is clear that it wants nothing better than the liberty to work out its own destiny within the Indian secular society. Here one should mention that this opinion is more vocal in the North and East than in the West or South, because it is there that Muslims have felt the brunt of the effect of the massacres, the migrations and the continuing anti-Muslim propaganda. Elsewhere the Muslims have long

[21] *Rashtriya Swamyam Sevak Sangh:* a Hindu youth organization of militant tendencies.

[22] This was the demand of the Sikhs for a separate Panjabi-speaking and Sikh majority state to be carved out of the previously existing Panjab state. This was agreed to in 1966 by the central Government, the remainder of the Panjab state being renamed 'Haryana'.

been peaceable minorities (except the Moplahs in 1921 and the Pathans of the Bombay mill areas) so that partition has not vitally changed their position. It is not mere fear which prompts this view. The Muslims of the West and South have been 'accepters' of non-Muslim rule for two centuries. In the North the 'non-accepters', those who believed that the Muslim religion required a Muslim society and state in which to flourish, were creamed off from the upper and middle classes by the partition. Those who remained were consciously, as with Muslim Congressmen, or passively, as with many members of the middle class, accepters of life in a non-Muslim world. They were therefore, as it were, non-aggressive by definition. They wish to become an established and respected community within Indian society. They desire freedom for their religion and the retention of their group consciousness, but no political connexion with Pakistan. They view the Kashmir dispute as a disaster because of its implicit threat to their progress and safety.

The Indian Muslims desire no special aid or patronage from the Government. They recognize that it is better for them to stand on their own feet and rise by their own exertions. So there is no talk of special electorates, reserved seats or quotas in the services. An index of the possibilities of this attitude when passions are dormant is the election of Muslims in Uttar Pradesh for constituencies containing a majority of Hindu voters. In the political sphere they would appear to have their share of appointments, for both the Congress and the Government are anxious to maintain their reputation for impartiality. Lower down the scale, however, it is different. It is widely believed that none but the most brilliant can expect appointment to the services. And this arises not from any set policy, but from the normal working of the Hindu social system, with its weight of family and clan obligation, and its interlocking relationships, set in conditions of permanently threatening unemployment. This may be resented by many, but the wiser leaders recognize it as inevitable in the circumstances and ask only for freedom from interference both external and internal. In the conditions of the prewar years Muslims denied the opportunity of government service would indeed have felt themselves hardly used. But today there are other opportunities. The professions, including engineering and other modern skills, trade and commerce, have all rapidly expanded. None are yet dominated by caste rings or social inhibitions. These are fields open to the minority groups which offer rewards to the enterprising.

It is easy to think of the prospects of the Indian Muslims in gloomy terms. Long ago denied the sceptre, which many thought essential to their existence, and now suspected by many for their religion and regarded as second-class citizens, is there any future for them other than eventual absorption in the Hindu mass? I think this view overlooks three factors. The first is the resilience historically displayed by many Muslim communities when placed in alien or even hostile surroundings. Muslim minorities have long existed in China, Russia, the Balkans, and elsewhere without fading away. Indeed, Islam has often grown not so much by conquest prefacing conversion as by infiltration leading to conversion and then seizure of power. Islam believes in political expression, but is not dependent upon the secular arm. The second reason is that the bulk of the present Indian Muslims represent the 'accepting' stream of Indian Muslim thought. The South has lived on 'accepting' terms as a minority for generations, while the Muslim survivors in the North may be called the 'accepting remnant'. Thirdly, the pressure of the modern world on India means that secularism is likely to increase in spite of occasional orthodox reactions. Such a process must soften communal consciousness and acerbities and tend towards tolerance. In this sense it can be argued that the Indian Muslims are a people of the future rather than of the past.

If it does not seem reasonable to expect the disappearance of Indian Islam, we could still envisage a sort of twilight existence for the foreseeable future. Will not the suspicion and resentment of important sections of Hindu opinion continue as long, at least, as the present strained relations with Pakistan persist? And will not this mean, as soon as the present generation of Muslim Congressmen have disappeared, a second-class existence compounded of profuse professions of regard with practical neglect and discrimination? It is difficult to deny this possibility in the short or to sustain it in the long term. The suspicions engendered by present Pakistan relations are an obvious handicap and a provocation to aggressively minded Hindus. But it can hardly be believed that Indo-Pakistan relations will remain at their present low level or that a *modus vivendi* can never be achieved. More positively the march of secularism comes in. As it becomes less important to belong to a particular caste or even to be a Hindu it will be less shocking or irritating to be a Muslim. Therefore it would seem that the prospects of the Northern Muslim, though clouded at the moment, are brighter in the long run. His community should in time become an accepted part of an integrated secular Indian society, as his Southern brethren are now on the way to becoming. Hindu society is not intolerant of any group who performs a useful function, as the history of the Malabar Moplahs shows. The community may have to pass through deep waters first, but this is the prospect on the other side. Four conditions are necessary for its realization. One is the spirit of acceptance of life in an alien cultural environment. The second is initiative to make use of any opportunities which occur and the third a determination to reform and adapt within the community itself. The last is the endurance to carry the community through the years of adverse opinion and suspicion which may still lie ahead. The new Indian Islam will be very different to the imperial Islam of the Mughals or the decayed Koranic 'Promised Land' Islam of the nineteenth century. With these conditions fulfilled, there is no reason why it should not become a vigorous and integrated body, making a creative contribution to a new India.

BIBLIOGRAPHY

AHMAD, Aziz, *Studies in Islamic Culture*, Oxford, Clarendon Press, 1964.

CHAND, Tara, *Influence of Islam on Indian Culture*, Allahabad, University Press, 1952.

HUNTER, Sir W. W., *The Indian Musulmans*, London, Trubner and Co., 1876.

HUSAIN, S. Abid, *National Culture of India*, London, Asia Publishing House.

LEVY, R., *The Social Structure of Islam*, London, Cambridge University Press, 1957.

QURESHI, I. H., *The Muslim Community of the Indo-Pakistan Subcontinent*, The Hague, Mouton, 1962.

ROSENTHAL, E. I. J., *Islam in the Modern National State*, Cambridge University Press, 1965.

SMITH, D. F., *India as a Secular State*, Princeton, N.J., Princeton University Press, 1963.

SMITH, W. C., *Modern Islam in India*, London, Gollancz, 1946.

idem, Islam in Modern History, Princeton, N.J., Princeton University Press, 1957.

TITUS, M. T., *Islam in India*, London, Oxford University Press, 1930.

III

Language and Region Within the Indian Union[1]

BY W. H. MORRIS-JONES

Professor of Commonwealth Affairs, and Director, Institute of Commonwealth Studies, University of London

WISDOM about India begins with the obvious: it is a very large country. The next step is through the well known: it is not an area of recent settlement but one of the most ancient civilizations. Moreover, even when in the hands of alien masters, it has not for long been subject to ruthless government as a simple unit from a single centre. These given, we should know what to expect: a continuous political problem of cohesion. It is therefore inappropriate to feel (or affect) shock and despair whenever the problem manifests itself as, for instance, in the question of language. For it is rather the relation of the problem to the 'resources' for dealing with it that merits attention.

Even to speak of 'dealing with' the problem of language is misleading. It suggests the removal of a difficulty—whereas this may be unnecessary as well as impossible. It may instead be a matter of containing and limiting a difficulty and learning to live with it. Cases differ: Quebec was not Louisiana, Belgium is not Switzerland. Assimilation, suppression, coexistence, strife—all have happened in the field of language 'policy'. Predictions about the future of language in India must be founded on a review of the particular shape and texture of the Indian language problem and its relation to the types of 'equipment' or 'resources' available to meet it.

Language is perhaps the most important mark of group identification. But it is more precisely discriminating than either colour or race, for whereas the latter may be overridden by other forces so that they cease to refer to any real interacting community of persons, language so long

[1] Written before the *Report* of the Education Commission (1966) was available.

as it is used is a working link; a means of communication is inescapably a delineator of group boundaries. To say this is not necessarily to endorse the view of language taken by doctrines of nationalism; nothing concerning political organization need follow as of right or as of logic from the fact that language identifies a group. Quite evidently, states can be durably constructed in defiance of this particular group formation. It is equally evident, however, that when this happens those who direct governments have to give careful attention to language policies. That 'intimate and fateful link between language and politics' which is proclaimed in the theory and ideology of nationalism[2] is not broken when the theory is rejected.

Indeed, many more of the assertions which were made about language by the nineteenth-century doctrinaires of nationalism have to be acknowledged as valid—and can be so acknowledged without entailing acceptance of their political conclusions. For the identification of language group with nation and the further identification of nation with self-determining state rested on a separate set of metaphysical propositions. The advocates of nationalism were right, however, to stress that language is even more than an instrument of communication and a badge of identification. Language does more than act as a channel through which universal experiences are expressed and passed from one to another within a group; it comes to reflect and reinforce experience and character peculiar to the group. The imperfections of translation are necessary, the traditions carried and conveyed by a language are particular and distinct. 'Every language is a particular mode of thought and what is cogitated in one language can never be repeated in the same way in another . . . Language . . . is an expression of a peculiar life which contains within it and develops through it a common body of language.'[3] Each language is a vehicle for a particular literature; each literature embodies a tradition born of a set of experiences; each set contains universal as well as peculiar elements, but even the universal elements are perceived to some extent in distinctive ways; a language 'fits' a way of life. Ways of life, to be sure, are not all equally distinct. Many experiences have 'overlapped', are shared. And languages faithfully reflect this by their familial relations. They are not equidistant one from another, but are rather related in varying degrees, so that transition and translation from one language to another may be relatively easy or difficult.

[2] E. Kedourie, *Nationalism*, London, Hutchinson, 1960, p. 61.
[3] Schleiermacher, quoted in Kedourie, op. cit., p. 63.

It should thus be a matter not for wonder but for ready comprehension that in questions of language emotions are often strongly engaged. From this it should not, however, be concluded that attachment to language is 'merely' a question of sentiment. Arguments about language policy on the contrary normally refer to issues of interest in even the narrowest sense of the term. This is especially and increasingly the case as governments extend the sphere of their activities and thus their impact on people's lives. By its language policy a government may be able to dictate the medium of instruction throughout the educational system, to control entry into its employment, to influence access to its processes. When a government approves and supports one language and not others for purposes such as these, it injures interests and disturbs expectations, by altering the relations between these language groups. It can also damage social ties within such groups, as when the young get drawn by opportunities or led by education into a language group other than that of the home. That it simultaneously offends deep sentiments serves to intensify the conflicts.

India has not one language problem, but a complex of language problems. It has them, moreover, in a situation of political and social revolution. Its difficulties are so unlike those of any other country in the world that direct comprehensive comparisons are worthless.[4] It is not a question of establishing an equilibrium between mainly two equally prominent languages, as in Belgium and Pakistan; nor of giving equal status to two or three languages spoken by unequal numbers of citizens as in Canada and Switzerland. The experience of the Soviet Union is of limited relevance for the reasons that Russian is the mother tongue of the great majority of the people and that it was already the established language of imperial administration and cultural hegemony within the territories of the State. Turkey and Japan have had to reform and modernize—borrowing words and changing scripts—but they had one language to deal with. In some African states English is in effect the official language, while also serving as 'link' language across tribal areas and medium of the bulk of education, but in these areas there are no developed indigenous languages with their own literary traditions.

---

[4] Only by playing dangerously complicated 'if' games can one get a little close to 'parallels': if the political unity of the Roman Empire had survived over wide areas of Europe and if the lingua franca of the tiny Pan-European administrative elite had been Chinese while the priestly culture was in Greek . . .

The Linguistic Survey of India[5] gives 179 languages and 544 dialects. But most of these are spoken by very small numbers of people. The Constitution lists fourteen 'languages of India' and the 1961 Census gives the following numbers of people returning each as their mother tongue.[6]

TABLE I

THE FOURTEEN LANGUAGES OF INDIA (CENSUS, 1961)

Language	Population (millions)		% of total population (439 million)	
Hindi	133.4		30.4	
Urdu	23.3		5.3	
Panjabi	10.9		2.5	
		167.6		38.2
Bihari	16.8		3.8	
Rajasthani	14.9		3.4	
		199.3		45.4
Telegu	37.7		8.6	
Bengali	33.9		7.7	
Marathi	33.3		7.6	
Tamil	30.6		7.0	
Gujarati	20.3		4.6	
Kannada	17.4		4.0	
Malayalam	17.0		3.9	
Oriya	15.7		3.6	
Assamese	6.8		1.5	
Kashmiri	1.9		0.4	
Sanskrit	0.002		0.00045	

[5] Calcutta, 1927. The main official documents on language questions in the post-Independence period are *Report of the Linguistic Provinces Commission*, New Delhi, Constituent Assembly, 1948; *Report of the Linguistic Provinces Committee*, New Delhi, Indian National Congress, 1949; *Report of the States Reorganization Commission*, New Delhi, Government of India, 1955; *Report of the Official Language Commission*, New Delhi, Government of India, 1957; *Report of the Committee of Parliament on Official Language*, New Delhi, Government of India, 1959; *Report of the Committee on National Integration*, New Delhi, Government of India, 1962; and the (annual) *Report of the Commissioner for Linguistic Minorities*, New Delhi, Government of India, 1959–65. Against this volume of official reports, other studies are surprisingly few: S. Harrison, *India: The Most Dangerous Decades*, Princeton, N.J., Princeton University Press, 1960; Joan Bondurant, *Regionalism versus Provincialism*, Berkeley and Los Angeles, University of California Press, 1958; Paul Friedrich, 'Language and Politics in India', *Daedalus*, Vol. 91, Summer 1962.

[6] 1961 Census, Table C-V (A). Bihari and Rajasthani are *not* in the Constitution's listed fourteen, but have been included here because they are so much more important than any of the other unlisted languages and because they are closely related to Hindi. These sixteen languages account for 414 millions out of a total population of 439 millions. A group of fifteen languages each spoken by over half a million account for a further 19 millions; nineteen languages with between 100,000 and 500,000 speakers are spoken by 4 millions; and 673 other languages cover only under a further 2 millions.

To this must be added the fact that the 1951 Census gave just under 4 million persons literate in English (1 per cent of the population, $6\frac{1}{2}$ per cent of all literates). Thus it can be seen that Hindi, strictly defined, is spoken by 30.4 per cent of the population, while the Hindi group, if taken to include Urdu and Panjabi,[7] accounts for 38.2 per cent of the population, and if this category is further extended to include Bihari and Rajasthani the coverage is 45.4 per cent. Four other languages (Telegu, Bengali, Marathi, and Tamil) are spoken by very large numbers of people, but none of these by itself accounts for more than 7 per cent to 9 per cent of the population. The Dravidian family, comprising Tamil, Telegu, Malayalam, and Kannada, accounts for just under one-quarter of the whole.

Alongside these statistics are to be placed less easily quantified social facts. For a century English has occupied a position of peculiar importance. In the first place, it was the language of government—not, admittedly, at the informal lower levels, but generally throughout the civil and military services and the judiciary. It was also the language of politics and public life, excepting again some of the activities at local level and in some princely states; as such, it was the language of much national protest and even when it ceased to be the cherished mark of distinction of the early leaders, it continued to be the unavoidable means of all-India communication in the independence struggle. Next, English was the language of higher education; this created an intellectual elite on an all-India basis with access to a rich world literature and to modern scientific knowledge. But at the same time it enhanced and emphasized the gap between the society's leading elements and the rest of the people. It also had this serious consequence for most of the Indian languages: they were by-passed by the tide of modernization and neglected by the vanguard of their own people. Possession by a few of English as a route into a new world provided independent India with a modernizing leadership; the other side of this was that the bulk of the people and their own languages were effectively insulated from change.

Such a situation could survive independence only if the English-educated could maintain an almost monopolistic position. But everything was against this. Already in the 1930s extension of the franchise and the creation of power centres in the provinces had provided a

---

[7] The combining of these admittedly begs some questions. Urdu is not so much a regional as a (Muslim) community language, similar to Hindi, but with borrowings from Arabic and Persian rather than Sanskrit and written in a different script. Panjabi is closely related to Hindi; the demand for a separate Panjabi-speaking state, to which the Government agreed in 1966, was inspired more by the fears of the Sikh community than by linguistic aspirations.

political challenge. The rise of regional business classes during the war years was continued afterwards. The expansion of Primary and Secondary education increased literacy in the Indian languages; literacy in English probably increased also, but less rapidly; certainly the knowledge of English available among university students was said to decline and the switching of the medium of instruction in at least some universities away from English has not only recognized this trend but furthered it. In all, it seemed as if an artificial dam had now burst under the pressure of forces held back by special circumstances.[8] In that situation someone was bound to get hurt, and it was the English-educated. But more important was the question as to whether the unity of the country would suffer a deadly blow. What could protect cultural and political coherence against 'the upsurge of the regional languages' released by 'a new mass social consciousness'?[9] Many observers, inside India and outside, could see only a choice between some form of central authoritarianism and a fragmentation of the body politic. Neither has yet happened, even though India has moved into the dreaded 'after Nehru' era. Some would say that indeed there is a loosening of all-India's hold on the minds of the people and a matching weakening of the central Government's power in relation to the states. The evidence, however, does not point all in that direction and the movement, if it is there, is very slight. What are the containing forces?

The pressures from the newly politicized classes and the accompanying demands for the cutting down of English to its proper size as a foreign— albeit important—language were real and evident. But is the metaphor of the bursting dam historically correct? The change was, in fact, less dramatic and requires a less sensationalist presentation. In Ceylon it does indeed appear true to say that not until after Independence did any challenge confront the small English-educated elite; when it came, it came suddenly and swept all before it—though later, even here, there seems to have been some retreat. India's development was different. First, it is important to remember that some of the Indian languages—notably Bengali and Marathi—were vehicles for a cultural renaissance associated with political and social movements of reform and liberation as long ago as the turn of the century. Secondly, it must

---

[8] A different water metaphor was used with respect to the switch from English in universities by the *Report of the University Education Commission*, Government of India, New Delhi, 1949, when it said (p. 478) that this was 'a plunge . . . attended with unusual risks', but 'inevitable'.

[9] Harrison, op. cit., Ch. III, 'The New Regional Elites'.

not be forgotten that the interwar extension of the nationalist movement, while more limited than it appeared or pretended at the time, did entail the mobilization by an all-India leadership of groups whose political work was at least in substantial part performed through regional languages. Gandhi preached Hindustani as the national language, operated a machine which worked mainly in English, and reorganized the units of the party on the basis of regional languages. That capacity for sustaining the incompatibles is a clue worth bearing in mind.

It must nevertheless be admitted that the campaign for the reorganization of the states on linguistic lines developed to such a degree over the first decade of independence that it produced convulsions in the body politic. That it did so was in large measure the result of the opposition to the change on the part of Nehru and a few of his colleagues, but their resistance was itself an indication of their fears. It is likely that if the creation of more or less homogeneous linguistic states had been conceded quickly and quietly less damage would have been done to all-India loyalty. However, this was not done and India suffered her first bloody encounter with the problem of language in politics. The present decision to create some form of Panjabi-speaking state by cutting off portions from the existing state of Panjab is best seen as the postponed last stage of that operation.[10] The new states that emerged from the reorganization have in the main justified themselves as viable and coherent entities. True, the position of language minority groups within these new assertively linguistic states has nowhere been easy and the latest *Reports of the Commissioner for Linguistic Minorities* give an account which is less than reassuring; the recommended safeguards for minority groups in the state public services have been inadequately implemented. Further, the position of a few particular language minorities—for instance, Marathi-speakers in Mysore, and Bengalis and tribal groups in Assam—causes tension and dominates the local political scene. On the other hand, the creation of linguistic states has released energies which had previously been consumed by every form of struggle between linguistic groups within the multi-linguistic states. There no doubt remain several sources of conflict and faction within state politics

[10] It must be admitted that *Panjabi Suba* has been a primarily communal campaign of Sikhs dressed up as a language plea. It can also be allowed that the calm view taken here is not widely shared; the concession of Panjabi Suba is insistently seen as a sign of weakness and a prelude to a further series of dreadful strains. It is India's fate to attract prophets of gloom. (Perhaps she encourages them by her own self-criticism, perhaps by her very success in maintaining stability in face of gigantic difficulties—most infuriating for the 'news'-hungry lovers of alarm and crisis.) It is her achievement to disappoint them.

and there are few states which present a picture of harmonious cohesion, but at least one important cause of bitter dissension was removed.

The emergence of these more easily consolidated state units, however, raises other questions. The first concerns the balance between centre and states. The fears of those like Nehru who resisted linguistic states were that the increased strength of state governments would imply a weaker position for the Union Government. This does not, of course, necessarily follow if the centre is simultaneously strengthened, nor should one accept the implication that the centre gains in power if states are helplessly torn by internal strife; after all, the states are in many respects the agents of the centre, and a paralysed state government is at least as weakening to the centre as a strong and stubborn one. Whether in practice the fears have been realized is, as suggested already, a moot point. To measure change in federal balance is extremely difficult; the relationship is a bargaining one and a shift in political 'terms of trade' is not so easily detected. A great deal depends on whom you talk to. Like all good canny businessmen the participants in the political and administrative 'dealing' process do not like to admit to making great 'gains'. From their conversation you would conclude that times are hard and 'profit margins' negligible: the man at the centre bemoans the weakness of his position, the man at the state end makes out that he comes off worse. The matter is complicated by the fact that the position of the states is far from uniform and both could be right. Some states—by reason of size or leadership or other determinants of 'league table position'—are stronger than others. The general impression is, no doubt, that the rising power of the states was held in some check so long as Nehru was in effective control at New Delhi, but that subsequently the ugly harvest of states' reorganization has been fully reaped. Attention, for example, is drawn to the manner in which in the food crisis of 1965–6 certain surplus states managed to evade their obligations to pass grain on to deficit areas.

On the other hand, it must not be overlooked that the central leadership—taking Cabinet and Congress Working Committee together—now contains a greater proportion of the strong and senior leaders than during most of the Nehru period. Moreover, these men—Kamaraj, Reddy, Chavan, for instance—are masters of state politics and by their side many of the Chief Ministers are beginners. It was Nehru who wielded the axe that cut down six state leaders in one blow, but it was Kamaraj who fashioned the weapon. Also, it was Shastri who afterwards forced without much difficulty the resignation of the Orissa

Chief Minister. One has to remember that the Nehru era was by no means one of unambiguous central dominance; in relation to certain states, the great man put up with a great deal for the sake of peace and quiet and from his weakness some state rulers profited. Thus the generally accepted impression may be mistaken and it is probably nearer the mark to say that, both state reorganization and the removal of Nehru notwithstanding, the federal balance has undergone remarkably little change.

But the creation of linguistic states also reacts back on the language situation itself. The obvious effect of the new practically single-language units was to advance still further the regional languages as the media of state public life—at the expense, naturally, of English, which had enjoyed a role as common ground between Marathi and Gujarati in undivided Bombay and between the Dravidian languages in un-divided Madras. The change is marked in some fields—that of legis-lature debates notably—but has been slower and more limited than might have been expected in others. For example, while the use of the regional language in the administration has somewhat increased, the medium of examination for entry into state public service remains English *alone* in Assam, Bengal, Andhra, Kerala, Mysore, Madras, Gujarat, Maharashtra, and Panjab, while even in Uttar Pradesh, Bihar, Rajasthan, and Madhya Pradesh it is still English or Hindi. Again, while the importance in circulations of the regional-language newspapers has undoubtedly increased, there is no decline in the English Press. The force of habit is part of the explanation, but it is also that a language does not at once become equipped for new functions. As fresh responsi-bilities are imposed on the regional languages, so they will grow to be able to fulfil them. Indeed, it is precisely in this way that, over time, the arrested development of these languages will be resumed.

Now it is this gradually but surely growing importance of regional languages which calls for compensating emphasis on an all-India language if national issues and loyalties are to find adequate expres-sion. In this way are the two main aspects of the Indian language problem related: the assumption of full responsibility and 'adult status' by the regional languages comes about at the expense of English, and the capacity of English to serve as an all-India medium is thereby reduced; at the same time, Hindi as a regional language shares in the prosperity and development of the whole group of regional languages, but its capacity to replace English as the all-India medium is limited. The limits are mainly three. First, even more is required of an all-India language than of a state language in so far as the issues and styles of

national public life are more sophisticated than those of the states; bu
Hindi, so far from being the most developed of the Indian languages, i
rather less developed than some. It is of more recent growth, its litera
ture is less notable, its literacy figures are poor,[11] and its homeland fel
the impact of scientific and cultural change rather less and later than di
the areas around Calcutta, Bombay, and Madras.

Secondly, the necessary modernization of Hindi gives rise to specia
problems. For one thing, Hindi enthusiasts were already engaged in
struggle to 'purify' the language—to increase the distance betwee
itself and its Muslim 'partner', Urdu—by the replacement of word
derived from Persian and Arabic by words constructed from Sanskri
This 'communal' urge aggravates the difficulty of the gap betwee
ordinary spoken Hindi and the emerging refurbished product of th
scholars. It also entails a resistance, stronger than might otherwise b
the case, to both the romanization of the script and the incorporatio
of words, especially technical ones, from English. Finally, and mos
marked of all in its political implications, there is the limit set by th
very fact that Hindi is a regional language.[12] Its selection as all-Indi
medium is naturally seen by people of the non-Hindi areas as inevit
ably giving its region an advantage over others. It is around this issu
that Madras in 1965 caught fire.

Language policy has been a matter of fairly active political concern i
India for the last twenty years. Before 1946, it is fair to say, the probler
was pronounced upon from time to time, but scarcely thought throug
Of all the nationalist leaders only Gandhi from the beginning of h
impact on the movement gave it serious attention.[13] In his insistence
from as early as 1918, on Hindustani as India's national language h
never wavered. It was necessary for the movement—and later th
national Government—to be able to speak as the people spoke an
here was the best available means, understood at least over the Norther

[11] The Hindi states come low in the table: Bihar, 18 per cent; Uttar Pradesh and Madh
Pradesh, 17 per cent; Rajasthan, 15 per cent. (Quoted in 'Our Language Problem'
symposium) *Education Quarterly*, Government of India, December 1963.)

[12] Outside the Hindi zone, broadly defined as including Central and Northern India, t
percentage who have Hindi as a second language drops sharply: Maharashtra, 8.9 per cen
West Bengal and Assam, 6.7 per cent; Gujarat, 3.5 per cent; Orissa, 1.8 per cent; Mysor
1.3 per cent; Andhra, 1.2 per cent; Kerala and Madras, 0.2 per cent.

[13] His writings on the subject are collected in *Thoughts on National Language*, Ahmed
bad, Navajivan Press, 1956. Nehru's pre-Independence essay, 'The Question of Languag
is in his *The Unity of India*, London, Lindsay Drummond (3rd impression), 1948. Mu
of the limited preparatory thinking finds expression in Z. A. Ahmed's symposium, *Nation
Language for India*, Allahabad, Kitabistan, 1941.

wo-thirds of the land. It was necessary also to use language to heal Iindu-Muslim communalism; Hindustani, the half-way between Iindi and Urdu, could achieve this. Finally, English had to be dis-placed—given a different role no doubt—if that self-respect as a nation vhich was the real object of political independence was to be gained. Iowever, despite the pronouncements, the activities of language-propagating societies, and even the rules about the conduct of business nside Congress, little real change had taken place by 1946 in the relative ositions of Hindi and English.

When the Constituent Assembly met decisions had to be taken, first n respect of the deliberations and proceedings of that body, next on the anguage in which the document was to be drawn up, and finally on the ctual provisions to be included in the fundamental law of the land. At nce sharp divisions appeared.[14] It is most important to note that these lid not take the form of explicit confrontation between Hindi and .nglish as rivals for the position of national language. Rather, the rgument was about the *timing* of the switch, the *nature* of the Hindi anguage to be employed, and the *extent* of legal and governmental provision on its behalf. The designation of some form of Hindi as ational language at some stage and for some purposes was not ques-ioned at that time, nor has it been successfully challenged in any clear ashion subsequently.[15] Briefly, the Constitution (Part XVII, Articles 43–51) established a number of positions: evading the term 'national anguage', it designated Hindi in Devanagari script as 'the official anguage of the Union' and the use of international numerals; it stipu-ated that English could continue to be used for fifteen years (from 1950) or official purposes; it empowered the President, *within* the fifteen-ear period, to authorize the use of Hindi and of Devanagari numerals longside English; it empowered Parliament, *after* fifteen years, to

[14] The first detailed account of these is contained in Chapter 12, 'Language and the .onstitution—the Half-Hearted Compromise', of Granville Austin's valuable study, *The idian Constitution : Cornerstone of a Nation*, Oxford, Clarendon Press, 1966.

[15] As Austin (op. cit.) shows, the Assembly's decision-making process on the language sue was most tortuous and obscure, but it is clear that no straight vote as between English nd Hindi was ever called for. Ambedkar's statement (in his *Thoughts on Linguistic States*,)elhi, Ambedkar, 1955, quoted by Austin) that 'Hindi won its place as the national language y one vote' was irresponsibly misleading and has been copied by others. It appears, in fact, 1at the Assembly's language decisions were taken by 'overwhelming majorities', the real ght having taken place inside the party. Even here the key vote in the Congress Assembly arty on 16 July 1947 was 63–32 in favour of Hindi *simply as opposed to Hindustani*. The ne-vote myth, Austin concludes, can only refer to a Party-meeting decision of 26 August 949 which at one stage in its confused proceedings gave preference to Nagri against .nternational' *numerals* (op. cit., p. 300), a decision in any event reversed in the final :rsion.

provide for the use of English and of Devanagari numerals for specified purposes; it laid down a time programme for review and recommendation by Commission and Parliamentary Committee; it left to the state legislatures the matter of official language at state level, insisting only that the language used for Union official purposes be used for state-Union communication and also for inter-state communication (unless states concerned agreed to use Hindi); it protected English as the language of the Supreme and High Courts and of authoritative texts of Bills, Acts and Orders of Government; it gave a general direction to the Union to develop and promote the spread of Hindi.

The first review of the problem took place when the Official Language Commission was duly set up in 1955 and reported in the following year. The twenty-man body representing all the major languages of the country concluded, subject to a 'minority report' by one member and a minute of dissent by another,[16] that despite all the difficulties the place envisaged by the Constitution for Hindi represented 'the only practicable course'. It went on to spell out the implications, even though some of these went beyond its strict terms of reference. So far as the educational system was concerned, while the medium of instruction in schools should be the regional language or mother-tongue, Hindi should everywhere be introduced as a subject in Secondary education though the timing of compulsion in this should be left to states to determine; Hindi areas should be merely 'encouraged to provide facilities' for non-Hindi languages to be taught. In universities, a change from English as medium of instruction and examination was firmly envisaged, but the decisions as to stages, differential treatment of subjects, and the choice between Hindi and regional languages should be left to universities to decide. In the administration of the Union Government, the advance of Hindi depends on the preparation of standard terminology and the training of staff in its use; the Commission thought the Government would be justified in imposing Hindi tests on existing personnel and new entrants provided it gave sufficient warning. But it did not favour restrictions on the use of English and it left the timetable of change to the Government.

The language of legislation and the law courts would eventually have to be Hindi, but it was clear that much preparatory work had to be done before any change-over—including the establishment of an authoritative Hindi version of the statute book—could be attempted. In the Union Public Services examinations, Hindi should be introduced

[16] A third member appended a 'separate note' which set out how he would have wished the Report to go further in pressing Hindi forward.

first as a compulsory subject ('offset' by a paper for Hindi candidates chosen from 'a variety of options' including South Indian languages), then as an alternative medium of instruction. It was conceded that as regional languages developed as university media, they would have to be accepted as public service examination media—thus producing impossible problems of standardization and raising the question of regional quotas of entrants as the only solution; the Commission hoped that before this happened the teaching of Hindi in the South might have advanced so that competitors from the South would be at no disadvantage with a Hindi medium of examination.

The minority report by Dr. S. K. Chatterjee (Bengal) urged that the progressive use of Hindi be 'kept in abeyance for the time being' because (mainly) of the differential advantages this would confer on citizens of Hindi areas; he added, however, that effort should be concentrated on the spread of Hindi in non-Hindi states. The minute of dissent by Dr. P. Subbarayan (Madras) was couched in very similar terms but with rather more emphasis on the very distant future—'long time to come', 'many years', 'ultimately'—prior to which not only would non-Hindi India be unprepared for Hindi but Hindi would be unready for its role. The Committee of thirty Members of Parliament who examined the Commission's report added little. Apart from six 'minutes of dissent' and 'notes'—including a most vigorous one by Sir Frank Anthony, the Anglo-Indian Member of Parliament—they only insisted that the Union Government should 'prepare and implement a plan of action for the progressive use of Hindi' in official business and discouraged the notion of public service examinations in languages other than Hindi and English.

These reports, while cautious in tone, reflected some of the pressures which continued to be made by the Hindi enthusiasts. They implied that if 1965 could not be a date of dramatic change-over, nevertheless things could not be allowed to stay unaltered. But this mood only increased the anxieties of the non-Hindi areas, especially the South. Nehru was looked to for resistance to any speed-up in the Hindi programme and he responded by a number of statements in which he spoke of the need to have English 'for an indefinite period . . . as an associate additional language . . . for official purposes' and also stressed that the pace of Hindi's advance could not be imposed but had to be determined by the views of the non-Hindi people. These statements, however, were usually in the form of highly personal reflections —as if he could not yet make the go-slow on Hindi a matter of government policy. Nevertheless, it was sufficient—when coupled with fresh anxiety about 'national integration'—to bring about a change of emphasis in a series of official statements and reports. Thus the Government of India Resolution of 1959 referred to the need for 'a flexible approach' to the switch away from English, one that would 'take into account' the views of the non-Hindi areas. The Presidential Order of 1960 stated that after 1965 Hindi would be the 'principal' official language while English would continue as 'associate' official language with no restrictions on its use; Hindi would become an alternative medium of examination for entry to the Union public services but for the present only a qualifying paper in Hindi was required. The National Integration Conference of 1961 expressed the shift of position in several ways: English would have to serve as 'link language' because it would 'take some time' before Hindi could be ready; English was in any case important for higher, especially scientific and technological, education and for international contacts, and its study should not be neglected; Hindi areas were expected under the 'three-language formula' for Secondary education[17] to be more serious about the teaching of other Indian, and preferably South Indian, languages. The Committee on Emotional Integration added two further points: the pace at which regional languages were increasing in importance made it necessary to reinforce the positions of both Hindi and English by introducing them at the later stages of Primary education, by ensuring their continuation steadily through Secondary schools and above all by maintaining them in those universities that are switching to instruction in regional languages,[18] second, to make easier the teaching of Hindi in non-Hindi areas, permission should be given to teach it in Roman instead of Devanagari script and there could even be experiments in teaching it in various regional scripts. Finally the Official Languages Act of 1963 restated the assurances that even after January 1965

[17] Originally put out in a rather complex form by the Central Advisory Board of Education in 1956, this was simplified and endorsed by the 1961 Conference of Chief Ministers to mean that the languages to be taught in secondary schools (where the medium of instruction was, of course, the regional language) would be: (a) regional language (and mother-tongue if different); (b) Hindi or, in Hindi areas, another Indian language; (c) English or other modern European language. See *Report of the Committee on Emotional Integration*, Appendixes 19–22. It is clear that both 'sides' were cheating: Northern states were teaching Sanskrit or some neighbouring North Indian language while Southern states were similarly often avoiding Hindi.

[18] The Committee's *Report* gives, in Appendix 23, a statement of the position in forty universities. This shows that in eleven of these some degree of Hindi instruction had come in, in three others instruction in a regional language. It would appear that the Committee's main concern was about the loss of standards and intellectual isolation arising out of the switch away from English in the Hindi areas. The same point received some emphasis at the fourth Annual Conference of Vice-Chancellors (*Report*, 1962).

English would continue to be used in addition to Hindi for all official business of the Union for which it was already being used as well as for parliamentary business.

In view of this painful but not insignificant retreat, it may be asked why the South's distrust not only remained but grew until it exploded in fury in February 1965. The answer must in part be that the retreat had left too many ambiguities and the death of Nehru had removed the personal guarantor of the interests of the South. English was by law to continue, but in practice would the life of the non-Hindi Union government servant be made impossible by his Hindi colleagues, by Hindi superiors and Hindi Ministers? It does indeed seem that the circulars which began to go out at the end of 1964—prescribing Hindi for correspondence with Hindi states and Hindi translations to accompany letters done in English—might have been differently worded under a watchful defender of the South. But the new leadership was finding its feet and, despite the presence of Kamraj of Madras near its elbow, evidently did not take adequate account of Southern fears.

What of the aftermath of 1965's violence? The extraordinary fact is that by mid-1966, although nothing had happened to change the legal position with regard to language policy, all had become quiet again. Part of the explanation is that the war with Pakistan silenced all dissension, at least for some time. But it seems that the South is satisfied that the Northerners have received a real shock, above all that the party leadership has been firmly alerted to the dangers of attempting any kind of imposition. The resolution which eventually emerged from the Congress Working Committee in June 1965 went quite far: the three-language formula is to be strictly applied and extended even to the university stage; steps are to be taken to conduct Union public service examinations in *all* regional languages (including Hindi) as well as English, while the examinations will include compulsory papers in English and Hindi (or, for Hindi-speakers, another regional language); regional languages are to become as soon as possible not only the languages of state administration but also the medium of university instruction; while the importance of English-language teaching is stressed, a phased programme for the development and use of Hindi is to be prepared. This scheme clearly attempts to remove fears of differential advantage, advance all regional languages in their areas, and at the same time guarantee the existence of effective link languages for all-India purposes.

It is too early to say how far the resolution has been implemented,[19]

[19] Although the resolution made no reference to amending the Official Languages Act

but its adoption by the leaders following months of argument should assure its importance. The central point is that it comes from the dominant party, which is determined not to lose its hold on any part of the country. It may have secured two vital things: an atmosphere of confidence in which the natural processes of language development, together with the necessary measures of deliberate language *reform*,[20] can take place, and more time so that the adjustments to avoid suffering and loss of efficiency can be made.

The difficulties of India's language problem, in other words, are not unevenly matched by the political resources she can bring to their handling—not least a body of shrewd and seasoned politicians, trained in the states but conditioned, in layers as they move up the party ladder, to think in all-India terms. The Madras violence admittedly revealed flaws in their communications systems, but on the whole their sensitivity and balance are highly developed. The 1965 resolution is neither a perfectly safe nor an easy solution; it is another groping step. But if the language question is one to be lived with, this may be more possible by tentative small moves taken over time. Time is the essence here; to gain it is to gain all.

Two recent events point to the measure of success so far achieved. In July 1965 the Jan Sangh, associated with extremist Hindi sponsorship, announced that it welcomed the three-language formula and in deference to the views of its units in the South had decided not to press for the switch to Hindi for the next ten years, trusting that this would give time for the language to develop in the South.[21] In February 1966, Kamraj, the Congress President, stood up to give his address to the annual Session of the Party. He explained that his address was in Tamil and he would not read it, but would hand over to the translator, who would deliver the Hindi version. As he walked to his seat Hindi Congressmen protested and begged him to read it first in Tamil —which he smilingly agreed to do.

---

in such a way as further to protect the South against the imposition of Hindi, Party and Government spokesmen did give the impression that this would be done. So far as the present writer knows, no amending legislation has yet been passed. The war with Pakistan followed close on these discussions and the matter appears not to have been taken up subsequently.

[20] On this subject, see Alfred Pietrzyk, 'Problems in Language Planning: The Case of Hindi', in B. N. Varma (Ed.), *Contemporary India*, London, Asia Publishing House, 1964.

[21] It may be suggested that this reflects not merely that Party's desire to retain an all-India status which it was in danger of losing but also its determination to keep in line with its Congress Party sympathizers who had been persuaded by the leaders to go along with the Working Committee formula. In such ways does a dominant party influence others as well as (more often indeed) receiving influences from them.

IV

The Cohesive Role of Sanskritization

BY M. N. SRINIVAS

Professor of Sociology, University of Delhi

I

SANSKRITIZATION has been an important cultural process ever since the Vedic Aryans established themselves in India. Professor S. K. Chatterjee has written: 'The progressive Sanskritization of the various pre-Aryan or non-Aryan peoples in their culture, their outlook and their ways of life, forms the keynote of India through the ages. And in the course of this "Sanskritization" the affected peoples also brought their own spiritual and material milieus to bear upon the Sanskrit and Sanskritic culture which they were adopting and thus helped to modify and to enrich it in their own circles.'[1] Sanskritization is not confined to any single part of the country, but widespread in the subcontinent, including remote and forested regions. It affected a wide variety of groups, both those within the Hindu fold and others outside. (It was even carried to neighbouring countries such as Ceylon, Indonesia, and Tibet.) With the absorption of each new group not only did the corpus of Sanskritization as well as its prestige increase, but absorption actually became easier.

British rule set in motion a vast array of forces, some of which greatly strengthened Sanskritization, while others were either hostile or indifferent to it. It was also during British rule that the Westernization of India began, a complex and wide-ranging process, and one whose importance is likely to increase in the future.

Sanskritization may be briefly defined as the process by which a 'low' caste or tribe or other group takes over the customs, ritual,

---

[1] '*Kirata-Jana-Krti*—The Indo-Mongoloids, their Contribution to the History and Culture of India', *Journal of the Royal Asiatic Society of Bengal*, 3rd Series, Vol. XVI, 1950, p. 148. It is interesting to note that Professor Chatterjee used the term 'Sanskritization' as far back as 1950. At that time he was not aware of my use of the term. I used it for the first time in 1947 in my D. Phil. thesis, and this was not published until 1952.

beliefs, ideology and style of life of a high and, in particular, a 'twice-born' (*dwija*) caste. The Sanskritization of a group has usually the effect of improving its position in the local caste hierarchy. It normally presupposes either an improvement in the economic or political position of the group concerned or a higher group self-consciousness resulting from its contact with a source of the 'Great Tradition' of Hinduism such as a pilgrim centre or monastery or proselytizing sect.

The existence of a highly systematized hierarchy both favours and inhibits the Sanskritization of the lower castes. The culture of higher castes is a matter of prestige, and ambitious lower castes would like to take it over. As against this, however, the locally dominant caste, wherever one existed, would want its culture to be its exclusive property, and not usurped by a low caste. But in spite of this, Sanskritization did spread, over the centuries, to groups in every part of the country.

In the case of a group external to Hinduism such as a tribe or immigrant ethnic body, Sanskritization resulted in drawing it into the Hindu fold, which necessarily involved its becoming a caste having regular relations with other local castes.

Sectarian movements often acted as agents of Sanskritization, and when they attracted members from low castes they helped to raise their status. But, as is well known, a sect was regarded as a caste by outsiders, and within it there were endogamous castes. This situation is typical of the caste system in which the internal divisions of a caste are ignored by outsiders.

The above remarks apply to sects which popular opinion regards as firmly within the Hindu fold. In the case of sects which are either marginal or outside, conversion failed entirely to dissolve caste distinctions among the converts.

Sanskritization is a profound and many-sided cultural process only a part of which has structural relevance. Its impress is seen in language, literature, ideology, music, dance, drama, style of life and ritual.[2] Its influence is not confined to Hindus, but is visible even in sects and religious groups outside Hinduism.

II

In order to assess properly the contribution of Sanskritization to Hinduism and India it is necessary to remember certain features of Hinduism which mark it off sharply from other world religions. Hinduism does not have the kind of overarching formal structure that Roman

[2] See V. Raghavan, 'Variety and Integration in the Pattern of Indian Culture', *The Far Eastern Quarterly*, Vol. XV, No. 4, August 1956, pp. 497–505.

Catholicism, for instance, has, nor a body of trained missionaries who are devoted to convert the unbelieving. There is no body of dogma to which all Hindus are required to subscribe. Hinduism is also not a 'congregational' religion and Hindus are not required to gather together for weekly prayers as are Muslims or Christians.

Hinduism is best described as a loose confederation of innumerable cults, the connecting threads of which are found in Sanskritization, and, in the last resort, Brahmins. There are cults of ancestors, of caste, village, and sectarian deities, and of the great gods of Hinduism. There are centres of pilgrimage which draw pilgrims from regions varying in extent from the entire subcontinent to a local area composed of a few neighbouring villages. These centres may be temples, rivers, river sources and confluences, the sea at some places, tombs of saints, and places associated with epic heroes. Centres may be visited throughout the year, or only on certain special occasions. The calendrical festivals observed by Hindus may again vary from the strictly local to those common to Hindus everywhere. In the case of the latter there are regional variations in ritual, myth or belief, or all three. Occasionally, what is common is nothing but the festival name.

The sacred literature of the Hindus, in Sanskrit (or inspired by Sanskrit, but in a regional or other language), has played a vital part in enabling Sanskritic Hinduism to absorb local cults. The two epics, *Ramayana* and *Mahabharata*, and the *puranas*, which are popular stories about the great gods of Sanskritic Hinduism and their relatives, retainers, and followers, have been especially significant in this connexion. According to J. Dowson:

The *Puranas* succeed the *Itihasas* or epic poems, but at a considerable distance of time, and must be distinguished from them. The epics treat of the legendary actions of heroes as mortal men, the *Puranas* celebrate the powers and works of positive gods, and represent a later and more extravagant form of Hinduism . . .[3]

The contribution which the *puranas* have made towards the production of a common religious culture out of a vast and heterogeneous mass of local beliefs, myths, and cults has been well described by Professor Raghavan:[4]

In religious dogma and cult *puranas*, *agamas* and *tantras* show how the great tradition absorbed different local cults and made a pattern and system out of the heterogeneous practices functioning at different levels. A common phenomenon is the sudden emergence in relatively full-fledged form of a

[3] *A Classical Dictionary of Hindu Mythology*, London, 1961, p. 245.
[4] Raghavan, op. cit., p. 500.

deity and its worship, for example, Ganesha, Durga and Rādha, and of cults and schools of thought like the Shaivite and Vaishnavite sects, the adoration of Kārtavīrya, Dattātreya, etc. Though philosophers and Sanskrit religious authors ignored them, they were winning status among the people, and the time came when they first entered the popular books, the *puranas*, which provided a liaison between the learned classes and the masses. The accepted eighteen *puranas* were revised, eighteen minor *puranas* came into being, and many other *Samhitas* and *purana*-like compilations were composed which incorporated all this growing material. As the locale of this culture expanded, new holy spots, shrines and sacred waters (*ksetra* and *tirtha*) in newly occupied regions were designated. *Purana*-like accounts (*Mahatmya*) described the new sites, linking them by significant legends to epic heroes and gods and to episodes mentioned in the *itihasas* and *puranas*, and thus sanctifying them.

The superficial observer of Hinduism is apt to be bewildered by its seeming lack of form, its great complexity, its multitude of gods and its heterogeneous modes of worship. To take but one example: the idea of a single supreme being originally became crystallized towards the end of *Rig Veda Samhitas*, and was fully developed in the period between the *Samhitas* and *Brāhmanas*.[5] But it was significant that the development of monotheism did not result in the rejection of polytheism and henotheism. They all existed together, but the position of Brahmins in the caste hierarchy and the prestige of Sanskritic Hinduism were such that henotheism and monotheism were preferred to polytheism by upwardly mobile groups. The fact that alien groups could enter, over a period of time, the Hindu fold, and that there were prospects of social mobility for groups already inside Hinduism, meant that they had to take over the beliefs of the higher castes.

Polytheism, henotheism, and monotheism constitute a continuum. In both polytheism and henotheism a number of deities are propitiated, but in henotheism the deity who is being worshipped at the moment is regarded as supreme. In other words, henotheism may be regarded as temporary monotheism. According to Dowson, there was, in Vedic religion, '. . . a constant tendency to elevate now this one now that one to the supremacy, and to look upon him as the Great Power.' Temporary monotheism may either lead to permanent monotheism or be a substitute for it. Here again it must be pointed out that Hindu monotheism is profoundly different from Islamic or Christian monotheism. All gods are true gods, but as a group develops it sees that there is only one god who is called by different names by different people

[5] Dowson, op. cit., p. xi.
[6] Ibid.

According to the *Rig Veda*: 'God is one but sages call him by different names.' The daily *sandhya* prayer of Brahmins includes the hymn: 'Just as all the rain-water pouring down from the sky reaches ultimately the ocean, salutations to various gods reach ultimately Keshava [one of the names of Vishnu].'

In this connexion the existence of a certain division of labour among deities forces the usually monotheistic Hindu to be 'polytheistic'. Thus when success is wanted in any enterprise the elephant-headed Vināyaka, the son of Shiva, is worshipped. Lakshmi is worshipped for wealth, Saraswati for learning, and so on. In addition, in popular Hinduism, innumerable deities have a reputation for granting such tangible benefits as children, the cure of cattle diseases, and particular ailments of human beings. Village goddesses in several parts of India preside over the epidemics of plague, cholera, and smallpox, and even Brahmins learned in Sanskrit worship them.

The average Hindu, then, worships a multiplicity of deities, but the idea that all of them are only manifestations of the one god who is present everywhere and who has many forms, makes Hindu polytheism qualitatively different from other polytheisms.

It is in sectarian Hinduism that a spirit of exclusiveness is visible, but even there it is not great enough to insist on the exclusive propitiation of only one god. To take the example of an extreme sect: the Shri Vaishnava Brahmins of the South worship only Vishnu. Orthodox Shri Vaishnavites boast that they will not visit a Shiva temple even if dragged by elephants. But Vishnu himself has many *avatars* and manifestations, and Shri Vaishnavites worship Vishnu in each of his manifestations.

A popular mode of worshipping a deity is to chant his 108 (*ashtothara*) or 1,000 (*sahasranama*) names. These names refer to the various attributes, forms, and manifestations of the deity who is being worshipped. The idea of manifestation which resulted in a deity or even an historic personality being made out to be a great god was a potent source for the absorption of the deities of low castes and tribal people. Village goddesses in most parts of India have been identified with Shakti, who is in turn a manifestation of Pārvati, the wife of Shiva. The cobra deity is identified in South India with Subramanya, the warrior son of Shiva. The Kaveri River is identified with the Ganga (River Ganges). Rama and Buddha are both regarded as *avatars* of Vishnu. And so on. Identification not only enabled wide cultural gulfs to be spanned, but also provided a means for the eventual transformation of the name and character of the deity, and the mode of worshipping him.

Many Sanskritic deities worshipped in India today began their existence in the dim past as the deities of low castes or tribes.

The deities of the Sanskritic pantheon are very much family men,
except Ganapati (or Vinayaka), the remover of obstacles, and Hanu-
man, the monkey devotee of Rama. The god's wife or wives are also
worshipped. The two sons of Shiva, Ganapati and Subramanya, are
great gods in their own right. The animal or bird on which a god sits
(*vahana* or 'vehicle') also becomes an object of worship. The Brahmani
kite is the 'vehicle' of Vishnu; the peacock, of Subramanya; the bull,
Nandi, of Shiva; and the rat, of Ganapati.

The pantheistic idea that all things are animated by god provides a
philosophic rationale for the worship of such objects as stones, trees,
animals, and rivers. But it should be noted that where a tree, for
instance, is worshipped, there is usually present a myth linking it with a
Sanskritic deity or epic hero. The *ashwatha* tree (*ficus religiosa*), for
instance, is regarded as the abode of Vishnu in his form as Narayana.
All the major rivers of India have myths which testify to their sacred-
ness and to their sin-cleansing virtues, and linking them with Sanskritic deities, or famous seers (*rishis*) or epic heroes.[7]

The epics also have been responsible for the spread of Sanskritic
Hinduism: they have not only transmitted to the people a knowledge
of the great gods of Hinduism and certain basic theological ideas, but
have also helped to spread a common culture throughout the country.
The epics, and the innumerable stories included in them, constitute the
foundation of the literature in every Indian language. The fact that the
institution of *harikatha*, or public reading of the epics and *puranas* by
trained masters of the art, was a popular pastime made it possible for
Sanskritic Hinduism to reach even the illiterate masses.

In the Tamil country, however, there has been an attempt to reject
the older epic *Rāmayana* on the ground that it is Northern, Aryan, and
anti-Dravidian. The organized hatred for the *Rāmayana* is part of the
Tamil non-Brahmin movement, a cultural and political movement
which began towards the end of World War I.[8]

Thus far I have concerned myself with those characteristics and
aspects of Sanskritic Hinduism which enable it to absorb local cultural

---

[7] See, e.g., 'The Kaveri Myth', in my *Religion and Society among the Coorgs of South
India*, Bombay, 1965, pp. 213–28.

[8] One of the literary products of this movement is a play called '*Keemayanam*', in which
the tables are turned on the epic hero Rama and his followers. The performance of this
play has been banned in Madras State on the ground that it offends the religious suscepti-
bilities of large numbers of Hindus.

beliefs. When a local cult is so absorbed there is an addition to the corpus of Sanskritic Hinduism and, historically speaking, Sanskritic Hinduism has grown by such addition. McKim Marriott has called this process 'universalization', and its opposite—the process by which an element of Sanskritic Hinduism becomes localized—as 'parochialization'.[9] Just as a local element becomes transformed in the course of its ascent into Sanskritic Hinduism, a universal element similarly alters its identity in the course of descent into 'parochial' Hinduism. Another term for 'parochialization' is 'de-Sanskritization'.

The complex character of the processes subsumed under Sanskritization is illustrated when it is seen that occasionally ideas which have been developed through the regional language but under Sanskritic inspiration have returned to Sanskritic Hinduism often transformed in the process.

An example of this is seen in the name of the shrine of the famous Nataraja at Chidambaram. The shrine embodies the Daharavidya of the Upanishads. *Dahara* or *dahra* or *dobhra* means '*small*' and *dabhra-akasa* is the small or microscosmic space, the image of the macrocosmic *akasa*, of which the correct Tamil rendering is *Sirrambalam* or *siruambalam*. But when the *akasa* was also thought of as embodying *cit*, the principle of consciousness, the name *sirrambalam* was by a quasi-folk etymology remade as *cid-ambaram*, a freshly formed Sanskrit name, which still persists. Sanskrit devotional literature was also increased by re-absorbing in Sanskrit garb, material which was originally given the people in their own local tongues.[10]

III

I shall now mention the main agents of Sanskritization. Since Sanskritization is intimately related to social mobility, it is necessary to state here that, while the overall character of the traditional system was stationary, it did allow for the mobility of particular groups and families.[11] The sources of such mobility were the political system, which was characterized by fluidity, especially at the lower levels, and the ecological-demographic system which made it possible for families to move out and bring marginal land under cultivation.

Historically, the second *varna* or caste-category of *kshatriyas* or warriors seems to have been the one most open, accommodating all

[9] 'Little Communities in an Indigenous Civilization' in McKim Marriott (Ed.), *Village India*, University of Chicago Press, 1955, pp. 171–222.

[10] Raghavan, op. cit , p. 501.

[11] See in this connexion Ch. I of my *Social Change in Modern India*, Berkeley, University of California Press, 1966, and also my essay, 'Mobility in the Caste System', in a forthcoming volume of essays: M. Singer, B. S. Cohn and W. L. Rowe (Eds.), *Changes in the Caste System*.

kinds of groups, indigenous as well as alien, the only necessary qualification being the effective possession of political power. But, sooner or later, power has to be translated into authority, and it was precisely in this situation that Sanskritization was important. He who became chief or king had to become a *kshatriya* whatever his origins. In those areas where a bardic caste existed the chief was provided with a genealogy linking him to a well-known *kshatriya* lineage and even to the sun or moon. The chief's style of life, including the ritual he performed, had to be modelled on that of the classical *kshatriyas*, and in order to be able to do this he had to seek the support of Brahmins. The indispensability of Brahmins is pointedly seen in the fact that in areas where there was no established Brahmin caste the chief had either to import them from outside, offering them gifts of land and other inducements, or he even had to create Brahmins out of some ambitious local group.

On their side the Brahmins had a positive approach to anyone who wielded power. Here the well-known dictum '*na vishnuh prithvipatih*' ('One becomes a ruler by virtue of his embodying an element of the divine in him') came into play.[12] (This was extended even to Muslim and British rulers.) Brahmins were predisposed to reverence power and they helped to legitimize power into authority. They performed the essential Vedic rites which proclaimed the kingly status of the actual wielder of power, and they sang their praises in Sanskrit.

The ruler and his caste were in turn potent sources of Sanskritization both in the support and patronage they gave to priestly and learned Brahmins and in providing a particular model of Sanskritized life style to those who came under their influence.

Every great temple and pilgrim centre was a source of Sanskritization, and the periodic festivals or other occasions when pilgrims gathered together at the centre provided opportunities for the spread of Sanskritic ideas and beliefs. Several other institutions such as *bhajan*, *harikatha*, and individuals such as the *sanyasi*, and other religious mendicants, also helped to spread ideas and beliefs of Sanskritic Hinduism.

As I have stated earlier, the relation between Sanskritization and Westernization is intricate and many-sided,[13] and I shall not attempt its analysis here. It is enough to note that it is extremely complex, and that some new agencies such as the All-India Radio, school textbooks

[12] Raghavan, op. cit., p. 499, and see also in this connexion, D. R. Chanana's 'The Sanskritist and Indian Society', *Enquiry*, New Series, Vol. II, No. 2, Monsoon, 1965, pp. 49–67.

[13] For an attempt at such analysis, see Chs. III to IV of my *Social Change in Modern India*.

and films, spread *both* Sanskritic and Western ideas and beliefs. Dependence on local centres decreased with the great development of communications which occurred following the advent of British rule, and this again favoured the spread of Sanskritization as well as Westernization. As Marriott has stated:

But those few persons and groups of Kishan Garhi who have demonstrably in recent times taken on more Sanskritic, great traditional forms of religion seem in every instance to have obtained them, *not from the local higher castes, but from itinerant teachers of exotic cults, from urban-centred associations of recent growth, from new state schools, or from the market place.* A newly standardized great tradition is thus externally available to the people of Kishan Garhi as a transformed, now heterogenetic criticism of the indigenous religious order of the village. [*My italics.*][14]

The development of communications and the extension of Sanskritization to innumerable groups have resulted in a radical transformation of traditional culture. A highly simplified and uniform culture has emerged to suit the needs of a vast body of illiterate people in every part of the country.

IV

I shall now briefly consider the relation between caste and Sanskritization. I shall first consider the *varna* model of caste and then the *jati* model. The conceptual division of society into four distinct hierarchical categories is of Vedic origin, and finds clear expression in the sacred literature of the Hindus, including the law books or *Dharma Shastras*. The *varna* model may therefore be regarded as the literary or ideal model of the caste system, but that should not be understood to mean that it did not have any relation to existential realities. A relation did exist, though it varied in different parts of the country and during different periods of Indian history. (It has not yet been the subject of systematic analysis.) One of the interesting features of this relation is that with the enormous development of communications during British rule, and the rise of a Western-educated intelligentsia, the popularity of the *varna* model has been continuously increasing. The need to translate the *jatis* of different regions into a single India-wide framework is greater today than previously, thanks to the spread of education, and increased urbanization and spatial mobility.[15] As important is the fact that educated and urban Indians live only very partially in the universe

[14] Op. cit., p. 211.
[15] See in this connexion McKim Marriott, 'Interactional and Attributional Theories of Caste Ranking', *Man in India*, Vol. XXXIX, No. 2, April–June 1959, pp. 104–5.

of caste, and their relations with other individuals are not always, or even frequently, referable to caste. With the increase in secularization, ideas regarding pollution and purity are becoming weaker. This is more marked in urban than in rural areas.

Rural and urban castes differ significantly from each other, and are also gradually becoming part of a single system. In rural areas the inter-dependence of all the castes living in a village or group of neighbouring villages is emphasized, whereas in the towns the 'horizontal' character of a caste stands out. But this is becoming progressively less true. And, as Marriott has pointed out, with the increase of urbanization, education, and geographical mobility people will increasingly use the *varna* model of the caste system: 'Attributional analysis will tend to be more readily used . . . by persons who are not only urban, but also educated—who are strangers to the small community. Interactional ranking is more to be expected as the logic of untutored, untravelled villagers.'[16] That the *varna* idea distorts reality is only too obvious.

Existentially, caste may be viewed as a series of local systems of interacting *jatis* linked in an all-India framework by means of the idea of *varna*. The *varna* idea is influential in local systems of *jatis* in varying degrees, and within a local system different *jatis* show differential awareness of the *varna* idea. This in turn is related to their political, economic, and social position, and to the degree of their awareness of the wider society of which they are a part.

The local character of the caste system was even more pronounced in pre-British India.[17] Relations between castes or even between members of the same caste did not usually cross the frontiers of the smallest political unit. This was poignantly illustrated in the statement of a Nayar washerwoman of Calicut who told me that she had not crossed the bridge across the local River Kallai to the northern bank, as that would result in her losing her caste. (This was as recently as 1954.)

The local system was a 'vertical system' in the sense that the *jatis* living in it were, in the first place, constrained not to extend their rela-tions with their caste-folk living beyond the political frontiers, and this in turn was a factor in their having intimate relations with each other. A more important factor in local interdependence was caste-wise special-ization in occupation.

Each local system represented a unique hierarchy of *jatis*. Two

16 Op. cit., p. 104.
17 E.g. E. Miller, 'Caste and Territory in Malabar', *American Anthropologist*, Vol. XVI, No. 3, June 1954, pp. 410–20.

sections of a single *jati* could, for instance, occupy different positions in their respective, local hierarchies.[18] Such a situation was one of the many consequences of the mobility inherent in the system. A *jati*'s position in the local hierarchy was not always clear and this indeterminateness again was a function of mobility. In fact, in the traditional system, one of the functions of the king was to settle the rank of a caste when there was a dispute. It would be reasonable to assume that only a few disputes were serious enough to be taken note of by the king, and that the smaller disputes did not go beyond the council of the locally dominant caste.

The character of the locally dominant caste was important in determining the extent to which the *jatis* of a region were Sanskritized or otherwise. It provided an immediate model for the local, non-dominant castes to imitate, and in comparison the *varna* idea was distant. In fact, the *varna* idea had to be articulated only through particular, local *jatis*, and if these were not dominant, not only did they not exercise influence on the other castes, but they themselves ran the risk of being influenced by the culture of the non-Sanskritized dominant castes. This is indeed the familiar process of 'de-Sanskritization'.

But Sanskritization and de-Sanskritization are not entirely dependent upon local forces, and were not, even in pre-British India. Speaking generally, a certain amount of the *varna* 'aura' hung around Brahmins everywhere, and where a dominant caste of peasants wanted to pass for Kshatriya or Vaisya, it had increasingly to resort to the services of the Brahmin in the process of legitimizing its claim. It is even conceivable that the legitimizing role of Brahmins forced them to Sanskritize their style of life to a greater degree than would otherwise have been the case. In other words, Brahmin *jatis* in rural areas were subjected to opposite pulls: the tendency to imitate the locally dominant, non-Brahmin caste on the one hand and, on the other, to be Sanskritized enough to play their role as Brahmins. Where Brahmins were divided into priestly and lay Brahmins, the legitimizing burden fell mainly on the former.

I have referred earlier to the Sanskritizing role of the great temples, monasteries, and pilgrim centres, and all castes, including dominant ones, living within their cultural hinterland, came under their influence. The local hierarchy of castes was not, then, entirely local. It was penetrated by the wider system, and the degree of penetration

[18] See in this connexion D. F. Pocock, 'Inclusion and Exclusion—A Process in the Caste System of Gujarat', *Southwestern Journal of Anthropology*, Vol. XIII, No. 1, Spring 1957, p. 24.

varied with the state of the roads in the region and the fame of the pilgrim centre.

In those areas where a highly Sanskritized caste was dominant, the culture of the entire region underwent a certain amount of Sanskritization. But in a highly stratified society such as India's, there were—and still are—obstacles to the free and unfettered taking over of the customs of the higher castes by the lower. Indeed, traditionally, the dominant caste punished those low castes which were presumptuous enough to attempt it. But in spite of this there was a slow but steady seepage of the culture of the high castes to the low. The specific areas where this seepage occurred, and those which were immune to it, need to be identified in every region.

The mobility which was characteristic of the traditional system took mainly two forms: one in which a *jati* adopted, over a generation or two, the name and other attributes of a regionally prestigeful dominant caste which was not highly Sanskritized; and another, in which a *jati* called itself Brahmin or Kshatriya or Vaisya (usually with a prefix), and this was accompanied by appropriate changes in its diet, style of life, and ritual. The latter form became popular at the beginning of the twentieth century, when there was an all-round increase in caste-consciousness, and low castes sought to move up through Sanskritization. Soon they realized that the acquisition of education, and economic and political power, were far more important than Sanskritization in the struggle to move up. In actual fact, Sanskritization became easy once the reality of power—economic and political—had been acquired.

V

As I have stated earlier, British rule set in motion a vast number of forces which reacted with each other in a variety of ways and these forces continue to operate. Briefly, there are forces which strengthen or weaken one or both the processes. Occasionally, even a single force has contrary effects. Indian towns and cities, for instance, are centres not only of Westernization in all its aspects but also of Sanskritic Hinduism and Sanskritization. In them are housed big temples, trained priests, Sanskrit schools and colleges, and printing presses where Sanskrit books and their translations into regional languages are printed. Again, it is in the towns and cities that reinterpreted Hinduism has found organizations (Ramakrishna Mission, *Bharatiya Vidya Bhavan*, etc.) and individuals to perpetuate it. *Bhajan* groups and the cult of saints, old and new, have their headquarters in the cities. In recent years there has also been a tendency for individuals in towns to undertake the performance of such revivalist functions as Vedic *yajnyas* (sacrifices) and drought-breaking prayers (*parjanya japa*).

It is pertinent to note in this connexion that the discovery by the West of the richness, versatility, and vitality of Sanskrit literature and thought had far-reaching effects in moulding modern India's ideas, attitudes, and values. The fact that India had a great civilization over two thousand years ago gave Indians much-needed self-confidence in facing up culturally and intellectually to the West, and politically to the British. The Bhagavad Gita was reinterpreted to provide a charter for social and political action which was indispensable if India had to become free and prosperous, and Indian society rid of its many evil and inhuman customs. Finally, certain values embedded in Sanskritic Hinduism, such as vegetarianism, and *ahimsa* (non-violence), appealed to Westernized Indians as worthy of perpetuation and extension to all sections of Indian society and even beyond. They found a powerful advocate in Mahatma Gandhi.

In a word, then, Sanskritic ideology, especially in its reinterpreted form, emerged as the most prestigeful of indigenous ideologies. However, with the development of regional self-consciousness in the twentieth century there was an attempt in several Indian languages to discard Sanskrit words and phrases. This 'purification' movement went furthest in Madras, where Sanskrit was identified with Brahmins, and Tamil with non-Brahmins; and Brahmins were made out to be Aryan invaders from the North, who were bent on suppressing the indigenous Dravidian culture. This view found powerful advocates in two cultural cum political organizations, the *Dravida Kazhagam* (Dravidian Federation) and, its offshoot, *Dravida Munnetra Kazhagam* (Dravidian Progressive Federation). Along with a great deal of obscurantism, parochialism, and incitement of hatred towards Brahmins, both organizations, and especially the D.M.K., propagated a rational outlook, and even atheism. Leaving aside Communism, this is the only rationalistic philosophy in India, and, unlike Communism, it is of indigenous origin.

There were also other important, though indirect, sources of Sanskritization. The new economic opportunities brought about by British rule went, by and large, to the upper castes which had a literary tradition. This was due partly to the fact that knowledge of English was an essential qualification for employment as teachers, doctors, lawyers, clerks, and government officials. This increased further the cultural if not the social distance between the new elite and the 'backward' castes. Given, as the latter were, to looking up to and imitating the higher castes, they discovered that English education was essential if they had to acquire power and prestige in the new dispensation. But mastery of English was difficult for all, and even more so for those castes from the rural areas which had no literary tradition. It was at this juncture that the British started parting with power, in instalments, to Indians. The leaders of the 'backward' castes realized that the capture of political power was essential and that it opened the door to education and employment. Thus began the 'Backward Classes Movement', which was, in a sense, an all-India phenomenon, though it found its strongest expression in peninsular India, where the cultural and social gulf between Brahmins and others was more marked than elsewhere.

A crucial result of the Backward Classes Movement was to emphasize the role of secular factors in the upward mobility of caste groups and individuals. Implicit in such an emphasis was a downgrading of the importance of Sanskritization: it was something that followed on the acquisition of secular power and prestige. In the case of the dominant castes,[19] there was no longer any desire to pass for Vaisya, Kshatriya or Brahmin. On the contrary, it was prestigeful to be a member of a dominant caste, and groups which could in no sense be regarded as subcastes of the dominant caste tried to pass for the latter. In some areas, such as Gujarat, some dominant castes opened their ranks to lower castes in order to strengthen themselves politically. (It remains to be seen, however, whether and how far this will lead to the fusion of these castes.)

The overlap between the traditional high castes and the new elite was far from complete. There were instances, in many parts of the country, of low castes benefiting from the new economic opportunities. Such castes Sanskritized their style of life in the classical manner, and tried to pass for one of the 'twice-born' *varnas*. The example of these castes had a 'demonstration effect' on their neighbours. The urge to mobility became widespread and the path to be taken well worn.

The Western discovery of the greatness of Sanskrit literature and thought, and the systematic reconstruction of Indian history, both played a vital role in the development of Indian nationalism. India was thought of as 'mother India', *Bharat Mata*, and patriotism was love

[19] I use the term 'dominant caste' here to mean a caste which enjoys numerical strength, high status, and wealth—principally in the form of land. In recent years education has become increasingly important in contributing to the power and influence of a caste.

for one's mother, freeing her from the thraldom of an alien ruler. Hindu symbolism expressed itself in political situations. During the Civil Disobedience Movement, for instance, the resisters (*satyagrahis*) were garlanded, their faces marked with *tilak*, and *arati*, a solution of turmeric and lime powder kept in a tray, was waved before them. Mahatma Gandhi expressed himself in a Hindu, even Sanskritic idiom—he saw God Narayana in the poor (*daridranarayana*), the millennium which he wanted for India was conceived of as *Rama Rajya* (the reign of the epic hero Rama, when there was justice and happiness for all), and he shared the Hindu veneration for the cow. Two of his central ideas, *satyagraha* or civil resistance, and *ahimsa* or non-violence, had their roots in Hindu and Jain customs and thought. Gandhi also preached vegetarianism and teetotalism.

Indian nationalism thus expressed itself predominantly in a Hindu idiom, and this was a factor, though only one, in non-Hindu groups experiencing a certain sense of isolation. It must be recalled here that since the beginning of the nineteenth century Hindu reformers worked hard to rid their religion of its many evils and to reinterpret it to suit the needs of a modern world. A certain amount of revivalism, or what appeared to be revivalism to non-Hindus, was part of this process of reinterpretation, though it was much greater in some reform movements than in others. Similar 'revivalism' was present among Muslims.

It was not only at the national level that there was increased self-consciousness, but also at other levels; in religion, sect, caste, language, and region. One of the results of this heightened self-consciousness was 'communalism', the setting up of the interests of one's 'community' (i.e. religious group) before that of the nation as a whole. This was further complicated by the presence of an alien ruler. Hindu communalism stimulated Muslim communalism and vice versa, and a vicious spiralling of hatred followed. The partition of the Indian subcontinent was perhaps the natural result of such a process.

One of the most important tasks which confronts independent India is to draw all sections of India's heterogeneous population into the mainstream of national life while at the same time retaining what is valuable in Sanskrit thought and culture. To do this it is necessary for Hindus to accept the entire Indian tradition to which all sections of the population have contributed, and for the latter to regard the Sanskrit heritage as their own. This can only be the result of a slow process of cultural osmosis, and in this context it is significant that independent India has declared itself a secular state, while Pakistan is an 'Islamic

V

The Future of the Backward Classes: The Competing Demands of Status and Power[1]

BY ANDRÉ BÉTEILLE

Reader in Sociology, University of Delhi, and Simon Fellow, University of Manchester, 1965–6

I

THE Backward Classes[2] constitute an important section of Indian society. In all they account for more than 30 per cent of the total population of the country. Their condition is intimately linked with many of the basic features of Indian social structure and, as such, is likely to be affected by any significant alteration in these. Clearly, an assessment of the future of the Backward Classes cannot be made in isolation from social and political forces which operate through the entire range of Indian society.

Studies in social and political projection are faced with problems of a special nature. Predictions in the social sciences cannot be made with the same certainty or the same degree of probability as in the natural sciences. This is so even when the social scientist has at his disposal the entire body of data considered necessary for his analysis. For here the validity of the analysis depends not only on the quality of data but also on the values which direct one's research.

Sociologists such as Mannheim[3] and Myrdal[4] have shown how

---

[1] This chapter was first published in *Perspectives*, a supplement to the *Indian Journal of Public Administration*, Vol. XI, No. 11, January–March 1965, pp. 1–39. The author is grateful to Professor M. N. Srinivas for having allowed him to make use of his unpublished Tagore Lectures, from which some of the basic concepts employed here have been drawn. Although he has not made specific acknowledgement at every point, the author's debt to him will be recognized by anyone who is familiar with Indian sociology.

[2] Comprising the 'Scheduled Tribes', the 'Scheduled Castes' and the 'Other Backward Classes; the 'Denotified Tribes', who constitute a small minority, are not considered separately here. For a general account see Lelah Dushkin, 'The Backward Classes', *The Economic Weekly*, 29 October, 4 and 18 November, 1961, pp. 1665–8; 1695–1706; 1729–38.

[3] K. Mannheim, *Ideology and Utopia*, New York, Harcourt, Brace and Co., 1936.

[4] G. Myrdal, *Value and Social Theory*, London, Routledge and Kegan Paul, 1958.

different persons may arrive at different (though not necessarily contradictory) conclusions even when they analyse the same body of facts. The values and interests of the sociologist give a direction to his research and no method has as yet been devised which can eliminate their influence altogether. Values play a part not only in the formulation of the problems to be investigated but also in the selection and arrangement of data.

The problem of the Backward Classes may be posed in a variety of ways. Is it essentially a political problem or is the problem basically educational and cultural? Should the Backward Classes be treated as a homogeneous, undifferentiated unit or should one view separately the problems of the Scheduled Tribes, the Scheduled Castes, and the Other Backward Classes? Finally, does one accept the prevalent basis of classifying the Indian population into 'Backward' and 'Forward' as a rational one?

One is likely to have specific views on all these questions, not only as a sociologist but also as a member of Indian society. There are special problems inherent in the study of one's own society, particularly when such a study deals with issues which are of general and fundamental importance. The outsider has a certain advantage. He is able to approach the problem with a more open mind, relatively free of preconceptions. This, of course, is not to deny that an inside view of social problems has advantages of its own.

If value preferences tend to distort interpretations of the past, their role in projections is likely to be even more decisive. An effort at projection faces a bigger challenge in the matter of valuation. For here one has to evaluate the significance not only of elements and forces which have established themselves but also of those which are in a process of emergence. One has to uncover potentialities inherent in factors whose contemporary significance may not appear very great. Here the judgement of the social scientist is put to a kind of test which he is normally inclined to avoid.

It cannot be too strongly emphasized that objectivity in social research is not merely a question of good intention or even of professional competence. It is also a function of the social position of the person who conducts the research. As such, a full and objective picture of social reality can hardly be drawn with a single stroke of the brush. Rather, the area of objectivity can be expanded only by slow degrees as different people, occupying different social positions and representing divergent interests, examine the same problem from a variety of angles. It would be well to bear these limitations in mind while making an assessment of the analysis which follows.

II

Who are the Backward Classes? In India, the Backward Classes constitute a category of people who are for the most part officially listed and given special recognition in a variety of contexts. In every complex society, of course, there are individuals who may be considered as economically or educationally backward; generally such people have also a low social status. However, backwardness as understood in the Indian context has a number of distinctive features. Firstly, it is viewed as an attribute not of individuals but of certain clearly defined social segments in which membership is generally acquired by birth; thus, the Backward Classes may in theory include individuals who are highly advanced both educationally and economically. Secondly, membership of the Backward Classes entitles one to certain advantages and concessions specifically conferred by the Government.

In a sense, then, the Backward Classes are not classes at all but groups of communities. It is true that there is a good deal of overlap in reality between the Backward Classes and certain economic categories such as that of the agricultural labourers. But it would be a mistake to view the problems of the two as identical. The Backward Classes have as a set of communities certain distinctive problems which derive from the status ascribed to them in traditional Indian society. It is these distinctive problems which will engage our attention in the analysis which follows. The very nature of the Backward Classes and most of their special problems can be understood only in terms of the basic character of Indian society; namely, its division into a multitude of closed status groups of unequal rank, each associated with a variety of privileges and disabilities supported by traditional sanctions.

It may on a first examination appear tempting to restructure the definition of the Backward Classes and to view their problems principally in economic terms. This would, however, divert attention from the specific nature of backwardness in Indian society. In the first place, the Backward Classes are by no means homogeneous economically. Secondly, the Backward Classes as officially viewed are part and parcel of modern Indian social and political reality. They are a product of forces which are in many ways unique, and distinctive of Indian history. Their identity does not derive solely or even primarily from a common economic experience, but from the very nature of the traditional system of stratification to which economic, political, and ritual factors have contributed in various ways.

The term Backward Classes, which has been given currency through official publications, is not altogether a happy one. The word 'class' suggests not only an economic category but also one which is relatively open. In reality the Backward Classes are more in the nature of an aggregate of closed status groups. One's economic position is not a determining factor in one's membership of the Backward Classes; rather, membership is determined generally by birth.

The Backward Classes, as stated earlier, together account for more than 30 per cent of the total population of India. They are not a homogeneous category, but consist of three broad divisions, each having its own distinctive background and, to some extent, its own problems of transformation. The three broad divisions are the Scheduled Tribes, the Scheduled Castes and the Other Backward Classes. The first accounts for about a sixteenth of the population of the country, and each of the two others for a little less than a seventh of it. The Other Backward Classes appear to be the least homogeneous and the most loosely defined of the three subdivisions. Their problems also are in many ways different from those of the first two and it may be misleading to consider the three together beyond a certain point.

An element of confusion pervades the discussion on Backward Classes due to a certain misapplication of terms. In this essay the term 'Backward Classes' will be used to refer to the most inclusive category and the term 'Other Backward Classes' will be reserved for that section of the broader category which remains by exclusion of the Scheduled Tribes and Scheduled Castes. It seems to be a common practice, not only among scholars but also among politicians, to use the term Backward Classes as being synonymous sometimes with the Scheduled Tribes and Scheduled Castes and at other times with a somewhat broader category. This ambiguity in terminology leads to certain important issues and problems being obscured.[5]

The position of the Scheduled Tribes and Scheduled Castes is defined in a more or less specific manner in the Indian Constitution. Lists of these communities are drawn up by the Central Government, and can be revised only by presidential authority. There is, in addition, a Commissioner for Scheduled Castes and Scheduled Tribes to look into the affairs of these communities on a continuing basis.

The Other Backward Classes, by contrast, are a more nebulous category. They are mentioned in the Constitution in only the most general terms. There is no all-India list for the Other Backward Classes. They are not separately enumerated in the Census and, in fact, one has to work with only a rough estimate of their population. Their position

[5] M. Galanter, 'Equality and "Protective Discrimination" in India', *Rutgers Law Review*, Vol. XVI, No. 1, 1961, pp. 42–74.

was sought to be defined in more specific terms by the Backward Classes Commission set up in 1953 under the chairmanship of Kaka Kalelkar. The Commission, which was not a standing body, could not, in fact, come to any tangible or agreed conclusions.

The Scheduled Tribes or 'Adivasis' numbered 29.9 millions in 1961 out of a total population of 439.1 millions. They are popularly believed to constitute the aboriginal element in Indian society. They are generally concentrated in the hill and forest areas and until recently the political system of the different tribes enjoyed a certain measure of autonomy. Today, however, it is difficult to define the tribal peoples of India in terms of any single set of formal criteria, although attempts have been made at such a definition.[6] Elements which would have to be taken into account in such a definition are the ecological isolation of the tribal people, the relative autonomy of their political and cultural systems, and the antiquity of association with their present habitat.

The difficulty of applying a set of formal criteria in defining the Adivasis arises from the fact that tribes in India are (and have been for some time) tribes in transition. The political boundaries of most tribal systems had collapsed well before the beginning of the present century. A certain amount of cultural interchange between the tribal people and the outside world has apparently existed for centuries. Sections of the tribal population tend to get absorbed into Hindu society by a process which has been fairly widespread. In fact, it is often very difficult to say of a particular social unit whether it is a tribe or a caste. The complexity of the phenomenon defeats any attempt to solve such problems by means of precisely formulated definitions. Each case has to be examined on its own merits and in relation to the specific social and historical factors prevalent in an area before one can decide whether or not a particular unit qualifies as a tribe. Lists of the Scheduled Tribes have, in fact, been drawn up after careful consideration of a variety of individual cases.

The tribal population is concentrated in certain geographical areas. Speaking very broadly, they may be divided into three groups according to their distribution, namely, the tribes living in the Northern and North-Eastern zone in the mountain valleys and Eastern Frontiers of India. There is a second group which occupies the central belt of the older hills and plateaux along the dividing line between Peninsula India and the Indo-Gangetic Plains. In addition, there are tribes scattered over the extreme corners of South-Western India, in the

---

[6] A. Béteille, 'Question of Definition', in *Tribal India Seminar*, No. XIV, 1960, pp. 15–18.

hills and the converging lines of the Ghats.'[7] These tribes speak a large variety of dialects and there are enormous variations in their habits, customs, and arts. Historically one of the principal features of the tribal population has been its ecological and social isolation. For centuries the tribal people have been confined to hills and forests and this isolation has left a definite impress on their social systems. It has also given them, in spite of wide cultural variations, a common destiny in Indian society. For one of the crucial problems faced by all tribal communities in India is the problem of integration into the wider social, economic, and political systems.

The Scheduled Castes or 'Harijans' have not had a history of isolation comparable to that of the Scheduled Tribes. They have been segregated rather than isolated. Thus, whereas the tribal people are concentrated in blocks, the Harijans are scattered through every state and practically every district. The different distributional characteristics of the Scheduled Tribes and the Scheduled Castes lead to certain differences in their problems of transformation. It is easier to implement special programmes of development for the Scheduled Tribes who live in compact blocks than for the Scheduled Castes who are geographically scattered. On the other hand, the concentration of the tribal population in particular areas provides better scope for the development of separatist political movements among them.

The Scheduled Castes numbered 64.5 million at the 1961 Census, thus giving a figure which is more than twice that of the Scheduled Tribes. They are concentrated in rural areas and are found commonly in multi-caste villages. Although they live in close interdependence with the higher castes, many areas of social life have been (and continue to be) inaccessible to them. They generally live segregated in their own settlements, which are often a little distance away from the residential quarters of the upper castes. They have been debarred by tradition from full participation in many of the collective activities of the village and some of these restrictions are still operative. Their economic, social, and ritual status continues to be depressed, although there are certain indications of change which will be discussed later.

The Scheduled Castes have been known in popular parlance as the 'untouchables'. Their social condition has been governed in important ways by the Hindu concept of pollution. Although the practice of untouchability has been made an offence, the stigma of pollution has not by any means been entirely removed.

[7] B. S. Guha, 'Indian Aborigines and Who They Are', *The Adivasis,* Delhi, Government of India, 1955, p. 31.

The Other Backward Classes constitute a congeries of communities of rather uncertain status. Lists had earlier been prepared by the Ministry of Education and by the state governments. The Backward Classes Commission under Kaka Kalelkar reported a good deal of ambiguity in these lists. 'But there was no authoritative list of Other Backward Classes. The Census had assumed one list; the Ministry of Education had prepared another; and it was left to the present Commission to recommend an authoritative list.'[8] The recommendations of the Commission were not, in fact, accepted as authoritative. The State Governments have in general been allowed to use their own criteria in drawing up lists of the 'Other Backward Classes'. These, in turn, are not always held to be binding by the Supreme Court, which, in the case of M. R. Balaji and Others *versus* the State of Mysore, decided against the recommendation of the Nagana Gowda Commission.

The Central Government has, particularly since 1961, been pressing for the adoption of economic criteria in defining the Other Backward Classes. There has been some resistance to this from a number of state governments. It has to be recognized that some of the castes included in the earlier lists of the Other Backward Classes are fairly powerful in state politics and have therefore been in a position to exert pressure on the state governments to have the old criteria retained. The Lingayats of Mysore and the Ezhavas of Kerala provide good instances of powerful dominant castes which have exerted pressure on their respective state governments for the retention of caste as the basis for defining backwardness.

Although the Central Government has not insisted on the old lists being abandoned altogether, economic and other pressures have been exerted on the state governments for the adoption of economic criteria. Since 1963 they have made the use of Central Government funds for the award of scholarships to members of the Other Backward Classes conditional upon the use of economic criteria for defining such classes. By now the majority of the states have adopted this criterion for defining backwardness for the award of scholarships to the Backward Classes other than the Scheduled Castes and Scheduled Tribes. The Central Government has also since 1962 decided to use the term Backward Classes to refer only to the Scheduled Tribes and the Scheduled Castes.[9] However, the broader usage is retained in this paper, since the

[8] Government of India, *Report of the Backward Classes Commission*, New Delhi, 1956, p. 48.
[9] The author is grateful to Mr. L. P. Singh, Home Secretary, Government of India, for supplying this information.

Other Backward Classes continue to retain a certain amount of significance at the level of the state government.

It is difficult to give exact figures for the Other Backward Classes, because they are not enumerated separately in the Census and because such lists as do exist are subject to revision from time to time. Some estimate can, however, be made of their strength by projection of the caste returns in the 1931 Census. Speaking in very broad terms, then, the Other Backward Classes constitute about one-seventh of the total population of the country, being thus approximately equal in numerical strength to the Scheduled Castes.

The core of the Other Backward Classes consists of peasant castes of various descriptions. The position occupied by these castes in the wider society is rather different from that of the Harijans. Frequently they occupy a low position in the *varna* hierarchy and they have in general been devoid of traditions of literacy. Further, since they have also lagged behind in the pursuit of Western education, they are often poorly represented in government jobs and white-collar occupations in general. In spite of this, such castes sometimes occupy a dominant position in the economic and political systems of the village. Not infrequently they are small landowners. When they are also numerically preponderant, their control over a village, a group of villages or even a district may be decisive.

Dominant castes of this kind have developed a vested interest in remaining backward. It enables them to enjoy a number of benefits in education and employment. What is more, they sometimes have enough political power to exert pressure on the state government to have their names included or retained in the list of Backward Classes. The case of the powerful Lingayat caste of Mysore, which had first been excluded from the list recommended by the Nagana Gowda Commission and had later to be accommodated, has by now become well known.

This, then, is the broad social background against which we have to consider the issues which confront the Backward Classes in their efforts at transformation. The issues, it will be evident, are many and diverse. In many ways they are different for the three broad divisions considered: the Scheduled Tribes, the Scheduled Castes, and the Other Backward Classes.

The tribal people have had a history of isolation which gives in many ways a unique character to their problems. They are faced with the task of achieving integration without doing violence to their rich cultural and artistic heritage. In the case of the Scheduled Castes an important problem is to break through the barrier of untouchability, not simply in its formal legal sense, but in its widest social application. Both have to face the challenges of poverty, illiteracy, and social prejudice, and this is true to some extent of certain sections of the Other Backward Classes, too. But the latter also include a number of dominant castes who have 'arrived', so to say, at least politically, and have now to think of consolidating their power against politically weaker sections of society which may appear to threaten their dominance.

In the discussion which follows we shall try as far as possible to consider separately some of the distinctive features of each of the three sections of the Backward Classes, keeping in mind the more general problem of backwardness. This should not, however, be taken to mean that each section constitutes a homogeneous or undifferentiated unit. In fact, there are numerous social and economic differences within each section, but a detailed consideration of these would require a far more exhaustive study than the present one. Here we can provide only a few illustrations of these differences. The condition of tribal people in non-tribal areas, for instance, is likely to differ greatly from their condition in an area which has a predominantly tribal population. The Scheduled Castes in South India occupy a somewhat different position from their counterparts in North India; an understanding of these differences would require an understanding of the differences between the social systems of North and South India, including the differential importance of the idea of pollution in the two systems. Finally, everywhere there are great disparities of wealth and power within the all-too-loosely defined category of the Other Backward Classes.

III

That Indian society is passing through a phase of active social change will not be disputed by many. In a sense the impact of change appears more striking among the lower strata of society, partly because these strata had remained relatively immobile in the past. Changes in the status of the Backward Classes, which may appear limited in absolute terms, tend to acquire a different significance when viewed against the background of traditional society.

It is well to remember that the currents of change do not all run in the same direction. Sometimes they run counter to one another. There are on the one hand certain factors which tend to blur the outlines of the traditional structure and to bridge the gaps between the Backward Classes and the advanced sections of society. The modern educational system may be viewed as one such factor. On the other hand, the frequent use made in politics of the loyalties of caste and tribe tends in some measure to freeze the traditional structure.

In spite of the apparent confusion of currents and counter-currents, the scales seem to be decisively weighted in favour of a lowering of many of the barriers of traditional society. In the traditional system, society was divided and subdivided into a large number of segments which were kept rigidly separated from one another. New networks of interpersonal relations are now being created in every field and these tend increasingly to cut across the boundaries of the old, established groups. New areas of social life are being opened up in which individuals from widely different backgrounds are able to come together on the basis of achievement, interest, and personal choice. The change from a segmental and particularistic social order to a more fluid and universalistic one is bound in the long run to change the very character of the Backward Classes. But paradoxically enough, it seems that this change cannot be affected without widespread use being made of the particularistic loyalties of tribe, caste, and community.

Of the many changes which are taking place among the Backward Classes, we shall consider two in particular: changes in their style of life and in their relation to the political system.

The traditional order imposed many restrictions on the Backward Classes with regard to changes in their styles of life. These restrictions were progressively removed during British rule, although a few of them seem to be still in force. The advent of Independence and the introduction of adult franchise, and more recently of *panchayati raj*, have made political power far more accessible to the Backward Classes than it was in the traditional system. There can be little doubt that in the years to come the Backward Classes will participate more and more effectively in the political process at every level, from the village to the nation.

When members of a lower caste change their style of life and move up in the hierarchy of prestige and social esteem, we speak of this as mobility along the axis of status. When, on the other hand, they advance themselves by securing positions of political office in an organ of government or a party or a pressure group, we speak of this as mobility along the axis of power. Our analysis of the future of the Backward Classes will centre around the chances of their movement along these two axes.

British rule provided the Backward Classes with increasing opportunities to imitate with effect the styles of life of the upper castes. These opportunities were extensively used by the Other Backward Classes and also the Scheduled Castes and Scheduled Tribes who set about 'Sanskritizing' themselves with varying degrees of success. Since Independence, however, the emphasis seems to be shifting from Sanskritization to competition for positions of office and power. It appears that at many points the demands of prestige and power come into conflict and this conflict is likely to make itself felt more acutely among the Scheduled Tribes and Scheduled Castes. Present indications seem to suggest that in the years to come the latter will turn increasingly to politics as an avenue of social mobility.

IV

We shall first consider the changes which the different sections of the Backward Classes have been undergoing in their styles of life. It may be useful to fix our point of departure in the past in order to be able to see the future from a proper point of vantage. It must not be thought, however, that changes in the styles of life of the Backward Classes are likely to follow a regular path. In fact, one of the points of the present argument is that political forces of a certain kind tend to arrest some of the changes which had been taking place more or less continuously over the last several decades.

Traditional Indian society had a structure which was highly segmental and hierarchical in character. The segments within it were separated from one another by clear-cut boundaries and marriage; commensality and many other forms of social interaction generally stopped short at these boundaries. The social separation of the different segments was bolstered by the fact that Hinduism allowed within its fold the practice of a wide variety of styles of life. Each group of castes, each caste and sometimes even each subcaste was allowed to cultivate its distinctive styles of life in the matter of diet, dress, worship, marriage, etc. Hinduism tolerated a plurality of cultures, but the price of this was the maintenance of a certain structural distance between people traditionally associated with divergent styles of life; for example, between vegetarians and non-vegetarians, or between people practising different crafts or worshipping different gods.

Social separation between different segments, each pursuing its own style of life, could be kept intact so long as the world was fairly static or the pace of change not very rapid. In the traditional system, mobility—whether vertical or horizontal—was slow and limited. The expansion of transport and communication, the spread of education and new economic opportunities, and an increasing degree of political articulation are bringing about fundamental changes in the traditional structure. The system now tends to become relatively more open, allowing for greater mobility and greater variety in the combination of class, status, and power positions.

Culturally the distance was greatest between the Adivasis and the Harijans on the one hand and the advanced sections of society on the other. The tribal people, who were ecologically isolated, had developed their own traditions, habits, and ways of life. The Harijans also lived in a cultural world of their own, shut out in many ways from the world of the 'twice-born'. In the case of the Harijans there were often specific sanctions against the adoption of the styles of life of the upper castes. Even until recently the 'exterior' castes in South India were disallowed the use of sandals, umbrellas, and silken cloth; they were not allowed to live in brick and tile houses; and their women could not wear upper garments. These disabilities, it must be noted, were often enforced by powerful traditional sanctions.

Thus, the Adivasis because of their physical isolation, and the Harijans, for other reasons, were unable fully to identify themselves with the higher strata of society or to use many of their distinctive symbols of status. For all this, social forces have been at work, leading to a transmission of cultural elements from the more advanced sections of society to the more backward. Two of the most important of such forces are Sanskritization and Westernization.[10]

Sanskritization was an important feature of traditional Indian society, where it appears to have been the principal idiom of social mobility. Its role in contemporary Indian society was first analysed in detail by Srinivas in his study of the Coorgs of South India.[11] Sanskritization can be defined as a process by which a caste or a group of people move up the social hierarchy by adopting styles of life associated by tradition with the upper castes. The Sanskritic model should not be viewed as an undifferentiated one; in addition to the Brahminical model, people seem at various places or various times to have made use of a Kshatriya model and perhaps even a Vaisya model.[12] But what is of particular importance in this context is that the idiom of Sanskritization is essentially traditional in nature.

In the past, the process of Sanskritization was slow and gradual and

[10] M. N. Srinivas, 'Sanskritization and Westernization', Aiyappan and Bala Ratnam (Eds.), *Society in India*, Madras, Book Centre, 1956.

[11] Srinivas, *Religion and Society Among the Coorgs of South India*, Oxford, Clarendon Press, 1952, and Bombay, 1965.

[12] Srinivas *et. al.*, *Caste: A Trend Report and Bibliography*, Oxford, Basil Blackwell, 1959, p. 140.

it offered very limited possibilities to the lowest sections of society. Social horizons were narrow, the economy was relatively static and population movements were limited. This made it difficult for a lower caste quickly to acquire economic and political power, or, having once acquired it, to shed its traditional marks of inferiority. There were, in addition, legal and ritual sanctions which acted against a too radical change in styles of life. These sanctions operated with particular force upon the Harijans who were able to cross the barrier of untouchability rarely, if at all.

British rule released the Backward Classes (including the Harijans) from the grip of many of the traditional sanctions. The new courts of law refused to recognize the rights of the upper castes to the exclusive use of particular symbols of status. The avenues of Sanskritization were thrown open to ever-increasing sections of society. The first to seize the new opportunities were those whose social position had been low in traditional society but above the line of untouchability. These included many of the castes hitherto classified under the Other Backward Classes.

Castes which had been fairly low in the traditional hierarchy changed their diet, their social customs and sometimes even their gods in favour of those of the upper castes. The decennial Census provided them with opportunities to replace their traditional names with new and more high-sounding ones. Caste associations were formed throughout the country and these not only put forward claims to higher social status but also urged their members to abandon many of the practices considered degrading by the upper castes. Thus Sanskritization served to lower the barriers between sections of society which had at one time been clearly separated. It is paradoxical that this process, which in a way represents the distinctive idiom of traditional society, had to await the coming of the modern age before it could acquire its full momentum.

The increased pace of Sanskritization has been dependent upon a number of forces, some of which are likely to extend their influence in the years to come. These include improvements in transport and communication, greater mobility in non-traditional sectors of the economy, the spread of literacy and education among the lower strata and (paradoxically) the institution of a secular legal order. Each of these forces, however, has other consequences which are likely to alter the very meaning of Sanskritization and in the long run to undermine its significance.

The revolution in transport and communication has thrown open pilgrim centres to people from far and near. Every year more people visit such important centres as Mathura, Kashi, Gaya, Tirupathi, and

Rameshwaram. In the past a visit to a distant centre of pilgrimage was not only replete with hazards but also a costly affair. Now even the moderately poor find it within their means to undertake journeys by bus or train to places which in the past would have appeared remote. It seems that these facilities will be used to greatest advantage by the better-off sections of the Other Backward Classes in the years to come.

The mass media have been harnessed for the diffusion of Sanskritic values and ideas. Mythological films and radio broadcasts of devotional programmes are becoming increasingly popular in the villages. This trend in the direction of Sanskritization is likely to persist in the rural areas, particularly among castes which are above the line of untouchability. Among the top castes there seems to be a trend away from popular Sanskritic culture and towards new values and symbols of status. The Other Backward Classes are still too much within the grip of the traditional system to be able to follow the top castes in this regard. The Harijans and the Adivasis are, in turn, different from the Other Backward Classes; their commitment to the traditional system was never so intense as to prevent them altogether from seeking alternative avenues of mobility.

The Other Backward Classes include a number of castes which enjoy a certain measure of economic and political dominance. A good example of these is provided by the Okkaligas of Mysore, who have been studied by Srinivas.[13] Such castes, or sections of them, are often the ones to benefit most from the new economic opportunities. And they are also the ones most likely to Sanskritize their style of life in order to set the seal of social acceptance on their material success.

Sanskritization affects the culture of castes in the lower and middle regions of the hierarchy in a variety of ways. To begin with an example which may appear trivial, but is nevertheless of considerable significance, one may consider changes in personal names among them. These changes appear particularly striking in South India, where sharp linguistic differences exist between typically Brahmin names and names common among the non-Brahmin peasantry. Among the latter the most common personal names have been typically non-Sanskritic, such as Pazhani, Thangavelu, Nadugowda, or Puttappa. Today one encounters in increasing number such typically Sanskritic names as Narasimhan, Parthasarathy, and Srinivas. This change, trivial in itself, is symbolic of the penetration among the Backward Classes of a culture and a style of life which had virtually been a monopoly of a few upper castes.

[13] Srinivas, 'The Dominant Caste in Rampura', *American Anthropologist*, Vol. LXI, No. 1, 1959, pp. 1–16.

Other, more fundamental, changes are also taking place. There are changes in occupation, diet, and social practices of various kinds. Occupations considered degrading in the Sanskritic scale of values, such as distilling, oil-pressing, or tanning, are often forsaken and there is a tendency even to deny any past association with them. Items of food such as pork and the drinking of alchoholic beverages are often given up. There is a pervasive tendency to abandon widow-remarriage and to replace bride-price by dowry. Finally, castes which had done without Brahmin priests in the past now try to secure their services on occasions of birth, marriage, and death. The pace of Sanskritization has been heightened by the activities not only of caste associations but also of such organizations as the *Arya Samaj* and the *Sanatan Dharm Samaj*. The latter act as important agencies for the diffusion of Sanskritic styles of life among large sections of people, including the Backward Classes and especially in the rural areas. The *Arya Samaj* in particular combines Sanskritization with certain universalistic principles which create a special appeal among the hitherto underprivileged strata of society.

Sanskritization, which was the principal idiom of social mobility in the past, appears to have special significance today for castes in the middle and the lower-middle regions of the hierarchy. This is partly because the top castes are reaching forward to new social values and to new symbols of status. Thus, in Sanskritizing their styles of life, the Backward Classes are emulating models which certain sections of the traditional elite are already trying to put behind. And some of the forces which impel the latter to attach themselves to new models operate also among the Backward Classes. One of the most important of these forces is what Srinivas refers to as Westernization.[14]

Sanskritization can be seen not only as an idiom of mobility but also as an important source of continuity with the past. Its symbols and values are essentially those of the traditional order. At a time when a modernist elite is trying to push the country towards a secular and Westernized social order, it is not unlikely that those who had in the past occupied a fairly low social position may set themselves up as the bastions of traditional values. Unable to cope with the process of Westernization or the pace of rapid social change, such people may well throw in their lot with traditionalist or even revivalist movements and parties. It may appear ironical that the defence of the traditional order should become the burden of people who had in the past been denied a position of honour within it.

[14] Srinivas, 'Sanskritization and Westernization'.

The Sanskritization of the Backward Classes provides Indian society with a stabilizing influence whose significance under conditions of rapid social change can hardly be overestimated. Social change can be brought about without severe strain only when a certain continuity is maintained with the past. No society can reorganize itself completely and with success within a brief span of time. The Western-educated elite in India is often impatient with the slow rate of change in the country. But in order to bring about change effectively it will have to make many compromises with some of the hitherto backward communities which are beginning to develop a new sense of commitment to the values of traditional society.

It would, of course, be unreal to suggest that every section of the Backward Classes is developing a stake in the traditional order. What has been said above applies principally to the upper strata among them and in particular to dominant peasant castes such as the Okkaligas or the Ahirs. The lowest sections of the Backward Classes are often under the influence of forces of a very different kind. It is well to remember that there are sharp cleavages within the Backward Classes, some of which may have greater significance than the ones which separate the dominant castes among them from the advanced sections of society.

Sanskritization has thus never meant the same thing for the Harijans as it has for castes above the line of pollution. Everywhere the effective adoption of the Sanskritic style of life has depended upon a number of preconditions. These include a minimum of economic and political power and a not too inferior ritual status. A caste may adopt a new name and claim a high social status, but such a claim is not likely to be very effective where most of its members are landless labourers and are refused the services of the village barber or the village washerman. Dominant castes such as the Okkaligas develop a commitment to the Sanskritic style of life because their economic and political position enables them to adopt such a style with some effect.

In the past the Scheduled Castes were prevented from Sanskritizing their styles of life by a variety of sanctions. They were excluded from temples, bathing *ghats*, wells, and other public places. A large number of civic rights, necessary preconditions to Sanskritization or upward mobility of any kind, were denied to them by legal and ritual sanctions. The new courts established by the British introduced the principle of equality before the law and by doing so removed one set of restrictions to changes in the social life of the Harijans.

However, the removal of legal disabilities did not automatically enable the Harijans to exercise their civic rights. Various kinds of sanctions were applied to keep them in their inferior position. They were (and still are) economically dependent on the upper castes, whom they dare not offend by pressing too far their legal claims to equality. A Harijan tenant or agricultural labourer who dares to behave as the equal of his master on social or ceremonial occasions may find himself deprived of his source of livelihood. And here it should be pointed out that dominant castes among the Other Backward Classes rarely look with favour upon the Harijans' claim to equality of status.

Apart from moral and economic pressures, physical violence or the threat of it is a very effective deterrent, particularly in a village. It is not unknown even now for Harijans to be beaten by caste Hindus for attempting to exercise their civic rights. The dominant caste of an area is rarely (perhaps never) a Harijan caste. The dominant caste often has the strength of organized numbers and this can be used against Harijans who are too eager to appropriate the traditional symbols of honour. In the past the Scheduled Castes had accepted their civic deprivations as a matter of course. Now that a spirit of challenge has been kindled among them, it is likely that conflicts between the Harijans and dominant peasant castes will become more pervasive.

In order to gain an understanding of the issues involved in the conflicts between Harijans and caste Hindus it may be useful to go back a little in time. The growing emancipation of the Adi-Dravida untouchables from traditional disabilities had aroused the wrath of the Kallar as early as the 1930s. The Kallars are a dominant peasant caste in Tamilnad, classified among the Other Backward Classes. Hutton reports that: 'In December 1930 the Kallar in Ramnad propounded eight prohibitions, the disregard of which led to the use of violence by the Kallar against the exterior castes, whose huts were fired, whose granaries and property were destroyed, and whose livestock was looted.'[15]

The 'eight prohibitions' related, among other things, to the use of ornaments of gold and silver, the use of upper garments by women, and the use of umbrellas and sandals. Hutton further writes: 'In June 1931, the eight prohibitions not having been satisfactorily observed by the exterior castes in question, the Kallars met together and framed eleven prohibitions, which went still further than the original eight, and an attempt to enforce these led to more violence.'[16] It may be mentioned that one of the eleven prohibitions was that 'their children should not read and get themselves literate or educated'.[17]

[15] J. H. Hutton, *Caste in India*, Bombay, Oxford University Press, 1961, p. 205.
[16] Ibid., p. 205.
[17] Ibid., p. 206.

The attempt of the Harijans to change their social customs does not proceed by way of Sanskritization alone. There are many non-traditional elements in the styles of life of the upper strata which the Harijans also seek to imitate. Whatever may be the idiom adopted, the very fact of upward mobility requires the rejection of many of the civic disabilities imposed by the former upon the latter. The upper castes are likely to see in this a threat not only to their social status but also to their political and economic power. This being the case, conflicts between Harijans and caste Hindus are likely to continue for some time. Anthropologists who have done fieldwork in village India in recent years report the existence and sometimes the intensification of such conflicts. But one important point has to be borne in mind: the nature of these conflicts and in particular the issues over which they arise tend to change.

Even in South India the issue of wearing upper garments or constructing brick and tile houses is no longer a living one. In these matters the Harijans seem clearly to have won their battle. But other issues remain, and new ones tend to emerge as the hitherto untouchable castes press forward in their campaign to gain full social equality with the caste Hindus. Before taking up some of the issues which are likely to figure in the immediate future, it may be useful to take stock of the gains which the Harijans have accumulated over the last few decades.

Diacritical distinctions in the matter of dress, ornament and habitation are now rarely enforced by the caste Hindus upon the Scheduled Castes. When the latter continue to retain their former style of life, it is more because they lack the economic resources to acquire the symbols of upper caste society and less because they are coerced by the latter to retain their traditional marks of inferiority. While doing fieldwork in Tanjore district, I was struck by the difference in dress between Palla women of the younger and older generations. The younger women, particularly on festive occasions, now commonly wear blouses and saris of synthetic fibre. This does not any longer evoke violence from the upper castes; all that remains now is a faint attitude of mockery among the Brahmins at the extravagance and vulgarity of the new generation of Harijans.

The adoption by Harijans of some of the upper caste symbols of status is likely to become increasingly common. These symbols, however, are by no means all a part of the Sanskritic model. The Tanjore experience referred to above seems to be of widespread occurence. Bailey reports a comparable situation from Bisipara, a hill village in

Orissa. In describing the participation of Pan untouchables in an annual festival in 1959, he says:

Many of the men wore shirts and long trousers and shoes, certainly as a mark of status and emancipation because the normal dress of the villagers is a *dhoti*, and even sandals are worn only when the ground gets unbearably hot in April and May. The Pan women wore blouses and mill woven *saris*, and several of the younger ones had put on lipstick and face-powder.[18]

However, there are even now certain pockets where the old disabilities continue to be enforced. *The Report of the Commissioner for Scheduled Castes and Scheduled Tribes* for 1961–2 states:

The Scheduled Castes are not allowed to wear *dhotis* below the knees, and a Scheduled Caste bridegroom cannot put on a turban with a *turra* in some of the villages of *Madhya Pradesh*. In some areas of this State band music is not allowed to be played at the time of marriage among the Scheduled Castes, their women folk cannot wear bangles and other ornaments made of silver and the Scheduled Caste people are not allowed to ride a horse or use a bullock cart as means of transport.[19]

There can be little doubt, however, that the areas in which such restrictions are enforced are shrinking at a rapid rate.

There is a certain measure of ambivalence in the attitude of the Harijans towards the traditional status symbols of the upper castes. There is, on the one hand, an urge to adopt many of these symbols and, on the other, an undercurrent of resentment against the entire traditional order. The rejection of the traditional symbols of status is helped by the existence of alternative styles of life towards which the Harijans are likely to turn in increasing degree. Before discussing the significance of some of these it may be useful to consider briefly the part played by Sanskritization in tribal society.

It is clear that the tribal people have been isolated to a far greater extent from the broad stream of Sanskritization than have the Scheduled Castes or the Other Backward Classes. In spite of this, however, they have felt the impact of Sanskritic ideas and values and this impact has gathered momentum over the last several decades. This has no doubt been largely due to the opening of the tribal area to traffic from outside. One of the most general effects of Sanskritization in this case is that it leads to the integration of segments of tribal society into the

[18] F. G. Bailey, *Politics and Social Change: Orissa in 1959*, Berkeley, University of California Press, 1963, p. 51.

[19] Government of India, *Report of the Commissioner for Scheduled Castes and Scheduled Tribes for the year 1961–62*, New Delhi, 1963, p. 6.

wider caste structure. Historically there have been numerous examples
of this kind of integration. The Bhumij in Eastern India, the Raj Gond
in Central India and the Patelia in Western India provide instances of
tribes which have been integrated into the caste structure.

It needs to be pointed out, however, that the Sanskritization of
tribal communities and their integration into the caste structure cannot
be understood simply in terms of changes in rituals or styles of life.
Rather, these changes in styles of life usually symbolize a more fundamental transformation in their productive organization. Generally it
is only as tribal people get integrated more fully into the wider economic
system that Sanskritization begins to act in a significant way.

As a typical example of Sanskritization of tribal communities one
may consider the Bhagat movement among the Oraons of Chhotanagpur. Over the last several decades certain sections of the Oraons
have sought to mark themselves out from the main body of their tribe
by adherence to a style of life in which vegetarianism, teetotalism, and
ritual abstentions of various kinds are given a prominent position. The
connexion of these codes of conduct with Sanskritic Hinduism has been
noted by many anthropologists. That such movements are often defined
in opposition to the wider Hindu society should not be allowed to
obscure the fact of their absorption of many of the values of that society.

The Meenas of Peepulkhunt in Banswara district in Rajasthan offer
another striking example.[20] Until recently classified as a section of the
Bhils, they are now taking in a big way to the adoption of Rajput names
and other elements of the Rajput style of life. This leads in some cases
to the repudiation of their tribal ancestry, followed by claims to Rajput
status. In concrete terms, the consequences of this kind of 'passing'
can be seen in changes in dress, worship, rules of marriage, and so
forth. In this area also one encounters the development of Bhagat
movements comparable to the ones of Chhotanagpur.

The efforts of Harijans and Adivasis to Sanskritize their styles of life
do not always meet with success. The structural distance between these
communities and the upper castes is still too great for the former to
pass successfully into the ranks of the latter. In Indian society the rules
of caste endogamy ensure the maintenance of structural distance
between groups which are of widely different backgrounds. Even
when intermarriage does take place across castes, the barrier of untouchability is rarely crossed. Indeed, it continues to restrict intermarriage even after conversion to Christianity. Nor is the Adivasi, even

[20] The author is grateful to his colleague, Mr. G. S. Aurora, for the information on the
Meenas.

when he is highly educated, in a better position when he seeks inter-marriage with a caste Hindu.

Where attempts at Sanskritization fail, the consequence is often a feeling of deep resentment among Harijans and Adivasis against the upper castes. This resentment is born out of an attitude which is different from what prevailed in the past. In traditional society in-equality between communities was accepted as a fundamental value. This value has been formally rejected by the new legal and political order, and where it still exists it is challenged at every point.

The attitude of resentment against the traditional order is most easily perceptible among the younger generation of Harijans who have been exposed to the ideas of secularism and democracy. In some places it has been nourished by social movements of a fairly organized nature. In Tamilnad the 'Self-Respect' movement challenged the traditional social and ritual order and sought to emancipate the lower castes from the domination of the Brahmins. It played an important part in the creation of a new climate among the Backward Classes including the Harijans.

In Maharashtra a considerable section of the Harijans became con-verts to Buddhism. The Neo-Buddhist movement was spearheaded by the late Dr. B. R. Ambedkar, a Harijan leader who enjoyed an all-India reputation. Dr. Ambedkar was an indomitable critic of the traditional Hindu social order with its emphasis on inequality, segregation, and ritual pollution. The conversion to Buddhism can be seen as an asser-tion of self-respect on the part of Harijans who refused to accept the degraded position assigned to them in Hindu society. The Neo-Budd-hists have dispensed with some of the traditional rituals of Hinduism although in other regards their style of life has not altered v ry signi-ficantly.

Buddhism is not the only religion which has attracted the alienated sections of Hindu society. Islam, Sikhism, and Christianity have also attracted converts from the lower strata. Christianity plays a very active part today among many tribal communities. Throughout tribal India a variety of Christian Missions and, in particular, the Roman Catholic Church operate as active agents of social change. Besides providing an alternative system of religious values, the Missions have introduced many new features into tribal society, such as education and modern medical facilities. It is no accident that many of the leaders of tribal India are Christians or at least have been educated in mission schools. The Harijans also have been converted in large numbers to Christianity, particularly in South India.

The Harijans and the Adivasis—particularly the younger generations among them—seem to be groping for new symbols to which they might attach themselves. The symbols of traditional Hindu society are no longer adequate, and it is for this reason that the Adivasis (and sometimes also the Harijans) endeavour to re-create a largely imaginary past in which their life was more pure and had not been corrupted by the priest, the moneylender, and the other evils of uppercaste Hindu society. It should perhaps be emphasized again that the kinds of symbols to which these sections of the Harijans and the Adivasis are reaching forward are likely to be very different from the ones to which the upper layer of the Other Backward Classes tend to attach themselves.

But the Harijans and the Adivasis are not entirely tied to an imaginary past in their search for new symbols. The modern secular social order provides alternative symbols and values which are likely to become increasingly important in the future. In order to understand how this is likely to come about we have to consider the process of Westernization in contemporary India.

We shall not attempt here to give a precise definition of Westernization.[21] Broadly speaking, the process refers to the adoption by a community of Western elements in dress, habits, manners, and customs. An important agency of Westernization in this sense is the modern educational system, which is associated with new norms and values, and new symbols of prestige. The English language, which occupies a central position in the new educational system, is an important symbol of status in every sector of Indian society.

Fifty years ago Western education was virtually a monopoly of the Brahmins and a few upper castes. The Backward Classes made a belated start in the adoption of Western elements into their style of life. However, since the end of the First World War demands began to be made by the leaders of these communities for the benefits of Western education. In fact, the demand for educational concessions was a major plank in the Backward Classes Movement. These demands were put forward in a particularly organized manner in South India, especially in Madras and Mysore and also in Maharashtra.

The Backward Classes in general, and particularly the Other Backward Classes, have been trying consistently to narrow the gaps in Western education between themselves and the 'forward' classes. Mysore State offers a striking example where rapid strides have been taken in this direction by the two dominant backward castes, the

[21] Srinivas, 'Sanskritization and Westernization'.

Lingayats and the Okkaligas. Such gains (which may appear rather limited in absolute terms) have, of course, to be measured against the past, and the rather low *average* rate of literacy and education in the country. Further, whatever may be the results achieved so far, there is every indication of a continuous rise in the demand for education by all sections of the Backward Classes.

There is no gainsaying the fact that the levels of literacy and education among the Scheduled Tribes and the Scheduled Castes are still very low. But once again what has been achieved must be measured against the background of traditional society which denied almost wholly the benefits of education to these sections of society. And viewed by the light of the past, the progress of some of these communities, for instance, the Lushais of Assam or the Mahars of Maharashtra— appears remarkable. The benefits of education are most likely to spread with increasing speed among the Scheduled Tribes and Castes. For not only are demands being generated from within, but the Government is investing increasingly larger sums of money to meet these demands.

We may pause briefly to take stock of some of the progress made by the Scheduled Tribes and the Scheduled Castes under the auspices of the Government. Over the last two decades there has been a phenomenal rise in the number of scholarships awarded by the Government of India to members of these communities. In 1944–5 only 114 post-matric scholarships were awarded to members of the Scheduled Castes. The figure had risen to 10,034 by 1954–5 and to 60,165 by 1963–4. Corresponding figures for the Scheduled Tribes are: 84 for 1948–9, 2,356 for 1954–5, and 11,670 for 1963–4.[22] There can be little doubt that these figures will continue to rise (though certainly not at the same rate) over the next ten years.

There are indications that the Harijans and the Adivasis are making increasingly effective use of the facilities provided by the Government to better their economic and social positions. Formerly many of the posts in the higher services reserved for members of these communities could not be filled for want of suitably qualified candidates. This is no longer the case today and is not likely to be so in the future. To take one example, whereas only five of the sixteen posts reserved for the Scheduled Castes in the I.A.S. were actually filled in 1957, since 1962 all the posts reserved for them have been actually filled.[23] The position with regard to the Scheduled Tribes is similar.

[22] By courtesy of Mr. L. P. Singh.
[23] By courtesy of Mr. L. P. Singh.

Modern education acts in a very special way as a solvent of the barriers between different communities. The modern school is a most effective area of desegregation and this is of particular importance from the viewpoint of the Scheduled Castes. The school brings together in increasing numbers children from castes which are widely separated from one another. Even in the orthodox South, Brahmin, non-Brahmin, and Harijan children come together in the school. In the villages of Tanjore district, for instance, it is a new experience for Harijan children to sit with the children of their Brahmin masters in the same room and study and play together. This early experience, even when it is short-lived, creates a new sense of confidence among the Harijans which is almost entirely absent in the older generation.

The differences in attitude between the generations, and the future implications of these differences, were brought home to me vividly in the course of my fieldwork in a Tanjore village. In this village, which I shall refer to as 'Sripuram', the Brahmins live separately in their exclusive area of residence called the *agraharam*. The Harijans live apart, on the fringe of the village or a little away from it. Even today Harijan men almost never enter the *agraharam*. When a Harijan tenant has to deliver grain to his Brahmin landowner, he stands at the head of the *agraharam* and calls out until somebody (often a non-Brahmin) is sent to bring the grain. Now, the village school is situated in the same *agraharam*, although at one end. The school is attended by a number of Harijan children whose movements within the *agraharam* are now hardly noticed. While children freely come and go, a Harijan elder still considers it an act of daring—perhaps even a little impious—to enter the *agraharam*.

It has been noted earlier that there were in the past many differences in culture between the Scheduled Castes and the higher strata. These differences were symbolized in different styles of speech, including vocabulary, diction and accent. Such differences tend to be ironed out today as boys and girls from every caste are brought up together in the atmosphere of a common school.

In Madras State the 'midday meals scheme' has been a subject of much discussion and controversy. The scheme provides midday meals for all school-going children throughout the state. The children are generally served together irrespective of caste. This sometimes leads to abstention from the meals by boys and girls of the upper castes, particularly the Brahmins. But for all this, the experience is a new one and in view of the central importance of commensality in the Hindu scheme of values, it is likely to have considerable significance for the future.

Western education creates a hunger for white-collar occupations among the younger generation of Adivasis and Harijans. Those who succeed in getting jobs as teachers, accountants, or clerks tend to be cut off from their communities. Their position is, in fact, replete with uncertainty. Standing between two worlds, they are often unable to gain a foothold in either. Although their number so far is limited, it is bound to increase and this increase will render more acute the social problems of transition from the most backward sections of society to the new middle class.

The tremendous urge for white-collar jobs among the Scheduled Tribes and Castes cannot be explained solely by motives of economic gain. In every range of Indian society a very high value is attached to non-manual work and a white-collar job is universally viewed as a passport to respectability. This view is sometimes held all the more keenly by the Backward Classes, who have until recently been almost wholly excluded from such occupations. Now that white-collar jobs are almost within reach, no price appears to be too high for them.

It is largely for this reason that boys from the Scheduled Tribes and Castes are not attracted in very large numbers to the craft-training schools of the Government. A Harijan boy who has been through high school would normally prefer a clerical job even where higher earnings are offered by skilled manual work. Among people who have been tied to social degradation for generations, the appeal of respectability is particularly urgent.

Thus the values and status symbols of the upper castes tend to be progressively internalized by the Backward Classes. The competition for higher social status spreads and becomes intensified. This competition is waged sometimes in the traditional idiom, for instance when a lower caste tries to Sanskritize itself and sometimes in a more modern idiom, for instance when demands are made for higher education or Government jobs. In the past it was generally accepted that different styles of life were appropriate to different sections of society. Now the social aspirations of the Backward Classes tend to be pitched at an increasingly higher level.

It is clear that the competition for status cannot bring the same kind of success to all sections of society. None the less, this competition is an important feature of modern Indian society and its pace is likely to quicken. In the past, social mobility was slow and gradual because the symbols of high social status were often not open even in theory to the lower strata of society. The value system today offers an increasingly greater measure of choice to the individual, although it is evident that the channels through which this choice can be exercised are not equally open to all.

In the past the unit of social mobility was generally not the individual but a caste or subcaste. A caste had a more or less homogeneous culture and it was difficult for an individual to change his style of life effectively in the absence of corresponding changes in his caste or kin-group. Today there is increasing scope for individual mobility. Western education, the expansion of caste-free occupations, and the possibilities of geographical mobility—all enable the individual to change his style of life on his own. And the criterion of individual achievement is likely to play an increasingly important part in the emerging social order.

An increase in the tempo of individual mobility is likely to bring about a change in the very structure of caste. Closed status groups based upon birth are likely to yield increasingly to open status groups based upon education, income, and occupation. There is indeed a noticeable trend in this direction in large urban centres where the ties of caste are being slowly but gradually supplanted by those developed in the school, the office, or the club. However, these trends are as yet largely confined to a small upper layer of urban Indian society. It may take more than a generation of Harijans and Adivasis to gain full acceptance in these new status groups based on factors other than caste.

The rapidity with which members of the Backward Classes pass into the newly emerging status groups will depend to a large extent on two factors. It will depend firstly on the extent to which facilities of education and employment are made available to them, and secondly on the weakening of the traditional attitudes regarding purity and pollution among the upper castes. There are indications that both these tendencies are beginning to operate but it is unlikely that significant results will be achieved within a short time. And the rural areas are likely to lag considerably behind the urban centres in the emergence of status groups based primarily upon education, occupation, and income.

V

So far we have been concerned largely with the movement of the Backward Classes along one particular axis, that of social prestige or status. The internalization of the values, idioms and symbols of the wider society, whether through Sanskritization or Westernization, had a certain unifying effect. It tends to pull down the walls which in the past segregated the different sections of society. This it does by replacing clearly differentiated styles of life by ones which are more general and standardized. The different cultures of the multitude of castes and communities tend more and more to be replaced by a single culture in which the same aspirations, values and symbols are shared by an ever-widening circle of people.

The upward movement of members of the Backward Classes is not always a smooth or easy process. Many of the status symbols of the upper strata of society are inaccessible to the Backward Classes, if not in principle, at least in reality. The channels of mobility, whether in the status system or in the system of production, are still very restricted in Indian society. On the other hand, the new political system has thrown open many possibilities of advancement to people from the Scheduled Tribes, the Scheduled Castes, and the Other Backward Classes. Today, if a Harijan cannot find a place in a higher status group, he can still hope to become an influential political leader. The adoption of a democratic political order in a highly particularistic society ensures that people from every major section of it can aspire to positions of power and authority. And, as far as Harijans and Adivasis are concerned, the principle of reservation provides a sure method of political representation.

The success of the Backward Classes in the competition for power requires a certain assertion of particularistic ties. A Harijan must assert that he is a Harijan if he is to mobilize the support necessary for his political advancement. And it is here that the demands of power and status come into conflict. Whereas the Backward Classes are prompted to merge their identity with the higher strata to enhance their status, considerations of power and economic advantage lead them to define their identity in opposition to the advanced sections of society. This is the dilemma of backwardness. A low caste would like to acquire a high-sounding title, claim Kshatriya status, and assume the symbols of high social status; at the same time it would insist on its right to be officially classified as backward.

It would be of interest to examine the conflicting demands of prestige and power from the viewpoint of the Backward Classes. How have these demands been adjusting themselves and what shape are they likely to take in the future? Frustrated in their efforts to gain social acceptance, the Backward Classes are likely to turn increasingly to political action.

The new political system adopted since Independence offers vast possibilities to large minority blocks such as the Scheduled Tribes, the

Scheduled Castes and the Other Backward Classes. It cannot be said that these possibilities have as yet been fully exploited. The process by which the different sections of society become progressively inducted into the arena of politics is a slow and gradual one. In India politics was in the early stages confined largely to a few upper castes. They were the ones to take the lead in forming political association in order to bargain for power with the British.

But politics has not remained confined to a small coterie of upper castes. It has made its way into ever-widening areas of society. The three general elections since Independence have brought home to every section of the Backward Classes the importance of organized politics. There are many indications that they are going to make increasing use of political action to bargain for a better position in society.

In its formal aspects at least changes in the political order have been much more radical than changes in other spheres of Indian society. And changes in political form do have an impact on the intensity of political participation. As Myron Weiner writes: 'But it is also true that India has become tremendously politicized. Politics has become the avenue for personal advancement in a society in which commercial activities offer little status and administrative posts are relatively few in number.'[24]

There is thus a clear trend towards increasing participation in the political process by sections of society which have hitherto been excluded from positions of power. It is difficult, however, to assess how far there is as yet a real articulation of interests. There is widespread poverty, ignorance, and illiteracy among the Backward Classes, particularly the Scheduled Castes and Tribes. Most members of these communities have as yet only a dim awareness of the nature and strategy of organized politics. It is not unlikely, therefore, that those who now represent their interests do so in a narrow and short-sighted manner.

However, even the most backward sections of society have by now had the experience of three general elections. Their awareness of political parties, movements, machines, and election campaigns has grown steadily over the last fifteen years. By now the experience of being courted during elections by eminent leaders has become familiar even to the hitherto 'exterior' castes. This must in course of time create in them a new awareness of their strength in the political arena.

Recent field studies by social anthropologists often report a change

[24] 'The Politics of South Asia', in G. A. Almond and J. S. Coleman (Eds.), *The Politics of the Developing Areas*, Princeton, Princeton University Press, 1960, p. 192.

of mood among the Harijans, particularly of the younger generation. Bailey[25] indicates how even in a remote hill village in Orissa the Harijan Pans played an active and even aggressive role in the 1957 elections. In Tanjore district, where I did fieldwork in 1961–2, the Congress and its ally the 'Dravida Kazhagam' drew active support from many Harijan youths for the election campaign.

Participation in election campaigns and contact with party 'bosses' tend to create among the younger Harijans a sense of impatience towards the slow and uncertain process of social mobility through imitation of the styles of life of the upper castes. Young Harijans who are inducted into political machines may feel that they can dispense with Sanskritization. Indeed, for a person who aspires to be a political leader among Harijans and Adivasis, a repudiation of Sanskritization may have a high symbolic value. In Tamilnad, where the Dravida Kazhagam has had a strong appeal among the Backward Classes, it is not rare for young Harijans explicitly to reject the values and symbols of the upper castes.

Thus whereas a generation ago an ambitious Harijan might have tried to acquire social respectability by changing his style of life, his counterpart today is more likely to try to build political connexions. And young Harijans with ambition, drive, and initiative are in demand all around. They are sought by every political party, for they are not only valuable as vote-banks, but can also be put up as candidates for reserved seats from the *Zila Parishad* right up to Parliament.

The scramble for power among linguistic, religious, and caste groups has become an important feature of post-Independence India. Virtually every region, community, and caste claims special benefits for itself. And pressure is exerted at every level for the satisfaction of these claims. The Backward Classes have not lagged behind in this regard. In fact, the policy of protective discrimination pursued by the Government has encouraged them to put forward their demands with special vigour.

The institution of *panchayati raj* is likely to quicken the pace of politicization. Provisions have in general been made for the reservation of seats for the Scheduled Tribes and the Scheduled Castes at all levels of the three-tiered structure. The village *panchayat* is likely to become in many areas an arena for conflicts between Harijan members and those of the 'clean' castes. The latter are rarely prepared to treat on equal terms those who had been until recently excluded from many of the important spheres of social life. Conflict, therefore, is likely to multiply

[25] Bailey, op. cit.

in the near future. And, perhaps conflict is a necessary condition for the articulation of the interests of the hitherto underprivileged sections of society.

In this context it is well to remind ourselves that there are deep cleavages within the Backward Classes. It is likely that the most stubborn opposition against the attempts of Harijans to improve their social position will come from those who are immediately above them rather than from the top castes. It is a matter of common observation that competition for status is often most acute between segments which are structurally adjacent to one another. This is because such segments operate largely within the same social universe. It is for this reason that castes which are just above the line of pollution are more likely to be jealous of their privileges in relation to the Harijans than the Westernized upper strata of society.

Conflicts between Harijans and caste Hindus over civic rights are likely to play an important part for some time to come. The new generation of Harijans is no longer in a mood to accept with resignation the civic disabilities imposed upon them by the upper castes. Their contacts with politicians and officials have given them a growing awareness of their rights as citizens of a democratic society and they are rapidly becoming jealous of these rights. A show of strength on their part is a likely source of violence in the rural areas where, in spite of a superficial acceptance of democratic values, the structure remains by and large inegalitarian.

In 1957 severe rioting took place in Ramanathapuram district in Tamilnad between Harijans and Thevars, a locally dominant caste included among the Other Backward Classes. The riots centred around the Immanuel murder case, in which a young Harijan was stabbed to death, allegedly for offering rude remarks to a prominent Thevar politician. The setting of the incident was provided by a by-election in which Harijans and Thevars supported rival candidates.

The Ramanathapuram riots provide only a striking example of a phenomenon which is of widespread occurrence and probably on the increase. It would perhaps be unreal to expect the Harijans to become integrated into the wider social system with rights of full and equal participation without any conflict or violence. But the extent to which such violence can be contained will depend in large measure on the effectiveness of our machinery of law and order.

A special correspondent of *The Mail* wrote during the third general election:[26] 'Shrewd observers draw attention to the new trend in the

[26] *The Weekly Mail*, Madras, 18 February 1962.

political scene in the State, with emphasis shifting from the outdated Brahmin versus non-Brahmin to Harijan versus non-Harijans as a reaction to the numerous concessions made to the Harijans by the Government'. These remarks, made with regard to Tamilnad, seem to indicate a trend which has general significance.

As Harijans in increasing numbers enter the arena of politics, conflicts between them and the upper castes are bound to multiply. These conflicts will in all likelihood manifest themselves most clearly at the level of the village or the small local community. There are now many village *panchayats* where Harijans have a large representation. In rare cases the domination of the *panchayat* by Harijans may lead to the withdrawal of the 'twice-born' from participation.

Where Harijans are more or less evenly matched in numerical strength with caste Hindus, a certain amount of tension or even violence is likely to become a part of the system. During my stay in Tanjore district in 1961–2, several cases of violent conflict between Harijans and non-Brahmins (particularly of the dominant Kallar caste) came to my notice. There was one incident in a neighbouring village which culminated in the murder of a Kallar landowner by the Harijan president of the village *panchayat*. During the legal proceedings that followed, the Kallar tried to storm the court-room at Tanjore in an attempt to do violence to the offending Harijan.

Tribal politics differs in many ways from the politics of the Harijans or the Other Backward Classes. There are certain special problems in their case which arise partly from their geographical isolation and partly from their ethnic identity, which is even more sharply defined than that of the Harijans. We noted earlier how the process of Sanskritization was in the past responsible for the weakening of the cultural identity of tribal peoples in the different parts of the country. But here also the process of cultural assimilation is countered by a variety of forces (principally political in nature) which seek to reassert the identity of the tribal population.

The shift in emphasis from a ritual idiom of mobility to one which relies more on organized politics has been noted by various observers of tribal society. Discussing the trend of modern leadership in Chhotanagpur, Dr. Vidyarthi writes:

The most significant and obvious fact is the switch over from religious leadership to political leadership. This change corresponds to a difference in aims and a difference in methods. The modern leaders are representing the tribal people to an outside political world. They are not concerned primarily with raising the social status of the tribals by making ritual practices more closely resemble those of the Hindus. Their chief task is to improve the material conditions of the tribals and to obtain government funds and services. Their activities, then, are more within the realm of the civil and political and less within the realm of the religious and the social.[27]

The search for a new identity by leaders of tribal communities is understandable. There are important sections of people outside the tribal world who have warned against the loss of their social and cultural identity. In the case of the Adivasis, assimilation (as opposed to integration) has been viewed as a genuine threat by no less a person than the late Prime Minister. The attitude of 'progressive' Indians towards Harijans is fundamentally different in this regard and less ambivalent. Few voices would be raised in protest against the assimilation of Harijans into the wider social system.

Close observers of the Adivasis have, in consequence, noted the development of a spirit of 'tribalism' among them. This is due to a variety of factors, among which the special treatment policy of Government and the work of the Christian missions are of importance. Today the spirit of tribalism can be given expression through the processes of organized politics. The demand for a tribal homeland, and the growth of a political party to put it forward, indicate the politicization of tribal society. Professor N. K. Bose, till recently Anthropological Adviser to the Government, writes: 'Tribal communities formerly tried to better their condition by either identification with the Hindus or with the ruling class through Westernization and Christianity. Now power can be derived by political organization into parties.'[28]

Tribal groups may, of course, press their demands through parties committed to unity and integration or they may form separatist parties to represent their exclusive interests. The Jharkhand Party (in some of its phases) may be viewed as an example of the latter. On the other hand, the Congress Party has shown an extremely high degree of resilience in meeting the special demands of communities of every kind. The recent merger of the Jharkhand Party with the Congress in Bihar seems to suggest that the party in power has many devices for softening the tone of separatist demands.

The kind of compromises which the ruling party is prepared to make is likely to deflect it, to some extent, from its main aims and policies.

[27] L. P. Vidyarthi, 'The Historical March of the Jharkhand Party: A Study of Adivasi Leadership in Tribal Bihar', *Indian Sociological Bulletin*, Vol. I, No. 2, 1964, p. 5.

[28] N. K. Bose, 'Change in Tribal Cultures Before and After Independence', *Man in India*, Vol. XLIV, No. 1, 1964, p. 5.

The Congress is likely to continue its tolerance of tribal exclusiveness partly as a measure of political expediency; an uncompromising attitude is more likely to precipitate a crisis than to overcome it. It seems probable that the special treatment policy will slacken the pace of development for some time to come by creating an atmosphere of apathy and complacency. It is difficult, however, to foresee any radical change in this policy in the immediate future. And the policy remaining broadly the same, the chances of a crisis being precipitated by separatist forces appear rather limited.

It is most unlikely that the 'communal' element will be eliminated from Indian politics for some time to come. N. K. Bose writes: 'Under the climate created by special treatment, communal consciousness has been inordinately accentuated.'[29] But the significance of this development can be evaluated in different ways. The growth of 'communal consciousness' need not be viewed as necessarily an unhealthy or disruptive force. It may, on the contrary, be a precondition to the integration of the tribals into the wider body politic. For the measure of integration lies not so much in a passive acceptance of the *status quo* as in the adoption of a body of common political rules through which divergent interests are organized and articulated.

Thus what has been viewed by some as an increase in communal consciousness may be only one step forward in the politicization of Indian society. The years to come are likely to witness a fuller participation in the political process by larger sections of the tribal population, and a more effective articulation between tribal leaders and the masses. The wider political order can be brought close to the tribal masses only when their leaders at every level learn to put forward demands on their behalf. In a heterogeneous society where particularistic ties are of such importance, it is unrealistic to expect political integration to come about without large concessions to special demands.

It may be interesting in this context to re-examine the old controversy regarding isolation, assimilation, and integration as three alternative lines along which tribal communities might develop. The case for isolation seems to have been abandoned as both unrealistic and undesirable. The tribal people everywhere are being drawn increasingly into wider social, economic, and political networks. In addition to market forces of diverse kinds, the developmental activities of the Government are bound to make steady inroads into the world of the Adivasis. And the Adivasi leaders are rapidly coming to realize that

[29] Ibid., p. 7.

they can gain more for themselves and their communities by coming to terms with the Government and the ruling party than by remaining isolated.

Increasing articulation with the wider social, economic, and political system is likely to lead in the long run to the disappearance of many of the distinctive features of tribal life. The process of modernization has a certain standardizing effect and it may be too costly for the Government to keep alive in a hothouse atmosphere the picturesque or artistic elements of tribal culture. The search for an identity on the part of tribal leaders does not always involve a genuine revival of the traditional heritage; more often it is part of an attempt to come to terms with political forces which in the long run are bound to destroy the very bases of this identity.

The Harijans illustrate even more clearly than the Adivasis the mechanism of integration through the political process. At the height of the 'Depressed Classes Movement' under Dr. Ambedkar, it had at times appeared as if they might move further and further away from the wider social system. In the years since Independence the Congress has successfully absorbed their demands and integrated the bulk of the Harijan leadership into the structure of the party.

The Congress Party seems to have succeeded in winning over the loyalties of the Harijans by making numerous concessions to them. Although such loyalties may not go very deep, it is doubtful whether any other party can compete with the Congress in this regard. Bailey has recorded in some detail the nature of Harijan support for the Congress in Bisipara which he attributes to 'the ideological pull (or perhaps one should call it "enlightened self-interest") of Congress policy towards the Harijans'.[30] I found confirmation of Bailey's observations in the Tanjore village earlier referred to as Sripuram, more than a thousand miles away.

The integration of the Harijans into the wider body politic is, by comparison with that of the Adivasis, relatively easy. Unlike the latter, they are not geographically concentrated and there is hardly any question in their case of the demand for a separate homeland. But numerically they are far more important than the tribals and, for historical reasons, the problem of untouchability has caught the imagination of the Western-educated elite in the country. For this reason the Congress has been compelled to accommodate the demands of the Harijans at every level and these demands are likely to become progressively organized both within and outside the party.

[30] Bailey, op. cit., p. 44.

There is a curious dilemma in the position adopted by the Government and the ruling party towards the Harijans. On the one hand, the leaders among the latter are impatient of the limited and tardy nature of the concessions granted to their community. On the other, there is a growing resentment among castes of the middle region against the 'soft' attitude of the Government towards the Harijans. The Congress, in gaining the support of Harijans through accommodation of their demands, is likely to create increasing disaffection in the ranks of the upper castes.

VI

The arguments presented above suggest that the Harijans (as well as other underprivileged groups) are likely in the near future to seize their civic rights with increasing success and perhaps also get increasing representation in political bodies of various kinds. At this point it is possible only to raise the question as to how effective this representation is likely to be.

In the last analysis it may be argued that the fundamental problem facing the Harijans (and also, to some extent, the others) is an economic one. It is a problem of landlessness, poverty, and unemployment. How well can the Harijans or the Adivasis make use of their position of growing political strength to solve, or even tackle, some of these basic economic problems?

It is admitted on all hands that the economic transformation of the Scheduled Tribes and the Scheduled Castes has been taking place at a creeping pace, if at all. The Harijans and Adivasis by and large continue to be poor, indebted, and landless. Governmental measures to ameliorate their economic conditions have had, at best, a moral or symbolic effect. Given the magnitude of the problem it is doubtful whether any substantial change can be brought about solely through measures such as the allotment to a few Harijans of bits and pieces of land or the reservation for them of a certain number of jobs in the Government. The same, of course, applies in large measure to the tribals.

In the pre-British economic system Harijans had almost without exception been in the position of agricultural labourers. In certain areas their position was no better than that of serfs tied to the soil. British rule and developments since Independence have progressively emancipated them from their former servile status. But the change in legal status has rarely been accompanied by any real change in economic position. Most Harijans continue to be landless agricultural labourers. In some ways their economic position has been rendered more insecure than in the past. In the past, traditional obligations assured the Harijan labourer of some source of employment and sustenance. Today, with the collapse of traditional obligations, even this is threatened.

The economic position of the tribals is not very much better than that of the Harijans. Here, however, the issues and problems are a little different. There is, to begin with, the problem of wasteful techniques of cultivation. Attempts are being made by the Government to control these but the problem itself is particularly acute for only a small section of the tribal people.

Land alienation and moneylending are the two most important economic problems which confront the tribals (and indirectly the Government). The two problems are closely related, since the moneylenders are also the ones to whom land is most frequently alienated. They have been sought to be remedied by legislative as well as executive action, but the success so far has been very limited. Such action sometimes has the consequence of raising higher the barriers between tribals and non-tribals without bringing about any substantial improvement in the economic condition of the former.

When tribal people do become a part of the wider social order they generally occupy within it the lowest rungs of the economic ladder. They join as landless labourers, often without security of employment, working sometimes on the farms of other people and sometimes eking out a bare existence through the sale of baskets, mats or jungle produce. In such cases their economic problems are not significantly different from those of the Scheduled Castes.

It is rather difficult to visualize any radical transformation in the economic position of the Scheduled Tribes and Castes for some time to come. If such a transformation does come about it is unlikely that it will have its sources within tribal or Harijan society. Any significant change in their economic position will require major changes in the external system, in particular the agrarian class structure of the country as a whole. The Harijans and Adivasis are almost everywhere prevented by their insecure position from initiating any kind of major economic change. Nor can governmental intervention by itself bring about any quick and substantial improvement, the magnitude of the problem being what it is.

Changes in the economic position of the Other Backward Classes are, if anything, even more difficult to assess. For one thing, they appear to be a rather assorted category, including at one end castes which are similar in position to the Harijans and at the other end powerful dominant castes like the Lingayats and Okkaligas. Further, the Other Backward Classes do not form a sharply defined category in the social system, and in the absence of numerical data it is impossible to consider trends of economic change among them separately from such trends in the whole of Indian society.

The Central Government's policy to do away with the 'communal' definition of the Other Backward Classes and its refusal to draw up an all-India list of these communities is bound to affect their position in important ways. These communities had developed a separate identity partly as a consequence of policies pursued by the state governments of associating them with certain concessions and advantages. When these are given to individuals on the basis of income, and not to whole communities, the boundaries between the latter and the so-called advanced sections of society will cease to have their former social and political significance.

It is not within the scope of this paper to consider the prospects of change in the agrarian class structure of the country. Here it can only be reiterated that the future of the Backward Classes is intimately related to what happens to the economy as a whole. In this paper we have tried to consider the problems of the Backward Classes *qua* Backward Classes, as understood in the Constitution and recognized for specific purposes by the Central Government and state governments. Although it is true that the Backward Classes overlap in large measure with certain economic categories as defined in this country, these are not 'classes' at all but groups of communities.

The distinctive features of the Backward Classes are in large measure related to the very structure of Indian society. When this structure undergoes change, the Backward Classes are likely to lose much of their identity. There is ample evidence to show that Indian society is undergoing profound changes. The traditional segmental structure is losing many of its characteristics and a greater interpenetration of segments is coming about. Networks of interpersonal relations cutting across the boundaries of caste and community are becoming an increasingly important feature of the new economic and political systems. Finally, ritual values, which played a decisive role in keeping alive the concept of structural distance, are becoming progressively weakened.

It is true that the forces of modernization are as yet largely confined to a limited sector of Indian society. Their effects are felt primarily among the Western-educated middle classes, particularly in the urban

VI

Caste and Local Politics in India

BY ADRIAN C. MAYER

*Professor of Indian Anthropology, School of Oriental and
African Studies, University of London*

THE theme of this book is the unity and diversity of Indian society,
and I wish to consider as one of its aspects the role of caste in local
politics. How important a factor is caste distinction in elections and in
party organization and faction composition, and what influence does
it have compared to other factors? Does the present political system
encourage or inhibit the use of caste as a means of recruiting followers?
For some, there is a moral issue behind these questions. Caste is seen to
introduce an unwarranted idiom of birth and ascribed qualifications
into a system which assumes a diversity based rather on differences of
performance and achieved qualities. This is why the words 'caste' and
'casteism' are often used as pejoratives in India, and why there are legal
prohibitions on the exploitation of caste sentiments in elections. I am
not concerned here with this issue, nor with the degree to which formal
prohibitions are enforced. Caste distinctions still exist in Indian
society; and my aim is to indicate whether the evidence shows that they
influence present political alignments and activities, and to assess their
importance as compared to other factors.

Before starting, I must point out that the word 'caste' can be used
to denote two sociologically distinct entities. One is a group of interacting members; the other is a named population, often widely dispersed, whose members do not interact as a whole, but which is yet a
social entity, because members are aware that they belong to it and
thereby have specific kinds of relationships with other people. I shall
call the former a caste group and the latter a caste.[1] A man has political

---

[1] One or more levels of sub-caste groups and sub-castes can be distinguished within
most castes; but the distinction is often not made by people of other castes, and I shall for
the most part ignore such internal divisions in this article, though what I say about castes
can be applied, *mutatis mutandis*, to the various internal levels. There is a third referent of
caste, namely the *varna*. In politics, this generally has a connotation similar to that of the
caste population and can be included with it, again *mutatis mutandis*, for the purposes of
this general review.

roles as a member of one or the other at different times. I restrict my use of the term 'political' to cover activities in the formal political system of an Indian district. This is one of 324 such administrative divisions in India, varying enormously in population and size, but generally extending over between 1,000 and 5,000 square miles, and containing between 300,000 and 3,000,000 people.[2]

Political activities in a district take place in three spheres. There is the sphere of rural politics, that of municipal politics, and that of what one can call constituency politics.

The rural political system is based on three tiers of power. The lowest is the village committee (V.C.), elected by the population of one or a few near-by villages. The middle tier comprises representatives of the V.C.s in a 'block' of villages, as defined for the community development programme. These blocks may coincide with the subdivisions of the revenue administration (*tehsil* or *taluka*), but are often smaller than this. The highest tier is the district committee (D.C.), on which sit representatives of the block committees (B.C.). At each stage a number of members are co-opted to represent special interests and sections of the population. This structure now exists in most states and conforms in general to the principles enunciated by the National Development Council when it endorsed the proposal for democratic decentralization (*panchayati raj*) in 1958, although the distribution of power in the structure, and the distinction between compulsory and optional duties, may vary.

A few states already had such a three-tier system before *panchayati raj* was introduced in 1959, and it is from a district in one of these (Madhya Pradesh) that I shall draw examples from my own experience. This is the district of Dewas, containing 446,901 people (1961) in an area of 2,376 square miles, and having a rural political structure of one D.C., five B.C.s and 208 V.C.s in 1960, the year of my last extended fieldwork there.[3] I am interested here in the way in which aspirants to power win seats and maintain their positions on these committees, and the degree to which they rely on caste ties to do so.

In each district there are at least one or two towns in which municipalities or corporations exist, formed mainly by representatives elected from a number of wards. In Dewas district there is only one sizeable town, the district headquarters of the same name, with a population of

² D. C. Potter, *Government in Rural India*, London, Bell, 1964. pp. 10 ff.

³ The fieldwork was made possible by a research leave from the School of Oriental and African Studies, University of London, to which I express my thanks. A new *panchayati raj* Act has now been introduced in Madhya Pradesh, but owing to successive emergencies it had not been implemented at the time of writing this paper in January 1966.

34,577 (1961) and having a municipal council of sixteen elected and four nominated members. Again, is caste a factor in municipal elections and in the working of this urban government?

Thirdly, each district contains a number of constituencies of the State Legislative Assembly, and forms part of a constituency, or may contain one or more constituencies, of the central Parliament. Does caste enter into the elections to these bodies, and does it affect the relations of members (M.L.A.s and M.P.s) to their constituents? Dewas district contains four M.L.A. constituencies, and forms part of an M.P.'s constituency with a neighbouring district.

These three political spheres provide to varying extents fields for the activities of political parties. These parties may be organized at the district, block, and village or village-group level. They are most active at times of elections, being for the most part caucus-type parties with little effective branch organization.[4] Through the party organizations, district politics reaches up to the state, if not the national level. For, besides its links through any legislators belonging to it, each district party is represented in the state-wide party organization. Though I shall not deal with state and national political levels, I shall look upwards from the district, and shall consider how district leaders affect, and are affected by, the pattern of politics at the state level, and shall try to assess what part caste may play in this pattern.

Rural Politics

The role of caste in rural politics can be discussed in two contexts. One is that of village politics, and the other is that of the politics of the system of block and district committees.

The pattern of power in villages has been one of dominance by members of one or sometimes several caste groups. This dominance was based on the ownership of land which, in an agricultural and largely subsistence economy, brought direct power over tenants and craftsmen as well as the general power of wealth. Coupled with landownership was usually the possession of the hereditary office of headman, which brought with it not only statutory powers of tax collection and the maintenance of law and order, but also the advantages of being in touch with officials and other outsiders, and hence the generalized influence deriving from the role of mediator between village and town. It must be stressed that not all members of this dominant caste group were equally endowed with political offices and land. But to the extent that the less well-endowed members of the caste group shared in the

[4] M. Duverger, *Political Parties*, London, Methuen (3rd ed.), 1959, pp. 17ff.

prestige, and to a lesser extent the power, of their leaders, the dominant unit was the entire caste group in the village.[5]

The politics connected with the new system of rural self-government takes one of two forms. In one case, there is competition for power between sections of the dominant caste group. Where there are two headmen, for instance, they and their lineages are opposed; or else these traditional leaders may be challenged by members of the dominant caste group who have not been members of this elite. In such cases, members of factions within the dominant caste group recruit support among dependants in the rest of the village—i.e. among tenants, craftsmen, and others from whom they can expect a return for the favours they have shown them—as well as from villagers whom they may be able to recruit by promises of favours in the future. The lines of political cleavage, therefore, are vertical and the pattern may well be that the membership of every caste group in the village is divided into two sections by the division within the dominant caste group.

The other pattern is where the dominant caste group is not divided in this way and is opposed by men of another caste group, who have not been dominant under previous conditions, but who now have the strength to aspire to village leadership. Such men may belong, for instance, to a lower caste which due to its size has become influential in the new system of universal suffrage; or they may be from a caste whose members have seized upon new avenues of prestige and power such as education and urban occupations. In such cases the traditionally dominant and the aspiring castes may oppose each other as whole caste groups; other castes may be divided, but the main lines of cleavage are horizontal rather than vertical.

Where there is no single dominant caste in the village, but, instead a number of castes with land and more or less equal power, these either oppose each other as caste groups, or sections of each make intercaste alliances on the pattern of vertical cleavages. The two kinds of alignment can therefore be distinguished here also; but it should be stressed that they are not necessarily mutually exclusive in a village, and that both may exist simultaneously.[6]

I have been using the term 'caste group', but, in fact, it is difficult to assess the role of caste ties in these situations. For caste groups are often at the same time groups of kin (the exception being when several

[5] See, e.g., A. C. Mayer, *Caste and Kinship in Central India*, London, Kegan Paul, 1960, p. 113.

[6] See, e.g., the Ponnur example given by Weiner, when there was competition between dominant caste groups as well as ties of dominant caste men with dependants: M. Weiner, 'Village and Party Factionalism in Andhra', *Economic Weekly*, Vol. XIV, 1962, p. 1513.

endogamous subcastes are represented in the village's caste group) and, in so far as they hold the monopoly of an occupation or comprise all major landholders, are economic interest groups, too. Hence, the actions of people may not result from decisions made solely for reasons of caste. Nor may intercaste alliances be formed on a caste basis alone; for ties of common class interest cut across caste boundaries. Sometimes, it is true, there is what appears to be an explicitly caste-based action.[7] But it seems that an equally if not more frequent pattern is one in which there are factions within the caste group, although the trend towards a loosening of control by the village's dominant landowners has meant a less exact coincidence of caste and economic and political power, and a greater capacity for previously dependent caste groups to strive for political power. There is even now a considerable summation of roles in rural social systems; and it may be difficult to distinguish a specifically caste component of action on the one hand, and on the other difficult to say that economic, kinship, and other social relations are not indeed to some extent caste relations. It is, in any case, dangerous to generalize about village politics, because there are so many variations from region to region and from village to village, and constant changes occur in the position in any one place; but one can say that, in general, to call political relations caste relations, though up to a point true, is only to simplify the issue in a way which masks the real complexity of the system, and which therefore obscures the springs of social differentiation from which future developments in village politics will emerge.

Political activities are of a different kind at the higher levels of the rural system. In Dewas district, for instance, the B.C. representatives are elected from amongst themselves by the V.C. members; and these representatives then elect the B.C. chairman from amongst themselves and choose their representatives for the D.C., where the chairman is again elected by members. Hence above the V.C. level there is a system of indirect election, with two key posts to be striven for—the chairmanship of the B.C. and D.C.[8]

---

[7] E.g., in an election described by Opler, the Nonia caste group of Senapur village held a meeting and decided to vote as one man for the candidate of one, rather than another, section of the dominant caste group; see M. E. Opler, 'Factors of Tradition and Change in a Local Election in Rural India', in R. L. Park and I. Tinker (Eds.), *Leadership and Political Institutions in India*, Princeton, N.J., Princeton University Press, 1959, pp. 144–5.

[8] Other states have different procedures for election; in some, the V.C. chairman is *ex officio* the representative on the B.C.; in others, the B.C. chairman is elected by all V.C. members.

Under such a system, prospective candidates for the B.C. chairmanship should ensure that only their supporters are elected to the V.C.s. Actually, however, such control is difficult if not impossible to exert. Elections to the V.C. are based on almost endless variations of village alignments and oppositions over which a B.C. candidate may have little influence, and it is therefore seldom possible for candidates to control what goes on in all of fifty or more V.C. elections. I have seen contenders for block and district leadership content themselves by throwing their weight into crucial elections in which their main supporters are involved, trying to influence other elections as best they can.[9] For example, they may be able to intercede where their close kinsmen are involved. In this way, a prospective block leader with a widely flung kinship linkage—which means, in fact, a widely scattered subcaste group—stands a better chance of organizing an electoral machine at least partially based on caste ties than does a member of a caste represented in only a few villages. In some areas the dominant caste is found in all villages and would seem to have a great organizing potential in this respect;[10] in other areas there are several dominant castes and none is found in a majority of settlements.[11] But here again, common kinship and caste is only one factor; for there may be splits within the dominant caste which detract from its usefulness as the basis for an alliance over the block. An example is provided by the Rajputs of Dewas block. Almost all Rajputs supported their caste-mate in his campaign for the B.C. chairmanship in 1957. But even at that time, there were signs that such a unity might not last.[12] This was borne out by later events; in 1960 a split between Rajput leaders was papered over with an overt unity, but by 1962 it had become an open break.

Major efforts by candidates for block leadership in Dewas are made after the V.C. elections, therefore, when the electoral dust has cleared and V.C. members can be approached for support.

Elsewhere, I have analysed an attempt by candidates to influence the selection of the B.C. representative by V.C. members.[13] The example shows that several factors entered into the calculations of candidates—common caste was one, but also prominent were intervillage rivalry as

[9] Mayer, 'Local Government Election in a Malwa Village', *Eastern Anthropologist*, Vol. XI, 1958, pp. 189–202.

[10] D. N. Majumdar, *Caste and Communication in an Indian Village*, London, Asia Publishing House, 1958, p. 7.

[11] Mayer, 'The Dominant Caste in a Region of Central India', *South-Western Journal Anth.*, Vol. XIV, 1958, pp. 407–27.

[12] Mayer, 'Local Government Election . . .', p. 422.

[13] Mayer, ibid.

well as intracaste group rivalry. Aspiring rural leaders in Dewas built up sets of supporters on these and other bases (for example, economic obligation, ritual kinship). The evidence I have suggests that the traditionally politically dominant caste tended to control the composition of the B.C. and D.C., rather than the newly emerging castes,[14] perhaps because it had had more experience of political manoeuvring in the past. But whether or not this is widely the case, the increase in competition for block leadership[15] has meant that the present system of decentralization and devolution of power may not, in fact, result in a greater popular democratic control, but may well instead result in greater control by dominant interest groups, including castes.[16]

Because of the difficulties of organizing support, aspirants have been increasingly under pressure to bring in political parties as organizing mechanisms. Party leaders may well dislike becoming embroiled in village factionalism and advocate a policy of non-involvement,[17] but the trend towards party nominations (or 'tickets') in V.C. elections seems to be a strong one,[18] and the losers in the higher-level elections—which are indeed fought on party lines—tend to say that their defeats occurred because they had not given party tickets in the V.C. elections and so could not control the election of their supporters. It should be stressed, however, that ticket-giving by the parties would not necessarily provide leaders with a surer basis of support. Leaving a party when not given its ticket is by no means unknown, and there would be no guarantee that V.C. members elected on one party's ticket would not be persuaded to vote for the candidate of another party in a subsequent B.C. election. Again, because district party politics are often really factional politics, a V.C. member would have loyalties to a faction, and might well work against the party if this faction subsequently found itself in opposition in the district party organization.

I have had to bring party politics into this discussion of rural politics

---

[14] Mayer, 'Some Political Implications of Community Development in India', *Archiv. Europ. Sociol.*, Vol. IV, 1963, pp. 92–93.

[15] This is implied by the smaller number of unanimous elections to B.C.s, as compared with the larger number of non-contested V.C. seats filled (see, e.g., C.V.H., '*Panchayat Elections in Andhra*' *Economic Weekly*, Vol. XVI, 1964, pp. 979–80.)

[16] R. Kothari, '*Panchayati Raj:* a Re-Assessment', *Economic Weekly*, Vol. XIII, 1961, pp. 754–60.

[17] P. Brass, *Factional Politics in an Indian State*, Berkeley, University of California Press, 1965, p. 225.

[18] It may well be more advanced in other parts of India than in Dewas, e.g. the Bengal villages studied by Nicholas and Mukhopadhyay, where village elections were openly fought on party alignments; see R. W. Nicholas and T. Mukhopadhyay, 'Politics and Law in Two West Bengal Villages', *Bull. Anth. Surv. India*, Vol. XI, 1962, pp. 15–40.

because the two are closely connected, especially at the higher levels of the rural system. On the one hand, rural leaders would find it easier to control village politics were party loyalties and the prestige of party politicians (hitherto mainly townspeople) to be enlisted by turning V.C. elections into party political contests; on the other, the party politicians need rural leaders to help them gather votes at times of general elections, since parties are badly organized in the villages. This rural leaders can do, not only because of social links they may have with village leaders, but also because of their influence through their control of the large sums placed at their disposal for rural community development. To what extent may the patronage provided by these funds be controlled by one group, and may such a group be based on caste?

Development money is provided from several sources. The D.C.s and B.C.s have funds to spend themselves, and also decide which of the projects sent to them from the V.C.s should be granted funds from the community development budget. Parallel to the rural committee structure is the co-operative system, in which village co-operatives elect representatives to the board of the district's co-operative bank, whose elected chairman and secretary are powerful figures in the allocation of loans from the large sums at the bank's command. In fact, the chairmanships of the bank and the B.C. and D.C. are the prized positions in rural politics. There are also other social service agencies through which smaller amounts of money may be obtained, as well as the revenue department from which short-term loans may be taken. Elsewhere, I have analysed how some Rs. 678,000 was allocated during the first two five-year plans in one block in Dewas district.[19] In particular, I was interested to find out how much justification there was in the contention of urban politicians that the local government system and the funds at its control were dominated by a Rajput caste party.

My conclusion, after studying the pattern of allocations to V.C.s and villages dominated by chairman and traditional headmen respectively of various castes, was that local government elections had indeed been used to bring power to a predominant number of Rajputs (as I have already indicated), but that, because Rajputs were dominant in only a minority of villages, the Rajput D.C. and B.C. leaders distributed development money in a fairly unbiased way in order to obtain adequate support in future elections. Rajput caste feeling and use of caste ties were expressed in the use of these rural political positions for

[19] Mayer, 'Some Political Implications', pp. 86–106.

brokerage and mediation for Rajput clients with official agencies and other townspeople, rather than in directly favouring them with patronage within the rural sphere.[20]

Leaders also, of course, used their rural positions as steps on the ladder upwards into the district party system, which, in turn, could lead to election to the state legislature. This was shown in the 1962 general elections in Dewas. At that time, each of the two main Rajput leaders had his own sphere of power—one in the committee system as chairman of the D.C., and the other in the co-operative system as secretary of the bank. In order to oust the sitting Congress M.L.A. (a Brahman townsman) one of these Rajputs applied for the Congress ticket, supported by his caste-mate. But when the M.L.A. (the Brahman) refused the ticket, the other Rajput could not resist applying for it, too. After a great deal of persuasion the former Rajput withdrew; but he did nothing to support his caste-mate in the ensuing election (and may even have worked against him), and the seat was won by a townsman of a Bania (trader) caste on the Jan Sangh ticket. By 1965 the two Rajput leaders were opposing each other throughout the rural political system, and the 'Rajput party' had openly split.

The example suggests that alliances based on common caste will break up at the higher levels of the rural political system, just as they do at the village level. As Brass notes, discipline exists in parties and particularistic groups of the kind I have noted, mainly when there is a threat from outside; when this is absent, the alliance will dissolve into warring factions. Whether, in fact, the Dewas Rajputs should have allowed themselves the luxury of such factions after 1962 is doubtful; the next B.C. election may well show that Rajput leadership has lost its position due to such internal divisions.

The Rajput rural leaders in Dewas, then, formed a caste body only in the sense that the core was Rajput; overt benefits were distributed amongst a multi-caste set of supporters, and only the more private advantages of brokerage were perhaps gained mainly by Rajputs. Such a body differs from traditional caste bodies, as well as from parties at the V.C. level. It does not, in fact, represent a caste group. Only some of its members are kin interacting in non-political situations, and it is recruited for political purposes only, unlike traditional caste groups which have duties in many different contexts. I have, in fact, suggested that caste is here becoming a political rather than a ritual division of

[20] For the distinction between patron and broker, see Mayer, 'Some Political Implications of Community Development in India', p. 105, and a forthcoming article entitled 'Patrons and Brokers: Rural Leadership in Four Overseas Indian Communities'.

society,[21] in the sense that these factions are no longer based on the ritual distinctions underlying caste groups. Whether castes remain castes when they are only political or 'secular' groupings is a debated question.[22] Although Rajputs formed the core of a district rural 'party', mainly because they had been leaders in the previous system, they did not have a permanent place there. Castes rising in education and wealth could supplant the incumbents, and Rajputs therefore made alliances with members of other castes, not exclusively on a caste basis, but rather as politicians seeking support on a variety of bases.

Municipal Politics

Differences exist between urban and rural politics. Because urban wards are relatively small, the candidates are more likely to be personally known to the electors, and their abilities may make more impact than they do in the upper levels of rural and legislative politics.[23] Again, party organization is at present more important in municipalities than in villages. The political parties contest every seat, and their adherents usually form the majority of the municipal council. Hence, municipal politics has hitherto been more closely affected by the internal groupings of the political parties than has local politics. Ticket-giving in a municipal election produces the same sort of competition as it does in legislative elections.

The issues behind ticket allocation mainly concern faction membership; and the factional struggles for leadership in a municipality, and hence the basis on which leaders are selected are often largely unconnected with the social and economic issues affecting the public.[24] Factions tend to span a number of castes, and caste membership is one among several criteria of selection of municipal candidates. The need to have new candidates, uncontaminated by the mistakes of their predecessors, is at least as important as caste,[25] as may also be class or profession.

Although candidates may not be chosen for their caste, do they campaign and collect votes on a caste basis? From my own study of an

[21] Mayer, 'Local Government Election in a Malwa Village', p. 202.

[22] e.g. E. R. Leach, 'Introduction: What Should we Mean by Caste?' in Leach (Ed.), *Aspects of Caste in South India, Ceylon and North-West Pakistan*, Cambridge, Cambridge University Press, p. 6; and M. N. Srinivas, *Caste in Modern India, and Other Essays*, London, Asia Publishing House, 1962, pp. 6–7.

[23] e.g. R. Chakravarti, 'The Personality Factor in Local Politics', *Economic Weekly*, Vol. XVII, 1965, pp. 1027–30.

[24] e.g. Brass, *Factional Politics in an Indian State*, p. 209.

[25] Mayer, 'Municipal Elections: A Central Indian Case Study', in C. H. Philips (Ed.) *Politics and Society in India*, London, George Allen and Unwin, 1963, p. 119.

election in Dewas,[26] and from Gupta's study of an election in an Uttar Pradesh town,[27] I see three main contexts in which votes are sought and in which caste could be a factor.

First, where a single caste is concentrated in a separate ward or sub-ward of the town, it is possible to recruit a caste vote by promising major improvements to the physical amenities of the area, such as water supply, electricity, or tarred roads. This is particularly the case where the ward is inhabited by one of the lower castes, is on the out-skirts of the town, and has few amenities. This strategy has only two qualifications. One is that such promises can most plausibly be made by the party which can back its promises with the expectation of aid from the state government—and this has invariably meant the Congress Party; the other is that such promises will have to be supplemented by personal promises of aid to caste leaders where these are in opposed factions, and that the support of each leader must be gained in such a way that the other is not openly involved—a difficult, but not im-possible, task for the experienced politician. Here, the caste group is really acting as an interest group and, since there are no other castes in the area, there is no caste rivalry to be considered.

Second, where the ward has a population containing several castes, a candidate can recruit economic interest groups. Gupta, for instance, gives the example of sweetmeat-makers, scattered over a ward, who were persuaded to vote for one party by the promise to alter 'vexatious' municipal hygiene regulations. Such an economic interest need not coin-cide with caste, but will do so in cases where the traditional occupation is followed exclusively by some or all members of a caste in the ward.

In both of these cases, then, it is possible to recruit a caste vote, as long as one can square factional cleavages within the caste. Indeed, Gupta lays great stress on this type of vote, saying that some 10,000 of the Congress's winning total of 13,000 votes were acquired in this way, and estimating that about half the Congress's total vote was gained through what he calls 'manipulation', rather than on the strength of a candidate's personal qualities and the vote of habitual supporters. It should be noted, however, that this sort of caste vote is not a vote within a system of castes competing for power and status; rather it is a caste vote in terms of benefits which do not affect the position of other castes (though it may alter the position of the general public if, say, charges for dairy products were changed because of new by-laws).

[26] ibid.
[27] R. Gupta, 'How an Urban Community in North India Voted in Recent Elections', *Janata*, Vol. XII, Nos. 13–16.

Only seldom, would it seem, is there the chance of recruiting a caste's block vote on the basis of an actual caste issue. Such an instance would be that in which a Dewas candidate attempted to gather the support of a caste which wished to rise in the hierarchy, by promising to support its claim to higher status.[28]

The third way in which caste votes are collected is through specific linkages which the candidates has with members of the caste, or with a chain of one or more intermediaries who themselves have contacts with the caste, in which support is given in terms of personal obligation and loyalty or with the expectation of personal gain of some kind. If the leader of an extended family, or a faction within the caste, can be persuaded to lend his support on this basis, the rest of his followers may also give their votes, though it may be hard to recruit a really large number of votes by this method.

An example of this kind of recruitment comes from the Dewas municipal election. Analysing the election in one ward, I put forward a diagram of what I called the candidate's 'action-set'.[29] This consisted of the links which the candidate had with his main helpers, some of whom acted as intermediaries and in their turn recruited helpers. Chains of two or more intermediaries could thus be traced, with one, two, three, etc., linkages radiating out from the candidate to the voter. The linkages were based on a number of different factors; sometimes the candidate or his intermediary recruited a helper because of economic obligation, sometimes because of common party membership, sometimes, too, because of common caste. The action-set showed the following categories of linkage:

TABLE II

CATEGORIES OF LINKAGE IN A MUNICIPAL ELECTION (DEWAS)

Content of linkage	*Number of links and distance from candidate*					
	first	second	third	fourth	fifth	total
Caste	2	2	—	—	—	4
Kinship	—	1	4	4	1	10
Political party	5	—	—	—	—	5
Economic and occupational	1	3	3	1	—	8
Other	2	7	2	1	—	12
Total	10	13	9	6	1	39

[28] Mayer, 'The Significance of Quasi-Groups in the Study of Complex Societies', in M. P. Banton (Ed.), *The Social Anthropology of Complex Societies*, London, Tavistock Publications, 1966, p. 109.

[29] Mayer, op. cit., p. 107.

The table distinguishes between caste-based links and kin-based ones. In fact, of course, the latter are also links of common caste; but the distinction stresses the difference I have previously noted between links inside a caste group—actually a subcaste group—of kin, and those of common caste between subcastes of the same caste. It is interesting to note that 'caste' links are more likely to occur nearer the candidate, whereas 'kinship' links are more likely when voters themselves or secondary intermediaries are involved. As might be expected, the candidate tries to get large caste block votes, whereas his intermediary supporters recruit voters on a much more limited basis of personal kin ties.

On the whole, caste was only one factor in this Dewas election; even if 'kinship' is categorized as a caste link, caste accounts for only fourteen of the thirty-nine links in Table II. The candidates were selected for a number of reasons besides their caste; and in their dealings with the electorate they were not always successful in combating divisions within castes. They undoubtedly tried to get block votes from castes in their wards—but they also wooed occupational interest groups, the people of a street within the ward, and so forth.

I do not have data about the distribution of funds by the Dewas municipal council similar to those which I have produced for the Dewas rural system. Hence I cannot discuss whether areas inhabited by certain castes are more favoured by the municipal administration or not. My observations indicate that there is competition between councillors for municipal funds to be spent in their wards—mainly when elections are imminent!—but I cannot correlate this with any particular social feature. Nor did the meetings of the municipal council proceed on caste lines. The groupings of councillors within each party represented on the council were linked to their party's internal factional position, which in turn was affected by each of the three political spheres in the district. It was because of this interconnexion that rural leaders took a close interest in municipal politics and, to a much lesser extent, the councillors took part in rural politics; for the events of each sphere affected the structure of the party's factions and hence the ambitions of party leaders in the legislative sphere.

Constituency Politics

Political alignments in villages are based on parochial loyalties—loyalties to kin, to the local caste group, and to the village. I have pointed out that leaders at the higher levels of the rural political system find it hard to control these alignments in order to build themselves bases of support; and the same is even truer for politicians concerned with the entire district or the state or national constituency. Parochial loyalties are usually too small-scale and too socially diverse to be built either into a party machine by the district party organization or into an electoral machine by a M.L.A. or M.P. candidate, although such a candidate should be a local man who is seen to have strong parochial loyalties himself.[30]

The importance of caste in constituency politics varies, but rarely does it seem to be paramount. For one thing, there is seldom any single-caste population which is so large that it can be mobilized to form a majority party and, even where this exists, it may well be internally fragmented. Take, for instance, the case of an Uttar Pradesh district with a Jat majority; here, no fewer than seven Jat candidates competed for a M.L.A. seat in 1962—and a candidate who relied on non-Jat votes was consequently elected.[31] Again, constituencies without a single numerically dominant caste may yet have one caste holding power in most villages, as I have indicated. Here, the fact that all candidates are often selected from that caste has been said to show the importance of caste as an electoral factor. An example is the Andhra district in which the Reddi caste provided the major candidates in seven out of ten contests in 1962.[32] But one could also argue that the fact that candidates are of the same caste makes caste an 'equal' factor in these situations. Caste considerations may influence the selection of candidates; but in the actual recruitment of followers intracaste divisions and alliances between castes are exploited and there is no solid dominant caste vote. Finally, in districts where there is more than one powerful caste, most of the contests may be between the two or three powerful castes there. Gray, for example, shows that in a district having Velmas and Reddis as its main castes five out of the eleven main M.L.A. contests were between candidates of these two castes.[33] But he also shows that the vote of at least one of these castes was split in four of these contests; and, indeed, the Velma caste had already split within the Congress before the election, and formed the cores of the two main Congress factions. In none of the elections I have just cited were there solidary caste alignments. The caste factor is an important one, and its

[30] e.g., F. G. Bailey, 'Politics and Caste in Contemporary Orissa', in C. H. Philips (Ed.), *Politics and Society in India*, London, George Allen and Unwin, 1959, p. 102.

[31] Brass, op. cit., p. 160.

[32] H. Gray, 'The 1962 Indian General Election in a Communist Stronghold of Andhra Pradesh', *Journal of Commonwealth Studies*, Vol. I, 1963, pp. 296–311.

[33] Gray, 'The 1962 General Election in a Rural District of Andhra', *Asian Survey*, Vol. II, No. 7, 1962, pp. 25–35.

manipulation is often vital; yet this very manipulation means that we are dealing at least as much with factions *within* castes and alliances *between* caste leaders, which are made for political and economic as well as for caste reasons, as with *purely* caste factors. Just as at the village level, so it is difficult to disentangle the various strands in the relationships between district and constituency leaders; and one can only say that their caste status is an important but not usually the only ingredient therein.

At least as important as the caste, then, is a different unit of loyalty and recruitment. Such a unit may be based on ideology, party programme, and party membership; but at present it tends to be based on the individual's political interest and factional membership. As Bailey has observed, the recruitment of supporters is here a craftsman's job and not the simple application of a mass-produced blueprint.[34] By this, he means that the followings of the candidate or the district party leader are composed of people recruited on diverse transactional linkages, and that they vary over time according to people's perception of their own interests. They are not necessarily linked to events outside the level at which they are operating; for instance, the following built up by a district Congress leader in Dewas is not necessarily influenced by alignments in the state Congress organization or the Ministry, or by the rivalries which frequently occur between these two wings of Congress at the state level. Rather, it follows the requirements of the moment, which are evinced by the people directly involved in Dewas district Congress politics.[35] This applies to the process of giving tickets for M.L.A. elections just as much as to the running of the party during and between elections.

Clearly, caste is a factor in the recruitment and maintenance of such followings; but it is only one among several factors. The type of action-set which exists in the sphere of municipal politics can also be seen in the constituencies, for candidates construct the same sort of action-sets during their election campaigns. Over time, the people in a succession of such action-sets will show some consistency of membership and a faction can thereby be identified. Factional alliances can cut across caste divisions in the district. They may also be independent of the major lines of cleavage at the state level, whether the latter contain a

[34] Bailey, *Politics and Social Change*, Berkeley, California University Press, 1963, pp. 141–2.

[35] I mention the Congress Party mainly because other parties in Dewas at present have little organization.

caste component or not. In fact, the two levels are consciously kept apart where necessary. I witnessed an example of this in 1965, when the election of the President of the Madhya Pradesh State Congress Committee took place in Bhopal. Dewas district had five representatives in the State Congress Committee. These came from different factions, and comprised Rajputs and members of other castes; but they voted overwhelmingly for one of the candidates (a non-Rajput) rather than the other (a Rajput), being aware that district rivalries were here irrelevant. Only one man, although pledged to the former candidate, voted differently on a purely personal basis. This, be it noted, was partly due to his evaluation of the two candidates' capabilities, and partly because of his feeling of caste solidarity with the Rajput candidate. Hence, caste may cut across district- or state-level groupings, providing an example of the fact that one cannot necessarily relate caste membership with political alignment, either positively or, as in this case, negatively.

Attempts to transform castes at the district and state level into groupings with the same sort of membership obligations and controls as exist at the local level have occurred, through the organizing of caste associations and federations. The importance of these bodies for communication and political organization has been well argued by Rudolph and Rudolph.[36] More recently, Kothari and Maru have studied a caste federation, seeing such a body as a 'conscious creation of the urban-educated political elite seeking institutional bases and numerical strength for their support.'[37] In so far as these associations and federations succeed in organizing the caste population of a region, they are clearly important political bodies, which may well provide a unifying and centralizing factor in a population composed of large numbers of small local groupings. But, in fact, they do not as yet seem to have been very successful. Neither do they take an important place in Brass's[38] and Bailey's[39] analyses, nor in Gray's accounts of Andhra elections.[40] For Kerala, Spellman remarks that there 'is no such thing as solid communal voting for any political party'[41] in spite of the existence of caste associations among, for instance, Nairs and Ezhavas; and

[36] L. I. and S. H. Rudolph, 'The Political Role of India's Caste Associations', *Pacific Affairs*, Vol. XXXV, 1960, pp. 5–22.

[37] R. Kothari and R. Maru, 'Caste and Secularism in India', *Journal of Asian Studies*, Vol. XXV, 1965, p. 48.

[38] Brass, op. cit., p. 242.

[39] Bailey, *Politics and Social Change*, pp. 133–4.

[40] Gray, 'The 1962 General Election in a Rural District of Andhra' and 'The 1962 Indian General Election in a Communist Stronghold of Andhra Pradesh'.

[41] J. W. Spellman, 'A Survey of the 1963 By-Election in Trivandrum II (Kerala)', *Political Science Review*, Jaipur, Vol. III, 1964, p. 85.

Gough suggests that the main political cleavage is between people of propertied and propertyless classes, who belong to different political parties and at the same time higher and lower castes respectively; she goes on to note that, at least when people join the Communist party, 'men have greater *political* allegiance to it than to their caste or to *any organized communal association*'.[42]

In any case, caste associations and federations are faced with the same possibility of fission as are other caste groups, as Kothari and Maru note. In Dewas, for example, the Kshatriya Mahasabha was in 1960 challenged by the formation of a branch of the Rajput Parishad. The allegiance of local 'Kshatriyas', especially Rajputs, was thereby split—although most joined the latter body. A visit to Dewas in 1965 showed that the Parishad had not, in fact, been at all active, and it appears to have been an example of an association started because of the actions of politicians at the stage level, who wished to gain local support in precisely the way characterized by Kothari and Maru. In general, then, though caste associations and federations may be vitally important in bridging local diversity in the future, they do not appear to have been so yet. Even if and when they do become more important, moreover, it is likely that they will become part of multi-caste political parties rather than emerging as separate caste parties, as Morris-Jones suggests.[43]

Social organization, in Dewas district at least, is too diverse for there to be a predictable and 'orderly' coincidence of political and social divisions. Moreover, parties are usually weakly organized, and ideological differences, if any, are minor ones. Local organization therefore tends to be based on factions. The successful politician realizes that such a pattern means that followers should be recruited on a variety of bases; and he takes advantage of this diversification. Where the faction linkages are not diverse, caste parties (among others) may form, it is true, but these will tend to lose to more diverse formations. For instance, Roy[44] gives the example from Uttar Pradesh of a district Congress organization which relied too much on Brahman leadership (thirteen out of nineteen district committee members, and twelve out of thirty-three district board (D.C.) members were Brahmans); it did not take into account the rising leaders of other castes, and was defeated by a coalition of these.

[42] E. K. Gough, 'Village Politics in India—II', *Economic Weekly*, Vol. XVII, 1965, p. 415 (second italics mine).

[43] W. H. Morris-Jones, *The Government and Politics of India*, London, Hutchinson, 1964, p. 187.

[44] R. Roy, 'Congress Defeat in Farrukhabad', *Economic Weekly*, Vol. XVII, 1965, p. 897.

In speaking of factions, one must make clear which level of caste and which level of the political system one is referring to. The Rajput 'caste party' in Dewas, for instance, was a party mainly in terms of its brokerage potential and when seen from above, rather than when seen from below in terms of the rural base from which it had to draw support and to which it had to distribute patronage. Again, there may be a caste faction in control of a district party organization, which runs candidates for the legislatures but which is a caste party only when looked at from above, because it must be based on a diverse support of many castes if it is to maintain its position. A discussion of state level politics is outside this article, but one can suggest that what are seen as caste parties there when looked at from above, e.g. the Reddi and Kamma or the Vokkaliga and Lingayat parties discussed by Harrison,[45] may be based on diverse caste support from the lower levels.

This is, perhaps, to talk about a rather more 'rational' political situation than may often exist. I have found, for instance, that in Dewas there are more or less 'patternless politics' in terms of recruitment. The major constants are the existence of opposed factions, and certain basic personal antagonisms.[46] In Dewas, the men who provide these stable enmities happen at present to be of the same caste (though not of the same subcaste); but this need not always be so. Local politics can therefore best be understood in terms of coalitions, in which caste forms an important, but only one, factor, and in which the main variables are the number of people on each side, and the advantages to be gained by joining one of these coalitions. Advantages may be material, political, or those of personal prestige. At the same time, one must not ignore the fact that in some cases no specific advantages are gained. Here, support may stem from caste sentiment and a general feeling that a caste-mate is a better sort of man, because he has the same style of life and the same set of values. The case I have given of the dissentient Dewas voter in the State Congress election is an example of this; and it is this generalized kind of support to which many of the writers who stress the relation of caste to politics refer.

Conclusion

There is at present a fair degree of autonomy between the three levels of political activity I have distinguished. In village politics activities relate to the elections to and administration of the V.C. The second level

[45] S. S. Harrison, *India: The Most Dangerous Decades*, Princeton, N.J., Princeton University Press, 1960, Ch. 4.

[46] Cf. Brass, op. cit., pp. 55, 89, 168.

includes the politics of the higher stages of the rural system (block and district committees); the politics of larger municipalities (because most of the major protagonists here are district leaders); and those of the legislative elections. The third is that of state-level politics. I have already indicated that rural leaders do not exert—and cannot exert— very close control over many village political situations; and I have suggested that the alignments at state level can be quite different from those at the district level, and that opponents in the district may support the same state leader. The reason for this relative autonomy is that there is no strong party system reaching from the state to the village. Discipline in the party is often weak or even almost non-existent, and the basic units are not the party branches, but rather the changing factions within the party, based on prominent leaders.

Leaders use a number of bases to recruit support. One of these is caste. But I must again stress that caste means different things at different levels. At the village level a leader draws support from the actually operating caste group; and the basis on which he draws support may be one which is central to the system of caste defined as a hierarchy of interdependent local units. That is, it may come to him from a group which wishes for advancement within the local caste hierarchy in payment for its support, or from a group which hopes for his support in maintaining a status threatened by others. Such issues are much rarer in the district sphere: here, caste support is usually over matters which some would view as external to the caste system— licences, jobs, and so forth. Here, too, castes often act as interest groups based on the named caste population rather than on the locally interacting caste group. This is even more clearly the case at state level. In short, one must specify the level about which one is talking, and the kind of caste unit to which one refers, before one can speak of caste's role in politics.[47]

There is also an operational aspect of the question. Here, the problem is: under what conditions is it possible to gain the vote of an entire caste, and under what conditions will this bring political gain? The caste composition of the electorate in question, the likelihood that one may gain one caste's vote without losing that of another, the ways in which one may prevent splits within the caste—these are the questions which arise here. I hope that I have shown that no clear answer can be given to them: the answer varies at different levels of caste organization and of political action, and in different regions of India, according

---

[47] For a short discussion of the implication of distinguishing levels of caste, see A. Béteille, 'A Note on the Referents of Caste', *Archiv. Europ. Sociol.*, Vol. V, 1964, pp. 130–4.

to the nature of traditional caste relations, the history of political parties and so forth.

As to the question which is related to the theme of this book—whether caste is a divisive or an integrative force in India politics—I would say only this: politics is an activity which, by definition, presupposes divisions. For it concerns competition for power and disagreements over policies. Any idea that 'casteism' *creates* divisions is therefore mistaken. If divisions were not along caste lines, they would be along some other lines, as is often the case. As Menon puts it: 'Caste consideration is more often the occasion rather than the cause of a particular action.'[48] The question is therefore rather: Is it preferable to have divisions on a caste basis or on some other basis? This is a judgement which it is outside the scope of this chapter to make. But it must be stressed that, at least at some levels of politics, caste divisions are not of a traditional kind; that is, they are not hierarchical divisions based on ritual purity. Rather, they are divisions between political and economic interest groups of different status. Whether it is better to have such interest groups based in the final analysis on kinship or on some other social factor is a question which it is for others to answer. Dalton in his paper in this book (pp. 159–81) shows that some people have held that it is possible to have no divisions at all, under an ideally interdependent caste (*varna*) system. But he also suggests that India is going further away from this ideal into the realm of factionalism and the politicization of caste; and, if this is the case, such people should perhaps take comfort from Srinivas's view that 'there is no need . . . to be unduly frightened by the existence of "divisions" in the country. It is true that a person does feel that he is a member of a particular caste, village, region, state and religion but these loyalties can represent a hierarchy of values and are not necessarily inconsistent with being a citizen of the Indian Republic.'[49]

[48] V. K. N. Menon, 'Caste, Politics, and Leadership in India', *Political Science Review*, Jaipur, Vol. III, 1964, p. 103.

[49] M. N. Srinivas, *Caste in Modern India* . . ., p. 110.

BIBLIOGRAPHY

BAILEY, F. G., 'Politics and Caste in Contemporary Orissa', in C. H. Philips (Ed.), *Politics and Society in India*, London, George Allen and Unwin, 1959.

Idem, Politics and Social Change, Berkeley, University of California Press, 1963.

BETEILLE, A., 'A Note on the Referents of Caste', *Archiv. Europ. Sociol.*, Vol. V, 1964, pp. 130–4.

BRASS, P., *Factional Politics in an Indian State*, Berkeley, University of California Press, 1965.

CHAKRAVARTI, R., 'The Personality Factor in Local Politics', *Economic Weekly*, Vol. XVII, 1965, pp. 1027–30.

C.V.H., 'Panchayat Elections in Andhra', *Economic Weekly*, Vol. XIII, 1964, pp. 979–80.

DUVERGER, M., *Political Parties*, London, Methuen (3rd ed.), 1959.

GOUGH, E. K., 'Village Politics in India: II', *Economic Weekly*, Vol. XVII, 1965, pp. 413–20.

GRAY, H., 'The 1962 General Election in a Rural District of Andhra', *Asian Survey*, Vol. II, No. 7, 1962, pp. 25–35.

idem, 'The 1962 Indian General Election in a Communist Stronghold of Andhra Pradesh', *Journal of Commonwealth Studies*, Vol. I, 1963, pp. 296–311.

GUPTA, R., 'How an Urban Community in North India voted in Recent Elections', *Janata*, Vol. XII, 1957, pp. 13–16.

HARRISON, S. S., *India: The Most Dangerous Decades*, Princeton, N.J., Princeton University Press, 1960.

KOTHARI, R., '*Panchayati raj:* A Re-Assessment', *Economic Weekly*, Vol. XIII, 1961, pp. 754–60.

Idem, and MARU, R., 'Caste and Secularism in India', *Journal of Asian Studies*, Vol. XXV, 1965, pp. 33–50.

LEACH, E. R., 'Introduction: What Should we Mean by Caste?' in E. R. Leach (Ed.), *Aspects of Caste in South India, Ceylon, and North-West Pakistan*, Cambridge, Cambridge University Press, 1960.

MAJUMDAR, D. N., *Caste and Communication in an Indian Village*, London, Asia Publishing House, 1958.

MAYER, A. C., 'Local Government Election in a Malwa Village', *Eastern Anthropology*, Vol. XI, 1958, pp. 189–202.

Idem, 'The Dominant Caste in a Region of Central India', *South-West Journal of Anthropology*, Vol. XIV, 1958, pp. 407–27.

Idem, Caste and Kinship in Central India, London, Kegan Paul, 1960.

Idem, 'Some Political Implications of Community Development in India', *Archiv. Europ. Sociol.*, Vol. IV, 1963, pp. 86–106.

Idem, 'Municipal Elections: a Central Indian Cast Study', in C. H. Philips (Ed.), *Politics and Society in India*, London, George Allen and Unwin, 1963.

Idem, 'The Significance of Quasi-Groups in the Study of Complex Societies', in M. P. Banton (Ed.), *The Social Anthropology of Complex Societies*, London, Tavistock Publications, 1966.

MENON, V. K. N., 'Caste, Politics, and Leadership in India', *Political Science Review*, Jaipur, Vol. III, 1964, pp. 101–6.

MORRIS-JONES, W. H., *The Government and Politics of India*, London, Hutchinson, 1964.

NICHOLAS, R. W., and MUKHOPADHYAY, T., 'Politics and Law in Two West Bengal Villages', *Bull. Anth. Surv. India*, Vol. XI, 1962, pp. 15–40.

OPLER, M. E., 'Factors of Tradition and Change in a Local Election in Rural India', in R. L. Park and I. Tinker (Eds.), *Leadership and Political Institutions in India*, Princeton, N.J., Princeton University Press, 1959.

POTTER, D. C., *Government in Rural India*, London, Bell, 1964.

ROY, R., 'Congress Defeat in Farrukhabad', *Economic Weekly*, Vol. XVII, 1965, pp. 893–902.

RUDOLPH, L. I., and RUDOLPH, S. H., 'The Political Role of India's Caste Associations', *Pacific Affairs*, Vol. XXXV, 1960, pp. 5–22.

SPELLMAN, J. W., 'A Survey of the 1963 By-Election in Trivandrum II (Kerala)', *Political Science Review*, Jaipur, Vol. III, 1964, pp. 63–100.

SRINIVAS, M. N., *Caste in Modern India, and Other Essays*, London, Asia Publishing House, 1962.

WEINER, M., 'Village and Party Factionalism in Andhra', *Economic Weekly*, Vol. XIV, 1962, pp. 1509–18.

VII

Rural Cities in India: Continuities and Discontinuities

BY OWEN M. LYNCH

Assistant Professor of Anthropology, State University of New York at Binghamton, N.Y.

I: INTRODUCTION

In a challenging and stimulating article entitled 'Sociologies: Urban and Rural', David Pocock has hypothesized that it is false to presuppose dichotomy between rural and urban sociology in India. His reasoning is that they are essentially the same. Pocock writes:

Where it is recognized that city and village are elements of the same civilization, how does the question of their continuity arise? Is it not because the sociologist has assumed (almost unconsciously) a division which his later observations would lead him to mend? If we have posited the village from the outset we have automatically opposed it in our minds to the city. When we come to knit up what we have broken we can only do it by way of a description of the relationships between the two entities . . .
It would appear impossible to recognize the 'orthogenetic' character of India's cities and villages and at the same time to think of comparing them separately with their 'equivalents' elsewhere. The sociology of India's urban and rural population may not be divided between urban and rural sociologies.[1]

Taking up the challenge of Pocock's concluding sentence, I shall in sections II and III of this paper draw a picture of those continuities of North Indian rural-urban social organization that existed in the past and to some extent continue to exist in the present. In so doing I disregard the fact that cracks have appeared to mar the unity of what was once an urban landscape composed of rural institutions. Thus I adopt

[1] D. F. Pocock, 'Sociologies: Urban and Rural', *Contributions to Indian Sociology*, Vol. IV, 1960, p. 81. (The author wishes to state here that, throughout this chapter transliterations of Hindi words have been made to conform to the *popular* English-speaking usage. [Ed.])

the fiction of painting this picture almost entirely in the present tense. Thereafter, in section IV, I will show how, why and at what points these cracks (or discontinuities of rural-urban social organization) began to appear and how the colour of new social forms has been brushed in to replace the fading of old social institutions. Thus what emerges is a picture of that *mélange* of old rural-like institutions along side of new Western-like institutions which exists in many North Indian cities today.

While I cannot provide a total answer to Pocock's problem, I will examine it in the context of a single city, Agra City in the state of Uttar Pradesh. I will further limit much of the discussion to a single caste of Chamars called Jatav. Comparative data from cities and villages in North India will be cited to the extent that they illustrate the problem.

II : THOKS

Agra City is divided into well over 200 *mohallas* or *bastis* ('neighbourhood', 'ward'). One of the first continuities with village organization that one notices is the tendency towards residential segregation by caste and caste groups within these *mohallas* or *bastis*. There is a

. . . clustering of people on a caste basis. In the absence of any such statistics proper results may not be available; but a keen and observant eye can notice the concentration of Kayasthas in Mathurpura and Pipalmandi, Banias in Belanganj, Johribazar, Rajamandi, and Lohamandi, and Brahmins outnumber any caste in Moti Katra, Gokulpura, and Balka basti.[2]

The *mohallas* of the Jatavs tend to be either dominated or completely occupied by them. They live today residentially segregated *en bloc* into caste units much like the *pattis* and untouchable hamlets of the villages.

Some *mohallas* are subdivided into units called *thoks*. *Thoks* have an organization of their own, except when a *thok* and a *mohalla* are identical, in which case the organization of the *thok* is the same as that of the *mohalla*. Let us now turn to one of the Jatav *mohallas* in which there are *thoks*. This *mohalla* I shall call Bhim Nagar.

When one looks at the internal organization of a *mohalla* such as Bhim Nagar, one finds a second continuity with village organization in India. That is to say, the *mohalla* is composed of units called *thoks*, which function very much like similar units in a village, where they

[2] A. R. Tiwari, 'Urban Regions of Agra', *Agra University Journal of Research*, Vol. VI, No. 1, 1958, p. 106.

are called *bakals*[3] or *panas* with sub-units known as *thollas*[4] or *thoks*.[5] The earliest remembered evidence about the social organization of Bhim Nagar goes back to about 1920. At that time Bhim Nagar was composed of 100 households or *ghars*. A *ghar* is not necessarily a house; rather, it is the household which lives in or is associated with a house (*dehari*, lit. door lintel), such that if one member moves out he remains a member until he sets up a separate *ghar*. These original houses composed a *thok* (which literally means a group, an amount or a bundle of the same kind of merchandise). Structurally, then, a *thok* is a social unit composed of several *ghars* and under the leadership of one man (the *chaudhury*), whose position is inherited in one of the *ghars*. Functionally, a *thok* is a unit of social control, commensality, co-operation, and affective relationship.

The original 100-house *thok* has since 1920 split into eight *thoks* by a process of fission, and these eight have been joined by two other *thoks* which have settled on previously unsettled land, one of them occupying the place of an old butchery. Thus, there is now a total of ten *thoks* in Bhim Nagar.

Recruitment to a *thok* is either by ascription through birth in a member *ghar* or by achievement through acceptance by *thok* members. If an outsider comes and settles in a *mohalla*, he may enter a *thok* on payment of a small fee and with the approval of a *chaudhury* and a few leading men. If accepted, the man is enrolled in a *thok* book, if there be one, and he in his turn agrees to abide by the laws of the *thok* and its *panchayat* (court). After this, a man may give and receive *nyota* (invitations in the form of money; see also below, p. 145) and ask the *panchayat* (caste court) to settle cases for him. If two brothers of a *ghar*, or a son and father of a *ghar*, want to separate, then the younger brother or the son begins to receive and take *nyota* separately as a separate *ghar*. Furthermore, while a man may eat at a feast of another *thok* upon its invitation, and while he may give and receive *nyota* from a member of another *thok*, he has the obligation to abide by the rules of his own *thok*, and within it alone is he obliged to give and take *nyota*.

A *thok* is not strictly a territorial unit, because some of its members may live in the locations of other *thoks*. However, most members live in the location of their own *thok*. Nor is a *thok* strictly a unit of real

---

[3] A. Mayer, *Caste and Kinship in Central India*, London, Routledge and Kegan Paul, 1960, p. 133.

[4] O. Lewis, *Village Life in Northern India*, Urbana, University of Illinois Press, 1958, pp. 23–24.

[5] B. H. Baden-Powell, *The Indian Village Community*, London, Longmans, Green and Co., 1896, pp. 31 and 283.

relatives, though it tends to be so, since it includes the descendants of the first settlers, who were not all related, and many who have come and settled there because of some relatives within the *thok*.

The *thok* as a unit of social control has its own *panchayat*, under one or more *chaudhuries*. As in the village, the *panchayat* is formed of the *panches* (leading male members) of the *thok*. Formerly the *panchayat* would decide on all types of questions, chief among which were:

(1) cases of marriage and illegitimate sex relations;
(2) quarrels between members of the *thok*;
(3) making of new rules of behaviour for members of the *thok*.

The leader of a *thok* is its *chaudhury*, whose position generally passes from father to eldest son. However, if the incumbent is too young or does not want the position, or if a new *thok* is formed, or if the incumbent is deposed by the people of the *thok*, the *chaudhury* can be elected by unanimous consent.

The duties of the *chaudhury* are to keep order and peace within the *thok* and to reprimand offenders. Other duties of the *chaudhury* are to officiate at weddings and other ceremonies, to represent the *thok* at a feast of a poor person who cannot invite all, and to represent the *thok* and its members in cases external to itself, such as in the courts or with the police.

In addition to the *chaudhury* there is also his assistant, the *chari bardar* (mace-bearer), whose recruitment is also ascribed by birth. It is his function to summon all the men of the *thok* to a *panchayat*, to restore order and silence to the meeting when it gets out of hand, and often to announce publicly the decision of the *panchayat*. The *chari bardar* is allowed to show some force towards recalcitrant members of a *panchayat*.

Thoks also function as units of co-operation, self-help, and commensality. These functions are most evident at the time of marriage, though they may occur at other times. This is seen when there is giving or receiving of *nyota* (invitations). At such a time each *ghar* in the *thok* gives an amount of money to the *ghar* which is collecting it. Strict accounts are kept in a notebook by both the collector and the giver. This is done in the presence of the *chaudhury*, who is a public witness for the *thok* in all its transactions. He who has received is expected to return a sum somewhat over that originally received when, in turn, the original giver becomes a receiver. The manifest function of *nyota* is to allow for the accumulation of money at a specific time without going into debt to a moneylender. *Nyota* also functions latently as an integrative mechanism which defines the social boundaries of the *thok*.

Members of a *thok* are obligated to give and receive *nyota* only among themselves; outside the *thok* it is by individual choice. In return for the *nyota* collected, the collector is expected to give a feast called *jyonar* or *mara*.

Thoks also function as units of affective relationships. Each *thok* has a *panchayat* meeting-place which is usually an open space of some sort; the men congregate to talk, smoke, and sleep in the summer; the children play; and feasts and public entertainments are held. During the rainy season various types of entertainment are held here, such as *ras*, which is like a comic opera; *alha*, which is the singing of epic verse about culture heroes such as Alha and Dr. Ambedkar;[6] and *satsang*, which is the singing of devotional hymns. Members of other *thoks* may come and watch, but must do so as individuals, not as members of the *thok*. Women of the *thok* are expected to confine themselves to the area of the *thok* and to immediately contiguous neighbours. They will go out of the *thok* usually on four legitimate occasions: first, to get the daily water; second, to go to the hospital or to a doctor; third, to visit relatives; and fourth, to go to the latrine. Men are expected to do the marketing. The *thok* is, therefore, an effective unit bounding the spatial mobility and, to some extent, the face-to-face social interactions of women.

III: *MOHALLA*

In some *mohallas* in the city there is only one *thok*, and therefore the social organization of the *thok* and the *mohalla* is identical. However, in other *mohallas*, such as in Bhim Nagar, the *thoks* are only component parts of the total *mohalla*. What, then, is the *mohalla* as a unit of social organization?

As we have already noted, the *mohalla* or *basti* is a residential ward in the city. Outside the *mohalla*, people are identified as 'so-and-so of Bhim Nagar' or as 'such-and-such of *x mohalla*'. There is a definite identification of persons with their *mohalla*, just as villagers are identified with their village and its reputation.

The *mohalla* as a residential unit plays an important function in kinship and marriage. All the people of the *mohalla* are related, either

---

[6] Alha was a warrior of the twelfth century. He with his brother Udal fought for the King of Mahoba against the King of Delhi. The Jatavs of Agra believe them to have been untouchables. Dr. Ambedkar was a man of Mahar caste from the state of Maharashtra. He was an untouchable who, after gaining a Ph.D. from Columbia University in the U.S.A. and a law degree from England, rose to become the first Law Minister of Independent India and an important leader of the untouchables.

as real or as fictive kin. All such relatives are called the *bhaibandh*. Any widow, *divorcée*, or unmarried girl is called a daughter of the *mohalla* and is therefore under the protection of the men of the *mohalla*. Kinship terms are generally applied to all in the *mohalla*. For this reason, then, the *mohalla* functions as an exogamous unit just as does the North Indian village. The limits of the exogamous interdict apply to the immediately adjacent *mohallas* also. However, it is possible for two members of a *mohalla* to be wed. This occurred in one case where the children were born in two other *mohallas* but subsequently moved to Bhim Nagar with their parents. This kind of marriage is considered valid but it is not looked upon with favour. Thus, in the city the *mohalla* acts as a unit of exogamy just as the village does in some places of North India,[7] and we find another continuity between village and city forms of social organization.

As already mentioned, an individual becomes a member of the *mohalla* either by birth or by application for membership in a *thok*. The defining criterion of membership is whether or not one has the right to ask for *nyota*. Those who live in the *mohalla* but are not members of any *thok* are called *kirayedars* (renters), though a *thok* member may also be one who lives in a rented room or house. *Kirayedars*, who are better considered as outsiders, are always spoken of with some disparagement as outsiders and are somewhat looked down upon by the *gharwalas* (householders) or *thokwalas* (members of a *thok*). Just as many Indians retain an ancestral affiliation to a village, so too does the Jatav retain an affiliation to his ancestral *ghar* and its *mohalla*. As Cohn[8] has pointed out, in the village the Chamar's tie was to his *jajman* (patron), not to land. Being for the most part landless in the village, the Jatavs easily became an urban proletariat, because there were no roots to anchor them to the rural soil. In the city, however, roots were struck, because many have been able to buy their own land and/or houses and they have become an urban yeomanry.

In Bhim Nagar there is a barber shop, a tailor shop, a sweets shop, a small provisions shop, and a tea shop. While these shops are not as heavily patronized as they were in the past, they give evidence of a self-sufficiency and isolation that did exist. In the Chamar enclave of Regharpura in New Delhi a similar self-sufficient situation existed, but:

---

[7] Lewis, *Village Life*: p. 10; McKim Marriott, 'Social Structure and Change in a U.P. Village', in M. N. Srinivas (Ed.), *India's Villages*, London, Asia Publishing House, 1965, p. 111.

[8] B. S. Cohn, 'Chamar Family in a North Indian Village: a Structural Contingent', *Economic Weekly*, Vol. XIII, Nos. 27, 28, 29, 1961, pp. 1051–5.

Today the ironsmith need not supply his necessary accessories for the work. The Chamar can purchase it from the market located a few yards away. Similarly the barber's position in the village is of lesser importance now. Several modernized saloons are found outside, and generally the younger folk who were his important customers till recently visit them.[9]

In addition to the *panchayat* (court) which each *thok* had and has, there was also a *panchayat* for the whole *mohalla*. This *panchayat* attempted to solve inter-*thok* disputes, cases serious enough for a larger body to consider, and matters of importance to the whole *mohalla*. Furthermore, in pre-Independence days, the *mohalla* as a unit was linked to other *mohallas* in and around the city through the *panchayat* system. Each *mohalla* was in an intermediate level of *panchayats* called the *trepan*, *barah*, and *atharah mandi panchayats* (53-, 12-, and 18-*mohalla panchayats*). These were again all united into the highest-level *panchayat*, which covered the whole city, called the *caurasi mandi panchayat* (84-*mohalla panchayat*). These two levels were like a Court of Appeals and a Supreme Court. As was the seriousness of the case, so was the level of the *panchayat* which would be called. Normally only a wealthy man was in a position to try to summon such a *panchayat* on his own, because of the financial burden of entertaining the *panches* at such higher-level meetings. For each of these higher-level *panchayats* there was also a *chaudhury* and a *chari bardar* whose positions were hereditary. In North Indian villages upper-level *panchayats* are variously known as *bhaiband*, and *sabha*,[10] *dabas* villages,[11] *pankhera*,[12] etc. In the villages, too, there are at each level hereditary *chaudhuries* and also *panches*.

In these higher-level *panchayats* the status of a *panch* (member of a *panchayat*) was an achieved one in so far as one had to distinguish himself in oratory, wisdom, and astuteness in getting to real issues and finding workable solutions to the cases. It was these higher-level *panchayats* that took decisions on behaviour for that part of the caste under its jurisdiction as well as on matters that needed decision of the caste as a whole. They were, then, the leadership group of the caste. In addition to their leadership and problem-solving functions, these *panchayats* also functioned as outlets for personal ambition and as

[9] A. Bopegamage, *Delhi: A Study in Urban Sociology* (University of Bombay Publications, Sociology Series No. 7), Bombay, University of Bombay, 1957, p. 106.

[10] L. Levine, 'Speech Variation and Social Structure in a Group of North Indian Villages', unpublished Ph.D. dissertation, Columbia University, 1959, pp. 118 and 138–42.

[11] Lewis, *Village Life* . . ., pp. 24–30.

[12] Mayer, *Caste and Kinship* . . ., p. 252.

symbols of the unity of the caste. Finally, these *panchayats* also functioned as integrating mechanisms and as communications centres for
the caste, for it was in them that news was passed on, contacts made, and
friendships renewed.

The existence of *panchayats* in Indian cities was not an isolated
phenomenon. They have been noted in Dacca,[13] Delhi,[14] Kanpur,[15]
Dehra Dun,[16] Lucknow,[17] and even in Bombay.[18] It would be worth
while to quote Niehoff writing on Kanpur here, since he notes that the
existence of *panchayats* seems to be a lower-caste phenomenon in the
city as well as in the village:

Among the castes having permanent *panchayats* as listed by Blunt . . .
all are middle or low castes. The same situation still prevails in Kanpur.
The low castes of this group, without exception, had formally organized
panchayats, as had some of the middle castes. These low and middle caste
panchayats were organized usually on a local as well as a city-wide grouping.
One local neighborhood *panchayat* (Kuril) was made of 150 members. The
same caste group had a *panchayat* which covered the whole city. The Chamar
caste *panchayat* had a neighborhood grouping (*mohalla*), a city grouping, and
a district grouping, the seriousness of the misdemeanor deciding which
subdivision would be called upon.[19]

In addition to the structure and functions of the *mohalla*, *thok*, and
panchayat, as well the residential segregation of castes, there is also
one other continuity between rural and urban social structures. This
is in ascribed and mutually exclusive occupational status. As Chamars,
the Jatavs were traditionally supposed to be leather-workers, though
the majority of them in the villages were *kamins* (agricultural serfs).
In the city the Jatavs were originally labourers, tanners, scavengers,
and contractors for building homes, etc., all jobs which they traditionally did. However, at the turn of the century a tanning factory was
begun. By 1920, a full-scale industry for making shoes of European

[13] A. N. J. Den Hollander, 'Changing Social Control in a Bengal City', in *Transactions of the Third World Congress of Sociology*, London, International Sociological Association, Vol. VI, 1956, pp. 64–71.

[14] Bopegamage, *Delhi* . . ., p. 107.

[15] A. Niehoff, 'Caste, Class and Family in an Industrial Community in Northern India', unpublished Ph.D. dissertation, Columbia University, 1957, p. 82.

[16] G. S. Bhatt, 'Urban Impact and the Changing Status of the Chamars of Dehra Dun', paper presented at Indian Sociological Conference, Saugar [India], 1960 (typewritten).

[17] Census Commission of India, *Census of India—1911 : United Provinces of Agra and Oudh*, Vol. XV, Pt. II, Allahabad, Superintendent, Government Press, 1912, pp. 345–6.

[18] W. L. Rowe, 'Caste, Kinship and Association in Urban India', paper prepared for Symposium No. 26, *Cross-Cultural Similarities in the Urbanization Process*, Burg Warten-stein, 1964, p. 8 (lithographed).

[19] Niehoff, 'Caste, Class and Family . . .', p. 82.

design was present in Agra. As the industry grew, the Jatavs took more and more to the making of shoes, i.e. the occupation which is traditionally part of their status-set in the caste system. Since this was a traditionally polluting work, the Jatavs had a virtual monopoly of the shoemaker status. Shoemaking of the European type has become the primary and virtually the only occupation of the Agra Jatavs.

To sum up, it can be said that the Jatavs, at least until 1900, were tightly organized internally as a caste, but were loosely integrated externally into more inclusive institutions of power, opportunity, and wealth in the society at large, because the Jatav status of untouchable precluded such external integration.

IV: CHANGES IN *MOHALLA* ORGANIZATION

While the Jatavs have taken to an occupation traditionally assigned to them, this status is, nevertheless, integrated into a market economy which is very different from the redistributive economy of the village. Originally as labourers and contractors, and later as craftsmen and factory-owners, the Jatavs have been integrated into a market system of distribution and production. As owners of their own factories, many of them have become owners of the means of production. Others, as labourers, have been paid in cash, not in kind, and payment to them has been either through a piece-work factory system or through a putting-out system run by factors or middlemen. Therefore, neither for factory-owner (*karobar*) nor for labourer (*karigar*) has there been a *jajmani* or redistributive system of economy.

There have been four effects of this structural change. First, the Jatavs have become independent in the sense that they have not been bound to a hereditary *jajman* (patron) in a personal tie. On the contrary, they have been integrated into a more impersonal market system in which the productive components are almost completely in their own hands. Second, for some there was and is increased wealth which has allowed them leisure time to engage in caste uplift movements and to get an education. Third, many have been able to build brick and cement (*pakka*) houses, wear better clothes, and enjoy a better standard of living. This has reduced the low caste status characteristics by which the caste was known and therefore its 'visibility' *vis-à-vis* other castes. And fourth, in addition to residential segregation and isolation there has been occupational isolation. Since the production of shoes, at least until recently, has been completely in their own hands, the amount of their non-political interaction with other castes has been reduced to a minimum. Thus the 'observability' of Jatav behaviour, and control

ver it by other castes, have been minimal when compared to the control
ver them in the village with its *jajmani* system, its dominant caste, and
s village *panchayat*. Under this condition of minimum 'observability'
ew ideas and behaviour patterns have had a fertile ground in which
ey could grow. These new ideas were stimulated at one time by the
rya Samaj[20] and at another time by the Independence movement.

In addition to the market system there has been a structural change
n the Indian social system itself which has had deep effects on the
ocial organization of the urban Jatavs as I have described it. This was
ne introduction of parliamentary democracy and the universal franchise
fter Independence in 1947. The Jatavs at that time assumed the status
f citizens in the Indian Republic, and as such, under conditions of the
niversal franchise, they were related potentially, at least, to a whole
ew national and state structure whose channels of power and oppor-
unity were, in principle, now open to them.

Most Jatavs date the disintegration of the *panchayat* system from
ne introduction of parliamentary democracy and politics, though the
rocess had probably begun earlier. While this change was fundamental,
nere were other factors which seem important to me. These were:

(*a*) increased wealth through the involvement in the market system;
(*b*) increased education;
(*c*) the use of the courts as an alternative system of justice;
(*d*) the politicization of caste.

) Wealth   I have already discussed some of the effects of increased
ealth. One further effect was that it allowed or increased the means to
orrupt. Traditionally the disputants in a case gave a sum to the
anches for convening the *panchayat*. This sum was spent on food and
rink. Increased wealth, however, helped change these traditional sums
nto secret bribes. None of my informants felt that the *panches* were
ncorruptible. Thus, faith in the justice of the *panchayat* system has
ied. Furthermore, a rich man can outride even the severest of punish-
nents, for he can both pay the fine and remain independent of the
eed for *nyota* to finance major expenses.

) Education   Education has weakened the *panchayat* system and the
unctions which gave it the strength to enforce its decisions in the
ollowing ways. First, the educated man, or at least the literate man, is

[20] The *Arya Samaj* is a Hindu reformist sect founded in 1895 by Swami Dayananda
araswati. It preaches a return to the most ancient of Indian scriptures, the Vedas, and is
gainst idolatry, polygamy, non-marriage of widows, and caste status ascribed by birth.

more adapted to the new social environment in which he exists. Ther
has been a partial replacement of one of the criteria for leadership an
authority—namely, respect for the aged man and his experienti
wisdom—by respect for the educated man and his literate advantag
in dealing with the new socio-political order. The educated son is ofte
leader of or adviser to the uneducated father. The educated themselve
have less fear of using the courts, since they have some measure c
control over the written procedures used therein. To this advantag
is added the fact that for the educated it is a matter of prestige to us
the courts rather than the *panchayats*, i.e. the traditional system of th
uneducated. Thus, education gives the educated, or literate, man a
advantage both to engage in 'bridge actions'[21] between the old syster
of the *panchayats* and the new system of the courts, and to confound h
illiterate caste-mates.

Second, considering education in the broadest sense as the commun
cation of new ideas, there is the fact that the urban Jatavs have bee
exposed to new egalitarian and individualistic ideals through the Inde
pendence movement, through the teachings of Ambedkar and Gandh
through integration into the schools for the young and, most important
ly, through integration into party politics for all. Thus, there has bee
an undermining of the old ideas of caste and traditionalism by the ne
ideals of socialism and democracy. Since the Jatavs, under the influenc
of the Buddhist movement,[22] are also anti-Hindu, there is also a
undermining of the religious belief that the *panchayat* speaks wit
sacred authority and thereby has power to enforce its sanctions. Thes
new ideas are institutionalized in the courts and politics, and therefor
it is through them, rather than through the traditional *panchayat*, th
people prefer to relate themselves to others.

(*c*) *The Courts* Another important reason for the decline of th
panchayat system is that the courts now furnish an alternative syster
of justice. Thus, there is the opportunity to engage in 'bridge action
and thereby either to manipulate the *panchayat* or to ignore it alt
gether.

---

[21] F. G. Bailey, *Tribe, Caste and Nation*, Manchester, Manchester University Press, 196
p. 251, defines 'bridge actions' as situations in which '. . . the actor may play upon th
roles which he has in different systems of social relationships (i.e., caste and democra
socialism) so as to win for himself the support of more effective allies.'

[22] The Agra Jatavs followed Dr. Ambedkar into Buddhism in 1956. The relevant aspec
of this movement are treated in O. M. Lynch, 'The Politics of Untouchability: Soc
Structure and Social Change in a City of India', unpublished Ph.D. dissertation, Columb
University, 1966.

While there is definite evidence of the use of the courts in pre-Independence India for certain intercaste conflicts, I was unable to trace any intracaste court cases, though no doubt some of them existed. Yet, for both inter- and intracaste conflicts, it is probable that there was much reluctance to use the courts in pre-Independence India, first, because there were few elected Jatav officials who could intervene for them; second, because, as has been pointed out by Galanter, 'the local officials were almost uniformly unsympathetic to the claims of the lower castes';[23] and, third, because the Jatavs lacked education and knowledge of court proceedings.

While castes still retain under the new Constitution their right to discipline their own groups, their ability to do so has weakened because of the increased possibility of 'bridge actions'. This is first of all due to education, as I have mentioned above. Secondly, there is less fear of the courts, since the total external social environment of the caste has redefined the relationship of the Jatavs to the courts more in terms of the status of a citizen who has a right to use the courts than in terms of the status of an untouchable who has learned to fear the courts. 'One of the basic themes of the Constitution is to eliminate caste as a differential in the relationship of government to the individuals—as subject, voter, or employee.'[24] Since the courts need not judge the real issue at hand, and cases are often trumped up, one party can use the courts as a means to get even or to wear down another party and as a means to score a point. The threat of such action is sometimes enough to keep a poor man from appealing to the *panchayat*. In effect, the court is like a counter-sanction of greater force than that of the *panchayat*, since it can inflict jailing and/or fines. While it is the rich who can most easily resort to the courts and use them as a threat against the poor and their convening a *panchayat*, recourse to the courts is by no means confined to the rich. One who is dissatisfied with the decision of the *mohalla panchayat* may prefer to bring the case to the courts rather than to the upper-level *panchayats*.

The third reason why the opening of the courts has undermined the *panchayat* and its sanctions is that the courts also stand as a reference group from which new standards in the administration of justice are learned. This is evident in the statement of one reliable informant who said of the *panchayats*: 'They have become just like the courts. You pay the *peshgar* [the clerk who controls the order of presentation or

[23] M. Galanter, 'Law and Caste in Modern India', *Asian Survey*, Vol. III, No. 11, 1963, p. 548.
[24] Op. cit., p. 555.

docket of cases in the court] a little and he gets your case fixed on time. You pay your witnesses and you win your case.'

(*d*) *Politicization*   The fourth and final reason for the breakdown of the *panchayat* system has been the politicization of the Jatav caste. Before Independence a new leadership group called the *bare admi* ('big men'), parallel to the caste *chaudhuries*, had developed. They propagandized for the education of Jatav children and also for the Sanskritization of caste behaviour and practices. These new leaders gradually assumed the functions of problem-solvers and policy directors in matters external to the caste, because they were better adapted to the changing socio-political environment. They also acted as advisers to the caste *chaud-huries* in the *panchayats*. As one informant put it, in describing one of the most famous of these leaders: 'He was like a lawyer at the side of the *sarpanch* [head of a local *panchayat*].'

After Independence the importance of these parallel leaders, whose position is achieved, not ascribed, has increased to the point where they are virtually the only leaders of the caste in the city. However, among them can now be distinguished the old *bare admi* (big men) who are the wealthy businessmen of the caste, and the new *neta log*, who are the politicians. Not all *neta log* are *bare admi* and vice versa. The structural fact on which the status of the *neta log* is based is the introduction of parliamentary democracy and the universal franchise in India. The most influential men of the caste now are the M.L.A.s (Members of the Legislative Assembly), the elected city Corporators, and the workers and officers of political parties. These men are influen-tial in dispensing political patronage in the form of grants for co-operatives, grants for improvements in the *mohallas*, recommendations for the special privileges of the Scheduled Castes under the 'protective discrimination' policy of the Government, and also in many informal practices wherein influence is needed to open doors or grant privileges. Since the *neta log* have assumed part of the role-set of the old *chaud-huries*, other members of the caste have gradually transferred to them aspects of the *chaudhuries*' role-set which have to do with problem-solving internal to the caste. An omnicompetency is now imputed to them in all matters, some of which they can aid in and some of which they cannot aid in. However, the *mohalla panchayats* do have their *chaudhuries* and their *panchayats* which continue to operate in a limited way. They still settle cases of marriage and will settle a dispute when both parties promise to abide by the decision. It is the *caurasi mandt* and middle-level *panchayats* that have virtually completely disappeared.

What is happening, then, is that the hereditary caste *chaudhuries* are being supplanted by the *neta log*. The functions of leadership, problem-solving, and adjudication of disputes have been differentiated out of the caste and integrated into the institutions of the city and the nation (i.e. party politics, the legislatures and the courts), as well as the whole structure of patronage and influence involved in the developmental programmes of the modern Government.

That this process may not be confined to Agra is hinted at in a study of Kanpur:

There were some amalgamating tendencies in caste *panchayats*. These developments ran parallel with the caste-like behavior of the semi-political organizations such as the Scheduled Castes Federation. This occurred among the low castes, and again it was the Chamars, the most numerous of the low caste groups in the labor population of Kanpur, who had made the first movements in this direction.[25]

The semi-political movement mentioned by Niehoff has now become a political party, the Republican Party. There is no reason to suspect, therefore, that the course of development that has occurred in Agra has not also occurred in Kanpur.

In addition to the weakening of the *panchayat* system, there have been other factors which have also tended to weaken the internal structure of the *mohalla*. I have already noted how the *thoks* were units of affective relationships. In the past, men used to congregate to smoke the *hookah* (Indian pipe) at the *panchayat* meeting-place. The *hookah* was a symbol as well as a mechanism of social integration within the *thok*. However, as one informant put it, 'Before people began to smoke *bidis* [Indian cigarettes], the *hookah* kept everybody together to talk. Now one lights up a *bidi* and walks away.' While there is some truth in the replacement of the *hookah* by the *bidi*, what has really happened is that there now exist alternative sources of entertainment and affiliation. First of all there are the ubiquitous films. Most of the young men are fond of them and they frequently see them. Secondly, there are the shoe factories outside the *mohalla* or in other *mohallas*, which are not only places of work but also loci of social interaction and social communication. Correlated with the factories are the markets, where men meet to do more than buy and sell shoes. Here they meet to talk, discuss, and gather news. For the young there are the schools, both private and public, which draw the children out of the exclusive *mohalla* environment and enlarge their horizons to some degree. And finally, there is politics. Throughout the year there are various political

[25] Niehoff, op. cit., p. 83.

meetings and rallies either for the political elite or for the whole community. There are also the various *melas* (fairs) in the city, which are always a source of amusement. Most importantly there are the new communications media of the radio, the post, and the newspapers, of which the Jatavs are making increasing use. All of these factors tend to integrate the Jatavs into an urban and national culture in such a way as to weaken the internal unity and structural control of the *mohallas* and *thoks*.

I might, in passing, also mention one more factor. In Bhim Nagar there now stands a Buddhist temple. This shrine, the size of a small room, was built by voluntary subscriptions of wheat, flour, and money by all the people of the *mohalla* in about 1957–8. The importance of this edifice is that it symbolizes not only the unity of the *mohalla* as a group but also the integration of the Jatavs into an all-India Neo-Buddhist Movement of at least nominally converted ex-untouchables. This movement has opened the *mohalla* to influences and ideas which are more than purely local. In its attack on caste and the caste system, the movement has indirectly attacked the whole traditional basis of Indian society and has further weakened the unity of the *mohalla* and the *panchayat* system. The goals of the Jatavs are no longer to preserve the inner order and integration of their caste and their *mohallas* but, rather, their goals are to become more integrated into the urban culture of Agra and the national culture of India. The real problems of social disorder and social control, according to the Buddhists, are those of the caste system itself, not those of internal caste cohesion and control.

V: CONCLUSIONS

(1) The implication of this paper is that it seems to confirm Pocock's hypothesis that it is false to presuppose a dichotomy of rural and urban sociologies in India because they are essentially the same. The qualifications we would add are that this seems true for some castes, in some cities, and at certain historical periods. The more challenging question now is to identify the conditions under which this is so. My own study and the literature I have cited would seem to suggest that it is probably truer for lower than for upper castes and probably exists under a social system where caste and caste-based institutions and not citizenship and the institutions of parliamentary democracy are present and functioning.

(2) While continuities of rural and urban social structure were and are present, we have also demonstrated that discontinuity between the social structure of the villages and Agra City began first and funda-

mentally for the Jatavs in the market system.[26] There was in the city no *jajmani* system based on a redistributive economic system, at least for the Jatavs during the period covered by this study. As shoemakers the Jatavs were and are in control of their means of production. This means that they were not integrated into a hereditary system of reciprocal rights and duties which is fundamental to the caste system. With the opening of educational institutions and the introduction of parliamentary democracy, party politics and the courts, the *panchayat* system and to some extent *thok* and *mohalla* solidarity began to break down. Leadership of the caste is now in the hands of the politicians (*neta log*), whose position, unlike the traditional *chaudhuries*, is achieved not ascribed. The *mohalla* and the *thok* as units of integration and interaction have lost much of their importance, due to education, alternative sources of entertainment, local and national politics, and the Buddhist movement. These functional alternatives are now more open to Jatavs to exploit, because of their occupation of new statuses such as citizen, voter, politician, student, civil servant, Buddhist, etc. And these alternatives are opted for by Jatavs, because they promise a greater share in the scarce resources of wealth, power, education, and prestige. In other words, discontinuities in urban and rural social structure are due to the fact that the functions performed by traditional forms of social organization are being integrated into urban and national institutions such as the schools, the courts, the market system, political parties, and other forms of association such as the Buddhist movement.

(3) My final conclusion is that I must go a step further than did Dr. Srinivas when he noted that, with the Pax Britannica, came a horizontal spread of caste organization.[27] After Independence and the introduction of parliamentary democracy, there has also been a vertical integration of castes into more inclusive institutions at city, state, and national levels of integration.

[26] This is not to say that there are not elements of the *jajmani* system in the cities and that the Jatavs were not involved in such a system at a time prior to the information in this study. Many of the Sweepers of the city still continue to receive payments, both in kind and in money, that are traditionally given. For many, the areas in which homes that they clean lie continue to be hereditary.

[27] Srinivas, *Caste in Modern India, and Other Essays*, Bombay, Asia Publishing House, 1962, p. 16.

BIBLIOGRAPHY

Works in English

BADEN-POWELL, B. H., *The Indian Village Community*, London, Longmans, Green and Co., 1896.

BAILEY, F. G., *Tribe, Caste and Nation*, Manchester, Manchester University Press, 1960.

BHATT, G. S., 'Urban Impact and the Changing Status of the Chamars of Dehra Dun', paper presented at Indian Sociological Conference, Saugar [India], 1960.

BOPEGAMAGE, A., *Delhi: A Study in Urban Sociology* (University of Bombay Publications, Sociology Series No. 7), Bombay, University of Bombay, 1957.

COHN, BERNARD S., 'Chamar Family in a North Indian Village: A Structural Contingent', *Economic Weekly* [of Bombay], Vol. XIII (27, 28, 29), 1961, pp. 1051–5.

DEN HOLLANDER, A. N. J., 'Changing Social Control in a Bengal City', *Transactions of the Third World Congress of Sociology*, London, International Sociological Association, VI, 1956, pp. 64–71.

GALANTER, MARC, 'Law and Caste in Modern India', *Asian Survey*, Vol. III, No. 11, 1963, pp. 544–59.

INDIA. *Census of India—1911. United Provinces of Agra and Oudh*, Vol. XV, Pt. II, Allahabad, Superintendent, Government Press, 1912.

LEVINE, L., 'Speech Variation and Social Structure in a Group of North Indian Villages', unpublished Ph.D. dissertation, Columbia University, 1959.

LEWIS, O., *Village Life in Northern India*, Urbana, University of Illinois Press, 1958.

LYNCH, O. M., 'The Politics of Untouchability: Social Structure and Social Change in a City of India', unpublished Ph.D. dissertation, Columbia University, 1966.

MARRIOTT, McKIM, 'Social Structure and Change in a U.P. Village', in M. N. Srinivas (Ed.), *India's Villages*, London, Asia Publishing House, 1960.

MAYER, A. C., *Caste and Kinship in Central India*, London, Routledge and Kegan Paul, 1960.

NIEHOFF, A., 'Caste, Class, and Family in an Industrial Community in Northern India', unpublished Ph.D. dissertation, Columbia University, 1957.

POCOCK, D. F., 'Sociologies: Urban and Rural', *Contributions to Indian Sociology*, Vol. IV, 1960, 63–81.

ROWE, W. L., 'Caste, Kinship and Association in Urban India', paper prepared for Symposium No. 26: Cross-Cultural Similarities in the Urbanization Process, Burg Wartenstein, 1964 (lithographed).

SRINIVAS, M. N., *Caste in Modern India, and Other Essays*, Bombay, Asia Publishing House, 1962.

TIWARI, A. R., 'Urban Regions of Agra', *Agra University Journal of Research*, Vol. VI, No. 1, 1958, pp. 101–14.

VIII

The Gandhian View of Caste, and Caste after Gandhi

BY DENNIS DALTON

Lecturer in Politics with Special Reference to Asia, Department of Economic and Political Sciences, School of Oriental and African Studies, University of London

Just as nature is unity in variety . . . so it is with every man; the microcosm is but a miniature repetition of the macrocosm; in spite of all these variations, in and through them all runs this eternal harmony, and we have to recognize this. This idea, above all other ideas, I find to be the crying necessity of the day.[1]

The inmost creed of India is to find the one in the many, unity in diversity.[2]

In this harmony between our unity and our diversity lies the secret of life.[3]

WHEN Gandhi is discussed, the tendency is often to assess; and so assessments of his significance are in abundance. Was he 'a religious genius',[4] the embodiment of 'truth, compassion, courage, and simplicity',[5] the 'Yudhishthira of his age'?[6] Or, was he rather 'one of history's magnificent failures'?[7] Indeed, even one who 'far from being infallible, committed serious blunders, one after another, in pursuit of some Utopian ideals and methods which had no basis in reality'.[8] Answers

[1] Swami Vivekananda, *The Complete Works*, Calcutta, Advaita Ashrama, 1955, Vol. VI, p. 181.

[2] Rabindranath Tagore, 'Society and State', in *Towards Universal Man*, London, Asia Publishing House, 1961, p. 65.

[3] Sri Aurobindo, *The Ideal of Human Unity in The Human Cycle: The Ideal of Human Unity, War and Self-Determination*, Pondicherry, Sri Aurobindo Ashram, 1962, p. 564.

[4] W. N. Brown, *The United States and India and Pakistan*, Cambridge, Mass., Harvard University Press, 1955, p. 80.

[5] S. A. Wolpert, *India*, New York, Prentice-Hall, 1965, pp. 129–33.

[6] R. C. Zaehner, *Hinduism*, London, Oxford University Press, 1962, p. 235.

[7] F. Moraes, *India Today*, New York, Macmillan, 1960, pp. 89–91.

[8] R. C. Majumdar, 'Gandhi's Place in the History of Indian Nationalism', in *Gandhi, Maker of Modern India?*, Boston, D. C. Heath and Co., 1965, p. 56. These estimates, *pro* and *con*, are given only as a random sample. For a recent extensive appraisal by numerous (sympathetic) writers, see G. Ramachandran and T. K. Mahadevan (Eds.), *Gandhi: His Relevance for our Times*, Bombay, Vidya Bhavan, 1964.

will not be attempted here; rather, the object of this essay is to consider Gandhi's main purpose as a political thinker and moral reformer, the sense in which this purpose was directed by a desire for social harmony, and how this is evident in his views on caste. The only judgement offered will come with 'Caste after Gandhi', the concluding section of the chapter, and the concern there is with how Gandhi might himself have regarded certain developments in caste after Independence.

Gandhi's central purpose, as seen here chiefly in his views on caste, may be considered broadly within the context of three questions. How is this purpose related to aspects of the recent Western intellectual tradition? How is it related to the modern Indian tradition? And how is it related to the 'Gandhian tradition' itself, that is, to his approach to the problems of contemporary India? The interpretation developed here is that Gandhi was committed, above all, to the reconciliation of the divergent ideas, attitudes, and interests which surrounded him; and that his purpose is best described as a quest, not for *Satya* or even *Swaraj*,[9] but pre-eminently for harmony. Other thinkers of modern India have shared in this quest, and perhaps none more than Tagore, whose words express well Gandhi's central concern: 'The task before us today is to make whole the broken-up communal life, to harmonize the divergence between village and town, between the classes and the masses, between the pride of power and the spirit of comradeship.'[10]

GANDHI, THE STYLIST: WESTERN PARALLELS

What is meant by a political 'style' or 'stylist'? The quality is, perhaps, as difficult to define in the abstract as it is easy to perceive in the particular. Style, in general, suggests, as Chesterfield tells us, 'the dress of thoughts'; and, for political thought, this means a study of 'the history, not of political ideas, but of the manner of our political

---

[9] *Satya* may be translated as 'truth' and *swaraj* as 'self-rule'. Both terms, however, had for Gandhi complex meanings. *Satya* was conceived as an impersonal abstraction (as in his oft-quoted remark, 'God is Truth and Truth is God'); yet it was an abstraction with which he could carry on daily 'experiments'. Thus, his autobiography was called, 'A Story of My Experiments with Truth', and his method of political and social action was named *satyagraha* ('truth-firmness', or 'clinging to truth'). The meaning of *swaraj* was equally complex, since it meant *individual* as well as national self-rule, and these two goals were seen as inextricably interwoven. Two points may be made about the use, here, of 'harmony' as embodying the meaning of Gandhi's central purpose. First, the word may be best translated, in Gandhian terms, as *sarvodaya*, the 'welfare, equality, and uplift of all'. Second, it should be emphasized that Gandhi saw the concepts of *satya*, *swaraj*, and *sarvodaya* as necessarily interrelated or complementary. The society that has perfectly realized the *sarvodayan* ideal, becomes, by virtue of this, a society based on Truth. Moreover, each of its members will have achieved self-rule, or a knowledge and subsequent mastery of themselves as individuals.

[10] Tagore, *Towards Universal Man*, p. 306.

hinking',[11] that is, the characteristic mode of expression which a given political thinker adopts. The style of a political actor is easier to dissect. The most striking recent example may be seen clearly in the contrasting political styles of the late President Kennedy and Lyndon Johnson; styles that may be identified in terms not only of speech and personal mannerisms but also of their respective approaches to the operation of government and basic understanding of the nature of politics. The determinant of their styles, in each case, is found in their relationships to their particular traditions; Johnson's Texan background and Kennedy's New England heritage go further than anything else in explaining their political orientations. Moreover, tradition as the determining factor of political style applies to political thinkers as well. Among the latter, the relationship is more complex, since the tradition has usually become the subject not merely of behavioural expression but also of considerable reflection. The contrasting styles, however, among three thinkers as representative of their respective traditions as Hobbes, Hegel, and Machiavelli, should illustrate that the main concern is with the way in which ideas are expressed; symbols, language, and images used; and the past, as well as the present, interpreted.

When Gandhi is considered as a stylist, difficulties may seem to arise. On the one hand, he was not a systematic or sophisticated political philosopher and his significance is missed if he is considered exclusively in terms of political thought; on the other hand, he was not primarily a politician, in the restricted sense of pursuing goals essentially political in nature. With Gandhi, it can only be said that the moral concern remained dominant; and because of the circumstances in which he chose to think and act, his style not only had political implications but possessed as well a political component. Moreover, the main factor of analysis, the element of tradition, applies to a study of Gandhi's style as much as to other political thinkers and actors: primary attention must be given to Gandhi's relationship with his tradition, the manner in which his thought and action express and interpret that tradition within the context of the contemporary Indian situation.

If the great purpose of Gandhi's life is seen in his quest for harmony, then the dominant note that pulsates throughout this theme, giving it a distinct rhythm and rich appeal, is the style which he developed so brilliantly. If he has any claims to being a 'religious genius', then it must rest with his stylistic achievement. The quality of this style was

[11] M. Oakeshott, 'Political Education', in *Rationalism in Politics*, London, Methuen, 1962, p. 130.

peculiarly Indian. It depended, above all, on the ingenious use of indigenous religious symbols, images, language, and beliefs; as such, it
invites comparison with Indian rather than Western sources. Yet in
one sense the nature of Gandhi's style is illuminated as much by
Western as by Indian writers.

Among Western thinkers, Gandhi's name is most often associated
with Tolstoy, Ruskin, and Thoreau since these were, as Gandhi himself
says, important influences imbibed during his South African experience.
Such comparisons, however, throw no light on the nature of Gandhi's
purpose or the style that expressed it. One comes much closer if his
purpose and style are compared to quite different thinkers of the last
century. Philosophers like Nietzsche, Comte, and Marx, for example,
faced the divergent streams of thought and attitude of their age and
sought to produce coherent patterns. Henry Aiken sets forth suc-
cinctly the aim of these philosophers when he remarks that, for them,
'history and science are themselves instruments of cultural change, to
be used deliberately for the purpose of reconstituting Western man's
attitudes toward his tradition and, hence, toward himself'.[12] Unlike
these Western thinkers, Gandhi's motive was not to subvert his religious tradition but to reconstruct it; hence, his 'instruments of cultural change' were not 'history and science' but religion itself, and
associated symbolic forms. Like these thinkers, though, Gandhi's aim
was also to 'reconstitute' his fellow Indian's 'attitudes toward his
tradition and, hence, toward himself'. Above all, Gandhi sought, in so
far as it was possible for a moral reformer in India, to promote social
harmony and not to provoke abrupt change with violent consequences.
Continuity, no less than innovation, was his goal, since he believed that
the latter without the former was doomed to impermanence. Thus
Gandhi could say, with all the force of a revolutionary: 'What I am
aiming at is the greatest reform of the age.'[13] But the real spirit of his
teaching, which in turn directed the quality of his style, is best expressed in that Sermon which remained with Gandhi to the end:
'Think not that I am come to destroy the law, or the prophets: I am
not come to destroy, but to fulfil.'

Gandhi's purpose and style, then, when seen in this broad sense, represent nothing unique: more often than not, when sensitive men experience 'the shaking of the foundations', a search for melody in the chaos

[12] H. D. Aiken, *The Age of Ideology*, New York, Mentor, 1963, p. 25.
[13] M. K. Gandhi, '*Harijan*, 12 August 1933', in *Hindu Dharma*, Ahmedabad, Navajivan,
1950, p. 311.

begins, new symbolic forms and patterns of order are conceived, and a reconstitution of tradition is sometimes achieved. Today we are more aware than ever before of the reinterpretation of especially religious symbols. Gandhi developed a body of beliefs which may be called a political philosophy, and he was a master-manipulator of symbols; but his *forte* was certainly not theory. His achievement rests rather with his style as seen within the context of the modern Indian experience, with the way in which he used his tradition in an attempt to reconstitute Indian attitudes toward it, and, finally, with the way in which he applied the results to a programme of political and social reform.

What was Gandhi's relationship to his tradition? When his critics point out his dubious interpretations of classical texts, they imply that his interest was, or should have been, that of an historian, committed to an objective appraisal of data. No one was more aware than Gandhi that quite the opposite was true: that he was subjectively involved in his tradition and found psychological support in this involvement. If this kind of relationship is common anywhere, then it is in Asia; Gandhi, however, cultivated and refined it. His moralist outlook was formed early in life; and it was gradually reinforced, during the South African experience, by his interpretation of the 'spirit' of Hinduism. Refinement came largely after his return to India, with the development of a poetic sense, 'a perception, not only of the pastness of the past, but of its presence',[14] and the ability to express this sense in rich symbolism. If the historian looks at his past with objectivity, then Gandhi treated it with affection, drawing from the classics old words—*swarajya*, *karmayoga*, *ahimsa*[15]—charging them with fresh meaning, until they became symbols of both the past and the future. Few examples illustrate better the thinking behind Gandhi's style than his approach to the Gita:

What, however, I have done [he wrote in 1936] is to put a new but natural and logical interpretation upon the whole teaching of the Gita and the spirit of Hinduism. Hinduism, not to speak of other religions, is ever evolving. It

[14] T. S. Eliot, 'Tradition and the Individual Talent' in *Selected Essays*, London, Faber and Faber, 1951, p. 14.

[15] The concept of *karmayoga* ('way of action') as found in the *Bhagavad Gita* was first developed in the modern Indian context by Vivekananda. The ideal of *karmayoga* was interpreted by him as a call for disinterested service to society. Tilak and then Gandhi reinterpreted it further, applying it to political reforms. No less important than this conceptual development, however, were the symbolic forms that the idea of *karmayoga* assumed in Gandhi's personal style of leadership. As one writer on Gandhi aptly expressed it, he became 'the *karmayogi par excellence*', the embodiment of disinterested action for the welfare of India. *Ahimsa* may be translated as 'non-violence', but Gandhi also defined it as 'love' and 'charity'. Once again, the concept was taken from traditional Indian sources, and then reinterpreted for the nationalist movement.

has not one scripture like the Quran or the Bible. Its scriptures are also evolving and suffering addition. The Gita itself is an instance in point. It has given a new meaning to *karma*, *sannyasa*, *yajna*, etc. It has breathed new life into Hinduism.

The Gita is not an aphoristic work; it is a great religious poem. The deeper you dive into it, the richer the meanings you get . . . With every age the important words will carry new and expanding meanings. But its central teaching will never vary. The seeker is at liberty to extract from this treasure any meaning he likes so as to enable him to enforce in his life the central teaching.[16]

This passage holds the key assumptions behind Gandhi's approach to his tradition. Hinduism is seen here as 'ever-evolving', and Gandhi views his own contribution as giving it a 'new interpretation', clarifying the 'spirit' of its teaching. The Gita, through its own reinterpretation of more ancient concepts, 'has breathed new life into Hinduism'; but, more than this, the Gita is itself 'a great religious poem', subject to continuing reinterpretation, and 'with every age the important words will carry new and expanding meanings'. 'The seeker is at liberty to extract from this treasure any meaning he likes': a more radical use of a religious text could hardly be conceived. The crux, then, of Gandhi's approach was this: to 'reconstitute' his tradition (or, in current anthropological terms, the 'Great Tradition')[17] in a manner that would meet the demands of the Western cultural impact, and yet maintain continuity with his past. In a word, then, Gandhi's purpose was to harmonize; to create unity out of cultural diversity.

GANDHI AND HIS PREDECESSORS: THE INDIAN CONTEXT

The problem of cultural diversity was, of course, present in India long before the advent of the British. Never before, however, had the problem reached, in a cultural sense, such acute proportions, throwing the

[16] Gandhi, *Harijan*, 3 October 1936, in *Hindu Dharma*, p. 157, and Mahadev Desai (quoting Gandhi) in *The Gita According to Gandhi*, Ahmedabad, Navajivan, 1956, pp. 133–4.

[17] In the last decade several stimulating anthropological and politico-sociological studies have appeared which offer valuable insights into modern Indian political and social thought. Themes, for example, like 'Sanskritization and Westernization', 'the Great and Little Traditions', and dynamics of leadership, particularly at the village level, all bristle with implications for an analysis of Gandhi's ideas, as well as those of some of his contemporaries. See especially M. N. Srinivas, *Caste in Modern India, and Other Essays*, London, Asia Publishing House, 1962; McKim Marriott (Ed.), *Village India*, Chicago, University of Chicago Press, 1955; R. Park and I. Tinker (Eds.) *Leadership and Political Institutions in India*, Princeton, Princeton University Press, 1959; and M. Singer (Ed.), *Traditional India: Structure and Change*, Philadelphia, American Folklore Society, 1959. This, however, is to cite only a few books, and to omit many important articles. If, though, one of the latter were to be singled out for its exceptional worth it would be Susanne H. Rudolph's 'Conflict and Consensus in Indian Politics', *World Politics*, April 1961.

challenge and response mechanism into full gear. Long before the birth of Gandhi the scale of the problem had been realized; and by the time of his maturity the sense of purpose conceived to meet the cultural challenge from the West had come to dominate Indian political and social thought. The Western ideological impact on India had reached its high-water mark in the nineteenth century with the introduction of the ideals of social and political freedom and equality; and much of the subsequent thinking took the form of a response to these twin concepts. It was with an eye to these that Tagore wrote, 'We shall be swept away and into oblivion if we cannot achieve harmony between our social conditions and the demands of the modern age.'[18] The response, undertaken by Tagore and others, was characterized chiefly by the type of 'reconstitution' of Indian tradition already described. Aurobindo called it 'preservation by reconstruction':

And the riper form of the return [to the Indian tradition] has taken as its principle a synthetical restatement; it has sought to arrive at the spirit of the ancient culture and, while respecting its forms and often preserving them to revivify, has yet not hesitated also to remould, to reject the outworn and to admit whatever new motive seemed assimilable to the old spirituality or apt to widen the channel of its larger evolution. Of this freer dealing with past and present, this preservation by reconstruction, Vivekananda was in his lifetime the leading exemplar and the most powerful exponent.[19]

When Vivekananda (1863–1902) turned to the problem of caste, and more particularly the Western attack on caste,[20] he employed the same approach to this as to other issues. This approach involved the reinterpretation of a traditional Indian ideal, the ideal of *varnashramadharma*.[21] This, it was hoped, would not only accommodate but also reinforce the Western demand for freedom and equality, and, if

[18] Tagore, op. cit., p. 126.

[19] Aurobindo, *The Renaissance in India*, Pondicherry, Sri Aurobindo Ashram, 1951, pp. 39–40.

[20] For a brief examination of Vivekananda's views on caste, see R. Chowdhary, 'Sociological Views of Swami Vivekananda', in R. C. Majumdar (Ed.), *Swami Vivekananda Centenary Memorial Volume*, Calcutta, 1963, pp. 362–76 .Also in this volume, A. T. Embree, 'Vivekananda and Indian Nationalism', pp. 521–3.

[21] The ideal social order was set forth, in ancient Indian thought, in the theory of *varnashramadharma* (often shortened by Gandhi to *varnashrama* or *varnadharma*). The system of the four *varnas* or social orders ensured, in theory, the harmonious interrelationship of four social functions: those of the *brahman* (spiritual authority and instruction), *kshatriya* (temporal power), *vaisya* (wealth), and *sudra* (labour). The working of society depended upon the fulfilment by each of these *varnas* of its social role as prescribed by *dharma* or the sacred law. For a statement on the meaning of this theory see, especially, A. L. Basham, 'Some Fundamental Ideas of Ancient India', in C. H. Philips (Ed.), *Politics and Society in India*, London, Allen and Unwin, 1963.

possible, even go beyond this by demonstrating the exceptional value of the ideal precisely because of its traditional Indian base. This line had been anticipated, to some extent, by Vivekananda's predecessor, Swami Dayananda Saraswati (1824–83), founder of the *Arya Samaj*. Dayananda introduced the argument that became important not only for Vivekananda, but for Gandhi as well. The Vedas, he declared, provided no justification for any notion of superiority or inferiority among the four great divisions of Hindu society; each *varna* was equal to the rest, and passages from various texts are interpreted to maintain this position.[22]

The fact that a Swami argued this view carried far more weight than if it had come from a Westernized reformer; so that by 1907 Bal Gangadhar Tilak, the incarnation of Hindu orthodoxy among political leaders, could maintain that 'the idea of superior and inferior castes is foreign to Hindu religion', and this is followed with the by now customary selections from the classics. Tilak, moreover, moves on to express fears that had been voiced before him:[23] 'The prevailing idea of social inequality is working immense evil. Capital is made out of the ideas of inequality and class is set against class. Such disintegration, if unchecked, will involve us in utter ruin. The saints and prophets once averted the danger and we are now called upon to play the same role.'[24]

By distilling the 'spirit' of Hinduism as found in the ideal of *varnash-ramadharma*, Vivekananda sought 'to play the same role' as India's 'saints and prophets', a role in which he urged on the Hindu community the gospel of social harmony.[25] Not only, though, did Vivekananda respond to the needs of his own society by condemning the divisive influence of caste as 'don't touchism';[26] he directed his response at the West as well. Like Dayananda, he incorporated the alien concept of social equality into the *varnashramadharma* ideal; but unlike his predecessor, he declared that it was this very ideal which the West itself badly needed. Beginning with a criticism of 'that horrible idea of competition',[27] which was not merely tolerated but idealized in

[22] Dayananda Saraswati, *Light of Truth or Satyarth Prakash* (trans. C. Bharadwaja), Lahore, 1927, pp. 85–92. Also Charles H. Heimsath, *Indian Nationalism and Hindu Social Reform*, Princeton, Princeton University Press, 1964, pp. 299–300.

[23] The divisive influence of caste had been criticized, among modern social reformers, as early as Ram Mohan Roy and perhaps most strongly by R. G. Bhandarkar. See Heimsath, op. cit., pp. 11, 197.

[24] B. G. Tilak, *The Mahratta*, 15 September 1907.

[25] Vivekananda, *Complete Works*, Vol. IV, pp. 474–80.

[26] Ibid., Vols. III (1960), pp. 167, 173–5; V (1959), pp. 22–23, 26–27, 311; VI (1963), p. 394; VIII (1959), p. 136, 139.

[27] Ibid., Vol. V, p. 278.

the West, Vivekananda set the Indian against the Western theory of society: 'Competition—cruel, cold and heartless—is the law of Europe. Our law is caste—the breaking of competition, checking its forces, mitigating its cruelties, smoothing the passage of the human soul through this mystery of life.'[28] Later, in this century, precisely the same sentiments were expressed by Tagore.[29]

Like Vivekananda, Gandhi combined a strong criticism of 'don't touchism' with an insistence that India's salvation could come only through a reconstruction of her own traditional foundations. His ideas on the contrasting traits of Indian and Western civilizations, and the unique value of the former, were formed in the period of Vivekananda's eminence, and are set forth in his first book, *Hind Swaraj*. To a much greater extent than Vivekananda, however, Gandhi concentrated on harmonizing the divisive forces within Indian society itself. There he launched a grand attempt at reconciliation of the Western ideals of freedom and social equality—in the face of Hindu orthodoxy—with main elements of the Indian religious tradition. This attempt illustrates the keynote of Gandhi's political and social thought, the passionate yet unending patience of his pursuit of cultural harmony; and this note is particularly evident in his approach to the problem of caste.

GANDHI'S CONCEPTION OF CASTE

Gandhi's views on caste changed considerably during his lifetime, and perhaps because of this they have been the subject of considerably confused commentaries. On the one hand, Gandhi has been unduly attacked for his ambiguity and inconsistency, in his remarks on caste, as well as for an excessive deference to Hindu orthodoxy.[30] On the other hand, sympathetic interpreters have seen his conception of caste as undergoing a rational evolution, moving gradually from an orthodox stance in 1920 to more liberal views in the 1930s, and culminating in a radical position at the end of his life.[31] This latter interpretation is the more nearly correct; but since it has nowhere been developed fully, it suffers from oversimplification. By emphasizing the evolutionary nature of Gandhi's approach to caste, it moves too far, thus projecting too much orthodoxy into his earlier position, and purging his later ideas

[28] Ibid., Vol. III, p. 205.
[29] See the quotation from Tagore and the comments on it in an article to which the writer is himself much indebted: H. R. Tinker, 'The Uniqueness of Asia', in R. N. Iyer (Ed.), *The Glass Curtain*, London, Oxford University Press, 1965, pp. 270–2.
[30] S. Natarajan, *A Century of Social Reform*, New York, Asia Publishing House, 1959, pp. 150–1.
[31] L. Fischer, *The Life of Mahatma Gandhi*, London, Jonathan Cape, 1957, pp. 362–4.

of all orthodox elements. First, though, it would be well to examine the other interpretation mentioned, and its basis for the attack on Gandhi's treatment of the question of caste. Critics have focused on Gandhi's allegedly specious distinction between *varnashramadharma* and the caste system; reform will inevitably founder on such subtleties, it is argued, and a total condemnation of the whole system, whether called *varna* or caste, is absolutely essential for effective change.[32] Milder criticism has observed that Gandhi said nothing new, but merely repeated arguments of his predecessors, most notably Dayananda.[33] The main effort, here, will be to set forth Gandhi's conception of caste, in both its fundamental and its changing aspects; it will not be to defend that view. However, a brief comment should be made on the two criticisms of Gandhi just mentioned.

Each of these criticisms may in turn be criticized on the same account: they ignore the significance of style in his approach to caste reform, and thus miss much of his purpose as he saw it. The distinction between caste and *varna*, and the subsequent idealization of *varnashramadharma* as an order of equality and harmony, emerged in Gandhi's thought in the 1920s, and it eventually provided the basis of his approach to the caste problem, as distinguished from the problem of untouchability. A similar approach to caste by Dayananda and Vivekananda has already been observed. Indeed, Vivekananda, and later Gandhi, too, pointed to the ancient roots of this position on caste in the teachings of Buddha; and a noted Indologist has confirmed the similarity between Gandhi's view of caste and that of Buddha and many of his successors.[34] It is true, therefore, that there is little novelty in Gandhi's position on caste. Except, that is, for the element of style: and, in Gandhi's case, this makes all the difference. For Gandhi amplified this aspect of style with all the force of his creative skill, and the symbols he conceived were unknown to his predecessors.

Gandhi's symbolic language comprises a study in itself,[35] but a glance at the origin of one of his key terms, 'Harijan', may offer one good example of his use of words. The movement against untouchability has a long history in India, and Vivekananda was among its most recent champions. If Vivekananda's writings and speeches are examined,

[32] G. S. Ghurye, *Caste and Class in India*, Bombay, Popular Book Depot, 1957, pp. 220–1. And O. C. Cox, *Caste, Class and Race*, New York, Doubleday, 1948, p. 35.

[33] C. Heimsath, op. cit., pp. 344–5.

[34] Louis Renou, 'Gandhi and Indian Civilization', in K. Roy (Ed.), *Gandhi Memorial Peace Number, Visva-Bharati Quarterly*, Shantiniketan, 1949, p. 237.

[35] See the approach of Indira Rothermund, *The Philosophy of Restraint*, Bombay, Popular Prakashan, 1963, Ch. II, 'Gandhi's Terms and Symbols', pp. 17–36.

the references to untouchables are usually in terms of 'pariah' or the victims of 'don't touchism'. Subsequent reformers relied on equally uninspired terminology. For years, Gandhi himself used *'bhangi'*, 'untouchable', 'unapproachable', *'Panchama'*, or *'Antyaja'* (the last-born). Then, in August 1931, he wrote that he had at last found the right word: 'Harijan' (man of God). 'It was a word', he tells us, 'used by the great saint, Narasinha Mehta', a Nagar Brahmina 'who defied the whole community by claiming the "untouchables" as his own'. Gandhi, however, is not willing to leave it at that; from this moment implications of the word begin to develop in his mind. 'I am delighted to adopt that word', he continues, 'which is sanctified by having been used by such a great saint, but it has for me a deeper meaning than you may imagine. The "untouchable", to me, is, compared to us, really a "Harijan"—a man of God, and we are *Durjan*, men of evil.'[36] Thus not only is Gandhi 'at least spared the use of a term which is itself one of reproach', but the substitute itself grows in esteem.

When Caste Hindus have of their own inner conviction and, therefore, voluntarily, got rid of the present-day untouchability, we shall all be called Harijans; for, according to my humble opinion, Caste Hindus will then have found favour with God and may therefore, be fitly described as His men.[37]

By 1934 the famous Harijan journal had been founded as the main vehicle of Gandhi's ideas, Harijan Boards had been formed, Harijan Day proclaimed, and the Harijan Sevak Sangh organized, all to promote the reform of untouchability. Perhaps most noteworthy, Gandhi decided, in 1932, to employ his 'fiery weapon', the fast, on behalf of the Harijans. Symbolic language was thus reinforced by symbolic action;[38] few instances manifest better Gandhi's use of his tradition. It is in terms of such a style that the significance of the use of *varnashra-madharma* itself lies.

Before discussing the evolution of Gandhi's views on caste, the constant elements in his conception should be noted. First, Gandhi was himself predominantly liberal in his own personal indifference to caste restrictions. Thus in 1917, for example, while he is unequivocally defending the caste prohibition on interdining for Indian society as a whole, he is setting a personal example of indifference to this restriction, and in

[36] Gandhi, *Young India*, 6 August 1931, in *The Removal of Untouchability*, Ahmedabad, Navajivan, 1954, p. 14.
[37] Gandhi, *Harijan*, 11 February 1933, in op. cit., p. 15.
[38] Op. cit., pp. 58–59.

this way is converting his closest associates.[39] In typical traditional style he explained this in terms of his *sannyasin*[40] attitude, adopted early in South Africa. As a result, Indian society saw Gandhi, and Gandhi regarded himself, as occupying the peculiar position of a figure above the discord around him, and uniquely capable of harmonizing it. This view has the deepest possible roots in the classical Indian tradition. The second constant element that should be noted is his commitment to the idea of equality. 'All men are born equal', he insisted, and the four great *varnas* must be seen as equal orders. In South Africa, as early as 1909, Gandhi had publicly decried the caste system for its inequalities: its 'hypocritical distinctions of high and low' and 'caste tyranny' which had made India 'turn [her] back on truth and embrace falsehood.'[41]

However much Gandhi condemned inequality of castes in South Africa, shortly after he returns to India the emphasis falls on the generally beneficial aspects of caste, and a strong defence of it for its 'wonderful powers of organization'.[42] It is on the basis of his remarks on caste in this five-year period, from 1916 to 1921, that he acquired the reputation of orthodoxy; and certainly it is true that at this time he was most sensitive to that community of opinion. Caste prohibitions on interdining and intermarriage are upheld, since they foster 'self-control'; and the system itself is regarded as a beneficial, 'natural institution'.[43] Gradually the term *varnashramadharma* is used more frequently; still, it is indicative of this early undeveloped stage of his views that caste and *varnashramadharma* are used together with no attempt to distinguish between them.[44] Gandhi is at this point searching for an approach to caste that will allow him to reform it effectively from within, without alienating the orthodox. The remark that he makes at this time on the issue of intercaste marriage is suggestive of his attitude; he advises that a beginning should be made with inter-marriage not among different *varnas* but among members of different subcastes. 'This would satisfy the most ardent reformers as a first step and enable men like Pandit Malaviya [an orthodox Hindu] to support

[39] See Rajendra Prasad, *At the Feet of Mahatma Gandhi*, Bombay, Hind Kitabs, 1955, p. 152.

[40] The *sannyasin* or 'holy man' of Hinduism is above caste distinctions.

[41] Gandhi, *Collected Works*, Publications Division, Ministry of Information and Broadcasting, Government of India, 1963, IX, pp. 180–1.

[42] Gandhi as quoted in C. F. Andrews, *Mahatma Gandhi's Ideas*, London, Allen and Unwin, 1931, p. 123.

[43] Gandhi, *Works*, Vol. XIII, pp. 301–3.

[44] Ibid., pp. 94, 325, 522.

it.'[45] The remark signals the approach taken for almost another decade, an approach which continues to sanction prohibitions on intermarriage and interdining, but gradually builds *varnashramadharma* into a social ideal independent of caste.

After 1919, when Gandhi assumes effective control of the Congress, signs appear that he has begun the long process of gaining confidence as a national leader. He is now the 'Mahatma', and while, for the orthodox, his credentials as a 'Sanatani Hindu' remain in question, and his writings are still replete with defensive remarks, there is none the less evident now a surer sense of purpose. Echoing Vivekananda's earlier defence, he urges the caste ideal as the right path to social harmony: 'If we can prove it to be a success, it can be offered to the world as a leaven and as the best remedy against heartless competition and social disintegration born of avarice and greed.'[46] This defence of caste, however, is significantly qualified in December 1920 by distinguishing between 'the four divisions' and 'the subcastes', and also by stressing his earlier insistence on equality among the four orders:

I believe that caste has saved Hinduism from disintegration. But like every other institution it has suffered from excrescences. I consider the four divisions alone to be fundamental, natural and essential. The innumerable subcastes are sometimes a convenience, often a hindrance. The sooner there is fusion the better. The silent destruction and reconstruction of subcastes have ever gone on and are bound to continue. Social pressure and public opinion can be trusted to deal with the problem. But I am certainly against any attempt at destroying the fundamental divisions. The caste system is not based on inequality, there is no question of inferiority, and so far as there is any such question arising, the tendency should undoubtedly be checked. But there appears to be no valid reason for ending the system because of its abuse. It lends itself easily to reformation. The spirit of democracy, which is fast spreading throughout India, and the rest of the world, will, without a shadow of doubt, purge the institution of the idea of predominance and subordination. The spirit of democracy is not a mechanical thing to be adjusted by abolition of forms. It requires change of the heart.[47]

Writing in October 1921, Gandhi reinforces the distinction between the four divisions and caste; and now, significantly, he begins to use the term *varnashrama* quite consistently. With a view to the orthodox, he maintains his support of restrictions on interdining and intermarriage,

[45] Gandhi, *Works*, Vol. XV, pp. 122–3.

[46] Gandhi, *Young India*, 5 January 1921, in N. K. Bose (Ed.), *Selections from Gandhi*, Ahmedabad, Navajivan, 1948, pp. 232–3.

[47] Gandhi, *Young India*, 8 December 1920, in *Caste Must Go and The Sin of Untouchability*, Ahmedabad, Navajivan, 1964, pp. 12–13.

for Hinduism 'does most emphatically discourage interdining and inter-marriage between divisions', in the interests of 'self-restraint'. Indeed, he goes so far as to say that 'Prohibition against intermarriage and inter-dining is essential for a rapid evolution of the soul'. This seems to have been an extreme statement which he was later forced to qualify. 'But', he continues, now playing to his other audience, 'this self-denial is no test of *varna*. A Brahmana may remain a Brahmana, though he may dine with his Shudra . . .' 'The four divisions define a man's calling, they do not restrict or regulate social intercourse.'[48] The Gandhian tech-nique is here in full swing: on the one hand, he holds that since man's *varna* is, as the orthodox contend, inherited, 'I do not believe that interdining or even intermarriage necessarily deprives a man of his status that birth has given him.' (Although immoral conduct may do so.)

On the other hand, the two key pillars of caste, interdining and intermarriage, are neatly separated from the concept of *varnashrama*. It is precisely on this basis that Gandhi can argue, six years later, '*Varna* has nothing to do with caste. Down with the monster of caste that masquerades in the guise of *varna*. It is this travesty of *varna* that has degraded Hinduism and India.'[49] This unambiguous indictment of caste had begun as early as January 1926,[50] and as caste comes under an increasingly scathing attack the idea of *varnadharma* moves in to fill the vacuum, replacing one traditional concept with another. The admixture of continuity and innovation which always characterized his style is evident in this passage—a statement which offers an outstanding example of Gandhi's use of language:

When we have come to our own, when we have cleansed ourselves, we may have the four *varnas* according to the way in which we can express the best in us. But *varna* then will invest one with higher responsibility and duties. Those who will impart knowledge in a spirit of service will be called Brah-manas. They will assume no superior airs but will be true servants of society. When inequality of status or rights is ended, every one of us will be equal. I do not know, however, when we shall be able to revive true *varnadharma*. Its real revival would mean true democracy.[51]

Gandhi is thus able to urge on the orthodox a 'democratic' ideal derived from the classical Indian tradition; while he opposes as 'excrescences' those caste practices which he has separated from *varnadharma*. The

[48] Gandhi, *Young India*, 6 October 1921, in *Varnashramadharma*, Ahmedabad, Navajivan, 1962, pp. 34–35.

[49] Gandhi, *Young India*, 24 November 1927, in op. cit., p. 13.

[50] Gandhi, *Young India*, 21 January 1926, in *Caste Must Go*, p. 16.

[51] Gandhi, *Harijan*, 4 April 1936, in *Varnashramadharma*, p. 26.

ideal with which he replaces caste, however, could hardly have been seen by the orthodox as a suitable substitute:

Fight, by all means, the monster that passes for *varnashrama* today, and you will find me working side by side with you. My *varnashrama* enables me to dine with anybody who will give me clean food, be he Hindu, Muslim, Christian, Parsi, whatever he is. My *varnashrama* accommodates a Pariah girl under my own roof as my own daughter. My *varnashrama* accommodates many Panchama families with whom I dine with the greatest pleasure—to dine with whom is a privilege. My *varnashrama* refuses to bow the head before the greatest potentate on earth, but my *varnashrama* compels me to bow down my head in all humility before knowledge, before purity, before every person, where I see God face to face.[52]

Gandhi's views on caste during this initial decade (1916–26) following his return to India have been treated in some detail here because it was in this period that the real change in his position occurred; the crucial distinction between the caste system and *varnashramadharma* emerged then. Throughout this decade, it should be stressed, Gandhi was constantly harassed by Hindu conservatives, especially in his reform of untouchability; and the pace as well as the content of his views on caste reform must be seen in the context of his response to the Indian orthodox as well as to Western liberalism.

The last two decades of his career (1927–47) represent a progressive movement toward a radical view of caste. In September and October of 1927, Gandhi made two noteworthy speeches on *varnashramadharma* at Tangore and Trivandrum where the orthodox elements were formidable. The emphasis in both speeches is on social equality, justified, as always, with an appeal, not to Western ideas, but to the traditional concept of *advaita*. The caste system's most vicious feature, he argues, is that it has upheld the idea of inherited superiority; and this is inconsistent with the spirit of Hinduism in general and the ideal of *varnashramadharma* in particular. 'There is nothing in common between varnashrama and caste.' Gandhi concludes his earlier speech with a remark that is especially relevant to his political thought:

You would be entitled to say that this is not how *varnashrama* is understood in these days. I have myself said times without number that *varnashrama* as it is at present understood and practised is a monstrous parody of the original, but in order to demolish this distortion let us not seek to demolish the original. And if you say that the idealistic *varnashrama* which I have placed before you is quite all right you have admitted all that I like you to admit. I would also urge on you to believe with me that no nation, no individual, can possibly live without proper ideals. And if you believe with me

[52] Gandhi, *Young India*, 22 September 1927, in *The Removal of Untouchability*, p. 44.

in the idealistic *varnashrama*, you will also strive with me to reach that ideal so far as may be.[53]

This comment suggests that balance of 'practical idealism' which Gandhi struggled to maintain: practical rather than fanciful because of the style that reinforced it and the technique of *satyagraha* devised to implement it; idealistic rather than sophistic because of the intense search, evident here as elsewhere, for a right, a truthful, conception of caste.

Not until 1932, however, does the vestige of orthodoxy seen in his support of caste restrictions on intermarriage and interdining disappear. These restrictions are now criticized as being 'no part of the Hindu religion', serving only to 'stunt Hindu society'.[54] Writing in 1935 on this issue under the title 'Caste Must Go', he insists that 'in *varnash-rama* there was and should be no prohibition of intermarriage and interdining'.[55] His views on intermarriage, once loosened, culminated in the announcement of 1946 that couples 'cannot be married at Sewagram Ashram unless one of the party is a Harijan'.[56] 'If I had my way I would persuade all caste Hindu girls coming under my influence to select Harijan husbands.'[57]

In only one respect, it seems, does his reinterpretation of *varnashra-madharma* retain what may be called an element of orthodoxy; this concerns his view of the hereditary nature of *varna*. *Varna*, he explained in 1927, 'means the following on the part of us all the hereditary traditional calling of our forefathers, in so far as the traditional calling is not inconsistent with fundamental ethics, and this only for the purpose of earning one's livelihood'.[58] This position is never contro-verted, although it is qualified by his assertion that in the perfect social order all men would be Harijans. Whether considered with or without this qualification, however, the view still significantly manifests his dominant concern for social harmony. An egalitarian society, he believed, in which no one was oppressed or driven to envy by the privi-leged status of another, would foster a co-operative spirit; provided, that is, that each individual accepted his father's vocation 'for the pur-pose of earning one's livelihood'. Then no energy would be wasted in

[53] Gandhi, *Young India*, 29 September 1927, and *Young India*, 20 October 1927, in *Hindu Dharma*, Ahmedabad, Navijivan, 1950, pp. 321–5.

[54] Gandhi (citing a statement of the previous October) *Harijan*, 29 April 1933, in *The Removal of Untouchability*, p. 71.

[55] Gandhi, *Caste Must Go*, p. 3.

[56] Gandhi, in *Hindustan Standard*, 5 January 1946, in *Selections*, p. 237.

[57] Gandhi, *Harijan*, 7 July 1946, in *The Removal of Untouchability*, p. 76.

[58] Gandhi, *Young India*, 20 October 1927, in *Varnashramadharma*, p. 9.

a competitive pursuit of material gain; it would be turned instead into some form of social service. 'The law of *varna* is the antithesis of competition which kills.'[59] Weaving these two beliefs in equality and heredity together, he writes of his organic conception of the harmonious social order:

The four *varnas* have been compared in the Vedas to the four members of the body, and no simile could be happier. If they are members of one body, how can one be superior or inferior to another? If the members of the body had the power of expression and each of them were to say that it was higher and better than the rest, the body would go to pieces. Even so, our body politic, the body of humanity, would go to pieces, if it were to perpetuate the canker of superiority or inferiority. It is this canker that is at the root of the various ills of our time, especially class war and civil strife. It should not be difficult for even the meanest understanding to see that these wars and strifes could not be ended except by the observance of the law of *varna*. For it ordains that every one shall fulfil the law of one's being by doing in a spirit of duty and service that to which one is born.[60]

Viewing Gandhi's activities as a reformer of the caste system over this entire period, the most striking change might appear in his attitude towards orthodoxy. In 1924 he urges the leaders of the Vykom *satyagraha* 'not to overawe the orthodox';[61] this in a campaign against untouchability that had, in fact, the most modest and limited of aims. When this is compared with Gandhi in those final hours, dauntlessly throwing down the gauntlet before an enraged orthodoxy, the transformation seems complete. Yet, on reflection, what is most remarkable is not how much Gandhi himself changed, but indeed, in such a period of history, how he managed to remain in purpose, strength, and method, so fundamentally constant.

Nowhere are these aspects of Gandhi's constancy more evident that in his advocacy of the Constructive Programme, through which he wished to forge a spirit of harmony in three major areas of Indian society: between the untouchables and caste Hindus, the Hindus and Muslims, and the villages and the growing urban areas. In each of these areas, he felt that untouchability had left its ugly stain. 'The monster of untouchability' has turned 'caste against caste, and religion against religion'.[62] And 'for the city-dweller the villages have become untouchables'.[63] If the central purpose of his life and thought is clearly

[59] Gandhi, *Harijan*, 6 March 1937, in *The Removal of Untouchability*, p. 52.

[60] Gandhi, *Harijan*, 28 September 1934, in *Varnashramadharma*, pp. 8–9.

[61] Gandhi, *Young India*, 8 May 1924, in *Removal of Untouchability*, p. 112.

[62] Gandhi, *Harijan*, 16 February 1934, in ibid., p. 261.

[63] Gandhi as quoted in D. G. Tendulkar, *Mahatma*, Delhi, The Publications Division, Government of India, 1961; new ed., Vol. IV, p. 2.

revealed anywhere, then it is in his view of the broader implications of untouchability:

The ulcer of untouchability has gone so deep down that it seems to pervade our life. Hence the unreal differences: Brahmana and Non-Brahmana, provinces and provinces, religion and religion. Why should there be all this poison smelling of untouchability? Why should we not all be children of one Indian family and, further, of one human family? Are we not like branches of the same tree?[64]

'I, for one, shall not be satisfied', he concludes, 'until, as the result of this movement [against untouchability] we have arrived at heart-unity amongst all the different races and communities inhabiting this land . . .'[65] This, if anything, was Gandhi's message to Independent India.

CASTE AFTER GANDHI

Much has been written about Gandhi's ideas being out of joint with the times: the 'time spirit' (to use an expression of his more cosmopolitan contemporary, Tagore) has seemed, in many ways, to have been against him. Gandhi always liked those lines from Thoreau's Conclusion to *Walden*: 'If a man does not keep pace with his companions, perhaps it is because he hears a different drummer. Let him step to the music which he hears, however measured or far away.'[66] Gandhi himself felt, at the end, out of step with the nation; and those in India devoted to his ideas today seem indeed to be listening to a different drummer. Even in academic seminars, where unreal or unorthodox subjects die the hardest of deaths, 'Gandhian Economics' is seldom treated today as a topic of serious discussion; and in government circles no aspect of Gandhi's thought has been dismissed with more aplomb than the 'cult of the spinning wheel'—unless it be his teaching of non-violence.

Gandhi often expressed the wish to live 125 years. If he had, perhaps he would have then seen a government and society emerge in India more responsive to his ideals. Today, as his centenary approaches, many Gandhian forms or symbols remain; but much of the substance departed with him. One can never know to which challenge he might have first turned today. With his anarchic spirit and persistent moral perspective, however, it seems likely that two fundamental developments would have troubled him above all: first, the profound sense of discord that has grown within India since Independence—not only in her external affairs but especially, Gandhi would have felt, in the divi-

64 Gandhi, *Harijan*, 10 February 1946, in *Removal of Untouchability*, p. 263.
65 Gandhi, *Harijan*, 16 February 1934, in ibid., p. 261.
66 H. D. Thoreau, *Walden and Other Writings*, New York, Random House, 1950, p. 290.

sive forces within the country itself. And second, the preoccupation in India with politics; as if, now that the major political reform of Independence had been achieved, her political interests had been forced to feed elsewhere, and found lush growth everywhere. The first of these features may be called factionalism; the second, politicization. Both are enemies of the anarchist in general, as well as of the particular Indian anarchist considered here; both, too, are historically identified by anarchism as foes of social welfare, and by Gandhi as threats to realization of *sarvodaya*, the *varnadharma* ideal. This concluding section will focus on each of these elements as they are related to caste today.

After the prayers are over, we talk. The people present in the room express only unalloyed, violent bitterness. Neither the spirit of Gandhi nor that of the Buddha is here; only resentment, hatred and suspicion.
    Saddest of all, the village is riven into two hostile blocs, one of caste-Hindus and the other of Buddhists who were previously Harijans. There is complete segregation and social boycott between them. There has been no improvement in the status of the Harijans since they embraced a new religion. They continue to be treated as untouchables. And where in Gandhi's time the two sections had lived in amity and oneness, since he was insistent on abolition of untouchability and caste distinctions, there is bitter and open antagonism now, which extends even to the precincts of the *ashram* school. No work is done together. 'Therefore we have made no progress in development work or anything', I am told, though the village is covered now by the Community Development programme. 'Our economic condition is very poor; worse than what it used to be.'
    Obviously, though the 'revolution' came to Sewagram under the personal direction of Gandhi himself, it has proved to be of a wholly transient character. Almost everything that was achieved in the village in Gandhi's time in the social and economic fields is lost already, in less than a decade after his death.[67]

This is Kusum Nair, relating her impressions of Sewagram, the Mahrashtrian village which Gandhi made his headquarters after 1936. This is a judgement on Gandhi's influence by a writer who shows, throughout, a sympathetic appreciation of his ideas. The verdict is given, moreover, in terms that Gandhi himself would have chosen as most relevant: 'resentment, hatred and suspicion', the division of the village 'into two hostile blocs' as a result of caste antipathies; the persistence of 'untouchability and caste distinctions', 'bitter and open antagonism', and the complete breakdown of social co-operation. The judgement, in short, is given on the basis of the growth, after Gandhi, of all those evils which he combated. He himself would have been the first to ask: If here in Sewagram, then what of all India?

[67] Kusum Nair, *Blossoms in the Dust*, London, Praeger, 1963, pp. 186–8.

Gandhi extolled *varnadharma* as an ideal of social harmony; a principle rooted in the conception of the four *varnas* as constituting an organic social order.[68] Yet Gandhi, as much as any of his Indian contemporaries, was fully aware of the divisive influence of caste, and condemned this, where it occurred, as another manifestation of untouchability. For Gandhi knew the villages as well as any national leader, and he accepted the force of factionalism as a basic fact of life. *Satyagraha* may be seen (and, indeed, has been brilliantly analysed)[69] as a weapon designed to reduce factionalism in all its forms; that is, as an effective technique of conflict-resolution.

What Gandhi does not seem to have appreciated, though, is the way in which the politicization of Indian society, and particularly of caste, has stimulated new and reinforced old varieties of factionalism; that is, he did not anticipate those political trends in language and caste after Independence so well described by Selig Harrison:

> Independence was an invitation to each language territory to come into its own, invoking the memory of the golden age that each can summon forth from the millenia of Indian history. Each caste group, too, saw in a free India dedicated to equality a chance in Orwell's sense to be more equal than the rest. Caste, a social order, has provided a basis for the new economic and political competition, and the new caste competitors form ranks, according to native linguistic regional ties. As economic competition grows, and as the political victors set the ground rules for the economic competition, so the unity and militance of regional lobbies and regional caste lobbies will grow.[70]

Not that caste and language represent the sole means through which the forces of factionalism and politicization find expression in India today; quite the contrary, the latter are manifest in many forms. Professor Mayer, in his contribution to this book (pp. 121–41), finds that the 'existence of opposed factions', emerges as a 'constant', while 'caste forms an important, but only one, factor' in the political situation under analysis. His essay, substantiated by recent studies like that of Paul Brass, demonstrate convincingly the pervasive nature of factionalism and politicization in the contemporary Indian scene.

[68] For a recent anthropological assessment of 'the caste society' as 'an organic system', in which intercaste competition must be regarded as action 'in defiance of caste principles', see E. R. Leach, 'What Should we Mean by Caste?' in *Aspects of Caste in South India, Ceylon and North-West Pakistan*, Cambridge, Cambridge University Press, 1960, pp. 5–7. This view, which is similar to Gandhi's in certain respects, is mentioned in connexion with Durkheim's social theory.

[69] Especially in the admirable analysis of Gandhi's *satyagraha* by Joan Bondurant, *Conquest of Violence*, California, University of California Press, revised ed., 1965.

[70] S. S. Harrison, *India: The Most Dangerous Decades*, Princeton, N.J., Princeton University Press, 1960, p. 5.

If the spirit of the times was allied with Gandhi in any sense, then it was with him as a nationalist. Whatever practical success he had as a political leader came when his own intuitive genius merged with the tide of Indian nationalism. Yet it is ironic that this nationalist should have so quickened India's political awareness, when he himself was so deeply distrustful of politics; participating in it only because: 'Politics encircle us like the coil of a snake from which one cannot get out, no matter how much one tries. I wish therefore to wrestle with the snake.'[71] During the period of Gandhi's Congress leadership the country, through nationalism, became increasingly politicized. E. M. Forster, for example, returning to India in 1945, after twenty-five years' absence (a period thus covering almost all of Gandhi's reign) wrote: 'The big change I noticed was the increased interest in politics.'[72] This seems understandable enough, considering the force of the nationalist movement. But to Gandhi, the idea of politics assuming such a pervasive form in India seemed a reprehensible prospect. His last official act can only be seen as a crying out against it: hours before his death he drafted a resolution directing the Congress Party to transform itself into a *Lok Sevak Sangh* ('People's Service Organization')—that is, to renounce politics. The fact that this advice, which has been symbolically called 'Gandhi's last will and testament', was thought absurd is indicative of the status that the political party system had attained in India by 1948.

This phenomenon of politicization is clearly evident in changing aspects of caste since Independence. As Mayer has observed, writing of the politics of local elections, '. . . caste becomes a political division of society, at the same time as it is losing its position as a ritual division'.[73] This judgement has been confirmed by numerous anthropologists and political scientists in the last decade. At the village level this has led M. N. Srinivas, for example, to stress the political significance of the local 'dominant caste'. Others have emphasized the importance of caste in local elections, or caste as the key determinant of village leadership.[74] Above the village, political scientists have

[71] Gandhi, *Young India*, 12 May 1920, in *Selections*, p. 45. The depth of this distrust of politics may be appreciated if seen against the background of other modern Indian thinkers like Vivekananda, Aurobindo, R. Tagore, M. N. Roy, and J. P. Narayan.

[72] E. M. Forster, *Two Cheers for Democracy*, London, Penguin Books, 1965, p. 324.

[73] A. C. Mayer, 'Local Government Election in a Malwa Village', in *Eastern Anthropologist*, Vol. XI, 1958, p. 202. See also Mayer's own reference to this point in his contribution to this volume.

[74] Two books especially relevant are Marriott (Ed.), *Village India*, and Park and Tinker (Eds.), *Leadership and Political Institutions in India*. In the former, the contribution of Srinivas; in the latter, those of Morris Opler and R. Bachenheimer.

described the formation and the operation of 'caste associations' and 'caste federations', thus illustrating the variety of forms that caste power may take, and the strength of its political implications. Once caste became politicized, it was understandable that factionalism should find expression through it at the village level.

But this aspect has not been confined to the rural areas; urbanization has often not led to a reduction of caste influence, for 'immigrants from rural areas . . . often tend to settle in distinct caste "colonies" within the cities [and] the consequence is greatly improved facilities for organizing. Moreover, cities teach men to forget caste as a co-operative element making for interdependence; caste becomes instead the unit in which men associate for competition against others.'[75] Finally, in reference to the larger caste associations and federations, a recent study of this subject observed that

. . . caste is shedding some of its old-time character and is acquiring a new emphasis and orientation. While still retaining a good part of the traditional modes of integration, it has entered a phase of competitive adjustment in the allocation and re-allocation of functions and power among various social groups. The institutions of caste association and caste federation are the media through which such an adaptation in roles is taking place.

The important thing is the motivation that lies behind such a process of group assertion. Here caste consciousness no doubt plays an important part in mobilizing and consolidating group positions. But the motivation behind it indicates an important shift in emphasis, from the preservation of caste traditions and customs to their transformation through political power. It is essentially a secular motivation in which mobilization of group support follows rather than precedes individual competition for power. Caste always had a political aspect to it but now the political aspect is gaining in emphasis more than ever before, especially in regard to individualized rather than group orientations to power. The network of kin and caste relationships is by stages drawn into personal networks of influence and power, and in the process greatly politicized. To this extent, caste identification and caste consciousness become means in the power struggle, the latter also influencing the normative orientation of such consciousness.[76]

The arguments set forth in this passage, as well as those points made by the sources cited above, tend to reinforce the view of caste conflict developed by Selig Harrison. He wrote in 1960: 'for caste to become the basis of economic and political competition . . . is to magnify all of

[75] W. H. Morris-Jones, *The Government and Politics of India*, London, Hutchinson, Home University Library, 1964, (cited above), pp. 65–66. See also K. Gough's essay in *Village India* for a view of a village affected by modernization and the resultant stimulus to caste competition.

[76] R. Kothari and Rushikesh Maru, 'Caste and Secularism in India: Case Study of a Caste Federation', in *Journal of Asian Studies*, Vol. XXV, November 1965, p. 49.

its worst features. Where it once exercised social control at the level of functionally integrated villages, caste now reinforces economic and political conflict. . . .[77]

In all of these developments academics have discovered much grist for research and politicians knowingly agree that politicization is a quite understandable trend. Gandhi, however, was neither an academic nor a politician (one does not notice, now or then, members of either species behaving the way he did in the months following Independence). Gandhi was a moral reformer who would have deplored the manner in which caste has found a new home in factional politics since Independence; but his technique of *satyagraha* leaves little suggestion of how he might have resisted it. Gandhi conceived the method of *satyagraha* precisely because he was involved, above all, in a quest for harmony; not a harmony which produced (in Aurobindo's words) 'a single white monotone', but rather (in words echoed as well by many of Aurobindo's contemporaries) 'a great diversity in the fundamental unity'.[78] May such a quest as Gandhi's be measured against ordinary criteria of success or failure? No more, perhaps, than a nation may be fairly judged in terms of his extraordinary demands.

[77] S. S. Harrison, op. cit., p. 101.
[78] Sri Aurobindo, *The Life Divine*, Pondicherry, Sri Aurobindo Ashram, 1960, p. 1057.

IX

The Position of the Tribal Populations in Modern India

BY CHRISTOPH VON FÜRER-HAIMENDORF

Professor of Asian Anthropology, School of Oriental and African Studies, University of London

THE coexistence of fundamentally different culture patterns and styles of living has always been a characteristic feature of the Indian stage. While in most other parts of the world rising civilizations replaced those that had preceded them, and conquering populations either eliminated or absorbed earlier inhabitants of the land, in India the arrival of new immigrants and the spread of their way of life did not necessarily cause the disappearance of earlier and materially less advanced ethnic groups. The old and the new persisted side by side, and this phenomenon of cultural and ethnic heterogeneity was only partly due to the great size of the subcontinent and the dearth of communications. There are certainly many comparatively inaccessible hill-regions where primitive tribes were sheltered from the pressure of more advanced populations, but the persistence of the tribes in a state of material and social development such as elsewhere hardly survived the end of the Neolithic age was not only due to the nature of their physical environment. More important than this was an attitude basic to Indian ideology which accepted the variety of cultural forms as natural and immutable, and did not consider their assimilation to one dominant pattern in any way desirable. A social philosophy based on the idea of the permanency and inevitability of caste distinctions saw nothing incongruous in the continuance of primitive ways of life in close proximity to centres of the highest and most sophisticated civilization. Even at times of the greatest efflorescence of Hindu culture there were no organized attempts to draw the aboriginal tribes into the orbit of Hindu caste society, for the idea of missionary activity was foreign to Hindu thinking. This does not mean, however, that none of the tribes ever became incorporated in the systems of hierarchically ranked castes. Where economic necessity or the invasion of their habitat by advanced communities led to continued interaction between aboriginals and Hindus, cultural distinctions were blurred, and what had once been self-contained and more or less independent tribes gradually acquired the status of castes. In many cases they entered the caste system on the lowest rung of the ladder. Some of the untouchable castes of Southern India, such as the Cherumans and the Panyers of Kerala, were undoubtedly at one time independent tribes, and in their physical characteristics they still resemble neighbouring tribal groups which have remained outside Hindu society.

There are some exceptions, however, and tribes such as the Meitheis of Assam achieved a position comparable to that of Kshatriyas. Aboriginals who retained their tribal identity and resisted inclusion within the Hindu fold fared on the whole better than the assimilated groups and were not treated as untouchables, even if they indulged in such low-caste practices as the eating of beef. Thus the Raj Gonds of Middle India, whose rulers vied in power with Rajput princes, used to sacrifice and eat cows without debasing thereby their status in the eyes of their Hindu neighbours, who recognized their social and cultural separateness and did not insist on conformity to Hindu patterns of behaviour. This respect for the tribal way of life prevailed as long as contacts between the aboriginals and the Hindu populations of the open plains were of a casual nature. The tribal people, though considered strange and dangerous, were taken for granted as part of the world of hills and forests, and a more or less frictionless coexistence was possible, because there was no population pressure, and the advanced communities did not feel any urge to impose their own values on people placed patently outside the sphere of Hindu civilization.

This position remained unchanged during the whole of the Muslim period. Now and then a military campaign extending for a short spell into the wilds of tribal country would bring the inhabitants temporarily to the notice of princes and chroniclers, but for long periods the hill-men and forest-dwellers were left to themselves. Under British rule, however, a new situation arose. The extension of a centralized administration over areas which had previously lain outside the effective control of princely rulers deprived many of the aboriginal tribes of their autonomy, and though British administrators had no intention of interfering with the tribesmen's rights and traditional manner of living, the very process of the establishment of law and order in outlying areas exposed the aboriginals to the pressure of more advanced populations. In areas which had previously been virtually unadminis- tered, and hence unsafe for outsiders who did not enjoy the confidence and goodwill of the aboriginal inhabitants, traders and moneylenders could now establish themselves under the protection of the British administration, and in many cases they were followed by settlers, who succeeded in acquiring large stretches of the aboriginals' land. Admin- istrative officers who did not understand the tribal system of land tenure introduced uniform methods of revenue collection, and these had the unintended effect of facilitating the alienation of tribal land to members of advanced populations. Though it is unlikely that British officials actively favoured the latter at the expense of the primitive tribesmen, little was done to stem the rapid erosion of tribal rights to the land.

In many areas the aboriginals were unable to resist the gradual alienation of their ancestral land and either gave way by withdrawing farther into hills and tracts of marginal land, or accepted the economic status of tenants or agricultural labourers on the land their forefathers had owned. There were some tribes, however, who rebelled against an administration which allowed outsiders to deprive them of their land, and as early as the end of the eighteenth century there were tribal revolts, the suppression of which necessitated prolonged military opera- tions. In Chhotanagpur and the Santal Parganas such rebellions of desperate tribesmen reoccurred throughout the nineteenth century, and there were minor risings in the Agency Tracts of Madras and in some of the districts of Bombay inhabitated by Bhils. In some of the fighting the aboriginals, who were determined but badly armed, suffered heavy casualties. Thus the Santals are believed to have lost about 10,000 dead in the rebellion of 1855. None of these insurrections were aimed primarily at the British administration, but they were the reaction to the exploitation and oppression of the aboriginals by Hindu landlords and moneylenders who had established themselves in tribal areas, and were sheltered by a Government which had instituted a system of land settlement and administration of justice favouring the advanced com- munities at the expense of the simple, illiterate aboriginals.

In some cases these rebellions led to official inquiries and to legis- lation aimed at protecting the aboriginals' rights to their land. The effect of such legislation varied from province to province and district to district, but seen in historical perspective it appears that land alienation laws had, on the whole, only a palliative effect. In most areas encroach- ments on the land held by aboriginals continued even in the face of protective legislation. It is one of the ironies of history that before, and even after, 1947 Indian nationalist opinion blamed British policy and British officials for unduly favouring the aboriginal tribes, and isolating them as a protected and sheltered minority from the main body of the Indian people. In fact, the deterioration of the aboriginals' position was largely due to the effects of the system of administration introduced by the British, even though this result was certainly not intended. It is true that many British officials sympathized with the tribesmen, to whose character and way of life they were greatly attracted, and some of the most fervent advocates of tribal rights were certainly found among officers of the Indian Civil Service. Yet their recommendations contained in numerous reports of commissions of inquiry were only seldom implemented in full, and even where they were incorporated in legislation they did not often prove very effective.

There was only one part of British India where a policy of non-interference and protection enabled the tribal populations to persist to a considerable extent within the framework of their traditional culture. In the hill-tracts of Assam, both to the south and to the north of the Brahmaputra Valley, the situation was different from that prevailing in peninsular India. Tribes such as the Nagas, Abors, and Daflas were the sole inhabitants of a vast region of rugged and largely wooded hills into which the population settled in the plains of Assam had never penetrated. A small volume of barter trade between hills and plains was carried on by tribesmen from the foothills visiting some villages on the edge of the plains, but most of the hill-people never set foot in the Brahmaputra Valley. When in the second half of the nineteenth century and during the first decades of the twentieth century the British extended their administrative control over part of the hill-regions, they did not encourage the entry of plainsmen, but devised a system of administration which allowed the hill-men to run their affairs along traditional lines and left the government of the villages in the hands of their own tribal dignitaries. Apart from such superior officers as the deputy commissioners and subdivisional officers, a few clerks to do the office work, and a small force of Assam Rifles, no outsiders were posted in such areas as the Naga Hills District, and the settlement of traders and shopkeepers was strictly controlled. No plainsman was allowed to acquire land in the hills, and the indigenous system of land-tenure was retained virtually unchanged. The one major intervention in tribal affairs was the prohibition of head-hunting and the suppression of intervillage warfare. But even this limited interference extended only to the fully administered areas. Both on the Assam–Burma frontier and along the Assam–Tibet frontier there remained regions over which the Government of India exercised no administrative control, and where the old tribal life continued without any outside interference.

As a result of this policy the hill-people of Assam suffered none of the exploitation and loss of land which so many of the aboriginals of peninsular India had experienced. This did not mean, however, that the hill-tribes of Assam remained totally isolated from developments in other parts of India. The establishment of schools, partly maintained by the Government and partly by Christian missions, brought a measure of education to the hill-men, and for the past fifty years there have been Nagas who had been sent outside the Naga Hills for further education, and had then returned to work as doctors, schoolteachers, or clerks. No such development had occurred in the hill-tracts north of the Brahmaputra, where a loose system of political control did not include any substantial educational or development work.

During the last years of British rule in India the policy to be adopted *vis-à-vis* the aboriginal tribes became a matter of passionate controversy. Certain anthropologically minded administrators, such as J. H. Hutton, J. P. Mills, and W. V. Grigson, advocated a policy of protection, which in some specific cases involved even a measure of seclusion, and this policy was ably defended by the well-known anthropologist and social worker Verrier Elwin. Indian nationalists and Congress leaders, on the other hand, attacked the idea of segregation and seclusion on the ground that it threatened to perpetuate a division within the Indian nation, and delayed the integration of the aboriginals with the rest of the Indian population. Advocates of this view saw in any measure designed to prevent a tribal community from being swamped by more advanced Hindu populations a British plot to create new minorities, and one of the critics of the protectionist policy invented the slogan of the 'anthropological zoo' in which the aboriginals were supposedly to be kept. This controversy had mainly been sparked off by the creation of the so-called 'Excluded Areas', backward regions inhabited by tribal populations to which, according to the Government of India Act, 1935 (para 91, 92), Acts of the Dominion Legislature or of the Provincial Legislatures were to apply only if the Governor of the province so directed. The intention of this provision had been to prevent the extension of legislation designed for advanced areas to backward areas where primitive inhabitants might be adversely affected by laws unsuitable to their special condition, but Indian nationalists saw in it a device to retain British control over selected areas, some of which were of strategic and some of special economic importance. We shall see, however, that after the attainment of Independence the Government of India adopted a somewhat similar policy. The North-East Frontier Agency (generally referred to as N.E.F.A.) was established as an area excluded from the State of Assam, and placed under a special administration responsible to the President through the Ministry of External Affairs, and within several states regions inhabited mainly by aboriginal tribes were notified as Scheduled Areas, for which the Governor of the state had a special responsibility.

Thus in 1947 a 'tribal problem' had already crystallized, and this was acknowledged by the architects of the Indian Constitution, who provided for the notification of 'Scheduled Tribes' and their protection by special legislation. But before we review the policy adopted by the Government of India and the individual states *vis-à-vis* the tribal populations, it is necessary to set out the details of the problem in greater detail.

According to the Census of 1961 the total population of Scheduled Tribes was 29,446,300, and this represented an increase of over 7 million compared with the figure for 1951. Thus nearly 30 million people were officially recognized as standing outside the Hindu caste system and forming a minority deserving of special treatment. Though compared with the total population of the Indian Union of 437,313,115, 30 million more or less primitive people spread unevenly over most of the states are numerically not a very important element, they nevertheless add appreciably to the heterogeneity of the Indian nation, and demographic developments over the past fifteen years do not suggest that there is any immediate prospect of their absorption within any of the larger sections of the population. The greatest concentrations of Scheduled Tribes are in the states of Andhra Pradesh (1.3 million), Assam (2 million), Bihar (4.2 million), Gujarat (2.7 million), Madhya Pradesh (6.6 million), Maharashtra (2.4 million), Orissa (4.2 million), Rajasthan (2.3 million) and West Bengal (2 million). The compact tribal population of the North-East Frontier Agency was only partly included in the Census operations of 1961, and those not enumerated would have to be added to the total figure for Scheduled Tribes.

Though set apart from the great mass of the Hindu population, the aboriginals are themselves divided into numerous ethnic groups differing, in race, language, and culture. As the most ancient population element in the subcontinent, the aboriginals belong clearly to very archaic racial strata. The oldest of these is formed by the Veddoids, so called after the Veddas of Ceylon. They represent a racial type which extends from South Arabia eastwards across India, and as far as parts of the South-East Asian mainland and Indonesia. The Veddoids are dark-skinned, and often curly-haired; their faces are roundish or heart-shaped, with broad and depressed noses, a low forehead, and pronounced superorbital ridges. Intermixed with more progressive racial types, the Veddoid element is found in nearly all the tribes of Southern and Middle India, but is virtually absent among the hill-tribes of Assam and the North-East Frontier Agency. These tribes belong to a racial stratum usually described as Palaeo-Mongoloid, which extends over wide areas of South-East Asia. Not only the hill-tribes of Burma, such as Chins and Kachins, but even the Dayaks of Borneo and the Ifugaos of the Philippines have close racial affiinities with some of the tribal people of North-East India. A slight Mongoloid element is discernible also among some of the hill-tribes of Bihar and Orissa, such as the Saoras and Bondos, and it is not unlikely that in prehistoric times, before the invasion of India by waves of peoples of Europoid race, there was some marginal contact between the Veddoids inhabiting Middle and Southern India and the Mongoloids who occupied the Himalayan region and the North-East.

In the discussion of the prospects for the integration of the aboriginals within the majority of the Indian population, these racial factors are often overlooked. Many of the aboriginals, whether they are of Veddoid or of Mongoloid type, diverge in appearance considerably from the dominant population of their respective regions, and even complete cultural and linguistic assimilation cannot remove the fact that a Naga looks very different from the member of an Assamese Hindu caste, and a Kadar stands out from the general Hindu population of Cochin. It is all the more remarkable that despite racial differences no less fundamental than those found in countries with acute race problems, there have never been any cases of racial tension in India. While religion and language have frequently been factors in political discussion and controversy, distinctions in physical make-up have never been of any political significance. One of the causes of this racial harmony may be inherent in the ideology of Hindu caste society, which accepts that humanity is divided into totally and intrinsically distinct groups. As E. R. Leach has pointed out, in Hindu eyes 'people of different caste are, as it were, of different species',[1] and racial differences are therefore accepted as natural. Since the endogamy and social exclusiveness of Hindu castes are by themselves a bar to close

[1] E. R. Leach (Ed.), 'Aspects of Caste in South India, Ceylon, and North-West Pakistan', *Cambridge Papers in Social Anthropology*, No. 2, 1960, p. 7.

intergroup relations, there is no need to place social distance between racially distinguished groups. The normal operation of the caste system is quite sufficient to prevent intermarriage, commensality, and intimate social intercourse between members of different tribes, and prejudices against racial mixture such as exist in South Africa or America do not arise in a situation where even castes of identical racial characteristics abstain from intermarriage. Indeed, in the present state of Indian society there is very little likelihood of any substantial miscegenation involving people of basically different racial groups, and whatever progress in the cultural assimilation of tribal communities may be made, there can be no doubt that for a long time to come most tribes will persist as groups of distinct racial characteristics.

The fact that despite its great racial diversity India has been free of racial tensions does not signify an indifference to racial characteristics. Certain features, such as lightness of skin colour, are socially highly valued, and the folk-image of the man or woman of high social status is associated with a specific physical type in which Europoid features predominate. It would be unrealistic to assume that the aboriginals' divergence from this ideal type will not be to the disadvantage of individuals whose educational and personal qualifications should enable them to compete for positions of prominence and social prestige.

Another factor which separates many of the aboriginal tribes from the majority of the Hindu population of their respective states is that of linguistic diversity. The Census of India, 1961, lists a total of 1,549 languages spoken by Indian as their mother-tongues, and the majority of these are unwritten languages spoken by tribal communities. Among the tribal languages, sixty-five belong to the Austro-Asiatic group, and are spoken by 6,192,495 persons. While in India there are only 377,993 speakers of Mon-Khmer languages, those of the Munda group are spoken by 5,814,496 persons, and among these there are 3,247,058 speakers of Santal, 736,524 of Mundari, and 648,066 of Ho. The greatest number of speakers of Tibeto-Burman languages is only 3,183,505, of which some 200,000 speak various Tibetan dialects. Most of the languages of these groups are unwritten tribal tongues, such as the languages of the various Naga tribes, and it is among them that we find the greatest diversity. While some languages, as, for instance, Garo, are spoken by as many as 300,000 persons, others are current only in very limited areas consisting perhaps of three or four villages.

The Dravidian language family contains, besides languages possessing a great literature, such as Tamil, Telugu, Kannada, and Malayalam, a number of unwritten tongues spoken by tribal communities. The number of speakers of these tribal tongues varies between figures of over 1½ million, in the case of the Gonds, and a few hundred in that of the 765 Todas and 862 Kotas, small tribes of the Nilgiris, each speaking a language of its own. Even among the Aryan languages there are some which are scheduled as tribal, Bhili with 2,439,611 speakers being the most important.

Language, however, is not an immutable feature, and while a tribal community cannot change its racial make-up in order to conform to the characteristics of the caste groups dominant in the region, it can become proficient in the main regional language. The first step in such a process of assimilation is usually bilingualism, and many aboriginals in contact with advanced populations are fluent in one, and sometimes even in two, languages other than their mother-tongue. Sometimes bilingualism is only a transitional phase followed by the decline, and ultimate extinction, of the tribal tongue. A process of linguistic assimilation has gone on for hundreds and probably thousands of years, and many tribal communities have lost their original tongues and speak today one of the main languages of India. Thus more than half of the Gonds of Middle India do not even know Gondi any longer, but speak Hindi, Marathi, or Telugu, according to the region in which they are settled.

The smaller a tribal community, the greater is the likelihood that it will lose its original language and adopt the language of economically stronger and culturally more advanced neighbours. Examples of the displacement of one language by another are numerous. Telugu, one of the written Dravidian languages, is steadily gaining ground at the cost of minor unwritten tribal tongues, which also belong to the Dravidian language group. This process can be observed in the Telingana districts of Andhra Pradesh. The Koyas of some groups of villages still speak their tribal Gondi dialect, but use Telugu as a second language for communication with their Telugu-speaking neighbours. The majority of Koyas, however, have given up Gondi altogether and speak Telugu, also among themselves. In the Adilabad district the Kolams living on the plains have similarly lost their tribal language and speak only Telugu, while in the hills there are still flourishing Kolam communities speaking Kolami. In the western part of the Adilabad district, which after the break-up of Hyderabad State was incorporated in Maharashtra, Kolams have come in contact with Marathi-speaking populations, and these same groups no longer speak Kolami, but only Marathi. The result in this case is a fragmentation of the Kolam tribe into a Kolami-speaking, a Telugu-speaking, and a

Marathi-speaking section. Members of the two latter are no longer able to communicate with each other, and the two sections have hence become endogamous subdivisions of the tribe. Both the Telugu- and the Marathi-speaking Hindu castes form in their respective areas the politically, economically, and socially superior populations, and the loss of the Kolams' tribal language is followed by a rapid acculturation to the locally dominant culture pattern.

The contact zones between tribal and non-tribal populations provide instructive examples of the manner in which a new language may infiltrate into the speech of small communities. The Bondos of the Orissa highlands, for instance, speak a Munda language, but in communications with their lowland Hindu neighbours they employ Oriya. As such contact is mainly in the sphere of commerce, it is not surprising that the Oriya terms for the higher numerals, for weights and measures, and other concepts connected with trade, have been incorporated into the Bondo speech. It is more remarkable, on the other hand, that many prayers and magical formulae are always spoken in Oriya, because the Bondos think it proper that such superior beings as deities and spirits should be addressed in a 'superior' language. Thus Oriya is fast becoming the ritual and not only the trade language of the Bondos. One can easily foresee that with the introduction of Primary-school education imparted through the medium of Oriya the original Munda language of the Bondos will increasingly lose importance, and that the $2\frac{1}{2}$ thousand Bondos will ultimately become entirely Oriya-speaking.

What happens if the language of a tribal community is displaced by that of a dominant neighbouring population? The language of the latter may not have terms for certain key concepts of the tribal culture. It is possible that some of the terms will be retained and incorporated in the adopted language, and by analysing such terms linguists can identify a substratum. But more frequently terms for specific culturally significant concepts are lost, together with the rest of the language, and in that case the ideas which they reflect may be transformed in the process of being clothed in a new linguistic medium. To take an example, the Gondi word *pen* has the meaning 'supernatural being, god, spirit'. Among the different categories of supernatural beings described by this term, there are benevolent deities as well as spirits which are potentially both benevolent and malignant, according to the manner man approaches them. If for such an inherently neutral spirit the Hindi and Marathi term *bhut* or the Telugu term *dayam* is used, there is at once a change in attitude, for *bhut* and *dayam* signify malevolent spirits invariably hostile to man, and not spirits of an ambivalent nature such as Gonds describe as *pen*. Conversely the Hindi term *deo* means a divinity rather more exalted than a Gondi *pen*, and by applying the terms *deo* and *bhut* to the various figures of the Gond spirit-world, as it is done by the Hindi-speaking Gonds of such areas as Chattisgarh, a division into two contrasting categories originally foreign to Gond thinking is brought into a tribe's religious system.

Whereas in this case linguistic change has led to a modification of concepts, the adoption of a new language may also involve the acquisition of entirely new concepts. If the members of a primitive tribe lacking pronounced pollution concepts change over to the use of a language possessing an elaborate vocabulary for distinct grades of ritual status, ranging from extreme pollution to a high degree of ritual purity, they will necessarily adopt some of the corresponding concepts and become, so to say, pollution-conscious. In such a case the spread of a language is accompanied by a diffusion of ideas and also, resulting from their acceptance, by a diffusion of behaviour patterns.

Whatever the results of linguistic change for the development of tribal cultures may be, there can be no doubt that in an age of rapidly improving communications extreme diversity of languages cannot persist unmodified. In some parts of the Naga Hills one could, even when travelling on foot, pass through three different language areas in a single day's march, and this state of affairs could only prevail because villages were isolated from each other by long-standing feuds, and there was no real need for any common language to enable people from distant areas to converse with each other. The pacification and opening up of tribal areas has put an end to the isolation of tiny communities, and there is now a need for a common language. In most cases the regional dominant language can fulfil the role of a lingua franca, and in Assam and the adjoining hill-tracts, for instance, Assamese is used not only for communications between the hill-men and the plains people, but also often for communication between members of different tribes.

Yet not everywhere is the situation as simple as in Assam, where only one language can possibly qualify as a suitable medium of intertribal communication. In other regions the position is far more complicated, for several languages may at one time or other have been in competition with each other. A concrete example may elucidate this point. When I began to work in the Adilabad district of Hyderabad, no less than seven languages were spoken within that district, and it was not unusual for aboriginals to be fluent in as many as four. There were, first of all, three tribal languages, namely, Gondi, Kolami, and Naikpodi, all Dravidian tongues listed as separate languages in the Census of India. Of these three Gondi was the most important and most widely spoken. Most Kolams and many Naikpods were proficient also in Gondi, but it was rare for a Gond to know either Kolami or Naikpodi. In the southern and eastern parts of the district Telugu was spoken by the Hindu peasantry, by itinerant merchants and some minor government employees, whereas in the northern and western parts Marathi held a comparable position. Throughout the district village records were kept in Marathi, for most of the village accountants (*patwari*) were Marathi Brahmans. The official language, however, in which the *taluq* and district administration was carried on was Urdu, and many of the officers of the Government knew no other language. It was not unusual, therefore, for a Gond to speak Gondi at home, Telugu to his money-lender, Marathi when dealing with the village accountant and many traders, and Urdu to government officials. That a good many Gonds were able to do this is a measure of the intelligence and resourcefulness of aboriginals pitchforked between the conflicting influences of different advanced populations. Today the former Adilabad district is divided between Andhra Pradesh and Maharashtra, and Telugu and Marathi have been gaining in importance, while Urdu, the previous state language, is of less relevance, though still used for communications between aboriginals and many of the older government servants.

The attitude of the Government of India and the various state governments to the tribal languages is ambivalent. In Andhra Pradesh the use of Gondi as the medium of instruction in Primary schools for tribal children, which the Nizam's Government introduced in 1944, has been virtually abandoned and no more school books in Gondi have been printed since the break-up of Hyderabad State. The avowed policy of the Government is clearly to educate all children through the medium of Telugu, and though the use of Gondi in the initial phases of Primary education has not been officially banned and Gond teachers still speak to Gond children in Gondi, there has been no encouragement for the use of tribal languages, and as soon as stocks of Gondi school books are exhausted Gondi will presumably become extinct as a written language.

Though educational experts in most Indian states are unanimous in advocating education in the mother-tongue, at least up to High School level, this principle is not applied to tribal children, even in the case of such large tribal groups as Santals or Hos, who speak languages not even remotely related to the dominant language of the state. Only in the North-East Frontier Agency have determined efforts been made to produce books and educational material in tribal languages and to begin instruction in the pupils' mother-tongue, though changing over to Assamese in the later stages.

The Scheduled Areas and Scheduled Tribes Commission set up by the Government of India in 1960 under Article 339 of the Constitution severely criticized the reluctance of state governments to satisfy the tribes' demand for Primary education in their own language. Under Article 350A of the Constitution it has to be the endeavour of every state to provide adequate facilities for instruction in the mother-tongue at the Primary stage of education to children belonging to linguistic minority groups, but the Commission pointed out that some of the states have taken this matter very casually, and failed to provide textbooks even in the major tribal languages. The Commission argued that:

...if it has been possible for the N.E.F.A. Administration to produce in five years well over a hundred textbooks in thirteen different languages, it should certainly be possible to have textbooks in Saora, Kui and Gondi. In Assam several of the many tribal languages are recognized for examination purposes by the University of Gauhati which has also recognized the Abor language used in N.E.F.A.[2]

Despite the progress achieved in Assam and some efforts of tribal leaders in Bihar, where there is a popular movement aiming at the creation of a literature in tribal languages, the prospects for the future of the tribal languages are poor, and it does not seem that the admonitions of the Commission have moved state governments to change their policy. Indeed, it can be foreseen that in most states, though probably not in Assam, they will gradually give way to the literate languages spoken by the dominant advanced communities which control the cultural, economic, and political life of the states in which the tribal populations are living.

In any context other than that of India the predictable disappearance of languages spoken by well over 12 million people would be considered a tragedy, and it is indeed tragic that not only these languages but much of the poetry and oral epic literature existing in these languages seem doomed to extinction. Yet, in comparison with the total population of India, the aboriginal tribes appear only as insignificant splinter groups, and there is very little public concern about the fate of their linguistic

[2] *Report of the Scheduled Areas and Scheduled Tribes Commission*, Vol. 1, 1960–1, p. 226.

heritage. The voluminous publications issued by the Office of the Commissioner for Scheduled Castes and Scheduled Tribes, and other agencies concerned with the welfare of the aboriginals, contain very little information on the problem of tribal languages, and it is difficult to avoid the conclusion that politicians and officials alike regard their ultimate disappearance as inevitable and even desirable in the interest of the integration of the tribes with the majority communities. It may be argued that the Census figures do not support the assumption that the tribal languages are bound to become extinct. The number of speakers of some of the major tribal tongues has not declined, and may even have risen on account of the general population increase. Thus there were about 4,601,000 speakers of Munda languages in 1931, and 5,814,496 were enumerated in 1961, while during the same period the number of Gondi-speakers fell from 1,865,000 to 1,501,431. Neither of these figures indicates dramatic changes in the position of the tribal languages, and the former indicates indeed the vitality of what is probably the most ancient language group in the subcontinent. But in the period to which they refer the tribal people were not yet affected by the programme of mass education which now brings the respective state languages to many of the remotest villages, nor, by that time, had the improvement of communications opened the areas of tribal populations to the incursions of outsiders who nowadays penetrate many of the last refuge areas of tribal culture.

Languages spoken by many hundreds of thousands of aboriginals inhabitating compact areas and the languages of the hill-people of Assam and N.E.F.A., where contact with non-tribal populations is relatively superficial, will probably survive for several generations. Other tribal languages were already in a state of rapid disintegration at the time of the Census of 1931, when several Census superintendents, among them those of the United Provinces, Mysore, and Baroda, commented on the displacement of tribal tongues by the languages of advanced communities. Under present conditions bilingualism will undoubtedly rapidly increase, for whenever school education is imparted in a language other than the children's mother-tongue a second language is soon acquired. Where the growth of political consciousness has led to a conscious evaluation of tribal identity, and hence the attachment to a tribal language, bilingualism would seem to be a solution which enables a tribal community to participate in the wider national life without losing touch with its own cultural heritage.

Besides the differences of race and language, there are various cultural factors which set the aboriginals apart from the bulk of Hindu society. Some of these are intangible and do not lend themselves to statistical assessment, but for many years the factor of religion was used as a criterion by which the tribes were distinguished from such communities as Hindus and Muslims. In the Census of 1931 about 8.2 million people were returned as adherents of tribal religions, but in more recent census reports tribal religions were not separately listed but were included under the head 'Others'. The reasons for the discontinuation of the heading 'Tribal Religions' are partly of a practical and partly of a political nature. Tribal religions are clearly not as easily definable as Islam or Christianity, and whereas usually no doubt exists whether a person is a Muslim or an adherent of a tribal religion, it is not equally easy to distinguish between some tribal cults and certain types of popular Hinduism. The political objections to the separate listing of tribal religions are based on the argument that Census statistics on religion tend to perpetuate communal divisions. In the 1931 Census the Commissioner had pointed out that 'the Census cannot hide its head in the sand like the proverbial ostrich, but must record as accurately as possible facts as they exist',[3] but his successors may have felt that the political arguments against the separate listing of tribal religions were too powerful to be disregarded, and the heading 'Tribal Religions' was removed from the Census reports.

The tables of the 1961 Census contain separate statistics only for Buddhism, Christianity, Hinduism, Islam, and Sikhism. All minor religions, including those previously classified as 'tribal', were collectively presented under the heading of 'Others', but from the figures for states and districts with a strong tribal element it is clear that many persons previously returned as adherents of tribal religions were now classified as Hindus. Thus in Andhra Pradesh, which contains a considerable population of aboriginals practising tribal cults, only 1,340 persons were classified under 'Others' in 1961, while in 1951 this figure was still 27,257. The fact that adherents of tribal religions were nearly all included among Hindus can be deduced from the figures for such districts as Adilabad, Mahbubnagar, and Warangal. The number of Gonds enumerated in Adilabad District in 1941 was 71,874, and virtually all of them professed a tribal religion and considered themselves entirely separate from Hindus. In my book *The Raj Gonds of Adilabad*[4] I have described the cult of the tribal deities of the Gonds, and recent visits to Adilabad have convinced me that there is no

---

[3] *Census of India*, 1931, Vol. 1: *India*, Part I: *Report*, p. 379.

[4] London, Macmillan, 1948.

change in Gond religion which would justify their classification as Hindus. Yet, in 1961 only two persons were returned under the head 'Other Religions' and there can be no doubt that all the Gonds were classified as Hindus. The same procedure must have been followed in regard to the Koyas of Warangal District, who in 1941 numbered 22,481 and in regard to the small tribe of Chenchus, primitive food-gatherers of Mahbubnagar District. For in Warangal only twenty-six members of 'Other Religions' were listed and in Mahbubnagar this category is represented by one single individual.

In West Bengal the number of persons classified under 'Other Religions' fell from 116,629 in 1951 to 39,727 in 1961, and in Bihar it dropped in the same period from 874,408 to 755,838. Detailed figures for Bihar are contained in the special tables for scheduled castes and scheduled tribes published as Part VA of the *Census of India*, 1961, Volume IV. In these tables the tribal religions of the Hos and the Santals are listed separately, and it is thus apparent how many Hos and Santals were returned as Hindus and how many as adherents of their original tribal religion. In the whole of Bihar 185,951 Hos were classified as professing the Ho religion, whereas 118,909 were returned as Hindus. But only 89,751 Santals were returned as adherents of their tribal religion, while 1,409,899 were listed as Hindus. Of the 735,025 Oraons of Bihar, on the other hand, 428,868 were classified as Hindus, 173,245 as Christians and the rest as members of 'other religions'. The tendency to include the aboriginals among the Hindus is here clearly noticeable, and it becomes even more obvious in the returns for some of the districts of other states. Thus in the Koraput district of Orissa, which is the home of such well-known tribes as Gadabas and Bondos, no single person was classified under 'Other Religions', and—with the exception of a few members of tribes who may have been converted to Christianity—all aboriginals must have been included among Hindus. Even in Nagaland, where Hinduism had long been unable to gain a foothold, of a total population of 369,700 persons only 137,484 were classified under 'Other Religions', which in this case certainly means the tribal religion, while there were 34,677 Hindus, as well as 195,598 Christians, representing the large group of Nagas converted to Christianity.

The officially inspired tendency to classify members of aboriginal tribes as Hindus and to play down the distinctions between tribal religions and popular Hinduism must not be taken as indicative of an organized movement for the conversion of the aboriginals to Brahmanical

Hinduism. Apart from the discouragement of such customs as cow sacrifice and the use of intoxicating liquor as an offering to tribal gods, there is on the part of the local Hindu communities little desire to make the aboriginals change their beliefs and religious practices. Though in areas where aboriginals and Hindus stand in close contact Hindu ideas and customs are gradually spreading to tribal communities, they usually find acceptance as an addition to tribal beliefs rather than as their replacement. 'Conversions' of tribesmen to Hinduism in a sense similar to conversions to Christianity or Islam are comparatively rare, even though in recent years Hindu missions have been active in some tribal regions of Middle India. Their efforts have been concentrated more on the modification of social customs than on the propagation of a new doctrine. As some of the more puritanical Christian missionaries, such as the American Baptists operating in the Naga Hills, set out to wean the Nagas from alcohol and introduced new types of dress, so have some of these Hindu missionaries interfered in matters of diet and clothing, and have thus brought about changes in cultural matters unconnected with religion. Even where there are no such agencies for the propagation of the Hindu way of life, schoolteachers and minor government officials, who are almost invariably non-tribals, tend to discourage tribal customs which appear objectionable to Hindu sentiment, and although India is officially a secular state, and great care is taken not to interfere with the practices of such major religions as Islam and Christianity, there have been instances of official interference with such tribal religious practices as animal sacrifices.

It would seem that in this respect there are certain discrepancies between the policies advocated by the Central Government and those pursued by individual states. The official policy of the Government of India is one of tolerance towards the beliefs, customs, and way of life of the tribal people, whereas some of the state governments have shown themselves less sensitive to the right of tribal communities to follow their traditional pattern of life even in matters not affecting the interests of other sections of the population.

The conditions under which aboriginal tribes have to adjust themselves to contact with other communities vary so greatly that generalizations applying to the whole of India cannot be valid. I propose therefore to discuss the present situation of the tribes in three specific areas with which I am familiar, and each of which presents certain problems of its own. The three selected areas are the hills of Travancore, the Telingana region of Andhra Pradesh, and the North-East Frontier Agency.

The forested hills of the part of Kerala which constituted the princely state of Travancore are the home of a number of tribes, some of whom are traditionally food-gatherers (for instance, the Malapantarams), while others are primitive shifting cultivators. Under the Government of Travancore they enjoyed special rights and privileges in the state forests, and the forest department was invested with wide powers to prevent the exploitation of aboriginals by outsiders. Today the situation has radically changed, for soon after 1947 the hills were invaded by large numbers of land-hungry plains people, who cleared the forests and settled on state land in defiance of the forest laws. With the consequent virtual disappearance of forest in many of the hill-regions which constituted the aboriginals' ancestral homeland, the protection which the tribes used to enjoy became largely illusory. Tribes which had persisted in their traditional way of life in the shelter of dense forests and of hills accessible only by footpaths find themselves today face to face with colonists from the lowlands who have denuded the forests and established their villages in valleys which, even ten years ago, were the haunts of elephant and bison. Against these settlers, hungry for cultivable land and indifferent to the far older rights of the tribesmen, the forest rules do not afford effective protection.

The type of shifting cultivation practised by most of the aboriginal tribes is dependent on the existence of large forest tracts, and the small patches on which the tribesmen used to cultivate millet and hill-rice made no appreciable inroads on the large forest reserves of the state. For they tilled every plot for only one or, at most, two years; as they did not remove the stumps of felled trees, little erosion took place, and when they abandoned a plot the forest quickly closed in on the fallow fields.

Today the areas still open for this type of shifting cultivation are few, and the destruction of forest through the more intensive cultivation of immigrants from the plains has deprived many aboriginals of their traditional means of livelihood. The establishment of tea, rubber, and cardamon estates in the last century resulted in an exodus of many aboriginals from large areas in the high ranges, but until some years ago there was still sufficient untouched forest in which they could find refuge. Now, however, the aboriginals are being squeezed out between the pressure of the old-established commercial estates and the uncontrolled waves of agricultural immigrants from the plains.

Incapable of competing with these new settlers on equal terms, the aboriginals are bound to lose in the scramble for land, and unless urgent and drastic measures for their protection are taken, they will be deprived of even the small areas of land which they now occupy. Their difficulties lie not so much in an inability to develop more efficient agricultural methods, but in their inability to preserve for their own use any land which they have made suitable for permanent cultivation.

Whether we investigate the economic position of the Muthuvans, the Mannans, the Uralis, or the Ulladans, we find that it is just in those localities in which the aboriginals had succeeded in constructing irrigated paddy fields, terraced garden plots, or cardamon lands that they lost the fruits of their labours to members of more advanced communities.

At this stage the prime need is therefore protection against the alienation of land still held by aboriginals, and the demarcation of areas from which they cannot be ousted. All other measures devised for the benefit of the tribals depend on the effectiveness of such a policy.

In Kerala there are no linguistic barriers between the tribes and other sections of the population. The aboriginals speak either Malayalam or, in the case of tribes living close to the Madras border, a dialect of Tamil. There is consequently no difficulty in extending normal Primary education to tribal children except for the distance of small isolated settlements from villages where a school can economically be maintained. In the whole of Kerala, which includes not only the former states of Travancore and Cochin, but also the Malayalam-speaking parts of Madras Presidency, there were in 1961 a total of eighty-four Primary schools and nineteen Basic schools specially for tribals. The state government has opened a number of Ashram schools, which are residential and have a craft bias, and these meet the problem of providing education for aboriginal children from widely dispersed settlements.

As the exploitation of the forests plays an important part in the economy of Kerala, and the aboriginals have an unrivalled familiarity with forest life, there are good prospects for their continued employment as forest labourers. With the progress of education the more skilled and responsible positions in the forest service should gradually come within their reach, but it would be unrealistic to assume that within a space of one or two generations people who until a few years ago lived in an economic style hardly superior to that of Neolithic man could adjust themselves by their own efforts to the complex economic and social system of Kerala. Protection and the continuation of special privileges will be required for many years to come if the former free forest-dwellers are not to sink even below the level of landless proletariat of untouchable caste.

The greatest danger facing the aboriginals of Southern India is a loss of the self-confidence which has enabled them to live fearlessly in forests inhabited by wild beasts. The distinguished Indian anthropologist Dr. A. Aiyappan describes how 'frustration and a feeling of inadequacy seem to make members of the small tribal communities in the South suffer from a severe inferiority complex', and how 'bold heroes of the jungle who for sport net and spear tigers, quake with fear in the presence of revenue inspectors'. This timidity is a result of the attitude of the Hindu plainsmen, who use any means to denigrate the tribes. Dr. Aiyappan tells how the Aranadans of the Nilambur forests, though ruthlessly exploited by Muslim forest contractors, prefer to work for these employers, because the Hindus treat the Aranadans as impure and keep them at a distance. The same author describes the plight of the Mudugas of the Attapady valley, who until recently had a fair degree of economic security as slash-and-burn cultivators, but are now being deprived of their ancestral lands as the hills where they used to live are being opened up by the construction of roads, and severe restrictions have been imposed on their traditional right to clear and cultivate the hill-slopes. The subsistence and survival of these and other tribes have been made problematic by the vacillations in government policy towards shifting cultivation. 'The matter has been discussed threadbare by national and international bodies of experts, and the discussions seem endless, but meanwhile the distress of the tribesmen is welling up.'[5]

While in Kerala the population of Scheduled Tribes is only 134,000, representing less than 1 per cent of the total population, the tribes of Andhra Pradesh number approximately 1½ million persons and constitute 3.68 per cent of the state's total population. The Andhra districts of the state, which were part of the former Madras Presidency, have a history of tribal development and administration different from that of the Telingana districts of the former Hyderabad State. The following more detailed account of the fortunes of tribal communities relates to parts of Hyderabad State where until the beginning of the century aboriginals were in undisputed possession of large tracts of land. In the district of Adilabad, for instance, the highlands between the valleys of the Godavari and the Penganga were almost exclusively inhabited by aboriginals. Gond rajas exercised judicial powers over groups of villages, and some tracts of land were recognized as the estates of such tribal chiefs. But the then prevailing system of land-tenure did not provide for individual rights to cultivate land, and as the population was sparse and land plentiful, Gond cultivators were free to clear and

[5] A. Aiyappan, 'In the South', in *Tribal India*, Seminar 14, Bombay, 1960, pp. 32, 33.

occupy any piece of fallow land they fancied. It was only when agricultural populations from neighbouring, and more developed, areas began to infiltrate into Adilabad District that competition for land became a serious problem.

With the gradual improvement of communications and the influx of experienced non-tribal cultivators, the land gained in value and began to attract persons of landlord class who acquired whole villages to be managed on a commercial basis. As few of the tribals had title-deeds to the land they cultivated, the new settlers found it easy to oust them from all the best areas, and within a period of thirty or forty years much of the land in the more fertile lowlands fell into the hands of non-aboriginals, while more and more of the Gonds withdrew into the hills, where, for some time, they remained comparatively unmolested. By the early 1940s this refuge area, too, had ceased to be safe for the tribals, for a policy of forest reservation deprived them of the possibility of extending the area of cultivation, and there were even cases of expulsions of whole village communities from areas notified as reserved forest without sufficient consideration to the needs of the local tribesmen. If this state of affairs had continued another decade, the majority of the Adilabad Gonds, as well as the members of several minor tribes, would have become landless and uprooted.

In 1945, however, the Nizam's Government decided on a bold policy of tribal rehabilitation. Large parts of the districts of Adilabad and Warangal were notified as Tribal Areas, in which non-aboriginals were banned from acquiring any more land. A staff of special officers was appointed to safeguard the aboriginals' interests, and regularize their right to the land. Within four years over 85 per cent of the tribals of Adilabad were given title-deeds to economic holdings of cultivable land, and the economic future of the Gonds appeared thus secure. Simultaneously with the assignment of land, other measures for the rehabilitation of the aboriginals were enacted. The most important of them was an education scheme, which provided for the training of Gonds and other tribesmen as teachers and village officers. School books were composed and printed in the Gondi language written in Devanagari script, and as soon as teachers were trained to a modest standard Primary schools for tribal children were opened in numerous tribal villages.

In order to protect the Gonds and other tribes from interference by outsiders likely to exploit them, tribal *panchayats* were instituted and invested with judiciary powers in civil as well as in minor criminal cases. All these measures were successful in raising the self-confidence of the aboriginals, and enabling them to recover their economic independence. The establishment of co-operative societies and grain-banks removed the need to rely on moneylenders, and within a few years many tribal villages were almost entirely free from indebtedness to outsiders

All these welfare activities were made possible by the creation of a special department initially attached to the Revenue Department. Some of the officers of this department, then known as Social Service, and now incorporated in a Social Welfare Department, had received anthropological training, and many of them learned to speak tribal languages. There was no abrupt change of policy *vis-à-vis* the tribal populations when after the so-called 'Police Action' of 1948 the Government of India placed the state of Hyderabad under a military administration. The subsequent democratically elected governments of the state pursued the development of tribal areas in a similar manner, and with some modifications this policy was continued even after the merger of the Telugu-speaking districts of Hyderabad State with Andhra Pradesh.

Today the aboriginals of the Telingana districts of Andhra Pradesh are in a much better position to defend their rights and protect themselves from exploitation than they were twenty years ago. But some of the special privileges have been withdrawn and the Tribal Areas Regulation of 1950, under which the tribals were removed from the jurisdiction of the normal courts, has been suspended. It is too early to say how much these developments will affect the status of the aboriginals, but when I visited Adilabad in 1964 I learnt that pressure on land owned by tribals was again increasing, and already two years earlier I found that land allotted to Koyas in Warangal district in 1947 had been alienated to non-aboriginal settlers from some of the Andhra districts. Thus it appears that the position of the tribals, though much better than in 1940, is by no means secure, and that any diminishment of vigilance on the part of those responsible for tribal welfare might well result in a new erosion of tribal rights.

The spread of literacy and education, however, has enabled the aboriginals to make use of the democratic machinery of the recently established *panchayati raj*, and some members of the old chiefly families have come back to prominence by being elected as chairmen of the new local councils. It thus seems that despite all the changes in the Gonds' fortunes, they still have confidence in their hereditary leaders, and are by no means on the way to losing their tribal identity. While in outward appearance and style of living the wealthier Gonds, as well as those who have attained to political positions or employment in government service, do not greatly differ from Hindus of comparable material status, such assimilation is, as yet, very superficial, and there are no signs of any breaking-up of the very tightly organized structure of tribal society. Contact with Hindus remains confined to economic and official relations, and Gonds continue to consider themselves as standing outside the Hindu caste system.

Totally different from the position of the aboriginals in Andhra Pradesh is the situation of the hill-tribes of Nagaland and the North-East Frontier Agency. In Andhra Pradesh, as indeed in most states, the tribes form a minority which is neither politically nor economically of much importance, and which Civil Servants as well as politicians can disregard with impunity. Indeed, many state governments seem to react to the frequent proddings of the Central Government and the Commissioner for Scheduled Castes and Scheduled Tribes with some impatience, and are often slow in spending the very considerable funds voted by the Union of Parliament for tribal welfare. In Nagaland and N.E.F.A., on the other hand, the tribes stand in the centre of interest, and the whole administrative machinery is geared to the various schemes for the development of the tribes.

The course of events in the Naga Hills since 1947 has been so bedevilled by political conflict and propaganda that no one without first-hand experience of the underlying causes of the Nagas' rebellion against the Government of India can assess the situation with any measure of accuracy. Here we are clearly not concerned with the rights and wrongs of a movement which has placed the Government of India in the embarrassing position of having to crush by superior military force a nationalistic upsurge which its leaders consider a war of national liberation. Without access to official records it is impossible to discover what went wrong in the Naga Hills immediately after the British withdrawal. The Japanese invasion of 1944 had certainly disrupted the previous administration, but the Nagas had, on the whole, proved loyal to the Government of India and the British district officers. In the past they had always enjoyed a special status and there had been very little interference with their internal affairs. Taxation had been light and the villages had been allowed complete self-government. Neither police subordinates nor forest and excise officials, who in other tribal areas have so often been a source of irritation, had ever disturbed the harmony of village life in the Naga Hills, and except for the ban on head-hunting and inter-village feuds, the administration did not concern itself with the way in which the various Naga tribes governed themselves.

After 1947 the Government of India pursued a policy which aimed at bringing all parts of its territory under a uniform administration. The Naga Hills were to be integrated into the State of Assam, and in order to achieve this the regular district administration, involving numerous officials of many different departments, was extended to the previously only lightly administered hill-tracts. While Assamese and other Indian officials posted in the Naga Hills saw themselves as the bringers of an altogether superior civilization and such benefits as schools and dispensaries, the Nagas saw in these new-comers novel rulers intent on depriving them of the virtual self-government the tribesmen had enjoyed in British days. This prospect they resented all the more as none of the Naga tribes had ever been conquered by the Assamese, who had lived in awe of the fierce hill-men. Indeed many Nagas felt that after the withdrawal of the British, who had imposed their rule over the hills, they should be allowed to run their own affairs. After protracted and fruitless negotiations between the Government of India and the leaders of the Nagas, hostilities broke out when in 1956 tribal extremists kidnapped and later murdered a pro-Indian Naga politician. A division of troops was dispatched to the Naga Hills to restore order, but many of the Naga leaders went underground, and ever since there has been a state of war between the regular Indian army and Naga guerillas. Unable to suppress the rebellion, the Government of India placed in 1957 the Naga Hills District and the Tuensang Frontier Division of N.E.F.A. under the Ministry of External Affairs, and in 1960 established a Naga state to be known as Nagaland within the framework of the Indian Union. This state was to have an administrative secretariat, a council of Ministers, and a legislative assembly, but for an interim period responsibility for law and order was vested in the Governor of Assam, who acted also as Governor of Nagaland.

The curtain of secrecy which screens events in Nagaland from the outside world prevents outside observers from understanding why the leaders of the Naga rebellion have felt unable to accept the limited autonomy granted by this arrangement, and are continuing to demand full independence and sovereignty. However unrealistic this demand may be, it is symptomatic of the desire of the tribal people to retain their cultural and national identity, even at the expense of having to forgo many developments in the material sphere. The demand is unrealistic, because material change has already gone beyond the point of no return, and only substantial financial support from the Union Government can assure the continuation of existing services, such as roads, schools, and hospitals. But it is obvious that the Naga rebels, and with them a large section of the Naga population, are convinced that political integration within the Indian Union is incompatible with the retention of their cultural characteristics and their own way of life. That they have come to this conclusion is not the fault of the Government of India, which has gone à long way in an attempt to reach a compromise, or even of the military officers trying to establish law and order, but it is the direct result of a certain arrogance found among many of the less-educated high-caste Hindus who look down upon aboriginals as savages and impure beef-eaters, and cannot see anything valuable or worth preserving in the tribal dress, art, social customs, and religion.

This attitude, often adopted by schoolteachers, medical personnel, and minor government officials, must have deeply offended the Nagas, who are a proud and independent people, used to being treated as equals by British officers such as J. H. Hutton and J. P. Mills, who had spent a lifetime learning about Naga culture. Considering the efforts made by successive Indian Governments to come to terms with the Nagas and the large sums provided for development—during the Third Five-Year Plan alone, a total of $71\frac{1}{2}$ million rupees—the continued resistance of the Nagas cannot be explained other than by the assumption of such a sense of grievance and deep-seated distrust. More information on the early course of the rebellion may prove this diagnosis wrong, but until Nagaland is opened to impartial observers, we have no alternative to guess-work, based on our knowledge of the Naga character and the fate of aboriginals in other areas where they were exposed to the influence of caste Hindus.

The tragic events in the Naga Hills have made the Government of India aware of the danger of disregarding the sensibilities of tribal populations, and in setting up the administration of N.E.F.A. special care was taken to avoid the mistakes made in the relations with the Nagas. Here it was possible to start with a clean slate, for of the 35,000 square miles of N.E.F.A. only a few hundred square miles had been under regular administration before 1947. At present N.E.F.A. is administered by the President of India through the Governor of Assam as his agent. The Governor is assisted by an adviser who is the head of the N.E.F.A. administration. Each of the five divisions (Kameng, Subansiri, Siang, Lohit, and Tirap) is administered by a political officer, who is in full control of all the entire staff of all departments, and responsible for the execution of all development schemes. The one-line administration has proved successful in co-ordinating a uniform attitude to the local tribesmen.

This attitude was largely shaped by Dr. Verrier Elwin, who until his death in 1964 held the appointment of Tribal Adviser to the Administration of N.E.F.A., and spent the last years of his life in inspiring the members of the Indian Administrative Frontier Service, as well as a group of young research officers and many officials of other departments, with his tolerant and appreciative approach to the culture and way of life of the hill-tribes. The effectiveness of his influence was partly due to the wholehearted backing which the Prime Minister Jawaharlal Nehru gave to this policy of trying to preserve as much as possible of the tribesmen's cultural heritage, and to prevent the forcible imposition of Hindu values on people whose roots lay outside the sphere of Hinduism. This policy has not remained without critics, and many Indian politicians levelled against the administration of N.E.F.A. the charge that it kept the tribals in isolation and forbade other Indians to settle, or even to trade, in the hills.

Yet from the point of view of the welfare of the tribesmen, the policy pursued during the first ten years of the existence of N.E.F.A. must be considered a great success. My assessment is based not on published accounts, which are usually rather rose-coloured, but on observations during a visit to the Subansiri and Tirap Divisions in 1962. When I first travelled in the Subansiri region in 1944, the local tribes, Apa Tanis and Daflas, had virtually no contact with the Government. The greater part of the area was unexplored and the political officer, stationed in the plains, had no control over the inhabitants of the hills except for the prevention of raids on the plains of Assam. By 1962 there was an administrative centre in the Apa Tanis valley linked by a motor-able road with the Brahmaputra valley, and attached to it were a hospital, schools, co-operative stores, and various other amenities open to the tribesmen. More impressive than these developments, however, was the fact that the local tribesmen seemed to be deriving considerable economic advantages from the activities of the administration without suffering any apparent damage to their cultural and social life. As no outsiders were allowed to settle permanently in the hills, they were secure in the ownership of their land, and improved facilities for trade greatly benefited the Apa Tanis, who had always been keen traders. Their adoption of new methods and commodities was selective. Thus there was no interest in bullock-drawn carts or the use of animals for ploughing, but Apa Tanis were quick to learn to drive trucks, and the more enterprising traders used motor transport for bringing up goods from the plains. Schools were well attended and many boys had ambitions to enter government service. Indeed, some of the officials expressed apprehension about the possibility of finding suitable employment for the many young men who were receiving education, and imagined that the newly learnt skills would enable them to attain a standard of living far superior to that of the ordinary villagers.

Whatever problems might lie ahead, the administration of N.E.F.A. has certainly succeeded in preserving the tribesman's self-confidence. Contact with other populations being slight, the tribesmen do not feel themselves to be a minority less privileged than other communities, and as long as they are secure in the rights to their ancestral land, the prospects for their future appear to be good. There is certainly a world of difference between the depressed status of many tribes of Middle and Southern India, and the material prosperity and vitality which strikes one so forcibly among a tribe such as the Apa Tanis of N.E.F.A. A measure of isolation combined with a sympathetic and imaginative policy of a progressive administration has here created a situation unparalleled in other parts of India.

This brief survey of the situation of the aboriginal tribes in three specific regions demonstrates the complexity of the problem of their integration within the wider Indian society. The conditions under which the tribes live in different parts of India are so varied that generalizations regarding their relations with other communities can have only a very limited validity, yet the populations notified as Scheduled Tribes all share the special protection guaranteed them under Article 46 of the Constitution, which reads:

The State shall promote with special care the educational and economic interests of the weaker sections of the people, and in particular of the Scheduled Castes and the Scheduled Tribes, and shall protect them from social injustice and all forms of exploitation.

Under Article 244 and the Fifth Schedule providing for the Administration and Control of Scheduled Areas and Scheduled Tribes, it is within the powers of the President to declare any tribal area as a Scheduled Area and to make administrative arrangements to give effect to the provisions of Article 46. The tribal areas notified as Scheduled Areas extend over 99,693 square miles, and though they are administered as part of the states in which they are situated, the respective governors are given powers to modify central and state laws in their application to them, and to frame regulations for their peace and good government and, in particular, for the protection of the rights of tribals to land, the allotment of wasteland and their protection from money-lenders. The Fifth Schedule also provides for the setting up of Tribes Advisory Councils in all states containing Scheduled Areas, and it is the duty of such councils to advise on matters concerning the welfare of the Scheduled Tribes. Although such Tribes Advisory Councils were set up in eleven states, their effectiveness has not been impressive, and the Scheduled Areas and Scheduled Tribes Commission of 1960–1 found that these councils met only once or twice a year, and that important items of legislation were not referred to them for discussion.

More important than the establishment of the Tribes Advisory Councils was the appointment by the President of a Commissioner for Scheduled Castes and Scheduled Tribes whose duty it is to investigate all matters relating to the safeguards provided for those castes and tribes. The Commissioner reports annually on the position of the tribes in the various states, and on the progress of the schemes initiated for their benefit. His annual reports are published and constitute a valuable source of information on all activities of the state governments concerned with backward classes and tribes. The fact, however, that the Commissioner and his assistants are concerned only with the gathering of information severely restricts the effectiveness of his office. Though he may tender informal advice to state governments and embody his views in reports to the President, he is not in a position to initiate any scheme or decide on the utilization of the vast funds which the Government of India provides for the betterment of the tribes.

At the centre the work relating to the Scheduled Tribes is attended to by the Ministry of Home Affairs, in which there are five sections specifically concerned with the Scheduled Castes and Scheduled Tribes. Moreover, the Planning Commissioner has a Social Welfare Division, which deals with the development aspect of tribal affairs, and the publications on the Five-Year Plans contain many data relating to the tribes.

It would appear that the provisions for the welfare of the tribes are strong on the constitutional and planning sides, but weak on the executive side. The concern of the Government of India and of Parliament for the rights and progress of the tribes is admirable, but by the time measures decided upon at the centre have filtered down to state and district level their impact is often weakened or outright lost. In all the reports of the Commissioner for Scheduled Castes and Scheduled Tribes, the Planning Commission and other bodies concerned with tribal affairs, there is the repeated complaint that the staff and administrative machinery provided by the states is not adequate to carry out the policy of the centre, even if the necessary funds are voted by Parliament. The welfare programme has been divided into 'State Sector Schemes' and 'Centrally Sponsored Schemes'. The latter comprise the schemes of tribal development blocks, co-operation, including forest co-operatives, tribal research institutes, and training scholarships. The State Sector Schemes, on the other hand, deal with the development of agriculture and cottage industries, education, housing, water supply, and public health.

Despite elaborate plans it appears, however, that in most states there is no clear policy for dealing with the problems of the tribal population. While it is generally accepted that departments responsible for forests, agriculture, fisheries, and health must have a staff of highly trained experts, there is little recognition of the necessity for experts in tribal welfare work. Other activities are given priority and therefore offer better promotion prospects, with the effect that officers who have proved efficient in tribal development are often diverted to other tasks which state governments consider more important.

One of the results of inefficiency on the executive level is the inability of states to spend the funds allocated by the Centre for Tribal Development. During the period 1950–61 no less than 493.5 million rupees were provided for the welfare of the Scheduled Areas, but the actual expenditure by the states fell very much short of this figure. In Madhya Pradesh, for instance, the Second Five-Year Plan made provision for close on 50 million rupees for tribal welfare, but less than 20 million were spent under the Plan.

A large part of the funds voted for the Second Five-Year Plan were to be spent on Community Development Projects, and it was planned to undertake an intensive development of compact areas having large tribal populations. Forty-three special multi-purpose Tribal Blocks, covering 23,540 square miles and containing a population of 1,685,000, were opened under this programme, and the Third Five-Year Plan envisages opening 450 such blocks, which have been renamed Tribal Development Blocks. In some of the blocks, however, the percentage of tribals was lower than that of non-tribals, with the result that funds sanctioned for the advancement of tribals were spent largely on non-tribals. The Commissioner for Scheduled Castes and Scheduled Tribes suggested, therefore, that in future only areas with a tribal population of not less than 66 per cent should be established as Tribal Development Blocks.

The hopes set on the Community Development Projects have only partially been fulfilled, and many Indian observers with first-hand experience of some of the Tribal Blocks take a pessimistic view of their usefulness. They point out that community development is basically a programme for directed and deliberate change, and that the people supposed to benefit have not been mentally prepared to accept changes. The tribesmen, like other Indian villagers, were used to looking to government officials for orders, and not for advice; though prepared to oblige the officers by paying lip-service to the development programme, they did not understand its implications and lacked the will for active co-operation. The Government's insistence on the fulfilment of specific physical targets laid down by planners without any knowledge of local conditions, led to the expenditure of funds on projects of little utility. Thus houses were built, but people would not live in them, roads were built only to be washed away in the rainy seasons, basketry centres started where there were no bamboos, and bee-keeping established where there are no flowers. Often all agricultural development was concentrated on the land of a few influential non-tribals, with the result that the aboriginals lost the little interest they had shown for the programme.[6]

The sort of difficulties into which community development could run in tribal areas can be gauged from an account of the situation in one such block in Bihar given by Dr. Sachchidananda, the Director of the Tribal Research Institute at Ranchi. He describes how the project officer and extension staff, who were all new to their jobs, found it difficult to comprehend their roles:

'Hitherto they had been accustomed to carry out orders, but now they were called upon to secure the co-operation of the people. Added to this was the difficulty of having to work in a totally unfamiliar area where the frame of reference to which they were used was inapplicable. Tribal culture had to be kept in the background of all development, but for them the pattern of work dictated from above was sacrosanct. They did not like to take upon themselves the responsibility of altering the programme to suit the peculiar needs of the area . . . there were also a number of administrative difficulties. The staff posted in tribal areas felt unhappy; . . . some of them went even so far as to say that they regarded it as penal posting. Some others regarded it as a golden opportunity of serving themselves rather than the people. It is they who continued the tradition of exploiting the poor and simple tribals who had some work to be done at the block level. . . . For some time there was great resentment against Project authorities. People complained that the latter did not do anything with the consent of the villages and that they had done nothing to improve the conditions in Mandar. In some villages which were

[6] Sachchidananda, 'Community Development and the Tribals', *Journal of Social Research*, Vol. VII, Nos. 1–2, 1964, pp. 70–78.

inhabited by influential non-tribals, much of the money has been spent. The general feeling everywhere was that the Project had benefited the non-tribals more than the tribals.'[7]

I have recently observed similar situations in some areas of Andhra Pradesh, and if it is the non-tribals who profit most from aid provided by the Government, one must assume that even in the tribal blocks the gap between the economic standards of the tribals and those of the rest is widening rather than closing. The root of much of these difficulties lies in the lack of communication between the development staff and the local aboriginals, and this is hardly surprising as long as officials are untrained and often recruited from castes which have a deep-seated prejudice against the tribal people.

The Planning Commission has clearly recognized the problem of finding suitable personnel for tribal development work, and in the Third Five-Year Plan the suggestion has been put forward that the Central Government and state government should co-operate in forming a special cadre comprising technical and other personnel for work in Scheduled Areas. The most significant aspect of such a policy would be that a body of trained persons would spend their entire period of service among the tribal people, so that their knowledge, experience, and sense of identification would become a vital factor in assuring rapid and uninterrupted service.[8]

This foresight and realistic assessment of the basic needs of an effective tribal policy are all the more remarkable as there is, even among educated Indians, a widespread unwillingness to face the fact that the 30 millions of aboriginals will for a long time to come form a separate and unassimilated element within the Indian nation. This became evident in a Tribal Symposium held in 1964 in Hyderabad, attended by anthropologists, administrators, and politicians. While the need for special protection was conceded by many of the participants, there was a general feeling that any privileges enjoyed by tribes were required only for a brief period of transition, and that within a span of about ten years the integration of the tribes within the rest of the population should be completed, whereupon there would be no more need for Scheduled Areas and the protection of Scheduled Tribes.

Most factual accounts of the situation in tribal areas and, above all, the Report of the Scheduled Areas and Scheduled Tribes Commission belie these facile assumptions, and make it clear that for a long time to come tribal communities will persist as minorities, distinct in culture,

[7] Sachchidananda, *Culture Change in Tribal Bihar*, Calcutta, 1964, pp. 114–16.
[8] *Third Five Year Plan*, Delhi, 1961, p. 711.

language, and way of life from the neighbouring majority communities. Rapid progress in the field of education, which is perhaps the most striking development in recent years, does not directly solve the problem of the aboriginals' economic backwardness. For the core of the tribal problem lies in the discrepancy between their economic potentialities and the growing wants stimulated by contacts with more advanced populations. Barring a few notable exceptions, the aboriginals of today have no greater economic capacity than had their fathers and grandfathers. Their agricultural methods have largely remained the same, and such crafts as they traditionally possessed have declined rather than developed, partly on account of the spread of cheap industrially produced commodities, and partly because contact with Hindu ideas of caste have made certain occupations appear socially undesirable.

It is paradoxical that in many areas where aboriginals are exposed to the influence of caste Hindus, just those features of Hindu society which modern India strives to discard are newly introduced among populations to whom they had hitherto been foreign. Thus not only the prejudice against certain occupations, but also dietary taboos, child-marriage, and restrictions on the remarriage of widows and *divorcées* are gaining a foothold among the hill- and jungle-folk at a time when they are losing ground in the larger urban centres. This development is almost inevitable as long as throughout rural India compliance with the more puritanical precepts of Hindu morality remains the principal criterion of social respectability.

Acceptance or denial of the necessity for assimilation with Hindu society is ultimately a question of values. Are the aboriginals to be allowed to follow their own inclination in emulating or rejecting the cultural pattern represented by their Hindu neighbours, or are they to be compelled or coaxed to abandon their own cultural tradition and values? In the past, Hindu society has been tolerant of groups that would not conform to the standards set by the higher castes. True, such groups were denied equal ritual status, but no efforts were made to deflect them from their chosen style of living. In recent years this attitude has changed. Perhaps it is the influence of the Western belief in universal values which has encouraged a spirit of intolerance *vis-à-vis* cultural and social divergences. Yet India is not only a multilingual and a multiracial country, but is also multicultural, and as long as Muslims, Christians, and Parsees are free to follow their traditional way of life, it would seem only fair that the culture and social order of the aboriginals, however distinct from that of the majority community, should also be respected. No doubt assimilation will occur automatically and inevitably where small tribal groups are enclosed within numerically stronger Hindu populations. In other areas, however, and particularly all along India's northern and north-eastern frontier live vigorous tribal populations which may well follow the path of the American Pueblo Indians and resist assimilation as well as inclusion within the Hindu caste system. Many of those who know these hill-tribes intimately are confident that, if encouraged to develop on the lines of their traditional culture, they can make a distinct contribution to the overall pattern of Indian civilization.

With the introduction of a system of Democratic Decentralization to take the place of the paternalism characteristic of the traditional form of Indian government, a new element has entered the relations between the tribes and the more advanced majority communities. The ability to vote in general elections for the Parliament in Delhi and the Legislative Assembly of their state did not make much difference to the tribals, because they did not understand the implication of the franchise, but the local elections aroused their interest to a much greater extent. The very fact that some of the most powerful people of the district approached the poorest villagers for their votes, and tried to gain their confidence, convinced them of a fundamental change. The very idea that they could choose their representatives was novel. At first, tribals only voted, for very few were sufficiently educated to stand for election. Even in areas with a preponderance of tribals, the elected representatives were often non-aboriginals and abused their powers by exploiting those who had voted for them. But as time passes and the aboriginals are gaining experience, they become more shrewd in the choice of their representatives, and tribal leaders have the opportunity of rising to positions of influence through the process of democratic elections.

Decentralization, however, has also its danger for the tribes, and the Commissioner for Scheduled Castes and Scheduled Tribes has expressed the fear that due to the existing pattern of concentration of social and economic power in the hands of a dominant section of the population, the Democratic Decentralization may lead to more extensive exploitation of the Scheduled Tribes. Moreover, the *panchayat samities* and *zila parishads*, which in some states have already taken over many of the functions of the former district officers, may be disinclined to support the implementations of tribal welfare schemes, for the simple reason that their leading members belong to the very classes which traditionally profited from the exploitation of the tribes. In his report for the year 1962-3 (pp. 9-10) the Commissioner proposed, therefore, that in order that the system of Democratic Decentralization might be smoothly introduced without endangering the interests of the tribals, 'the State Governments concerned should ensure that in the *panchayats* constituted in the predominantly tribal areas the Sarpanches [chairman] should invariably be elected/nominated from amongst the tribals only'.

A problem almost as important as the revolution of the district administrations by the introduction of *panchayati raj*, is the impact of industrialization on the tribes in areas rich in mineral resources. Certain areas within the tribal belt of Middle India, and particularly Orissa, West Bengal, Bihar, and Madhya Pradesh, have been found to contain rich deposits of minerals, and their exploitation and the establishment of great steel-works in the very centre of the aboriginals' homeland, threaten to lead to a large-scale displacement of tribal populations. The Scheduled Areas and Scheduled Tribes Commission expressed grave concern regarding the ultimate fate of the aboriginals, whose last refuge areas in hills and forests are now being turned into industrial regions. While the Commission accepts their 'substantial displacement' as inevitable, its report reveals (p. 271) that out of 14,461 tribal families displaced from an area of 62,494 acres, only 3,479 have been allotted alternative land.

The tribals were dislodged from their traditional sources of livelihood and places of habitation. Not conversant with the details of acquisition proceedings they accepted whatever cash compensation was given to them and became emigrants. With cash in hand and many attractions in the nearby industrial towns, their funds were rapidly depleted and in course of time they were without money as well as without land. They joined the ranks of landless labourers but without any training, equipment or aptitude for any skilled or semi-skilled job.

The Commission recommends that the Government, as trustee of the Scheduled Tribes, should not allow the tribes to go under in the process of industrialization, but should see that rehabilitation and training schemes enable the tribesmen to find employment in the industry growing up on the land from which they have been forcibly displaced. Judging from the situation in places such as Rourkela, Ranchi, and Jamshedpur, one cannot escape the conclusion, however, that the prospects for the tribesmen deprived of their land and virtually expelled

from their ancestral homes is by no means good, and that a real prole-
tarianization of the tribesmen of these areas appears as unavoidable.

Nirad C. Chaudhuri, the frank and provocative analyst of the present-
day Indian social scene, has expressed a similar assessment of the
tribesmen's probable fate under the impact of industrialization in
strong and colourful language:

> In an industrialized India the destruction of the aboriginal's life is as inevit-
> able as the submergence of the Egyptian temples caused by the dams of the
> Nile . . . As things are going, there can be no grandeur in the primitive's
> end. It will not be even simple extinction, which is not the worst of human
> destinies. It is to be feared that the aboriginal's last act will be squalid, instead
> of being tragic. What will be seen with most regret will be, not his dis-
> appearance, but his enslavement and degradation.[9]

It is to be hoped that this gloomy forecast will prove unduly pessimistic, but unless the detailed recommendations of the Scheduled Areas
and Scheduled Tribes Commission are acted upon, large numbers of
displaced aboriginals from the new industrial areas may indeed become
homeless vagrants unable to obtain any suitable employment which
could compensate them for the land they had to give up as a sacrifice
on the altar of India's modernization. The establishment of vast industrial enterprises in tribal zones lends urgency to the extension of protective measures to all tribals whose rights and way of life have been
placed in jeopardy. The framers of the Indian Constitution were clear
that while the Scheduled Tribes were to be brought out from their
age-old isolation, they should be saved from exploitation and from the
erosion of their rights to their ancestral land. This aim can be achieved
only by special legislation, and the Scheduled Areas and Scheduled
Tribes Commission ended its long report with the plea to 'secure the
advancement of the tribals without disturbing the essential harmony of
their life and secure their integration without imposition' (p. 499). The
manner of integration of the tribals within the wider Indian society
will ultimately depend on political decisions and these will be made on
the basis of moral evaluations. Unless the advanced sections of the
Indian population develop a spirit of cultural tolerance and an appreciation of tribal values, even the most elaborate schemes for the economic
settlement of the tribals are likely to prove abortive. It is for this reason
that the late Jawaharlal Nehru formulated the following five principles
for the policy to be pursued *vis-à-vis* the tribals:

[9] *The Continent of Circe*, London, 1965, p. 77.

(1) People should develop along the lines of their own genius, and the imposition of alien values should be avoided.

(2) Tribal rights in land and forest should be respected.

(3) Teams of tribals should be trained in the work of administration and development.

(4) Tribal areas should not be overadministered or overwhelmed with a multiplicity of schemes.

(5) Results should be judged not by statistics or the amount of money spent, but by the human character that is evolved.

Except in a few areas, such as N.E.F.A., these principles have seldom been put fully into practice. There are, moreover, indications that Nehru's extremely liberal ideas regarding the rights of the tribals and the preservation of their cultural heritage may not be shared by all of the present leaders of the Congress Party, and it is likely that pressure for a speedier and more complete assimilation of the aboriginals will gradually increase and lead to changes even in tribal areas such as N.E.F.A. The existence of a number of special agencies responsible for the protection of tribal rights, on the other hand, justifies the expectation that despite occasional attacks on these rights the tribals will continue to enjoy at least some of the privileges provided for them by the Indian Constitution.

BIBLIOGRAPHY

AIYAPPAN, A., *Report on the Socio-economic Conditions of Aboriginal Tribes of the Province of Madras*. Madras Government Press, 1958.
— 'In the South', *Tribal India*, Seminar 14, Bombay, 1960, pp. 31–34.
BAAGO, K., 'Religions in India according to the last census', *International Review of Missions*, Geneva, London, New York, Vol. LIII, 1964, pp. 169–72.
BANERJEE, HEMENDRA NATH, and DASGUPTA, S. K., 'The Santal of Modhupur, Purulia District', *Inter-ethnic Relation and Social Mobility Movements among some Tribes and Castes of Eastern and Central India c. 1900–1959*, in Surajit Sinha (Ed.), *Bulletin of the Department of Anthropology, Government of India*, Vol. VIII, No. 2, 1959, pp. 55–62.
BANERJEE, HEMENDRA NATH, 'The Kharia of Modupur, Singhbhum District and Neighbouring Regions', in Surajit Sinha (Ed.), *Inter-ethnic Relation and Social Mobility Movements among some Tribes and Castes of Eastern and Central India c. 1900–1959*, *Bulletin of the Department of Anthropology, Government of India*, Vol. VIII, No. 2, 1959, pp. 91–101.
— 'Statutory safeguards for Scheduled Tribes and Scheduled Castes', *Bulletin of the Cultural Research Institute*, Vol. I, No. 1, 1962, pp. 17–20.
BANERJEE, SWAPAN KUMAR, and CHOWDHURY, B. K. R., 1962 'Scheduled Tribes Population of West Bengal', *Bulletin of the Cultural Research Institute*, Vol. I, No. 1, 1962, pp. 23–33.
BANERJEE, SWAPAN KUMAR, 'Land Alienation: Causes and Effects thereof on Tribal Economy', *Bulletin of the Cultural Research Institute*, Vol. II, No. 2, 1963, pp. 19–20.
BARANGE, B. G., 'An Annotated, Bibliography on Tribal Indebtedness', *Bulletin of the Tribal Research Institute*, Chhindwara, Vol. III, No. 2, 1963, pp. 69–66.

BÉTEILLE, A., 'The Future of the Backward Classes: The Competing Demands of Status and Power,' *Perspectives: Supplement to the Indian Journal of Public Administration.* Vol. XI, No. 1, January–March 1965, pp. 1–39 (also reprinted as Chapter V of the present volume).

BISWAS, P. C., *Santals of the Santal Parganas (Bharatiya Adimjati Sevak Sangh)*, Delhi, 1950.

BOSE, NIRMAL KUMAR, 'Some Observations on Industralization and its Effects on Tribal Life', *Man in India*, Vol. XLII, 1962, pp. 5–9.

— 'On Communal Separatism', *Man in India*, Vol. XLIII, 1963, pp. 87–91.

— 'Integration of Tribes in Andhra Pradesh', *Man in India*, Vol. XLIV, 1964, pp. 97–104.

— 'Problems of National Integration', *Science and Culture*, Vol. XXX, 1964, pp. 157–60.

— 'Change in Tribal Cultures before and after Independence,' *Man in India*, Vol. XLIV, 1964, pp. 1–10.

BRYCE, L. W., 'Revolution and the Tribal Peoples', *Bulletin of the Tribal Research Institute*, *Chhindwara*, n.s., Vol. II, No. 1, 1962, pp. 15–18.

CHAKRAVATI, K. C., 'Nehru Government's Naga Policy', *Economic Weekly*, Bombay, 1958, pp. 939–40.

CHAKRAVORTY, BIRENDRA CHANDRA, *British Relations with the Hill Tribes of Assam since 1858*, Calcutta, K. L. Mukhopadhyay, 1964.

CHANDRA, VIMAL, 'The Constitutional Safeguards and Privileges accorded to the Tribals', *Vanyajati*, Vol. XII, 1946, pp. 161–72.

CHATTOPADHYAY, GOURANGA, 'The Application of Anthropology to Administration: Case Studies in Rural and Tribal Areas, *Journal of Social Research*, Vol. III, No. 1, 1960, pp. 48–54.

CHATTOPADHYAY, K. P., *Report on the Santals in Northern and Western Bengal*, University of Calcutta Press, 1946.

CHAUDHURI, NIRAD C., *The Continent of Circe: An Essay on the Peoples of India*, London, Chatto and Windus, 1965.

CHOUDHURY, N. C., 'Munda settlement in Lower Bengal: A Study in Tribal Migration', *Bulletin of the Cultural Research Institute*, Vol. II, No. 2, 1963, pp. 23–32.

CHOWDHURY, BIDYUT KUMAR ROY, 'Comparative Study of the Progress of Secondary Education among the Scheduled Castes and Scheduled Tribes of West Bengal', *Bulletin of the Cultural Research Institute*, Vol. II, 1963, pp. 40–52.

CULSHAW, W. J., *Tribal Heritage: A Study of the Santals*, Lutterworth Library, Vol. XXXIV, Missionary Research Series, No. XV, London, 1949.

DAS, AMAL KUMAR, 'Influence of City Life on Educated Tribals', *Bulletin of the Cultural Research Institute*, Vol. I, No. 2, 1962, pp. 69–78.

— 'Scheduled Tribes of West Bengal: A Panoramic Picture', *Bulletin of the Cultural Research Institute*, Vol. I, No. 1, 1952, pp. 34–47.

DAS, AMAL KUMAR, and BANERJEE, HEMENDRA NATH, *Impact of Tea Industry on the Life of the Tribals of West Bengal (Bulletin of the Cultural Research Institute*, Special Series, No. IV), Calcutta, Tribal Welfare Department, Government of West Bengal, 1964.

DAS, AMAL KUMAR, and BANERJEE, SWAPAN KUMAR, *Impact of Industrialization on the Life of the Tribals of West Bengal (Bulletin of the Cultural Research Institute*, Special Series, No. I), Calcutta, Tribal Welfare Department, Government of West Bengal, 1962.

— 'The "Family" of Tribals of West Bengal: Static and Dynamic Aspects of Composition', *Bulletin of the Cultural Research Institute*, Vol. II, 1963, pp. 12–21.

DAS, G. N., 'New Horizon', *Adibasi*, No. I, 1963–4, pp. 61–64.

DAS, NITYANAND, 'Reorientation of Ashram School Education', *Adibasi*, No. I, 1963–4, pp. 14–20.

DAS, T. C., 'Assimilation, Integration, Acculturation', *Journal of Social Research*, Vol. III, No. 2, 1960, pp. 6–10.

— 'A Scheme for Tribal Welfare', *Journal of Social Research*, Vol. III, No. 2, 1960, pp. 93–112.

— 'The Nature and Extent of Social Change in Tribal Society of Eastern India', *Sociological Bulletin*, Vol. XI (Decennial Celebrations Symposium), 1962, pp. 221–38.
DAS, T. C., 'Aspects of Tribal Culture under Modern Impact in Eastern India', in L. K. Bala Ratnam (Ed.), *Anthropology on the March*, Madras, The Book Centre and the Social Sciences Association, 1963, pp. 137–54.
DAS GUPTA, NARENDRA KUMAR, *Problems of Tribal Education and the Santals*, New Delhi, Bharatiya Adimjati Sevak Sangh, 1963.
DATTA-MAJUMDER, NABENDU, *The Santal: A Study in Culture-Change* (Memoir of the Department of Anthropology, Government of India, No. II), Delhi, Manager of Publications, 1956.
DHEBAR, U. N., 'Employment of Scheduled Tribes', *Vanyajati*, Vol. XII, 1964, pp. 1–2; 61–64.
DUBE, S. C., Approaches to the Tribal Problem in India, *Journal of Social Research*, Vol. III, No. 2, 1960, pp. 11–15.
DUBEY, S. L., 'Decentralization and its Problems', in *The Changing Tribes of Madhya Pradesh (Bulletin of the Tribal Research Institute, Chhindwara)*, Vol. II, No. 4–Vol. III, No. 1, 1959, pp. 44–56.
DUSHKIN, LELAH, 'The Backward Classes', *Economic Weekly*, Vol. XIII, 1961, pp. 1665–8; 1695–1705; 1729–38.
EHRENFELS, U. R., *The Kadar of Cochin* (Madras University Anthropological Series, No. 1), Madras, 1952.
ELWIN, V., *The Baiga*, London, John Murray, 1939.
— *The Aboriginals* (Oxford Pamphlets on Indian Affairs, No. XIV), Bombay, Oxford University Press, 1943.
— *A Philosophy for N.E.F.A.* (with a Foreword by the Prime Minister of India), Shillong, Sachin Roy on behalf of the North-East Frontier Agency, 1959.
— *A New Deal for Tribal India*, Delhi, Manager of Publications for the Ministry of Home Affairs, 1963.
— *The Tribal World of Verrier Elwin*, Bombay, Oxford University Press, 1965.
FRANDA, M. F., 'The Naga National Council: Origins of a Separatist Movement, *Economic Weekly*, Vol. XIII, 1961, pp. 153–6.
FUCHS, S., *The Gond and Bhumias of Eastern Mandla*, Bombay, Asia Publishing House, 1960.
FÜRER-HAIMENDORF, C. von, *The Naked Nagas*, London, Methuen, 1939 (revised ed.: Calcutta, Thacker, Spink & Co., 1963).
— 'Aboriginal Education in Hyderabad', *Indian Journal of Social Work*, Vol. V, 1944, pp. 87–106.
— *Tribal Hyderabad: Four Reports* (with a Foreword by W. V. Grigson), Hyderabad, Azam Steam Press, 1945.
— 'Aboriginal Rebellions in the Deccan', *Man in India*, Vol. XXV, 1945, pp. 149–86.
— *Progress and Problems of Aboriginal Rehabilitation in Adilabad District*, Hyderabad, Government Printing Press, 1945.
— *Ethnographic Notes on the Tribes of the Subansiri Region*, Assam Government, Shillong, 1947.
— *The Raj Gonds of Adilabad* (Aboriginal Tribes of Hyderabad, Vol. 3), London, Macmillan, 1948.
— *Himalayan Barbary*, London, John Murray, 1955.
GAFOOR, K. A., 'Legislation for Categories of Under-Privileged', *Indian Journal of Social Work*, Vol. XX, 1959–60, pp. 62–69.
GHURYE, G. S., *The Scheduled Tribes*, Bombay, Popular Book Depot, 1959.
GOULD, H. A., 'Some Preliminary Observations concerning the Anthropology of Industrialisation', *Eastern Anthropologist*, Vol. XIV, 1961, pp. 30–47.
GOVERNMENT OF BOMBAY, *Report on the Aboriginal and Hill Tribes of the Partially Excluded Areas in the Province of Bombay*, Bombay, 1939.

GOVERNMENT OF INDIA, *First Five Year Plan*, New Delhi, Manager of Publications, 1952.

— (L. M. Shrikant), *Report of the Commissioner for Scheduled Castes and Scheduled Tribes for the Year 1951*, New Delhi, 1952.

— *The Adivasis*, Delhi, Publications Division, Ministry of Information and Broadcasting, 1955.

— *Report of the Backward Classes Commission* (Chairman K. Kalelkar), New Delhi, Manager of Publications, 3 vols., 1956.

— *Memorandum on the Report of the Backward Classes Commission*, New Delhi, Manager of Publications, 1956.

— *Second Five Year Plan*, Manager of Publications, 1956.

— *Report of the Committee on Special Multi-purpose Tribal Blocks*, Manager of Publications for the Ministry of Home Affairs, 1960.

— *Report of the Scheduled Areas and Scheduled Tribes Commission 1960–1961* (Chairman, U. N. Dhebar), New Delhi, Manager of Publications, Vols. I and II, 1961.

— *Third Five Year Plan*, Manager of Publications, 1961.

— Language Tables, in *Census of India, 1961*, Delhi, Manager of Publications, Vol. I, Part II–C (ii), 1961.

— Language Tables, in *Census of India, 1961*, Vol. I, Delhi, Manager of Publications, Government of India, Part II–C (ii), 1962.

— 'Special Tables for Scheduled Tribes and Scheduled Castes; Ethnographic Notes', in *Census of India, 1961*, Vol. I, 'India', Delhi, Manager of Publications, Parts V–A and V–B, 1962.

— *Report of the Commissioner for Scheduled Castes and Scheduled Tribes for the Year, 1962–63*, New Delhi, Manager of Publications, Parts I, II, and IV, 1963.

GRIGSON, W. V., *The Aboriginal Problem in the Central Provinces and Berxar*, Nagpur, Government Printing Press, 1944.

— *The Challenge of Backwardness: Some Notes and Papers on Tribal and Depressed Classes Policy with Special Reference to Hyderabad State*, Hyderabad, Government Printing Press, 1947.

GUHA, B. S., 'Indian Aboriginals and their Administration', *Journal of the Asiatic Society*, Vol. XVII, No. 1, 1951, pp. 19–44.

HAZRA, DURGADAS, 'The Dorla of Bastar', in Surajit Singh (Ed.), *Inter-ethnic Relation and Social Mobility Movements among some Tribes and Castes of Eastern and Central India c. 1900–1959*, Bulletin of the Department of Anthropology, Government of India, Vol. VIII, No. 2, 1959, pp. 75–90.

HUTTON, J. H., 'Primitive Tribes', L. S. S. O'Malley (Ed.), *Modern India and the West*, London, Oxford University Press, 1941, pp. 417–44.

INTERNATIONAL LABOUR OFFICE, 'Report on India's Policy and Action on Behalf of Tribal Populations', *International Labour Review*, Vol. LVIII, 1956, pp. 284–98.

JAIN, J. D., *The Constitution of India*, Allahabad, The Central Book Depot, n.d.

JAY, EDWARD, 'Revitalization Movements in Tribal India, in L. P. Vidyarthi (Ed.), *Aspects of Religion in Indian Society*, Meerut, Kedar Nath Ram Naty, 1961, pp. 282–315.

KALIA, S. L., 'Sanskritization and Tribalization', in *The Changing Tribes of Madhya Pradesh, Bulletin of the Tribal Research Institute*, Chhindwara, Vol. II, No. 4; Vol. III, No. 1, 1951, pp. 33–43.

KARVE, IRAWATI, *The Bhils of West Khandesh: a Social and Economic Survey*, Bombay, Bombay Anthropological Society, 1961.

KURUP, A. M., 'Changing Phase of Tribal Economy: A Study of Tribal Coal Miners', in *The Changing Tribes of Madhya Pradesh, Bulletin of the Tribal Research Institute*, Chhindwara, Vol. II, No. 4; Vol. 3, No. 1, 1959, pp. 77–91.

— 'The Impact of Industrialization on Tribal Life', *Vanyajati*, Vol. XI, 1963, pp. 71–75.

MAJUMDAR, D. N., *The Fortunes of Primitive Tribes*, Lucknow, Universal Publishers, 1944.

— *The Affairs of a Tribe: A Study in Tribal Dynamics*, Lucknow, Universal Publishers, 1950.

MARMORIA, C. B., 'Tribes in India—Their Civil and Social Conditions', *Indian Journal of Social Work*, Vol. XVIII, 1957–8, pp. 115–24.

MATHUR, K. S., 'Some Problems of Tribal Rehabilitation in Madhya Pradesh,' *Journal of Social Research*, Vol. III, No. 2, 1960, pp. 113–20.

MEHTA, K. L., 'The North-East Frontier Agency Today', *March of India*, Vol. XIII, June 1956, pp. 8–12.

— 'New Life for NEFA', *March of India*, Vol. XI, February 1959, pp. 18–23; 41.

MILLS, J. P., 'The Effects on the Tribes of the Naga Hills District of Contacts with Civilization', in *Census of India, 1931*, Vol. III: *Assam*, 1932, Part I, Appendix A.

MITRA, A., 'The Castes and Tribes of West Bengal', in *Census of India 1951*, Vol. VI: *West Bengal, Sikkim and Chandernagore*, Alipore, West Bengal Government Press (supplementary vol.), 1953.

MUKERJI, SANKARANANDA, 'The Sundarban Shylock and the Tribal', *Bulletin of the Cultural Research Institute*, Vol. III, No. 1, 1964, pp. 73–76.

MUKHERJEE, BHABANANDA, 'Santals in Relation to Hindu Castes', *Man in India*, Vol. XL, 1960, pp. 300–6.

NAIK, T. B., 'What is a Tribe? Conflicting Definitions', *Bulletin of the Tribal Research and Training Institute*, Chhindwara, Vol. IV, No. 1, 1964, pp. 1–13.

NAIK, T. B. (Ed.) and BHOURASKAR, K. M. (revised), *The Changing Tribes of Madhya Pradesh*, Indore, Government Regional Press, 1961.

NATIONAL COUNCIL OF APPLIED ECONOMIC RESEARCH, *Socio-economic Survey of Primitive Tribes in Madhya Pradesh*, New Delhi, National Council of Applied Economic Research, 1963.

N.E.F.A. ADMINISTRATION, *A Brief Account of Administrative and Development activities in North-East Frontier Agency since Independence*, Shillong, Superintendent Government Press, 1957.

NEHRU, JAWAHARLAL, 'The Right Approach to Tribal People', *Indian Journal of Social Work*, Vol. XIV, 1953–4, pp. 231–5.

— 'Tribal Folk', in *The Adivasis*, Delhi, Publications Division, Ministry of Information and Broadcasting, Government of India, 1955, pp. 1–8.

ORAON, KARTIK, 'Tribes and Tribalism of India', *Journal of Social Research*, Vol. VII, Nos. 1–2, 1964, pp. 36–52.

ORISSA, GOVERNMENT, *Report on the Administration of Scheduled Areas for the Year 1958–59*, Cuttack, Tribal and Rural Welfare Department, Government Press, 1960.

PATNAIK, NITYANANDA, 'From Tribe to Caste: The Juangs of Orissa', *Economic Weekly*, Vol. XV, 1963, pp. 741–2.

RAMASWAMY, M., 'The Indian Constitutional Amendments', in T. S. Rama Rao (Ed.), *Indian Year Book of International Affairs*, Madras, Vol. XII, 1963.

RAVAL, INDUBHAI, B., 'Tribal Community Development Survey', *Indian Journal of Social Work*, Vol. XXI, 1961, pp. 369–71.

— 'Sociology of Tribal Economic Development', *Indian Journal of Social Work*, Vol. XXV, 1964, pp. 43–51.

ROY BURMAN, B. K., 'A Note on the Scheduled Castes and Scheduled Tribes of West Bengal', *Vanyajati*, Vol. IV, 1956, pp. 60–73.

— 'Basic Concepts of Tribal Welfare and Tribal Integration', *Journal of Social Research*, Vol. III, No. 2, 1960, pp. 16–24.

— 'Perspective of Tribal Welfare', *Bulletin of the Tribal Research Institute*, Chhindwara, Vol. I, No. 1, 1961, pp. 12–16.

RUSTOMJI, N. K., 'Tribal Administration in the North-East Frontier Agency', in *The Adivasis*, Delhi, Publications Division, Ministry of Information and Broadcasting, Government of India, 1955, pp. 139–45.

SACHCHIDANANDA, *Culture Change in Tribal Bihar. Munda and Oraon*, Patna, Bookland Private Ltd., 1964.

SACHCHIDANANDA, 'Community Development and the Tribals', *Journal of Social Research*, Vol. VII, Nos. 1–2, 1964, pp. 70–78.

— 'Tribal Education in Bihar', *Vanyajati*, Vol. XII, 1964, pp. 3–6.

SAHA, NIRANJAN, 'Human Factor in Agricultural Development: Study of a Tribal Community', *Economic Weekly*, Vol. VX, 1963, pp. 1641–3.

SAHAY, K. N., 'Christianity and Cultural Processes among the Oraon of Ranchi,' in L. P. Vidyarthi (Ed.), *Aspects of Religion in Indian Society*, Meerut, Kedar Nath Ram Nath, 1961, pp. 323–40.

SARMA, SATYENDRANATH, 'Assam's Relations with N.E.F.A.', *United Asia*, Vol. XV, 1963, pp. 358–64.

SAXENA, R. N., 'The Changing Tribes of India', *Journal of Social Research*, Vol. VII, Nos. 1–2, 1964, pp. 15–28.

SEN, G. E., 'Sortie over N.E.F.A.', *Economic Weekly*, Vol. XII, 1960, pp. 139–44.

SEN, JYOTI, 'Is there a Separate Tribal Problem?' *Man in India*, Vol. XLIII, 1963, pp. 351–2.

SHARMA, T. R., 'A Tribal Community in an Industrial Context (A Case Study in Jamshedpur City)', *Journal of Social Research*, Vol. V, No. 1, 1962, pp. 114–23.

SHARMA, V. S., 'The Scheduled Tribes of Himachal Pradesh and their Problems', *Vanyajati*, Vol. VI, 1958, pp. 117–22.

SHRIKANT, L. M., *Acts and Orders of Government of India and other important information relating to Scheduled Tribes, Scheduled Castes and other backward Classes and Anglo-Indians* (foreword by L. M. Shrikant), Bharatiya Adimjati Sevak Sangh Pamphlet No. VII, 1951, Delhi, Bharatiya Adimjati Sevak Sangh, 1951.

— 'The Integration of the Aboriginal Population of India', *International Labour Review*, Vol. LXXIII, 1956, pp. 241–51.

— 'Tribal Welfare under Panchayati Raj', *Vanyajati*, Vol. IX, 1961, pp. 136–44.

— 'Tribal Welfare with Special Reference to the Tribal Development Blocks', *Indian Journal of Social Work*, Vol. XXII, 1962, pp. 279–85.

SINHA, H. K., 'Tribal Education in Bihar: A Preliminary Statistical Analysis', *Journal of Social Research*, Vol. III, No. 1, 1960, pp. 85–92.

SINHA, SURAJIT, 'Tribal Cultures of Peninsular India as a Dimension of Little Tradition in the Study of Indian Civilization: a Preliminary Statement', *Man in India*, Vol. XXXVII, 1957, pp. 93–118.

THAKKAR, A. V., *The Problem of the Aborigines in India: R. R. Kale Memorial Lectures*, Poona, Gokhale Institute of Economics and Political Science, 1941.

— *Tribes of India: Being a Collection of 48 Articles contributed by Experienced Social Workers*, Delhi, Bharatiya Adimjati Sevak Sangh, 1950.

VARMA, KUMARI S. V., 'Working of the Multipurpose Tribal Blocks in Madhya Pradesh', *Vanyajati*, Vol. IX, 1961, pp. 48–55.

VARMA, S. C., 'Tribal Problems', *Bulletin of the Tribal Research Institute, Chhindwara*, n.s., Vol. I, No. 2, 1961, pp. 16–18.

VERMA, B. B., *Agriculture and Land Ownership among the Primitive People of Assam*, Delhi, Bharatiya Adimjati Sevak Sangh, 1956.

VIDYARTHI, L. P., 'Anthropology and Tribal Policy: A Case Study among the Maler Paharia; some Preliminary Thoughts', *Journal of Social Research*, Vol. III, No. 2, 1960, pp. 25–34.

— 'Approach to Tribal Integration in India', *Vanyajati*, Vol. XI, 1963, pp. 47–50.

— *Cultural Contours of Tribal Bihar* (foreword by N. K. Bose), Calcutta, 1964.

— 'The Changing Face of Tribal Bihar', *Journal of Social Research*, Vol. VII, Nos. 1–2, 1964, pp. 53–61.

VOLCHOK, B. Y., 'The Interaction of Castes and Tribal Communities in Central India', *Journal of Social Research*, Vol. VII, Nos. 1–2, 1964, pp. 104–12.

WILKINSON, T. S., 'Isolation, Assimilation, and Integration in their Historical Perspective, *Bulletin of the Tribal Research Institute, Chhindwara*, Vol. II, No. 1, 1962, pp. 19–28.

X

Elites, Status Groups, and Caste in Modern India

BY ANDRÉ BÉTEILLE

Reader in Sociology, University of Delhi, and Simon Fellow, University of Manchester, 1965–6

I

I DO not propose to spend too much time on questions of terminology, for the definition of each of my three principal terms might require a separate paper to satisfy a purist. Nor can I lay claim to being comprehensive within the scope of a brief paper devoted to a subject on which very little empirical material has been systematically collected. This chapter is not a result of systematic empirical investigation. It is impressionistic in character, and its principal object is to throw up a few ideas which may be tested in the future by a more rigorous examination of the available material, and by collecting new material where none is now available. It should be possible, given time and resources, to collect some quantitative data on many of the factors considered.

I shall not deal with every type of elite, and the ones which I shall exclude are not necessarily the least important in their economic and political power. Further, I do not have the competence to discuss in even the most superficial manner every region in India; I shall draw my examples mainly from Bengal and Madras (which are fortunately good examples, providing a number of useful contrasts); and, of course, New Delhi, making only occasional excursions into other areas.

It is necessary to give a brief outline of the kinds of problem with which I shall deal, and I think it is best to begin by indicating what I shall exclude. A major question in any comprehensive discussion of elites is that of the unity and cohesiveness of its different components; this question does not fall within the province of the present paper. Nor is it my intention to examine the part they play (whether openly or otherwise) in the decision-making process at various levels; or to consider what institutional checks exist against their arbitrary use of power. My main concern will be with the social background of certain sections of the elite, and with some of the changes taking place in it and in the social milieu in which it operates.

For certain analytical purposes it may be necessary to distinguish between rule and dominance. In terms of that distinction, I shall be dealing primarily (though not exclusively) with the 'ruling elite' rather than the 'dominant class'. The ruling elite consists of people who take, or appear to take, major governmental and administrative decisions; the dominant class, of those in whose interests such decisions are taken and whose power they help to sustain. The two categories may overlap to a considerable extent, but they are rarely identical. A study of the ruling elite does not provide a full understanding of the distribution of power in a society, although it may be useful as a first step in that direction.

In a recent excellent study, Bottomore has discussed the different meanings which have been attached to the word 'elite', and, following Aron, has sought to make a distinction between 'elites' (as 'functional, mainly occupational groups which have high status') and the 'political class'.[1] I find this distinction a little confusing, since the 'political class', which is earlier distinguished from elites (i.e. functional groups), is later viewed as including a 'political elite', composed, among others, of members of the top civil and military services, who are clearly to be viewed as functional groups having high status as well as a certain amount of power.

I propose to define the term 'political elite' more narrowly as comprising people in top positions in concrete political structures, such as Cabinets, parties, and legislatures; in short, people who are generally viewed as 'professional' or 'whole-time' politicians. My reason for limiting the use of the term in this way is that in India this component of the elite has certain distinctive features which mark it out from the bureaucratic and professional elites. This, of course, is not to deny the considerable measure of overlap in terms of social origin between the first and the last two; but it seems that this overlap, which was very high a few decades ago, is now being reduced.

The bureaucratic elite is not a unitary category. Its three main components (as I describe them here) are the administrative, the managerial, and the military elites. The distinction between the first and the second I draw from the one between public and private bureaucracies; and, while the army may certainly be viewed as a public bureaucracy, I

[1] T. B. Bottomore, *Elites and Society*, London, C. A. Watts, 1964, pp. 8–9.

consider it convenient to discuss separately the civil and military services. In addition to the political, the bureaucratic, and the professional elites, there are two other components: the business elite and the landed aristocracy; these, unfortunately, I am not able to discuss even cursorily.

I should like to say a few words about the typology which I have adopted. It is not exhaustive and, even within the limits which I have set myself, it would be possible to have alternative typologies. My primary distinction is between 'political' and 'non-political' elites. One could have a cross-classification into bureaucratic and non-bureaucratic elites,[2] for party leaders (whom I discuss as elements in the political elite) operate through bureaucracies and so do certain professional people; in this sense the categories are not mutually exclusive. Again, some of the elites which I consider, such as the Indian Administrative Service (I.A.S.) and army officers, occupy positions in clearly defined, unitary, corporate structures; others, such as intellectuals, constitute amorphous categories rather than groups. A comprehensive study of elites will, of course, have to take these distinctions into account. Here I ignore them, because the point which I wish to make can be most sharply made by contrasting, firstly, political with non-political elites; secondly, among non-political elites, bureaucrats with professional people (including intellectuals); and, thirdly, among bureaucrats, business executives, and army officers on the one hand with members of the I.A.S. on the other. My argument is that there are significant differences in the ways in which castes as well as categories defined in terms of other criteria of status are related to these various elites.

I am perhaps departing somewhat from conventional practice in my use of words such as 'political' and 'bureaucratic'; unfortunately, these words do not have very definite meanings. I base my distinction on the fact that in a democratic system bureaucratic positions are filled normally by appointment and political ones by election; or, at any event, the latter depend to a much greater extent than the former on some form of popular support. (In a one-party state, particularly if it is supported by a developed infrastructure, as in the Soviet Union, the distinction between 'bureaucrats' and 'politicians' is likely to be far less significant.) The differences between recruitment by election and recruitment by appointment are, in my view, largely responsible for such differences as there are in India between the social origins of politicians and those of bureaucrats. Training for appointment to top bureaucratic positions requires facilities to which, as we shall see,

[2] Or into national and regional elites.

different sections of the Indian population have very unequal access. Skills in mobilizing political support can be acquired without access to facilities of this kind.

I shall try in the interest of clarity to make my referents as concrete as possible. Under the political elite, I consider mainly the top leadership of the Congress Party and the central Cabinet. The administrative elite consists, for this discussion, of the I.A.S. The managerial elite here refers to top executives in the more important firms and commercial establishments. By 'professionals' I mean lawyers, doctors, writers, scholars, and the like; I find it convenient to distinguish them from 'bureaucrats', although some of them may be employed within bureaucracies, both public and private. The meanings of the other terms are either self-evident or explained at a later stage in the discussion.

I shall leave the discussion of the political elite (as defined above) to the end, and begin with a consideration of the bureaucratic and professional elites. High Civil Servants, managers with expense accounts and top-ranking officers of the armed forces share more in common than just occupation and income; they pursue, with certain variation, a similar style of life. This is less true of intellectuals (and other professionals) who are socially and economically more heterogeneous; it is least true of the political elite, whose members tend increasingly to come from widely different social backgrounds and cannot by any means be said to share a common style of life.

Bottomore[3] notes the connexion, first indicated by Mosca, between the elite and the 'new middle class' in modern democratic societies,[4] and this connexion is particularly marked in a country like India, where colonial rule retarded the growth of an indigenous industrial elite. But the 'new middle class' is an omnibus category; the most satisfactory way of viewing it in the present context is as an aggregate of overlapping status groups, our interest being in those which enjoy high social esteem.

The concept of status group (or *Stand* in the technical connotation given to it by Weber[5]) provides a useful link between elite and caste in modern India, because caste has been the status group *par excellence* and, in its hierarchical aspects, it has been markedly elitist in character.

In all societies there are bound to be significant elements of con-

---

[3] Op. cit., p. 5.

[4] Mosca, in fact, tends to equate the 'second stratum' of the elite (a crucial category in his scheme) with the 'middle class'; see Gaetano Mosca, *The Ruling Class* (trans. H. D. Kahn) New York, McGraw Hill, 1939, p. 408; also p. 404.

[5] H. H. Gerth and C. W. Mills, *From Max Weber: Essays in Sociology*, London, Routledge and Kegan Paul, 1948, pp. 186–91.

tinuity between traditional and contemporary elites, excepting perhaps a few with revolutionary experience. One cannot say that there has been any revolutionary change of a dramatic kind in Indian society between the end of the eighteenth century and the middle of the twentieth. There is therefore a natural tendency on the part of some to view contemporary social stratification in India as representing largely a perpetuation of the traditional system of stratification based on caste. But two things have to be kept clearly in mind. The principle of recruitment to the new elites is quite different from recruitment to castes: the son of a general today does not have a pre-emptive right to become a general or even a colonel. Secondly, it is now clear that even in traditional society both power and status could be achieved outside the caste system.

II

In examining the relationship between caste on the one hand and bureaucratic and professional elites on the other, one has to distinguish carefully between (i) recruitment to the elite group and (ii) its internal structure of roles and values. Recruitment still is to some extent selective in terms of caste, which, however, seems to play a rather less important part in the governance of internal relations. Thus, while Brahmins and Kayasths are more likely to get into the higher Civil Service than are members of the Peasant castes, the latter sometimes do succeed in being recruited. And when they are in, they are likely to be just as acceptable as the former, provided they have acquired the kind of education and social graces which are held in high esteem in the service, and which in themselves have little to do with caste.

The educational system plays a decisive part in recruitment to non-political elites in general and bureaucratic ones in particular. The new type of education, which is as indispensable to the barrister and the joint secretary as to the brigadier and the chief personnel officer, is little more than a hundred years old in India. Even though recruitment to it is still highly selective in terms of the traditional system of stratification, it is already showing signs of widening its base. And the educational institutions (particularly the more exclusive schools and colleges) not only recruit people, but also transform them by imposing on them their own values and styles of life.

The culture of these exclusive schools and colleges is of vital importance to the character of the elites we are here considering, and it is not entirely an indigenous culture. It is a culture in which the hierarchical values of caste are largely superseded by those of a different kind.

I am not suggesting that this is true of all schools and colleges in the country, or even of a majority of them. But it is certainly true of the 'public schools' and some of the exclusive colleges which provide a disproportionately large number of people in top bureaucratic and professional positions.

It is obvious that in a country where less than 30 per cent of the people are literate and only 0.2 per cent go to college opportunities for rising to the top in the professions and in the Civil and military services are very unevenly distributed. Where less than half the population is able to go to school, people from only a certain kind of social background can afford to go to exclusive schools in which fees may run up to Rs. 3,000 per year.[6] To what extent are opportunities of this kind determined by caste? Are there other, more important social factors which facilitate the use of these channels which carry people to the top of the bureaucratic and professional worlds?

It is difficult to say how far schools in different parts of the country are in practice open to members of different castes. One can, of course, say in a general way that members of the upper castes are more highly represented in them than those of the lower. We are, however, not concerned here with schools in general, but of a particular kind, those which act as training-grounds, so to say, of the bureaucratic and professional elites. These are, in the main, English-language schools, although a few vernacular schools, such as the well-known Ballygunge Government School at Calcutta, are also important.

The most important of the English-language schools bear a broad resemblance to the English public schools and have often been modelled on them. They are mostly boarding-schools, exclusive, very expensive, and generally train students (or until recently used to train them) for the Senior Cambridge rather than the Matriculation or Higher Secondary Certificate. The better-known ones are the Doon School at Dehra Dun, St. Paul's at Darjeeling, Mayo College at Ajmere, and the Lawrence Schools at Sanawar and Lovedale.[7]

The public schools—some twenty-five in number—irrespective of their location, draw students from all over the country, or at least have a large area of recruitment in the geographical sense. To the extent that particularistic factors are important in their internal structure,

[6] What this means in terms of salaries and incomes can be gauged from the fact that a lecturer in the best universities in the country starts on a basic salary of Rs. 400 per month. Before devaluation, Rs. 3,000 per year was £230; Rs. 400 per month was £360 per year.

[7] Details regarding public schools in India can be obtained from *A Handbook of the Indian Public Schools*, Bombay, The Times of India Press, M. N. Kapur, 1964. I am grateful to Miss Veena Monga for having brought this publication to my notice.

these are likely to be language and religion rather than caste. It would be difficult indeed for students in an institution such as Doon School to place each other in a *jati* framework, since they are likely to include Khatris from Panjab, Kayasths from U.P., and Nairs from Kerala. And one could not seriously suggest that they might try to solve the problem of placement by invoking the idiom of *varna*.

It is obvious that in the 'elite' schools caste status is likely to become ambiguous and, to that extent, irrelevant, although it is perfectly true that not all castes are likely to find equal representation in them. There are other factors, mainly ideological in nature, which also tend to overshadow caste as a basis of identity within the English-medium school. But what is perhaps more important is that the school system creates fundamental cleavages within each and every caste. Those who have been to a public school (or for that matter to any English-medium school) are privileged people, and, on the whole, they tend to be acutely conscious of their exclusive status; they form status groups of a new kind which cut right across caste.[8] However strongly Brahmins, Kayasths, and Nairs may be represented in exclusive boarding-schools, only a tiny fraction of boys from these castes can afford to go to them. Brahmin, Kayasth, and Nair men who have been to one of the select public schools are likely to feel closer to each other socially than to their respective caste fellows who have managed at best to pass out of vernacular schools in some village or small town. They are likely to know each other professionally, to live in the same kind of neighbourhood, to meet each other socially, and to cultivate similar styles of life.

A foreign degree is perhaps the most useful passport to elite status in the professions and in at least some of the bureaucracies. The most successful lawyer is likely to be a barrister, the most successful doctor a F.R.C.S. or M.R.C.P.; the best commercial firms are known to show a marked preference in the selection of their elite cadres for graduates of Oxford and Cambridge, or, failing that, the London School of Economics. Not all members of even the highest castes can afford to send their children abroad; and some at least of the middle-level castes can. This creates another cleavage (closely linked with the first) which tends to cut across caste in a major way.

Apart from public schools (and English-medium schools in general), certain vernacular schools play an important part in producing future members of the bureaucratic and professional elites. Obviously, there are great regional variations in the latter, but these also tend to be rather exclusive in character. I can speak only of vernacular schools in

[8] One can perhaps speak of these, too, as castes, but only in a metaphorical way.

Bengal, and some of the most outstanding of these are: Ballygunge Government School, Mitra Institution (Bhawanipore), Hindu School, and, until recently, the school at Shantiniketan. The more successful products of these schools tend to go to Presidency College, Calcutta, and quite a few continue their educational career abroad. Admittedly, there are important differences between persons who enter a British university through Doon School and St. Stephen's College on the one hand and through Ballygunge Government School and Presidency College on the other. But in both cases caste as an active principle of social orientation plays a relatively unimportant part.

III

Business Executives

Every year established commercial firms such as I.C.I., Hindusthan Levers, and Metal Box recruit to their elite cadres young people who have passed through the most exclusive schools and colleges in the country, including a fair proportion who have spent some time abroad, if not in study, at least in being there. These include persons from a wide variety of castes of the upper and middle levels. The Scheduled Castes and Tribes appear to be very poorly represented and the Peasant castes do not seem to contribute to this group in proportion to their numbers. This still leaves a good deal of room for the group to be fairly heterogeneous in its caste composition. Kinship and other personal connexions no doubt play an important part in recruitment to it, but they appear to do so in Britain and America as well.

The *boxwalas*,[9] as they are called, tend to be a very cosmopolitan set, and, along with officers of the armed forces, perhaps the most anglicized. The reason for this is largely that the best firms were until recently British firms, and the highest salaries are still paid, among Indians, to those who are 'home-covenanted' rather than 'firm-covenanted'; that is, people who were given appointments directly from Britain. The 'home-covenanted' Indians try to live up to the image of their British superiors, and the 'firm-covenanted' ones to that of the 'home-covenanted'. And, unlike I.A.S. probationers, covenanted staff do not have to go through the kind of rigorous training that might bring them face to face with Indian rather than Western culture.

[9] This term is widely used to refer to high-salaried business executives. Its origin is Anglo-Indian; the *memsahib* sat on her veranda and did her shopping from a 'box-wallah', or pedlar, who brought a box of silks, threads, and buttons. The term was applied to business people, in semi-jocular contempt, by the British bureaucrats. Canal engineers were similarly referred to as '*bhistis*', or water-carriers, and—in retaliation and with semi-jocular malice—the Indian Civil Service were 'the Heaven-Born'. (Ed.).

A position in even the best commercial firm carries less prestige than one in the Indian Administrative Service, although it is rather more lucrative. More often than not the executive tends to be a generalist with little specialized training to begin with. Family connexions (as opposed to caste status in the broader sense), social poise, and a certain kind of education are the most important criteria of selection. For the rising executive, fluency in the art of English conversation and familiarity with Western party manners are likely to be greater assets for mobility than a knowledge of the rituals of the twice-born.

In Calcutta and Bombay the social life of the *boxwala* centres around parties, clubs, and expensive restaurants. For them it is more important to belong to a smart set than to have been born into the highest caste. Domestic furniture, interior decoration, and tastes in theatre, films, and music show a pronounced Western orientation. As a mark of distinction, some may cultivate an interest in the plays of Wesker or John Osborne; a fortunate few may pile up copies of the *Oxford Gazette* or the *Cambridge Reporter*; and one or two may have an occasional letter published in the columns of *New Statesman*. These are the Bunties of V. S. Naipaul, with their public school or British university education, their near perfect English accents, and their sophisticated 'craze for foreign'.[10] On the whole, they are rather far removed from the centres of power.

Military Officers

Top officers of the armed services are certainly closer to the centres of power, and they have much in common in their social background and style of life with the group just considered. There are, I believe, only three Sandhurst-trained officers left in the Indian Army, but the Sandhurst model is still very much alive in the upper echelons of the service. Anglicized nicknames, common among *boxwalas*, recur in the army: 'Kipper' for Cariappa, 'Timmy' for Thimayya.

Merit and aptitude (as opposed to family connexions) appear to play a more important part in the selection of officers than in recruitment to commercial establishments, since the selection procedure involves competitive examinations which are both rigorous and elaborate. But, once again, promotion within the services depends in part on qualities of social poise and grace which derive less from caste than from the kind of social milieu out of which successful business executives emerge.

It is true that the British gave a certain recognition to particularistic

[10] See V. S. Naipaul, *An Area of Darkness*, London, Deutsch, and New York, Macmillan, 1964; the *boxwalas* seem to be far less disoriented than Mr. Naipaul makes them out to be.

principles in the organization of the Indian Army through the concept of 'martial race': there are regiments of Jats, Marathas, Gurkhas, etc.[11] But these principles play little or no part in the selection, promotion, and transfer of officers; certainly not in the higher echelons. In fact, service as an officer, with its frequent transfers and its long periods of exile from one's native social milieu, requires the individual to enter into close relations with fellow officers who are likely to belong to a wide range of linguistic and religious groups, not to speak of castes. Officers often tend to be primarily English-speaking and cosmopolitan, if only because the all-India character of the services forces them to be so.

One can get a fair idea of the styles of life of officers and of the more important criteria of status evaluation among them by observing their behaviour in the various messes and quarters in which they live. The Central Vista Mess for Air Force officers, situated on Janpath in the heart of New Delhi, may serve as a good example. There is much there to remind one of the glories of the British Raj: the silver, the cut glass, and the linen remain the same. Officers spend their evenings playing billiards or poker, and drinking beer, whisky, or rum. Informal groups are formed with an almost complete indifference to the principles of caste. One of the groups I knew well (and which was not perceptibly different from many of the others) consisted of a Bengali Kayasth, a Reddi from Andhra, a Tamil Brahmin, and a Lingayat from Mysore; Muslims and Christians were welcome to join if they wished.

The tone of social life in an officers' mess is in many ways highly anglicized, and parties and dating are important elements in it. In one such mess I was talking to the wife of an officer about an acquaintance, a captain in the army, whom she could not at first identify. 'Oh yes,' she said eventually,' the handsome fellow who had an arranged marriage.' It does not follow from this that arranged marriages are uncommon among officers of the Indian Army. What is true, however, is that the range of choice in the selection of spouses is far wider among officers of the armed forces than would be allowed by the traditional rules of caste (or, strictly speaking, sub-sub-subcaste) endogamy.[12] (This would be substantially true of the business executives discussed earlier.)

To what extent does family background count towards promotion in the army, and in what sense? To the extent that polish, manners, and social poise are important, an officer who comes from an upper middle-

---

[11] See M. S. A. Rao, 'Caste and the Indian Army', *Economic Weekly*, 29 August 1964, pp. 1439-43.

[12] See my 'Pattern of Status Groups', *Seminar*, No. LXX, June 1965, pp. 14-16.

class family and has been to a public school has an advantage over one who is lower middle-class in origin and a product of a vernacular school. Granted the fact that officers are more likely to come from the upper and middle levels of the caste hierarchy, the difference between, say, Brahmin and Khatri, or between Rajput and Kayasth is likely to be of little significance. The family backgrounds of those who are selected for higher command and staff training at the Staff College at Wellington are likely to be more homogeneous in terms of income, occupation, and education than in terms of caste.

The Indian Administrative Service

The Indian Administrative Service or I.A.S. (along with the Indian Foreign Service, or I.F.S.) constitutes the most important and influential service in the country. It consists of a small and very select group of around 2,000 persons who provide the country with its top administrators and Civil Servants. Recruitment to the I.A.S. is mainly by open competition, although a few posts are filled every year by departmental promotion. Some of the most talented young men (and an increasing number of women) compete every year for the I.A.S. examinations, which include written as well as oral tests of a fairly comprehensive nature. Successful candidates have to undergo probation for a year, during which they are trained in a wide variety of subjects ranging from language to law—and horse-riding.

The Indian component of the Indian Civil Service (I.C.S.)—of which the I.A.S. is the successor—was in its earlier phase made up almost entirely of members of two or three top castes. In Madras between 1892 and 1904, out of sixteen successful candidates for the I.C.S., fifteen were Brahmins.[13] In Bengal during this period all or almost all Indian members of the I.C.S. were either Brahmins or Kayasths. The position in Bombay appears to have been broadly similar.

The caste base of the I.A.S. has broadened considerably over the last several years. This broadening has come about as a result of several factors. First of all, the annual intake of the I.A.S. has risen significantly: 'The direct intake rose fairly steadily from 33 in 1947 to 73 in 1959 but the Krishnamachari Report (1962) makes it clear that the annual figure needs to be near 100.'[14] Fifty years ago, when the annual

[13] G. V. Subba Rao, *Life and Times of K. V. Reddi Naidu*, Rajahmundry, Addepally and Co., 1957, pp. 17–19.
[14] W. H. Morris-Jones, *The Government and Politics of India*, London, Hutchinson, 1964, p. 122.

intake was much smaller and the British component outnumbered the Indian, there were very few posts indeed to go between a very large number of castes. Secondly, English education (including public school education), which is so important for recruitment to the I.A.S., is no longer a monopoly of Brahmins and Kayasths to the extent that it was fifty years ago. Finally, the reservation of seats for the Backward Classes has ensured representation for a fairly wide range of castes. Until recently most of the seats reserved for them could not be filled for want of qualified candidates; since 1962, all posts reserved for the Backward Classes have been actually filled.[15]

While it is possible, within certain limits, to ensure the representation of castes belonging to a fairly wide range, it would be far more difficult to do this with regard to classes. It would not appear feasible to have seats in the Indian Administrative Service reserved for agricultural labourers or factory workers, or even their sons. Given the educational and other conditions required for competition, it would be safe to say that children of working-class parents are not likely to be represented in the I.A.S., and those of lower middle-class parents very poorly represented.

Professor Morris-Jones has provided certain interesting facts regarding the social background of I.A.S. officers in terms of occupation and education; unfortunately, similar facts relating to caste are not easily available. He says:

Of 350 appointees over a few years, 200 were sons of government officials and a further 100 were from professional families. Nearly 100 had a 'public school' education in India or abroad. Only 15 per cent came from rural areas. The predominance of certain universities—and, even more, of certain old-established colleges—is quite marked.[16]

The importance of education in a public school (and its counterparts the 'old-established college' and the British university) cannot be too strongly emphasized. People who have been through this kind of education stand out in any social context. In England the difference between a public school accent and an ordinary one is, after all, only a matter of subtle variation. In India it may well be a question of two different languages. Those who have been to a public school often speak English in a near perfect manner; those who have not may well find it difficult to make themselves intelligible in English. And the ability to

---

[15] A. Béteille, 'The Future of the Backward Classes: the Competing Demands of Status and Power', *Perspectives, Supplement to the Indian Journal of Public Administration*, Vol. XI, No. 1, January–March 1965, p. 23, also included as Chapter V of this volume.

[16] Morris-Jones, op. cit., p. 122.

speak English with fluency and poise is viewed as a most estimable quality in many higher social circles in India.

I.A.S. probationers can be differentiated into the public school type and the others. Anyone who has observed social life at the Indian Academy of Administration (where probationers spend their time, off and on, for a year) cannot fail to determine which is the dominant type. On one occasion, after I had given a talk at the Academy, I was visited in my hotel by a probationer who came from a lower middle-class family in a small town in Western India. After some time he asked me a question which had obviously bothered him a great deal. 'Tell me, sir,' he said, 'We who haven't been to Oxford or Cambridge, or even to St. Stephen's College, do you think that we have really missed something in life?' I gathered later that he was a Chitpavan Brahmin, which indicates that his status anxieties were clearly not on account of caste.

The dominance of the public school type among young officers of the I.A.S. is not accepted without challenge. The challenge may come from a number of sources of which I shall indicate only two. These are, on the one hand, the attractions of regional as opposed to Western culture; and, on the other, the demands of certain emergent political forces. Both these processes lead to what may be loosely described as the Indianization of the service, but this does not by any means imply that the role of caste in it is necessarily strengthened as a consequence.

People who come to the service from areas such as Bengal, Maharashtra, and Tamilnad, which have well-developed and highly self-conscious regional cultures, view with growing disdain the imitative Westernization of some of their colleagues. There are apt to be differences in taste between these groups in literature, music, and the other arts, accompanied by more pervasive differences in styles of life. In other words, the Western style of life, which was dominant in the old I.C.S., is likely to be opposed increasingly by secular, regional styles of life in which the Western element is less obtrusive.

The political scene in India has changed rapidly since Independence. District leaders and party bosses have much more power now and more effective contacts with the centres of power higher up than they ever had before. The I.A.S. officer has to begin his career in the districts where he has got to learn to come to terms on a new basis with elected political leaders whose styles of life are often very different from his own. Public school manners are not always likely to be helpful, and today a tactless officer is likely to come up against firm resistance from political leaders whom he cannot dismiss as lightly as his predecessor might have done during the British Raj. There seems to be a growing awareness of this, not only among the new generation of probationers, but also among those who are responsible for selecting and training them. How far this awareness will lead to a change in the character of the service is at this stage somewhat difficult to foretell.

Professionals : the Intellectuals

Lack of space compels me to confine myself in this paper to what may broadly be regarded as the 'intellectual' professions, although it would be very interesting to study, for instance, the legal profession and changes in its social composition and political influence over the last six or seven decades.[17] I shall consider only two main categories of intellectuals: those engaged in literary pursuits, including certain forms of journalism, and those who, as trained social scientists (primarily economists), influence directly or indirectly the policy-making process.

I shall ignore the literary works of authors who write in English and consider only some of the vernacular literatures which are not only more creative and seminal but also far more significant in the scope of their social and cultural influence. I shall choose my examples primarily from Bengali and Tamil literature. Literary works in Malayalam and Marathi are also of considerable significance, but I do not have the competence to discuss them.

Creative writers, particularly in the vernacular languages, appear to be drawn from a wider social base than the groups which we have so far considered. Although here, too, the top castes (or at least castes with traditions of literacy, such as Brahmins, Kayasthas, and Baidyas) are overrepresented, there is greater diversity in terms of education and parental occupation. A public school type of education is far less relevant to a literary career in Bengali and Tamil than to a position in I.C.I., the army, or even the I.A.S. Not only are many of the younger poets, short-story writers, and journalists in Bengal sons of clerks and schoolteachers, but several are themselves clerks and teachers, or started their career in similar occupations.

In Tamilnad, as is well known, the field of letters was until a few decades ago dominated even more strongly by Brahmins. But the last two decades in particular have witnessed a significant change. The Dravidian movement, and especially the D.M.K., has contributed profusely

[17] It would be interesting to ask, for instance, why people with a training in economics tend to have an increasingly greater say in the running of the country than those with a training in law. The situation was very different in the days of Motilal Nehru, C. R. Das, Gandhi, and Patel.

(if not richly) to modern Tamil literature. Many of the leaders of the D.M.K., which was (and still is to a large extent) a non-Brahmin movement, are popular literary figures. Among other things, they have sought to restore to the Tamil language its pristine vigour by eliminating from it what they consider to be superfluous Sanskritic accretions. Quite apart from their literary merits (which I have no competence to assess), the writings of authors such as Annadurai and Karunanidhi (both top leaders of the D.M.K.), have a very wide social appeal.

The influence of creative literary writers and also of journalists is, on the whole, diffuse; this is true of even such committed political writers as Karunanidhi and Annadurai. A somewhat different role is played by the trained social scientist who either works for the Government or acts in an advisory capacity through membership of various consultative committees appointed by it. In order not to draw the line too sharply between the first group and the second, one has to point to the academic social scientist who is interested in reaching a wider public through articles in periodicals of various kinds, while remaining aloof from committee work associated with the Government.

In a society which has adopted centralized planning in a large way, the need for trained social scientists to act as advisers to the Government is self-evident. The Planning Commission has a large staff of highly skilled personnel, and there are some in the Ministry of Finance and the Reserve Bank. Most of the top people (whether employees or members of various 'panels') are either economists or statisticians.

There are about ten or fifteen top economists[18] in Delhi who play a crucial part in the formulation of the Plans and in advising the Government in various capacities. What is the social background of these ten or fifteen persons? In terms of caste, they cover an extremely wide spectrum, ranging from Thiya through Patidar to Kayasth and Baidya and Brahmin. This small and select group is also very heterogeneous in its regional background; there are in it people from Gujarat, Maharashtra, Mysore, Kerala, Madras, West Bengal, and U.P.

I am not in a position to give precise data on the earlier educational background of this group, but almost all its members finished their education in one or another foreign university, the two most popular institutions being Cambridge and the London School of Economics. Since several of them also took a first degree at Cambridge, Oxford, or the London School of Economics it may be inferred that they came from professional or upper middle-class families.

---

[18] Including 'bureaucrats' who are heads of government departments as well as experts who are mainly academic people.

It is probable that the foreign training of most of India's top economic advisers leaves them with a certain lack of awareness of the realities
of social life in India. This is a criticism often voiced against them in the
context of the relative failure of Indian planning. I have neither the
time nor the competence to discuss here the validity of this criticism. I
can only quote the observations of a well-known economist who has
had some close association with Indian planning. In the words of
Wilfred Malenbaum:

> The Indian economist is a great admirer of the more developed countries.
> Despite their insistence that they are to do things 'their own way', it is hard
> to admit that an Indian way may in fact be different from the admired ways of
> the richer countries.
>   Leading Indian economists are held in high public esteem. There may be
> an unwillingness to admit how limited is the basis of their understanding of
> India's basic economic structure.[19]

It would be safe to suggest that there is a difference in orientation
between India's leading economists and certain powerful sections of its
political elite. I shall try briefly to indicate the nature of this difference
after considering some of the characteristics of the political elite in the
following section.

IV

The Political Elite

In a sense the most radical change in India during the last two decades
has been in its political institutions. The entire character of the formal
political structure was overhauled with the introduction of adult
franchise and the three General Elections held on its basis. Coupled
with this has been the effort to build up an infrastructure of democratic
institutions through the system of *panchayati raj* (the newly instituted
system of local government). Whatever may be one's evaluation of the
pace of these changes or the desirability of some of their consequences,
there can be no question that the changes have not been merely formal
in nature. More than one author has drawn attention to the widening
of the base of the political system and the increasing opportunities of
mobility provided by it.[20]

It is fairly well known that till the 1920s the Congress (along with
other political parties) was dominated to a very great extent by upper-

[19] W. Malenbaum, 'Who Does the Planning?' in R. L. Park and I. Tinker, (Eds.),
Leadership and Political Institutions in India, Princeton, 1959, p. 312.

[20] See Myron Weiner, 'The Politics of South Asia', in G. Almond and J. Coleman
(Eds.), *The Politics of the Developing Areas*, Princeton, Princeton University Press, 1960;
also Béteille, 'The Future of the Backward Classes', (pp. 83–120 of the present volume).

caste, professional, and landowning people. In Duverger's terminology, these were caucus parties rather than mass parties. How far did this kind of domination persist after Gandhi's radical reorganization of the Congress in the 1920s? Many would argue that the social composition of the top leadership has not altered basically, if at all. I shall present a few crucial facts to show that this is not altogether so.

Even in the 1920s and 1930s the top leadership of the nationalist movement was by no means homogeneous in its caste composition, although most of its members were either of upper middle-class background or professional people usually with British university degrees. There can be little doubt that the homogeneity of this group derived more from profession and education than from caste. In a recent book on leadership in India we are presented with pen portraits of three of India's most successful nationalist leaders, Nehru Subhas Bose, and Patel.[21] These, along with Gandhi[22] (and Jinnah),[23] should by any reasonable standard be regarded as a fair sample for the study of India's top political leaders in the two or three decades prior to Independence.

The castes of these four leaders cover an extremely wide range in terms of the categories of the traditional system. Nehru was a Brahmin, Gandhi a Bania, Patel a Patidar (who declared that Patidars were Sudras), and Bose was of the Kayasth caste, which in Bengal is generally held to belong to the Sudra (and *not* the Kshatriya) category. Yet there was much in common in the occupational backgrounds of these leaders. Three of them were barristers, and Subhas Bose was an I.C.S., with the added glamour of having turned down the appointment after being selected. Barristers and civilians[24] enjoyed in those days (even more than today) the highest status among occupational groups. Further, all the four men had finished their education in England: Nehru and Subhas Bose at Cambridge, and Gandhi and Patel at London.

Throughout the 1920s, 1930s, and 1940s, new leaders were being trained, largely as a result of Gandhi's mass movements, who not only came from a plurality of castes, but were socially heterogeneous in other regards as well. Many of these did not attain eminence till after Independence. In order to highlight the kind of change that has been taking place since Independence, I shall contrast two pairs of leaders: Nehru and Patel on the one hand, and Shastri and Kamraj on the other.

[21] Park and Tinker, op. cit.

[22] Gandhi is also discussed in the book, but in a separate section.

[23] I exclude Jinnah from this discussion, but his inclusion would strengthen, not weaken my argument.

[24] A word commonly used to denote officers of the I.C.S.

Morris-Jones has spoken of the duumvirate of Nehru and Patel.[25] If these two constituted a duumvirate in 1950, then the same label could be applied to Shastri and Kamraj fifteen years later.

There is no need to emphasize Nehru's Harrow and Cambridge background, or his familiarity with Western political ideas and Western culture and styles of life. It is sometimes forgotten how much of the Western social idiom had also been assimilated by Patel. Consider, for instance, the following picture of him, presented by one of his professional colleagues: 'A smart young man dressed in a well-cut suit, with a felt hat worn slightly at an angle. . . . Such was the new barrister who had come to Ahmedabad for practice.'[26] It is true that when the occasion demanded Patel could discard both Western clothes and manners; but so indeed could Nehru, though less unequivocally than the former.

It is difficult to visualize Shastri or Kamraj in Western clothes, and Western manners were perhaps only a little less strange to them than Western clothes. Kamraj represents the extreme case of a political leader of all-India stature who can barely speak English.[27] He would have been very much out of place, socially, among the genteel politicians who started the Indian National Congress in 1885 or the Justice Party in 1916-17. Yet it is undeniable that he has been one of the most successful leaders, not only in Madras but in India as a whole.

Shastri and Subhas Bose were both Kayasths by caste, but apart from that there was little else in common in their social background. Bose came from a wealthy professional family and went to Cambridge in his youth. Shastri was the son of a poor schoolteacher, who had never been outside India till he became Prime Minister. He was never fully at ease in the Western idiom, and yet, as events were to show, he was not wholly ineffectual as Nehru's successor.

It would be very misleading to view Shastri and Kamraj as representing the only dominant element in India's contemporary political elite. But the importance of such elements has clearly grown over the last two or three decades, and it has grown faster here than in the other elite is far more heterogeneous in its social composition than appears to the older elite and the new one, as the succession of Mrs. Gandhi to the office of Prime Minister clearly demonstrates. In effect, the political elite is far more heterogeneous in its social composition than appears to be the case with the bureaucratic or even the intellectual elite.

[25] Op. cit.

[26] Op. cit., p. 88.

[27] The case of Azad, who was a scholar of eminence, but refused to speak English as a matter of principle, is quite different.

The political elite is indeed very mixed in its social composition. The Cabinet, for instance, includes at one end individuals steeped in the Western idiom such as Indira Gandhi, M. C. Chagla, and Sachin Chaudhuri, and, at the other, men like D. Sanjiviya, Jagjivan Ram, and G. L. Nanda, whose cultural and political styles are much more traditional. These differences in style correspond to differences in social origins. The eighteen members of the Congress Working Committee are also heterogeneous in their social origins, the upper middle-class, professional elements being even less pronounced here than in the Cabinet.

It would be very difficult to discern any pattern in terms of caste in either the central Cabinet or the Committee. There are Brahmins, Non-Brahmins of various kinds, and members of the Backward Classes. At that level regional and religious representation becomes more important than caste, except that some representation of the Backward Classes (particularly the Scheduled Castes) is sought to be ensured, but they are generally groupings of a broader kind within which caste is subsumed.

Caste enters much more directly into the composition of political elites at the state level, where the regional (or linguistic) factor is a constant. Thus the Mysore Cabinet is dominated by Lingayats and Okkaligas, the Maharashtra Cabinet by Marathas, and some have referred to the Madras Cabinet as a federation of dominant castes. And at this level caste may be important not only in the process of recruitment but also in the internal structure of the political elite. Whether one is a Kayasth or a Bhumihar or a Rajput is likely to determine one's actions to a much greater extent in the Bihar Cabinet than among I.A.S. or army officers in Bihar. For politicians, being chosen by election, are dependent on public support to a much greater extent than administrators who are selected in an entirely different way.

The extent to which public support is given on the basis of caste is difficult to determine in an exact way. Clearly, there are great regional variations, and in every region caste has to compete increasingly with other factors as a basis for mobilizing support.

V

From what has been said in the foregoing it may appear natural to contrast the political and bureaucratic elites in terms of tradition and modernity. There is, in fact, a view widely held among Western-educated Indians that the new type of political leader is ignorant, semi-literate, and crafty in the arts of manipulating the loyalties of caste and community, in other words, traditionalist, obscurantist, and reactionary; whereas the planner and the administrator are seen as representing reasonableness, intellectual clarity, and modernity. Yet this contrast, when posed in terms of a simple dichotomy of tradition and modernity, may be misleading.

Modernization is not a simple process and it cannot be achieved by a set of simple imitative devices. It requires not only clarity of goals and objectives, but also deep sympathy and an understanding of the needs, limitations, and even prejudices of people. Planners and administrators who feel that the task demands no more than the most 'modern' kind of blueprint are bound to fail and, in the process, to attribute their failure to the perversity of the people.

No one can deny the indispensability in a developing society of a 'sober, task-oriented, professionally responsible stratum of the population,'[28] but there is more to it than just this. No amount of professional competence can be effective in the absence of enthusiasm, and it is doubtful how far this can be created by planners and administrators alone. It is easy to say that the enthusiasm of the masses can be misdirected by selfish or irresponsible political leaders, and this has been done often enough. But among those who turn away from the demagogy of the politician there are some for whom modernity is merely a matter of style, to be cultivated in private and exclusive circles; they are not likely to be very effectual.

In the final analysis it may be necessary to distinguish between modernity and modernism; and, correspondingly, between modernizing and modernistic elites. These categories are admittedly vague; they are not exhaustive; and they do not by any means correspond to the division between political and non-political elites. To the extent that an elite has acquired merely the symbols and styles of life, or even the skills of high status groups in more advanced societies, it is modernistic. It becomes modernizing only when it succeeds in utilizing these skills in a socially significant way, without attaching too much importance to styles of life which may have been historically associated with groups in which such skills originated.

The concept of modernization is an elusive one. It is easier to indicate what it is not than to say exactly what it is. It would be safe to maintain, for instance, that many of the cultural symbols which have historically emerged out of the public school and Oxbridge systems are

[28] E. Shils, in (ed.) L. W. Pye, 'Demagogues and Cadres in the Political Development of the New States', *Communications and Political Development*, Princeton, N.J., Princeton University Press, 1963, p. 69.

not necessary ingredients of modernity. The imitative adoption of such symbols in a society with a different cultural tradition may lead not to modernization but to its opposite. Taking the different categories described above, this tendency is probably most conspicuous in social circles dominated by business executives and officers of the armed forces.

Economists and other social scientists whose approach is dominated by foreign planning models are more difficult to place. Here there is generally a much clearer awareness of the issues involved and a more sophisticated grasp of the substance (and not merely the form) of Western culture. Planners in India are on the whole forward-looking people, but the desire to see the economy push ahead often creates in them an impatience (and a kind of psychological block) towards the demands of region, religion, and community which cannot just be wished away. Those who are responsible for planning will have to attune themselves not only to the goals of economic development but also to the ways of life of the people which the process of planning seeks to change.

Administrators have to face a task which in this regard is not very different from that of the planners. The Indian Administrative Service has so far been largely dominated by products of 'public schools' and a few 'old-established colleges'; such people have had in the past an overweening consciousness of their exclusive and elitist position. There are signs that this is changing. The I.A.S. is likely to fulfil its modernizing functions successfully only as its base of recruitment widens and its members rid themselves of the consciousness of belonging to a world which is different from that of the people for and with whom they now have to work.

In India, particularly among intellectuals, the modernizing role of the political elite tends to be underplayed. What is emphasized is the low level of education of the new generation of political leaders, and corruption, nepotism, and communalism, which, admittedly, are all likely to impede the process of modernization. It is true that the level of education and the debating skills of the Congress Working Committee in 1965 were below those of the people who started the Indian National Congress in 1885. But it is difficult to infer from this that a group of the latter kind would be more suited than the former to the task of modernizing a large and independent country, comprising a high proportion of illiterate peasants, within a democratic framework. This is not to deny the real dangers of demagogery and sectionalism, but merely to raise a question about the substance, as opposed to the form, of modernity.

XI

Cohesion and Division in Indian Elites

BY T. B. BOTTOMORE

Head of Department of Political Science, Sociology, and Anthropology, Simon Fraser University, British Columbia

THE elite groups in Indian society have not as yet been closely studied. The composition and recruitment of elites, the relations between them, their prestige and influence, the extent to which they are separated from the mass of the people, the degree of their internal unity, are all subjects upon which the available information is both scattered and incomplete. This essay is, therefore, exploratory in nature. I shall attempt to distinguish some of the important elements which make for cohesion or division in Indian elites, and to assemble what pertinent knowledge can be gleaned from recent studies.[1]

It is interesting, first of all, to observe some broad differences between elites in India and in the industrial societies. In the latter, according to one well-known study,[2] five major elite groups may be distinguished: political leaders, government administrators, economic directors (businessmen and managers), leaders of the masses (principally trade-union leaders), and military chiefs. Not all of these groups have the same importance in India. Thus, for reasons which B. B. Misra has elucidated in his book *The Indian Middle Classes*, no real bourgeoisie has developed in India, and although individual businessmen and specific interest groups may have some political influence, there does not seem to be, at present, a business elite exerting the kind of pervasive social and political influence which is apparent in the

---

[1] I have discussed the general characteristics of elites and their role in the developing countries in my *Elites and Society*, London, Watts, 1964; and the case of India more particularly in 'Modern Elites in India', Chapter IX of *Towards a Sociology of Culture in India* (edited by T. K. N. Unnithan, Indra Deva and Yogendra Singh, New Delhi, 1965).

[2] R. Aron, 'Social Structure and the Ruling Class', *British Journal of Sociology*, Vol. I, Nos. 1 and 2, March–June 1950.

Western societies. Similarly, the trade-union leaders, because of the slow growth of unions and the predominantly agricultural and rural character of Indian society, do not yet form an important elite. The position of the military chiefs is less clear. Until a few years ago most observers would have said that in India, unlike many other developing countries, the political role of military leaders was unimportant; but the border conflicts with China and Pakistan and increasing military expenditure have changed the situation, and the place of the military elite in Indian society now needs to be re-examined.

The two elite groups which are unquestionably important are the political leaders and the high government officials. These groups have borne the major responsibility for India's economic and social development thus far, and they are likely to bear it in the foreseeable future. It is with their position in Indian society that I shall be mainly concerned. There is, however, one other group which deserves attention: the intellectuals. In all literate societies, at least, intellectuals have an important place, whether as scribes, as experts, or as ideologists; and in the modern industrial societies they have become more influential both as experts in the fields of science, technology, and economic management, and as ideologists responsible for expressing and forming social doctrines and ideas in democratic régimes. Their role may well be of outstanding importance in the developing countries, where they are the rare possessors of scientific and technical knowledge, and where also, as ideologists, they may inspire radical movements for social change.

This discussion so far may suggest that since there are, in India, fewer elite groups at the national level—the major ones being the political leaders and government officials—there is probably less competition between elites than is the case in the Western industrial societies. A like conclusion may be drawn from the sphere of political leadership itself. India is not a 'one-party state', but it is a 'one-dominant-party system',[3] without any effective rival to the governing Congress Party. In these conditions, it is possible that divisions will emerge *within* the elites themselves, and this is made easier where there are already major social differences—such as those of caste and language—which provide a foundation. There have not been lacking scholars who have seen, in present-day India, the signs of profound disunity in the national elites. Two of the divisions which they discern are that between traditionalists and modernists, and those between regions; and I shall begin with a discussion of these issues.

[3] The phrase is used by W. H. Morris-Jones, *The Government and Politics of India*, London, Hutchinson, 1964.

The distinction between tradition and modernity is frequently made with reference to the developing countries, but it is not easy to set it forth in precise terms. It would hardly be illuminating if it meant only the contrast between a previously established form of society and the present conditions of change; that is, a simple chronological opposition. Generally, the distinction formulates the experience of the West European countries in passing from feudalism to modern capitalism, from the *ancien régime* to the *régime moderne*. On one side of this divide is a form of society in which religious thought is pre-eminent, technological and economic change is slow, the movement between social strata is limited, and the strata themselves are very clearly separated; on the other side is a type of society in which thought is mainly secular, and science and technology assume great importance, economic change is rapid, and there is considerable mobility between the various social strata. In these terms, a contrast may be drawn between the traditional system of Indian society, especially of Hindu society, and the new system which is being established through industrialization and political democracy. The question then is: are there now any influential traditionalist elites? Here the observation made by D. P. Mukerji seems to me just: 'Everywhere the old elite-groups have disappeared; here too they are going; and no new ones, barring the professional politician and the bureaucrat, are to be seen. To keep Brahminism as a going social concern in this universe is an old maid's dream. . . . Ten presidents can wash the feet of ten thousand Brahmins but the Brahmin's prestige in this field cannot be restored.'[4] There have been no significant Brahmin social and political movements, and even the more traditionalist religious groups have turned their attention increasingly to social welfare activities of a modern kind.

The absence of distinctive traditionalist elites—even the 'communal' political parties, where they have any strength, are not wholly traditional—means that the opposition between traditionalism and modernism, so far as it occurs, finds expression within the dominant elites. This opposition can be easily discerned, but not so easily evaluated, in political life. In the Congress Party, it was expressed in some measure by the differences between Gandhi and Nehru—but Gandhi was not simply a traditionalist, and Nehru was not simply a modernist. It is expressed at the present time by the coexistence of different 'styles' or 'idioms' of politics: the modern, the traditional, and the saintly, to use the terms which W. H. Morris-Jones has employed.[5] The modern

[4] D. P. Mukerji, *Diversities*, New Delhi, People's Publishing House, 1958, p. 73.
[5] Morris-Jones, op. cit., p. 52.

style is represented by the system of parliamentary democracy, by the courts and the higher administration. The traditional element is to be found largely in village politics, where caste, kinship, and factions have an important role. Finally, saintly politics has its basis in ancient religious ideals; it was one element in Gandhi's political thought, and it is expressed most fully today by Vinoba Bhave and J. P. Narayan.

This differentiation of political 'styles' refers primarily to the existence of levels or areas of politics which are in some degree self-contained and separate from each other. A study of Orissa, by F. G. Bailey,[6] illustrates this point and brings out some additional features. The author distinguishes between an 'elite arena' of politics, which is that of the state government, and a 'village arena'. The former is modern, the latter traditional. But there is also an intermediate region, that of constituency politics, where the two extremes meet and have to accommodate themselves to each other. In this process, Bailey suggests, the political activities of the state and the constituencies tend to absorb and transform (that is, modernize) those of the village. The elite itself appears to be more or less united—both socially and politically—and Bailey poses the question whether it could not be conceived as a middle class which is 'set in opposition to the peasants or the landless labourers or the industrial workers of Orissa'.[7] This idea is rejected mainly on the grounds that there is no corporate group of peasants and workers—and thus no clearly defined rival elite within the state—and also that the unity of the elite is, in fact, mainly displayed in its relations with external groups, with the elites of other states and with the Delhi Government.

A recent study of political leadership in Uttar Pradesh shows the Congress Party much more distinctly as a middle-class elite whose power is based upon property ownership:

In all four rural districts studied, the leadership and the major sources of support for the local Congress organizations have been drawn from the high caste ex-tenants of the *zamindars* and *talukdars* and from the petty and middle ex-*zamindars*. Power in the countryside rests upon control of the land. The power of the Congress rests upon its network of relationships—established through its leadership and through its control of local government and co-operative institutions—with the locally influential communities in the villages, with those who control the land.[8]

---

[6] F. G. Bailey, *Politics and Social Change: Orissa in 1959*, Berkeley, University of California Press, 1963.

[7] Op. cit., p. 228.

[8] P. R. Brass, *Factional Politics in an Indian State: The Congress Party in Uttar Pradesh* Berkeley, University of California Press, 1965, p. 229.

The unity of this leadership is continually threatened by factional
conflicts, which are a traditional feature of Indian society, and which
have their source in patron–client relationships such as those between
landowner and tenant, lawyer and client, leader and local community
(the latter involving caste loyalties, but extending beyond a single caste).
Factions have been able to flourish in Uttar Pradesh in part because
the political supremacy of Congress in the state has not been seriously
challenged. When there is a challenge, as in one district from the
Swatantra Party, the ruling group closes its ranks and factionalism
declines.

On the national level the political elite, and especially the governing
Congress Party, also has to deal with the traditional politics of the
village on one side and with the saintly politics of the *Bhūdan* movement on the other. But here, too, just as in the case of Orissa or Uttar
Pradesh, the influence of modern politics as practised by the elite seems
to be preponderant, while within the elite itself there is equally little
evidence of any profound division between modernists and traditionalists. No doubt some Congress leaders are more deeply concerned about
cow protection or the prohibition of alcoholic drinks, others about the
development of the steel industry or the provision of military equipment, but such differences have not produced any major rifts. If any
single issue could be pointed to as a source of disunity at the present
time, it would probably be the differences of opinion about the desirable scope of public as against private enterprise in India, or, more
broadly, the respective merits of socialism and capitalism as forms of
society—and this is a thoroughly modern question.

Among the high officials and military chiefs the problem of tradition
versus modernity scarcely arises, for both groups are entirely modern
in their education, their activities, and their professional outlook. The
case of the intellectuals is different and more complex. In most modern
societies intellectuals have formed a rather vaguely defined social
category, within which diverse groups have emerged and have coexisted
or contended with each other. From the eighteenth century up to the
present time one prominent line of division, in the Western societies
has been that between conservative and radical intellectuals. More
recently, the opposition has been complemented, or as some would
argue, supplanted, by a distinction between ' scientists' and 'humanists'
It is possible to trace some divisions of this kind in modern India; to
see, for example, in Ram Mohan Roy a progenitor of a radical intellectual class which reached maturity in the independence struggle, or to
observe the formation of a modern intellectual class through the intro-

duction of Western science and the establishment of Western Universities in India. But these developments in Indian culture have not produced such a rigorous opposition of doctrines, on such an extensive scale, as occurred in many of the Western countries. There has been no 'battle of the books', no influential group of *philosophes*, no general conflict between science and religion. In part this must be explained by the fact that Western thought was introduced into India by a colonial ruling power, and was diffused in a foreign language; with the consequence that the struggle for independence could be seen as demanding a reaffirmation of the traditional culture, perhaps interpreted in new ways and incorporating some elements borrowed from the West, but still fundamentally Indian. This contest between the indigenous and the foreign still continues, in discussions of the use of the English language, although it has lost the sharpness which it had for earlier generations, for Tagore or Nehru. Its outcome is well expressed by I. P. Desai when he writes: 'What we may have is a Western-influenced, Indian-oriented ideology and the large mass of the new intellectuals probably belongs to this category. Ideologically, we do not have genuine Westernization.'[9]

On the other side, Brahminism, which established the cultural unity of the traditional society, is incompatible, in many respects, with the conditions of life in a developing industrial society, and it has lost much of its vitality. Yet its influence is still considerable, and as M. N. Srinivas has observed on numerous occasions,[10] the processes of Westernization and Sanskritization are going on together in modern India. Thus, while some members of higher castes become Westernized—and this may be a very imperfect Westernization—members of lower castes are being drawn more fully into the traditional type of society by the adoption of Brahmin doctrines and practices. The result is a mixture of modern and traditional ideas, rather than a confrontation between them.

This is especially striking in a field where the pre-eminence of modern ideas might be expected to be uncontested, in the social sciences. It is often suggested that the sociologist or anthropologist and even the economist, working in India needs to have a peculiarly intimate acquaintance with the traditional society, regardless of the matter which he is studying. D. P. Mukerji claimed, for instance, that

---

[9] I. P. Desai, 'The New Elite', in *Towards a Sociology of Culture in India*, p. 154.

[10] See, for example, his *Caste in Modern India, and Other Essays*, Bombay, 1965, Chapter 2, 'A Note on Sanskritization and Westernization'; and also 'Changing Institutions and Values in Modern India', in *Towards a Sociology of Culture in India*.

'. . . the study of Indian traditions . . . is the first and immediate duty of the Indian sociologist', and further '. . . it is not enough for the Indian sociologist to be a sociologist. He must be an Indian first, that is, he is to share in the folk-ways, *mores*, customs, and traditions for the purpose of understanding his social system and what lies beneath it and beyond it. He should be steeped in the Indian lore, both high and low. For the high ones Sanskrit is essential . . '[11] This kind of obligation was not laid upon the early political economists and sociologists in European countries; it was not suggested, nor did they consider, that they should steep themselves in the culture of feudal Europe before proceeding to investigate the problems set by emergent capitalism. The difference marks the extent to which traditional ideas affect Indian social thought and produce a compound which is neither traditional nor modern.

It would be necessary to study much more closely than has yet been done[12] the development of intellectual occupations and of modern culture in India before judging how enduring this compromise between traditional and modern thought is likely to be. For the present, it undoubtedly exists, and the intellectual community is not rent by a struggle between modernists and traditionalists. Much more apparent is the diversity of regional cultures, and it is the divisive effects of regionalism which have now to be examined. The dangers of a 'balkanization' of India have been presented most forcefully in a recent book by Selig Harrison.[13] His argument runs as follows: India comprises diverse cultural regions which in the past were held together by the dominance of Sanskrit and of a national Brahmin elite, and subsequently by the dominance of English and of a British (or British-educated) political and administrative elite. Since Independence, English no longer serves as a national language, and the claims of Hindi to replace it are challenged and opposed; at the same time there has been a tremendous upsurge of the regional languages and cultures. These developments are likely to create insurmountable barriers between the linguistic regions, to impede mobility on a national scale, to intensify local loyalties, and to provoke demands for greater regional autonomy; in the end, they may give rise to separatist movements.

The strength of linguistic loyalties is undeniable, as is the vitality of the regional cultures. The first has been demonstrated by the mass

[11] D. P. Mukerji, *Diversities*, pp. 232–3.

[12] The most comprehensive attempt to date is E. Shils, *The Intellectual Between Tradition and Modernity: The Indian Situation*, The Hague, Mouton, 1961.

[13] S. S. Harrison, *India: The Most Dangerous Decades*, Princeton, N.J., Princeton University Press, 1960, especially Ch. III, 'The New Regional Elites'.

insistence upon establishing states based upon major linguistic areas, which resulted in the creation of Andhra, the partition of Bombay State between Gujarat and Maharashtra, and most recently the division of Panjab into Panjabi- and Hindi-speaking states. The second may be indicated by the fact that while no one has ever spoken of an Indian renaissance the Bengali renaissance in the early part of the century has been universally recognized, and that the revival of literature, music, and dance at the present time is primarily a regional phenomenon. Nevertheless, the conclusions of Selig Harrison's study, and in particular the analogy which he suggests between the situation in India and that in Eastern Europe when the Balkan states were created after World War I, are open to objection. In the first place the cultural unity of India is much more ancient and profound than was that of the Hapsburg Empire, and if its religious basis has become weaker in recent times it is still not negligible. On the other hand, it is a mistake to exaggerate the degree of unity in the past, and to overlook the new unifying factors which have appeared more recently. The cultural unity of India before the British period was not, for long periods, reinforced by a political and administrative authority which was securely established over the whole territory. It is in modern times that an effective Central Government and administration has been established and it has grown stronger in the last two decades by being founded upon popular consent.

Secondly, it should be remembered that India is, by intention, a federal, not a unitary state. In such a political system it is natural that the rights of the component states should be strongly asserted, and it is by no means evident that the Indian states are more intransigent, or more frequently in conflict with the Federal Government than are, for example, the states in the U.S.A. or the provinces in Canada.

Thirdly, it is misleading to suggest that the linguistic loyalties which are manifest in India are exceptional, or to be compared only with those in Eastern Europe half a century ago. Within the last few years there have been violent conflicts in Belgium between the two linguistic groups; there has been in Britain a remarkable growth of Welsh nationalism; and in Canada a linguistic minority in the province of Quebec has engendered a strong nationalist movement, which includes an active separatist wing. The Canadian example provides an instructive contrast with the situation in India. The cultural backgrounds of the French-Canadian and the English-Canadian communities are in most respects more diverse than those of the regional groups in India; for one community is Latin, the other Anglo-Saxon, one is Catholic, the other mainly Protestant in religion. Against this must be set the fact that there are only two major linguistic groups, and that a policy of bilingualism and biculturalism is conceivable, if optimistic. In India there are fourteen major linguistic groups, and the only solution of the language problem seems to be to establish one national language alongside the regional languages. Whether this is more or less difficult to achieve than bilingualism remains to be seen.

There can be no doubt that the existence of distinct cultural regions, which are also, within limits, separate political entities, affects the composition and the activities of elite groups. But how divisive its effects may be is a question that needs careful examination. Consider, first, the implications for intellectual life. It is true that in some aspects —in literature and music, for example, or even in the writing of history —the influence of the regional culture may be all-important. Even so, there is an element of unity in so far as the different cultures draw upon a common stock of themes derived from Hinduism. And if the Hindu religion itself should decline rapidly with the disintegration of the caste system, as some scholars believe is likely, there is still no reason to suppose that the accumulated cultural traditions which Hinduism animated will suddenly vanish, any more than the culture inspired by Christianity has disappeared in the predominantly secular modern Western nations. Furthermore, there are large and growing areas of intellectual life which are not influenced in any important way by a regional culture; the natural sciences do not have a 'national', let alone a 'regional', character, and even the social sciences, in spite of the attempts to connect them with specifically Indian traditions, are most likely to develop along lines which will make them part of a universal body of knowledge.

In this sphere, then, there seems to be no obstacle to the free movement of intellectuals throughout India. This would be facilitated by general use of a national language in higher education; and the spread of Hindi as a second language in non-Hindi-speaking areas, together with the continued use of English, suggests that the difficulties, although considerable, are not insuperable. Literary culture and art are bound to be closely dependent upon the regional language; the sciences, technology, management, and administration are not. In order to establish precisely the extent of regional divisions in the intellectual elite it would be essential to examine the degree of geographical mobility, and whether it is increasing or decreasing, among such groups as university teachers, scientists, and journalists. M. N. Srinivas has pointed out that in earlier times religious pilgrimages helped to unify Indian society: 'Linguistic barriers, and differences in customs and usage, do not seem to frighten pilgrims: on the other hand, they seem to enjoy the diversity of India.'[14] It may be that this unifying element in modern India will be supplied in part by the mobility of intellectuals; and it is worthy of note that university teachers, for example, have generally been hostile to the undue emphasis upon regional culture and in particular to the idea of an exclusive use of the regional language in higher education.

In the political sphere, it has already been shown, there are regional elites. But these elites are deeply involved in the national political system. The major political parties are all national parties, and even where their strength is mainly concentrated for the time being in particular regions—the Swatantra Party in Gujarat, the Communist Party in Kerala—they still contend for power on an all-India basis. Thus the political leaders are inescapably caught up in national politics, and many of those in the regional elites aspire to become national leaders. The politicians in the state governments are, of course, very much concerned with the development of their particular region, and they are frequently in conflict with the Delhi Government, especially with regard to the location of projects under the Five-Year Plans. But there is little in the activities or pronouncements of the regional elites which diverges from the ordinary representation of local interests in other federal systems. The state politicians in India do not insist more strongly upon their claims to a share in development projects than do, for example, the provincial governments in Canada when the allocation of federal funds in highway construction, electric power, or higher education is under discussion. Again, it is necessary to ensure, in the national Government and in governmental agencies, that the various regions are adequately represented, and in particular that a balance between North and South India is maintained. But is the distinction between North and South any greater than in the U.S.A., or the question of representation more delicate? The answer is by no means obvious.

The evidence at the present time seems to me to indicate a growing division in Indian politics, not between traditionalists and modernists, nor between regions, but between ideological groups of a modern kind. To some extent the development of ideologies has been obscured, and hindered, by the dominance of the Congress Party, which encompasses a considerable variety of social and political views; but in the last few years there has been a more vigorous conflict of doctrines, following the

[14] *Caste in Modern India, and Other Essays*, pp. 105–6.

growth of the Swatantra Party on one side and of the Communist Party on the other. The themes which dominate political discussion, as India's fourth general election approaches, are not those of traditional culture versus industrialism, nor of regional versus national development; they are the problems of economic growth, of the distribution of wealth and income, of planning and free enterprise. The effect of the growth of opposition parties is likely to be a greater unity of the elite in the Congress Party, and a development in India of competition between political elites which are much more clearly defined by their social and political aims.

An observer once remarked about the French Chamber of Deputies in the 1930s that there was a good deal less difference between two deputies, one of whom was a Communist and the other was not, than between two Communists, one of whom was a deputy and the other was not. A similar observation might be made about the Lok Sabha, with reference to the differences of region or caste among its members. It would certainly be true of the high officials in the Indian Administrative Service (I.A.S.). Their social background is diverse in terms of regional origins (although some regions are overrepresented), and in terms of caste (although the higher castes predominate, largely because of their advantages in secondary and university education, and in spite of the reservation of places for members of scheduled castes).[15] But any divisive consequences of such diversity are greatly diminished by the prevalence of common elements: the large proportion who have been educated in 'public schools', and still more, the intensive training given to probationers at the national Academy of Administration, and the ethos of a small elite group which has very strong traditions. The members of the I.A.S. are allocated to state cadres, but this does not divide the service on regional lines, partly because at least half the cadre in each state has to come from outside the state, and partly because officials are deputed for periods of service in the central administration. The I.A.S., although it has something of a federal character, is, like the *grands corps de l'Etat* in France, or the Administrative Class of the Civil Service in Britain, a very distinct, cohesive, and powerful elite.[16]

So far in this essay I have said little about the divisive influence of

---

[15] There is more information on the administrative elite than on most others. Sources include R. K. Trivedi and D. N. Rao, 'Regular Recruits to the I.A.S.—A Study', *Journal of the National Academy of Administration*, Mussourie, Vol. V, No. 3; a forthcoming study by V. Subramaniam; and W. H. Morris-Jones, *The Government and Politics of India*, pp. 121-3.

[16] Similar observations could be made about the Indian Foreign Service.

caste. The significance of caste, and the changes which it is undergoing in modern India, are questions of great difficulty and complexity, and in the present context I can only set out very briefly some suggestions as to the bearing of caste membership upon the formation and the stability of elites. It is necessary, first, to distinguish between the traditional castes (*jati*), which are local and small-scale groups, and the modern caste associations which endeavour to widen caste loyalties and to bring together in a single group '. . . those castes (*jati*) which form a category by virtue of a common name, a common traditional occupation, and a roughly common status position in their respective caste systems . . .'[17] The caste associations usually extend over a linguistic region or state, and in some cases they attempt to cover the whole of India. Their degree of organization and influence varies considerably in different parts of India, from the well-organized and powerful Nair Service Society in Kerala to the association of the Orissa Oilmen-Vaisyas, which, according to F. G. Bailey, is still in the formative stage and has little political influence.

The influence which a caste association may have on a national scale is revealed by M. S. A. Rao's account of the Yadavas,[18] who comprise a number of allied castes—Ahirs, Gopals, Gollas, and others—engaged chiefly in the occupations of cowherd and milk-seller in different parts of India; but who also claim to include a number of earlier ruling dynasties among their members. The All-India Yadav Maha Sabha, which was formed in 1924, has been especially active in pressing for the formation of a Yadav regiment in the Indian Army, and M. S. A. Rao suggests that the Yadav members of the Lok Sabha act together to sponsor the activities of the caste association.

Another national association which is active and influential is that of the Marwaris, the All-India Marwari Federation. Selig Harrison, in his account of the 'new caste lobbies',[19] discusses among other groups both the Marwaris and the Ahirs. Of the latter he observes that in Uttar Pradesh they have allied themselves with the Jats and some other castes to form an influential coalition; but this view has been questioned by Paul Brass, who notes that in the Meerut district of U.P., where the political influence of caste is strong, nevertheless all factions '. . . are multicaste in composition', and the diversity of castes '. . . makes

---

[17] F. G. Bailey, *Politics and Social Change*, p. 130. Bailey describes very clearly the differences between castes and caste associations, on pp. 122–35.

[18] M. S. A. Rao, 'Caste and the Indian Army', *Economic Weekly*, Vol. XVI, No. 35, 29 August, 1964, pp. 1439–43.

[19] S. Harrison, *India: The Most Dangerous Decades*, Ch. IV.

it impossible for a faction seriously interested in obtaining power to restrict its membership to particular social groups'.[20] A series of nine studies on the third General Election published in the *Economic Weekly* between July and September 1962[21] shows that the influence of caste affiliation upon voting varies greatly from place to place; that it is never the sole influence, but has to contend with economic interest, ideological commitment, attachment to individual leaders, and other factors; and that it is not usually pre-eminent.

Caste loyalties are undoubtedly strong in many regions, but they are probably most effective in village communities and become weaker in the larger caste associations which are active in state and national politics. Only detailed studies of the caste associations themselves and of their relations with the political elites in the states or at the centre —studies which, rather surprisingly, have not yet been undertaken— would make it possible to decide this point. Although some students of Indian politics foresee an increasingly important role for the caste associations in the near future, it does not appear that at present they play a major part in the selection of political leaders or in the creation of political divisions. To some extent, perhaps, they reinforce regional distinctions, but not all caste associations are organized on a regional basis, and some of them—the Marwari Federation, for example—have been opposed to regionalism.

The caste associations, so far as they are politically active, take part in state and national politics, and they may in this way affect the composition and the policies of the political elite. The *jati*, on the other hand, are mainly engaged in village politics, and so they are of less interest in the present context. It is worth noting, however, that even in village politics, where the sway of the traditional social organization is strongest, it is far from clear that caste loyalties always have a pre-dominant influence. A. H. Somjee has edited a series of village studies in Gujarat which show that although there is in some cases a major conflict between Patidars and Barias, this is overshadowed elsewhere by the opposition between kin groups or generations within one of the castes, or by the formation of alliances between castes on the basis of economic interests;[22] and André Béteille has concluded from a study of a Tanjore village that political power has to some extent detached itself from caste, that the balance of power is unstable, and that 'factors

[20] P. Brass, *Factional Politics in an Indian State*, p. 148.

[21] Reprinted as a pamphlet under the title *The Third General Elections: Studies in Voting Behaviour*, Bombay, *Economic Weekly*.

[22] A. H. Somjee (Ed.), *Politics of a Periurban Community in India*, Bombay, Asia Publishing House, 1964.

other than caste play an important part in maintaining it and changing it from day to day'.[23]

If the importance of caste in the political sphere is thus doubtful then it is even more so with regard to the other elite groups—the administrators, the military chiefs, and the intellectuals—for these groups are recruited on the basis of individual merit and achievement; they are not bound, as political leaders are, to the representation of various communities and interests in the society. In fact, caste distinctions do seem to play a small part in these elites. Among the high officials and the intellectuals the most apparent differences are those of region and language, but they are overcome, as I have suggested, by a substantial amount of geographical mobility, and by the influence of the standards which are established by the professional group itself. Caste loyalties, which may or may not be strong initially among those who enter the higher administration or the intellectual elite, seem to be overshadowed, if not extinguished, by a commitment to the more universal aims of these elite groups; and this process is helped by the fact that the functions of administrators and of intellectuals (at least, of those in the universities) are modern and 'Western', hence incompatible with the traditionalism of caste. In the case of the military it has been suggested that caste differences are more significant, in part as a legacy of British rule, with its concept of 'martial races';[24] but even if this is true at the regimental level, it is questionable whether it affects the upper levels of the military hierarchy. The military chiefs, like the high officials, are trained on Western lines and they probably have much more in common with each other than with other members of their respective castes.

The cohesion of these elites—political, intellectual, military, and administrative—is facilitated by the fact that entry to them depends in large measure upon property ownership, or educational qualifications, or both. Their members come predominantly from similar middle-class environments, have similar educational experiences, and deal with each other as middle-class, professional people. These common elements may well outweigh any differences of caste or language; and such evidence as there is, principally on the high officials, suggests that they do.

The elements which make for unity or disunity in the elites may now be summarized. Unity is fostered by the middle-class origins of elite

[23] A. Béteille, *Caste, Class and Power: Changing Patterns of Stratification in a Tanjore Village*, Berkeley, University of California Press, 1965, p. 200.
[24] See the article by M. S. A. Rao mentioned earlier.

members, by their similar educational experiences, by the particular training which they undergo and the traditions of their profession in the case of administrators, military chiefs, and intellectuals. In the case of political leaders, educational background is less important, and it is above all the ideology and organization of the Congress Party, the patronage which it dispenses, and the memories of its part in the independence movement, which serve to maintain unity. The divisive factors are those of region, language, kin group, faction, caste, and ideology. In the administrative and military elites all of these seem to be relatively unimportant at the present time. Among the intellectuals there are divisions arising from regional differences, and from the divergence between traditionalists and modernists, but these divisions are still not acute.

The political leaders are divided along many different lines—those of caste, of region, of kin group, of faction, of social doctrine (traditional versus modern, conservative versus radical)—but the fact that the Congress Party has governed India for two difficult decades, and has suffered only minor reverses, is an indication that the forces of unity have so far prevailed. It is partly, indeed, the existence of so many different lines of division, cutting across each other, which explains the cohesion of the political elite. A member of the elite may ally himself on one occasion with his caste fellows, on another with those from his region, on yet another with a particular faction, or with a group of those whose social philosophy is akin to his own; and this variability of alliances and groupings diminishes the likelihood of any major, irreparable division. There is still another factor which now promotes unity in the political elite; namely, the emergence of stronger opposition parties on an all-India scale. Many studies have shown how the Congress Party is able to overcome factional disputes when it is seriously challenged by rival political elites, and in the fourth General Elections it will have to confront, on a much more extensive scale, the opposition of the Swatantra Party and the Communist Party.

It is very likely that in the next decade the conflicts within Indian society will assume a more ideological character, and will come to resemble more closely those in other modern nations. The divisions of caste and region will add to the complexity of these conflicts, but I do not think they will be decisive in themselves. Probably the most important question is going to be which of the various elites, or combination of them—the political parties, the officials, the military chiefs, the intellectuals, or others which may emerge—can establish itself as the 'governing class'; and this depends above all upon the ability of an elite to assure India's economic development and to represent adequately the aspirations of the mass of the people. In this situation the Congress Party has still a decided advantage, because it has inspired and directed the economic progress of the last two decades, and through the scheme of *panchayati raj* has initiated a genuine extension of democratic government which has brought it more closely into contact with the people.

XII

Nationalism, Communalism, and National Unity in Ceylon

BY S. ARASARATNAM

*Senior Lecturer in Department of Indian Studies, University
of Malaya in Kuala Lumpur*

ON account of its geographic location, the island of Ceylon has been, over the ages, the recipient of diverse strands of social and cultural influences from many parts of the world. It has a continuous record of migrations, invasions, and settlements, all of which have determined the population as it is today with its many cultural patterns and social variations. Its proximity to India has meant that the major currents of influence and impact have proceeded from the subcontinent to whose broad cultural area Ceylon may be said to belong. Both the main ethnic constituents of its population and its classical culture have an Indian provenance. Its position as an island in the middle of the Indian Ocean and on the highway of sea-traffic from East to West has enabled other and more cosmopolitan elements to enter the cultural cauldron. From very early times there were contacts with the Mediterranean world, Western Asia, and South-East Asia, and in the modern period influences from Western Europe have come in quite extensively. In all these cases, social and cultural influences have resulted from commercial relations or imperial conquest.

In this way, through a recorded history of two and a half millennia, the island has been subject to intermittent doses of external influence —ethnic and linguistic, religious and social. The legacy of all these influences has been a country with a plurality of languages, religions, and ways of life, with many culturally separated groups of people alienated and, to some extent, isolated from each other. The diverse origins and character of external influences, the quick succession in which they came, and the intensity of their impact have rendered it difficult to assimilate them all into a coherent whole. Thus it was that many cultural pockets grew into existence, preserved their identity in an alien environment and could not be absorbed by elements that were already there.[1]

Today these many groups and subgroups exist in varying degrees of strength and are of great importance to the problem of national unity. The Sinhalese constitute about 70 per cent of the population of the island, occupying the western and southern coasts, the central highlands and north-central plains and parts of the eastern plains. They speak a language which belongs to the Indo-Aryan family of languages. Over 90 per cent of them profess the Buddhist faith. The Sinhalese community is again subdivided into those of the low country and those of the up country, the former constituting 62 per cent of the total Sinhalese population and the latter 38 per cent. The basis of the division is geographic, but certain historical circumstances give it a cultural force. The Sinhalese of the low country have been exposed for longer periods to external, especially Western, influences which have considerably changed their ways of life and value systems, while those of the interior are more traditional and less affected by the process of modernization.

The Tamils of Ceylon are another distinct community settled in the northern parts of the island and along the eastern seaboard, and constitute 11 per cent of the total population. The community referred to as the Indian Tamils are a more recent group of immigrants who came from the mid-nineteenth century onwards to work in the plantations. They are separated both geographically and socially from the Ceylon Tamils and also constitute some 11 per cent of the population. They live mainly in the upper reaches of the hills and are to some degree isolated from the rest of the population. Both these groups speak the Tamil language, which belongs to the Dravidian family of languages, and are predominantly of the Hindu religion.

The Ceylon Moor community, made up of Islamic settlers in the island, are scattered all over the country with a few concentrations on the east coast and certain districts of the west. They constitute about 7 per cent of the population and use an Arabized Tamil as their native language. Eurasians, Burghers (descendants of Dutch settlers), and Malays constitute tiny groups of under 1 per cent and exist mainly as urban communities. Four major religions of the world have struck

---

[1] For a discussion of the geographical background to historical developments in Ceylon, see H. T. Ray (Ed.), *History of Ceylon*, Vol. I, Part I, Peradenya, Ceylon University Press, 1959, pp. 8–19.

root in the island and have adherents in the following proportions: Buddhism, 64 per cent; Hinduism, 20 per cent; Christianity, 9 per cent; and Islam, 7 per cent.

With the beginning of modern political activity, these social differences asserted themselves in strength. The first forms of political organization were those that aimed to bring together specific communities in pursuit of their particular interest. The biggest attempt at nationalist politics, the Ceylon National Congress, did not remain national for long. Within two years after its formation in 1919, the Tamils walked out of it to form their own association. Every projected reform of the Constitution became a tug-of-war between communities to gain a greater voice in representative councils.[2] Mutual suspicion and fear were very great. As the colonial Government was persuaded to concede power gradually, Ceylonese politicians contended among themselves over the share that communal groups would receive. It was in an attempt to break through this community-orientated politics and induce a wider national view that the Constitutional (Donoughmore) Commission of 1929 introduced universal franchise and territorial representation.[3] Communal parties and politics lived on under adult suffrage and indeed became more entrenched with mass support. The first national party (the United National Party) that held office during and after Independence was a coalition hastily brought together from the many communal parties that were then in existence.

After Independence a conscious effort was made to lay firmer foundations for nationhood. Political power was distributed among all communities to an extent that gave them all a sense of participation in the building of the nation. National issues were placed in the forefront of political activity. Sectionalism and separatism preached by some groups in all communities were unpopular and did not gain widespread adherence. Admittedly communal issues flared up occasionally, such as over the disfranchisement of Indian Tamils of the plantations. But protest over such questions was muted and it was generally recognized that direct appeals to communal loyalties should, as far as possible, be avoided. Communalism was held to be dirty politics and it was felt that it should not blemish the efforts consciously made to promote a Ceylonese nationalism. To secure the highest common factor of agreement between communities, elements of Westernization were encouraged. By implication it was accepted that the roots of traditional

[2] G. C. Mendis, *Ceylon Under the British*, Colombo, Colombo Apothecaries Company, 1952, pp. 182–3.

[3] *Ceylon, Report of the Special Commission on the Constitution*, London, 1928, pp. 90–100.

culture ought not to be nurtured and fed to any substantial degree, as this would give rise to forces that divide and disrupt the newly found national unity.

By its very nature, this form of nation-consciousness was prevalent among only a limited section of people. It was based on a concept of nationalism as secular and territorially based, claiming the exclusive loyalty of the citizens to an entity called the nation-state which represented a geographical area, the home of the 'nation', and thus included within it all its inhabitants. Such a conception was derived from Ceylon's recent connexions with the West, and in that form it was comprehensible only to those who were familiar with the background of modern European history and political thought.[4] In the context of Ceylon this was the category of people who are variously referred to as 'middle-class', 'elite', 'English-educated', 'Westernized'—all of which terms convey the basic fact that they are a group of people who differ from the traditional social groups in that they are the product of the economic, social, and intellectual influences that have emanated from Western colonial rule. They have been estimated to consitute at the most about 7 per cent of the total population.[5] They are socially conspicuous because their habits of dress, speech, and ways of life are clearly distinguishable from the rest of the population. For about a decade after Independence their dominance over political and public life in Ceylon was complete. On account of this dominance, the deep social and communal divisions were papered over and ignored, with unfortunate consequences for the future.

These English-educated groups formed the upper layer of the elite groups of Ceylon. They were Western-oriented and monopolized the upper rungs of political power and social privilege. Separate from these, and below them in the social scale, was another layer of elite that stemmed from traditional sources of power and traditional institutions. Unlike the English-educated elite, they formed a link between independent Ceylon and the pre-colonial Sinhalese kingdoms. They were the Sinhalese literati, the specialists in traditional Sinhalese medicine, the Sinhalese schoolmasters, the Buddhist priest-teachers. In the years after independence they were content to play second fiddle to their social and intellectual betters, to act as a liaison between these holders

---

[4] For a study in depth of this phase of nationalism in Ceylon, see Sir Ivor Jennings, 'Nationalism and Political Development in Ceylon', *Ceylon Historical Journal*, Vol. III, No. 1, pp. 62–84.

[5] I. D. S. Weerawardena, 'The Development of a Middle Class in Ceylon', *International Institute of Differing Civilizations, 29th Session, London. Development of a Middle Class in Tropical and Sub-tropical Countries*, Brussels, 1956, pp. 280–92.

of power and the voting masses. They had not sufficient understanding of the Western-oriented democratic institutions that had been planted in the island for the past twenty-five years. They had as yet few strong political views of their own and no ways of making these felt in the highest councils of the state. They were not equipped to exercise or aspire for power in these new institutions.

The infiltration of the ideas of representative democracy propagated by the English-educated middle class in turn undermined their own position and finally brought them down from power. The Sinhalese-educated elite, who had so far functioned as catalysts for the English-educated, increasingly realized the strength of their position of direct contact with the mass electorate. They gained from the experience of the working of representative institutions from the lowest levels. Beginning with contests for power in local institutions such as village and district councils, rural development societies, and temple management societies, these second-rank leaders began to sense the power of the strength of numbers in democratic institutions. They also perfected a technique of dialogue with the 'masses' and of fashioning ideologies and slogans of direct relevance to the people, in a way the English-educated could not do.

The general prosperity and development in the country in post-war years, especially in the fields of education and mass communication, considerably improved the status of this partially submerged elite. With their rise in position and a growing awareness of their potential, they developed a national view of their own which differed markedly from the standpoint of the English-educated. The major changes that took place in 1956 mark it out as the year when the transfer of power was effected from the English-educated to the traditionalist elite, or at least the year when the latter group asserted themselves more vigorously and forced changes in national policy in line with their viewpoints. A growth in their influence could be noted even earlier when occasional concessions had to be made to them on many aspects of policy. A major extension in their political influence took place when sections of the more articulate and opinion-forming English-educated groups began championing their causes both for ideological reasons and out of sheer opportunism, to win their support against entrenched power groups from whom they had split away.[6] These developments saw the beginnings of fissions in the national consensus that had so far been fostered and the challenge of some of its basic assumptions.

[6] Jennings, 'Politics in Ceylon since 1952', *Pacific Affairs*, Vol. XXVII, No. 4, December 1954, pp. 338–52.

The basic difference between the nationalism of the Westernized middle class and that of the Sinhalese-educated groups was that while the former emphasized the nation as identified with state or country, the latter identified nation with 'race'. While the nationalism of the former was secular, that of the latter was very closely interconnected with religion. Herein lay the source of much subsequent fission in the national body corporate. Such an approach would divide Ceylon's heterogeneous population on ethnic and religious lines. As long as nationalism in Ceylon was Ceylonese rather than Sinhalese it was possible for the island's many groups to partake and be integrated in it to their satisfaction. Similarly, religion had discreetly been kept out of politics since the beginning of modern political activity in Ceylon. This did not mean, of course, that the position of the different religions in the country was determined to their satisfaction. What it meant was that, just as it was implied that it was not proper to talk and act on communal lines, it was equally agreed that political solutions should not be sought to religious grievances. From about 1955 these assumptions were eroded and gradually one moved to a position where ethnic and religious issues were at the heart of the new nationalism and such questions at the heart of national politics.

Students of modern Ceylonese politics and society are generally agreed in discerning here a new phase of nationalism,[7] a phase which rose to its peak in the troubled régimes of S. W. R. D. Bandaranayake (1956–9) and later of his widow Sirima Bandaranayake (1960–5) and now shows signs of subsiding. The years when this new nationalism was rampant was the time when social conflicts and fissions abounded in the Ceylon scene. They were, in fact, a direct consequence of the spread of Sinhala nationalism. The political aim of the new nationalism was to separate the Sinhalese element in the Ceylonese nation and seek to establish it above all other sections. This was not to be the natural and unconscious outcome of the status of a majority community in a democratic country, but a deliberate and conscious effort to enthrone the Sinhalese as the ruling community. The justification for this was not so much that the Sinhalese formed the majority; rather it was that the Sinhalese had been the island's original settlers, its ruling race in pre-colonial times, and had given it its distinctive culture. History and mythology were enlisted in support of this position.

[7] See, for example, B. H. Farmer, 'Social Basis of Nationalism in Ceylon', *Journal of Asian Studies*, Vol. XXIV, No. 3, May 1965, pp. 431–40; and R. N. Kearney, 'Sinhalese Nationalism and Social Conflict in Ceylon', *Pacific Affairs*, Vol. XXXVII, No. 2, Summer 1964, pp. 125–36.

Politics, in this nationalist phase, was strengthened by religion. In the same way that the Sinhalese community was to predominate in Ceylonese affairs, Buddhism, the historic religion of the Sinhalese, and still professed by a great majority of them, was to be the country's dominant religion. Here, too, this aim was to be achieved by deliberate action of the community and the state. The movement to rehabilitate Buddhism is anterior to the political movement to revive Sinhalese language and society. At the time that Western-oriented nationalism was in full cry, this movement worked in a modest and restrained fashion, aiming at gradual and voluntary reform of the various institutions of Buddhism. When the Sinhalese-educated intelligentsia began to assert themselves, the role of religion in nationalist thinking was magnified. The close relation between religion and social life in traditional society was now formalized and recognized in the new political movements. The political aims of the new movement were so successful because they were vindicated in the eyes of the common man by their association with religion. The justification for the emphasis on Buddhism was that Ceylon was the historic island of the Buddha Dhamma, an early recipient of the message of Buddhism which it has since carefully treasured.[8]

The new movement and its spokesmen attacked the liberal-national consensus on two of its weakest spots. In the first place, they criticized the established order for insufficient emphasis on the Sinhalese language and on Sinhalese interests generally. It was obviously to the advantage of this now depressed stratum of elite to transfer the conduct of national affairs and national education from English to Sinhalese. If such a change were fully effected, they would replace the English-educated from the upper layers of the hierarchy of power. They wanted Sinhalese to replace English as the official language of Ceylon. As they grew more in confidence and power they claimed that Sinhalese alone should be made the official language, to the exclusion of any other national minority language that prevailed in the island. In this way they rejected decisively any possibility of an alliance with similar traditionalist anti-Western groups in the minority communities. Secondly, they criticized the lack of sufficient importance given to Buddhism in the nation's affairs. They felt that the state should come forward more forcefully to fulfil its function as the protector of Buddhism and re-establish the historic connexion between the state and the Buddhist

[8] For an analysis of the Buddhist revivalist movement and its social implications, see M. Ames, 'Ideological and Social Change in Ceylon', *Human Organization*, Vol. XXII, No. 1, Spring 1963, pp. 45–53.

Church that existed under the pre-colonial Sinhalese kingdoms. They asked for an extensive programme of legislation by which the grievances of the Buddhist Church could be redressed. They wanted the state to use its resources and power to help Buddhist institutions to their feet, to put its various houses in order, and to lead the Buddhist revival that was taking place.

In the elections of 1956 the forces of the new nationalism found a spokesman, if not a champion, in Bandaranayake's coalition party and helped to the fullest extent to put him in power with a substantial majority. The forces of Sinhalese and Buddhist revival worked unanimously to overthrow the liberal-national order and prepared themselves for a period of change. The changes were to consist in the destruction of privilege and inequality and the evolution of practical policies that would enable them to achieve their positive aims. In spite of the decisive victory of these forces, Bandaranayake, during his administration, sought to temper the extremist Sinhala nationalism of his supporters with the older liberal nationalism in which he still partly believed. He attempted a legislative programme that would destroy the privileges of the middle and upper classes and the English-educated elite and do away with the gross forms of discrimination against the Sinhalese-educated intelligentsia. The most vaunted piece of legislation, and one most satisfying to this section, was the passing of the Official Language Act of July 1956, popularly known as the 'Sinhala Only Act'. It established Sinhalese as the one official language of Ceylon and imposed a period of up to five years when the transition was to be effected. Other changes swiftly followed, promoting the interests of the Sinhalese-educated by means of administrative regulations.

Two categories of people were adversely affected by these policies: the English-educated middle class and the communal and religious minorities. Though the English-educated middle class was drawn from all communities, a large majority of them were Sinhalese. Many of them were unable to adapt themselves to the new political climate. Their cherished values of liberalism, individual freedom, and secularism which they had striven to implant in Ceylon were now being undermined. Their own position was seriously threatened. Though many of them still held important political and administrative positions, it was clear that real power was passing over to the many new pressure groups that had grown around the new Government. The new men of power, mostly from rural Ceylon, worked through political and party officials and even through the Prime Minister, who was most responsive to their pressures.

The old administrative hierarchy, manned largely by the middle class, found themselves in positions of responsibility without power. Differing fundamentally in their thinking and outlook from the new power elite, they soon found themselves condemned as traitors to the nation (i.e. race) and enemies of the social revolution that these forces thought they were ushering in. In spite of this, however, the English-educated could not be dispensed with, as they were the repositories of all knowledge concerning the functioning of a modern state apparatus, and indeed of all modern learning. For the achievement of their aims of revival and rehabilitation of the Sinhalese people, the constructive thinking and ideas of the middle class were found necessary.

At this time a process of great soul-searching and considerable self-criticism was evident among the English-educated elite. It is reflected in the intellectual activity of the times—the seminars and discussions organized and the published works that appeared.[9] They were very concerned at this growing alienation between themselves and the new movement. They wondered how they could come to terms with these new forces and secure leadership over them so that they could channel them along constructive and fruitful lines. Sometimes this belated attempt to reorient themselves was artificial and unconvincing. A few took the easy way out and left the country. In the period 1958 to 1962 there was a considerable drain of talent from the country which was stopped only by restrictions imposed on foreign travel, by pressure on friendly governments not to recruit Ceylonese, and by a law which demanded that all those who had secured university education in Ceylon should serve the Government for a minimum period of five years. Many who were left behind in the country carried on as best as they could but there seems no doubt that they were and are a demoralized and dispirited class. Under the administration of Sirima·Bandaranayake pressures on them were more intense.

Very soon this class will cease to exist. It is not being added to with new recruits, as education is no longer imparted in the English medium. This makes the position of its remaining members very weak. But with the extinction of this class there will arise the problem of how a link is to be maintained with the outside world. A tiny country such as Ceylon cannot afford to live in intellectual isolation. The middle class, with all its faults *vis-à-vis* Ceylonese tradition, had been the ve-

[9] For a typical example of this, see 'The Role of the Western-educated Elite', *Community*, Vol. IV, No. 1, 1962, pp. 3–42; see also E. R. Sarathchandra, 'The Traditional Culture of Ceylon and its Present Position', in R. Peiris (Ed.), *Traditional Sinhalese Culture*, Peradeniya, 1956, pp. 99–103.

hicle through which the world had been interpreted to Ceylon and Ceylon to the world. How this function will be performed when the entire elite have been fully reoriented towards a national outlook, or whether this function will at all be considered necessary, remains problematic in Ceylon today. Politically speaking the discontent and disillusion of the middle class are not dangerous. They are a tiny minority, now politically disorganized, and can never emerge as an important pressure group.

As the new nationalism entered its constructive reformist stage and policies had to be underlined in detail fulfilling the general aims of this movement, its unity began to show signs of cracking. Neither the Sinhalese community nor the institutions of Buddhism were integrated in such a way as to function unitedly on the basis of the emerging concepts of nationalism. Historical developments and contemporary economic and social environment contributed to creating problems of quite a different character among various sections of the Sinhalese community. Among the Sinhalese of the coastal areas education had spread very extensively and they found the English-educated class and the privileged Christian groups an obstacle to their further progress. Here, too, subordinate non-agricultural castes had made their way up both economically and educationally and challenged the traditional high status of the agricultural caste. In the upper reaches of the hill country, the plantation area, Sinhalese peasants contrasted their plight with the prosperity of the plantations and the steady employment available to the Indian Tamils who laboured in them. They felt that their rise was associated with the attack on 'alien' capital and labour in the plantations. The disfranchisement of Indian labour in 1949 was a move to placate them.

Here, as well as in the paddy-farming plains lower down and northwards, there were feudal relationships still unsolved. Land hunger was most acute among peasants in these areas and many were burdened with irksome dues and service obligations to a landed and official nobility. These people would not be the beneficiaries of the shift of emphasis to Sinhalese language and Sinhalese education. They were more concerned with land reform and readjustment of relations within the Sinhalese community. At the first major steps to tackle land reform in 1958 the Cabinet was seriously divided, there was unrest in the country and a political move was started which eventually drove the Minister responsible out of the Cabinet.[10]

This necessity to balance sectional interests within Sinhalese

---

[10] W. H. Wriggins, *Ceylon: The Dilemmas of a Nation*, Princeton, N.J., Princeton University Press, 1960, pp. 294–5.

nationalism and share the spoils of power among many diverse groups led to political instability and inevitable dissatisfaction. In contrast to the period when the English-educated middle class was in power, the dominance of Sinhalese nationalism was marked by stormy politics. The assassination of Premier Bandaranayake in September 1959 was brought about by sections that were at one time his very strong supporters, but that were disillusioned when, after three years of power, they did not get all that they had expected.

The steps to rehabilitate and revive Buddhism caused the greatest furore. Everyone was agreed that the position of Buddhism in the country was unsatisfactory at the time of independence and that this situation was the result of centuries of colonial rule. The wealth of its temples had been frittered away; their properties alienated, sometimes to Christian churches; they lacked organization and unity of purpose. Buddhism, like Hinduism in India, had become a religious culture and thus reflected all the divisions of Sinhalese society. When reformation movements extended their activity after independence, they reflected the difference in outlook and ideology prevalent among the Sinhalese elite. The Western-oriented modernizers desired to refashion Buddhist institutions in keeping with the democratic ideals of responsibility and to keep Buddhist affairs independent of state. A section of the traditionalists wanted to see the re-establishment of the power and status of the Buddhist clerical hierarchy, as under the ancient Sinhalese kings, without any internal organizational reforms that would weaken their authority. The militants of the new nationalist movement desired sweeping changes in organization, to give them access to the power hierarchy within its institutions. They wanted these changes within Buddhism as well as the general assertion of Buddhist influence in the country to be made an essential part of state policy. These differences of approach were to be found not only among Buddhist laymen but were also reflected within the Buddhist clergy (*Sangha*) who had their supporters among the laymen. These sections attached themselves to political parties and Buddhist reform became an issue of politics, charged with emotion similar to the language controversy.[11]

After the assassination of Bandaranayake, these divisions in the nationalist and revivalist front which he had papered over with some success now widened and were more open. Bandaranayake had tried to keep the nationalist programme within the bounds of democratic concepts and preserve the fundamental liberal values of the state. His successor Sirima Bandaranayake was not saddled with any such

[11] Wriggins, op. cit., pp. 193–210.

ideological commitments. Her régime gave full play to the forces of Sinhalese and Buddhist revivalism. Attacks were made on various minority interests which these minorities felt went beyond the bounds of reducing privilege and redressing past wrongs. The State became a powerful instrument in promoting Sinhalese welfare and was made to extend its tentacles into many new avenues of economic and social life.

Here the nationalist forces secured a valuable ally in the Marxist Left who, after years in the political wilderness, abandoned their hostility to Sinhalese racialist nationalism and climbed on its band wagon, hoping eventually to direct it along lines favourable to themselves. The coalition of Marxist Communism and Sinhalese nationalism was formalized in 1964 when Sirima Bandaranayake reshuffled her Government and admitted Marxist leaders into the Cabinet with important portfolios. But this was the signal for the further fragmentation of Sinhalese nationalism. Both the conservative as well as the liberally inclined sections were upset at this trend and left the Government, seriously weakening it, and eventually causing its downfall.[12]

For a period of about a decade, from 1955 to 1965, the new Sinhalese nationalism dictated the pace of politics in Ceylon. If it was responsible for much instability, it was also the force that held together the Governments of this period and gave the country such authority and sense of direction as it had. It was fed in the early stages on a number of grievances, both real and imaginary. Lack of any recognition for many years had made it quite aggressive now and in this mood compromise and accommodation could not flourish. Minority groups like the Ceylon Tamils, Christians, English-educated middle class and Indian Tamils appeared as so many hostile forces arrayed in opposition to Sinhalese advance. The vernacular Press, politicians, and clergy helped to stir these feelings. In 1956 it was possible for the many strands in this new Sinhalese nationalism to work together politically and hence the remarkable electoral victory of Bandaranayake.

By 1960 this was not possible any more. Inner contradictions within the movement asserted themselves. The monopoly of control over these forces held by the Sri Lanka Freedom Party, the creation of Bandaranayake, was ended. The United Nationalist Party, so decisively defeated in 1956, was able to attract part of the new nationalist support. In the elections of 1960 and even more in those of 1965, the two parties were able to compete on equal terms. When the unanimity was gone, much of the sting was removed from Sinhalese nationalism. It now enters a new and as yet undetermined phase.

A consideration of the position of the minorities is important to demonstrate the effect the rise of Sinhalese nationalism had on national unity. The Tamils of Ceylon have settled in that island for centuries. Their immigration in small groups from Southern India occurred from the early centuries of the Christian era. More intensive and systematic migrations started from the eleventh century and by 1300 they were in a position to carve out a kingdom for themselves in the northern half of the island. This kingdom lost its independence to the Portuguese, who unified it with the rest of maritime Ceylon. Though today numerically a small minority, the Tamils' stake in the country is great. They have no connexions with the Indian mainland and have appropriated portions of the island as their traditional homelands. Here they have been able to develop their language, religion, and social institutions. Because of their isolation from South India, their society differs in its structure from that prevalent in Tamilnad. The lands where they settled were the least hospitable parts of the island. Assisted by independent political power and an integrated social structure, they developed forms of production and economic life that derived the best from this land and made it a self-sufficient and reasonably prosperous unit in the island. A little less than half the entire Ceylon Tamil population is concentrated in the small peninsula of Jaffna in the northernmost part of the island, with a density over twice that of the national average. The existence of an underground water table and fairly high utilization of land by rotation of crops and intense care have sustained this population at a level of subsistence. The increase in population and fragmentation of land have from the beginning of this century forced Tamil youths to look outside the peninsula for employment.

In such conditions, the spread of education, first by Christian missionary effort and later supplemented by Hindu associations, offered a valuable opportunity. This receptiveness encouraged Christians of all denominations to concentrate their educational efforts in Jaffna. Next to Colombo and the Western Province, Jaffna became the second most educationally advanced region in the island. The people of Jaffna made full use of these educational opportunities and this created a growing body of English-educated Tamils who could be used in the administrative services of the British Government in Ceylon and even in Britain's other tropical colonies. From the end of the nineteenth century these youths left Jaffna for Colombo and other southern cities, and later to Britain's Malayan territories, to fill lower grades of clerical employment.

This trek for employment was no migration; these people retained their ties with Jaffna. They kept their ancestral home, their kinship ties, and fulfilled all their social obligations. At the end of their tenures they retired to their Jaffna homes. Under British rule such development went on harmoniously; there was no serious competition for employment between communities. Facilities for English education were not widespread among the Sinhalese, and those who could offer themselves for such employment were proportionately few. In 1942 all education was made free and after Independence special attention was given to backward rural Sinhalese areas. This brought more Sinhalese into competition for administrative and commercial employment. The newcomers naturally suffered from the entrenched position of the Tamils of Jaffna, especially in certain special functions which the Tamils took to more than others. As long as there was open competition, and this, too, in the English language, there was nothing they could do except to equip themselves better.

The cry for the introduction of Sinhalese as the official language was to a large extent motivated by the advantage it would give in the struggle for employment. Those who would benefit immediately from it were in the forefront of the propaganda offensive. The introduction of Sinhalese at all levels of government business, and the gradual abandonment of the competitive principle, affected most the Tamils of Jaffna. With their limited holdings of land already overburdened, with no substantial capital being invested in their areas and no prospect of any new industrial ventures, and with the only existing outlet to employment blocked, they face a stark future indeed. Especially under the administration of Sirima Bandaranayake they were pressed hard. They had no access to the high policy-making bodies, absolutely no influence in government, and all their leaders were condemned to a perennial and sterile opposition.

From these recent events it is evident how dependent are the fortunes of the Tamil community on the ebb and flow of the tide of Sinhalese nationalism. When the forces of Sinhalese nationalism secure such ascendancy and unanimity as to be able to capture state power without the help of any non-Sinhalese elements, then the Tamils and all other minorities must go under. The hardship caused to the Tamils must be especially great as they have no means of economic self-sufficiency and are heavily dependent on state employment. Also, because of their social and cultural conservatism, they would find it most difficult to reconcile themselves to Sinhalese linguistic and cultural domination. In the darkest days of the Tamil community, separatism and autonomy for the Tamils were put forward as a practical solution to their problem. They had not a shred of loyalty at that time to the State and their feeling of belonging to a common Ceylonese nation was rudely shaken. The replacement of the present unitary Constitution with a federation of two states—Sinhalese and Tamil—has for some time been put forward and was now accepted by a great majority of Tamils. But such a Constitution and its many implications have not been fully considered, nor does this proposal take account of the fact that ultra-nationalist Sinhalese domination of the centre can always emasculate the prospective Tamil state.

A by-product of the alienation of the Tamils from the Sinhalese was the strengthening of Tamil nationalism and an intensive interest in the Tamil cultural tradition. This led to the forging of closer ties with the Indian Tamil community in Central Ceylon from whom the Ceylon Tamils had so far been isolated geographically and socially. Political parties and leaders representing the two groups of people began to have closer ties and discussed possibilities of joint action to safeguard common interests. Another more serious consequence to the integrity of the Ceylonese nation is the tendency of the Ceylon Tamils to forge links with the numerically larger Tamil community in the state of Madras. In an earlier day, this imaginary threat from 30 million Tamils across the Straits had been the propagandist's weapon to rouse Sinhalese nationalism. In its crudest form, the extremists of the Sinhalese nationalist movement presented the Sinhalese nation as subject to a continuous threat of extermination by the Tamils of South India for whom the Tamil communities of Ceylon would· act as a Trojan horse. It has been argued that the excessive anti-Tamil character of Sinhalese nationalism is caused by the fear of submergence by the Tamils of India. It is ironical that the actions of the nationalists brought about and strengthened the very factors they were fearing. When the Tamils were pushed hard, they began to look fondly towards India and the state of Madras as their saviour. In this way the extremes of Sinhalese nationalism and Tamil separatism fed each other, and the casualty was the Ceylonese nation.

Christian denominations constitute 9 per cent of the population, with Roman Catholics being the most numerous group among them: they are spread evenly among Sinhalese and Tamils. While they are geographically scattered all over the island, some heavy concentrations exist along the sea coast north of Colombo up to Mannar. Under British rule they had an early start with education and modernization, and equipped themselves faster to step into positions of authority. The educational structure set a premium on Christian advancement. Missionary schools, many of them of excellent quality, were strategically situated all over the country and were heavily subsidized from state funds. Supported by resources from the central organizations of these missions and by private contributions of the relatively affluent Ceylonese Christian community, the Churches and schools were able to function very effectively in the country and give the community a wide measure of social welfare. The educational system came increasingly under bitter attack by the Buddhist movement, which demanded nationalization of all schools and the denial of subvention to private schools that chose to stay out of the national system.

This radical change of the educational structure was effected in 1961, regardless of unanimous opposition from Christian denominations. Christians thought that the measure went beyond the scope of redressing the legitimate grievances of Buddhists to the extent of denying the fundamental right to choose the kind of education parents would want to impart to their children. The schools that stayed out of the state system could admit only children of the denomination that managed the school, were not entitled to state funds and could not charge fees from its pupils.[13] With these conditions it was not possible to manage a school without the greatest financial hardship. The few private schools in the island are now leading a tottering and shaky existence. In this, and in some other lesser acts directed at Christian institutions at the peak of Sinhalese nationalism, the community felt threatened and insecure.

The Indian Tamil community exist as an unassimilated and unassimilable element in the Ceylonese nation. They were brought by the British Government from Southern India to provide labour for the plantations that were opened up in the central highlands. They have continued to live here in isolation and are looked on with hostility by their neighbours, the Sinhalese of the hill country. They were yet another target of Sinhalese nationalist propaganda. The liberal franchise laws at the time of independence enabled them to send seven representatives to Parliament from the territorial electorates, much to the chagrin of the Kandyan Sinhalese, who bitterly resented this 'alien' representation.

[13] *Keesings Contemporary Archives*, 18–25 March 1961, pp. 17995-7.

Their disfranchisement and the rigorous citizenship laws of 1951 removed their voice from national political affairs.

The seriousness of the problem of national integration may be gauged from the fact that, out of 1,200,000 Indians resident in Ceylon, only 120,000 have been granted citizenship. About 130,000 opted for Indian citizenship and left the country. The balance of close upon one million people are termed 'stateless' and have an undetermined status. They have been the subject of much negotiation between the Governments of India and Ceylon. The most recent agreement between the two countries rather arbitrarily sets the figure that Ceylon will eventually absorb at 300,000.[14] In the meanwhile, pressures are mounting to enforce the gradual employment of Sinhalese labour in these estates and thus displace Indians. The plantation management is doubtful about the economic consequences of such action. Sinhalese extremists would gladly see all Indians out of the country as soon as possible, as they are an impediment to their aim of Sinhalese domination in the hill country. Here is another instance of direct opposition between the policies of Sinhalese nationalism and the interests of a minority community.

These observations illustrate how in this second phase of nationalism in Ceylon, sectional interests and loyalties of conflicting types within the Ceylonese nation have emerged. The chief among these is Sinhalese nationalism, which, because of the numerical superiority of the Sinhalese, must always predominate politically. Its present aim is to redress past grievances to the Sinhalese people and the Buddhist religion. In that sense it is a necessary adjustment of the colonial past and a necessary reconstruction of society when a nation becomes master of its own affairs. But such reform is always difficult to bring about and its path is strewn with many dangers. When the attempt is made to promote the interests of a community by legislation, the line between justice and privilege is blurred. Especially is this so when the aggrieved party is itself the sole arbiter of the proposed changes. At the height of its power Sinhalese nationalism had full control over Parliament and executive. Its leaders decided on measures that would do justice to the Sinhalese without consulting and accommodating many minority groups that were vitally affected by these measures. The privileged position hitherto enjoyed by these minorities for various historical reasons was considered justification for the imposition on them of present and future sufferings.

[14] Op. cit., 14–21 November 1964, p. 20405.

Most recent events since 1965 seem to indicate that the tide of Sinhalese nationalism has reached its peak and can now be contained by constructive and fruitful policies. Herein lies hope for the country's future. Many of the aims of Sinhalese nationalism have been achieved and the source of grievance and injustice eradicated. The Sinhalese language has become unquestionably the official language of state. The educational system has been reoriented to serve the interests of the Sinhalese. Employment opportunities are now made available to the Sinhalese in numbers more than proportionate to their ratio of population. The welfare of the Buddhist religion has been made the concern of the state and aided by it many voluntary organizations are carrying on the revivalist movement.

These are all achievements which no government can go back upon. They have been accepted by all major political parties and will therefore soon cease to be political issues. Parts of the Sinhalese nationalist programme have been accepted by more than one political party. In the elections of 1960 and 1965, ideological and social cleavages within the Sinhalese community showed prominently. Such divisions, natural in a democratic society, have been the saving of minority groups, which now begin to count in politics, can use their influence one way or the other and bring about solutions which tend to their own self-preservation and thus to the preservation of national unity. Likewise, the inability of Buddhist revivalist forces to present themselves as a unified movement is also a favourable omen for the future. The Buddhist clergy is now by no means a united body with a singleness of purpose. Many undesirable events have demonstrated the rashness of mixing religion and politics. Even if Buddhist *bhikkhus* are not fully forsaking the election platform for the pulpit, the fact that the Sangha support is divided between many political parties somewhat neutralizes their influence. The widely varied views among Buddhists on the role of Buddhism in a modern state make it impossible for the Buddhist revivalist movement to be enrolled in support of one single political party.

The dichotomous character of the elite of Ceylon, with English-educated and Sinhalese-educated pulling in different directions, is being eliminated. The entire educational system is geared to a common end. The causes of tension within the elite have been removed. The Sinhalese-educated elite have achieved power and now have an idea of the responsibilities that go with power. They have an idea of what is possible in a multiracial society and what is not. There is greater appreciation of the obligations of a majority community towards minorities, and that discontented minorities in a democratic state can obstruct the progress of majority interests. They should also now appreciate the international implications of national policies and the necessity to justify to international public opinion the actions of a government, especially if that state lays claim to protect all fundamental liberties. In brief, it is assumed that the Sinhalese-educated elite, by being brought in touch with government and with international relations, is not isolated and bitter and no longer looks inwards and backwards. It has now achieved a greater degree of sophistication in its ideas and experiences and has been politically modernized.

A related and equally healthy factor is the disappearance of the great gulf between urban and rural Ceylon. For a long time rural areas were just appendages of the urban centres which set the pace of politics. The rural voter has now realized his importance and political parties pay due attention to his interests in fashioning policies. Thus a balance has been struck in politics which will lead to the strengthening of democratic forms of government in the country. These factors, though operating mainly within the majority community, have removed potential sources of tension and, judging from the experience of some Asian and African countries, potential threats to unity and freedom.

A further factor of strength the nation derives from recent experiences is the fact that, in two decades of parliamentary government, almost every prevalent ideology has had a hand at guiding the destinies of the nation. The possibility of peaceful change by persuasion of voters has been demonstrated many times and the judgement of the electorate has come to be accepted. No doubt illegal seizure of power was sometimes attempted, but the general ineffectiveness and even ludicrous character of such attempts showed the strength of lawful institutions in the state. Even in the worst period of executive interference with personal liberties, the judiciary remained a firm guarantor of freedom and was sturdily independent of the executive and legislature. The democratic framework has emerged stronger after the strain of these recent years.

The minorities have felt the heavy hand of Sinhalese power and have learnt to moderate their demands. They can now distinguish between privileges and rights and will learn to live without built-in advantages. They now realize that, in a democratic state, the dominance of the interests of the majority community must be accepted. It is hoped that these moderating factors will operate on all groups in the island and that they will thus live together with greater mutual tolerance than they have recently shown.

XIII

Is There an Indian Nation?

BY HUGH TINKER

*Professor of Government and Politics with Special Reference
to Asia, School of Oriental and African Studies,
University of London*

To many people's way of thinking, to pose this question at all is to infer a negative answer. Indians began to think in terms of an all-India nationhood during the last quarter of the nineteenth century. Immediately, European writers—especially the British scholar-officials—advanced the contrary view that India resembled a continent rather than a nation, and the peoples of India reproduced as many significant differences as the peoples of Europe.[1] Moreover, these differences were treated not as elements of diversity (which many Indian intellectuals would accept) but as actual elements of division which must prevent any association between the peoples of India in any form of political union except that exercised by the restraining hand of Britain.[2] A variation upon this theme was the argument that because Indians were of a spiritual, mystical nature they had turned away from the challenge

[1] Probably the most vigorous expression of this viewpoint is contained in Sir John Strachey's *India*, London, 1888. A few sentences may be taken from Lecture I (pp. 2–3): 'What is India? . . . There is no such country, and this is the first and most essential fact about India that can be learned. India is a name which we give to a great region including a multitude of different countries . . . The differences between the countries of Europe are undoubtedly smaller than those between the countries of India. Scotland is more like Spain than Bengal is like the Punjab. . . . There are no countries in civilized Europe in which the people differ so much as the Bengali differs from the Sikh, and the language of Bengal is as unintelligible in Lahore as it would be in London.'

[2] This view was expressed by the most liberal-minded. See James Bryce, *The Ancient Roman Empire and the British Empire in India*, London, 1914, pp. 32, 77: 'Its political unity which depends entirely on the British Raj would vanish like a morning mist. Wars would break out . . . which might end in the ascendancy of a few adventurers . . . Pathans, or Sikhs, or Mussulmans of the north-west. . . . To India severance from England would mean confusion, bloodshed, pillage.' Or Graham Wallas, *Human Nature in Politics* (London, Constable, 4th ed., 1948), pp. 9–10: 'Now [in 1908, the English liberal] is becoming aware

of practical politics and, times without number, had stood by while their land was occupied and divided by the foreign invader. This theory was propounded even by European Orientalists such as Max Müller. To Indians struggling to govern themselves, any questioning of their identity as a nation made the questioner an enemy. National self-determination, like democracy, had been elevated throughout the world into what we now call a status symbol during the years between 1789 and 1918. To be advanced, to be civilized—to achieve any sort of recognition at all—a people had to establish a claim to be called a nation. Any European who questioned the claim of India to nationhood questioned its right to self-government and to acceptance in the world family. As the struggle for independence reached its climax, and the Indian Muslims aligned themselves behind leaders who denied that India was in a territorial sense a nation, the suspicion was confirmed: having failed to oppose the national movement fairly and squarely, Britain was attempting to defeat Indian nationalism by the ancient device of the Trojan Horse, the enemy within the gates. But the real enemy remained Britain, and the motives behind any Englishman's denial of India's nationhood became even more suspect. Being aware of this background, is there any good purpose in an Englishman posing the question again, twenty years after Independence—and Partition—had settled the question for all time?

Perhaps not: but the onlooker remains uneasily aware that nations have to be created by the deliberate forging of a national consciousness. The most sublime assumption of nationhood is not enough unless it is reinforced by genuine nation-building. The Declaration of Independence in 1776 satisfied Americans for eighty years: but then came the greatest fission in a nation-state which has ever occurred. The issue which brought this division to breaking-point—the role of the African slave, the Negro, in the United States—remains a cause of division still, one hundred years later. Some nations never succeed completely in creating a genuine overall national consciousness. Unity is preserved not through internal cohesion but merely through fear of the conse-

---

that there are many races in India, and that some of the most important differences between those races . . . are not such as can be obliterated by education. He is told . . . that the representative system . . . will never be suitable for India and therefore he remains un-easily responsible for the permanent autocratic government of three hundred million people. Even Arnold Toynbee asks in *A Study of History* (abridged ed., London, Oxford University Press, 1947), p. 463: 'Were the Gurkha mercenaries and Pathan raiders of that day [he speaks of 1930] marked out to be remembered in history as the fathers and grandfathers of barbarian conquerors who were to carve out on the plains of Hindustan the successor-state of the British Raj?'

quences of succumbing to external pressures. It may be an over-statement to suggest that the language divisions within Canada and Belgium never lead to total disruption merely because fear of being swallowed by a powerful external neighbour is greater than incompatibility with one's internal opponent: but it is hard to detect much positive sense of identity between French- and English-speaking Canadians, or even between French- and Dutch-speaking Belgians. Will India be content with a unity which is preserved only because of fear or dislike of external neighbours who threaten? This could be the situation if the sublime assumption of nationhood were accepted as a substitute for genuine nation-building.

Leading Indians are aware that nations do not just emerge because of words, but only through deeds. Let us listen to C. S. Venkatachar, formerly Secretary to the President of India, and India's High Commissioner in Canada, a scholarly official with a singularly detached and internationalist point of view. He holds that 'India is still a nation in the making', and he sees the process of integrating the separate regional groups as going on through 'the nationalist idea':

India, or for that matter, any new country, is not a territorial national society in a sense that the people in the West understand it. They are in the process of evolving themselves into a territorial national society. Where we are not able to integrate the various groups, which nationalism sternly demands, the result is a divisive force, as for example the case of Muslim minorities in India who did not agree to integrate themselves, so we had to agree to the creation of Pakistan . . . Nationalism can be a divisive force, but it can also be a great integrating force in the plural societies of cultural groups which exist in India and other Asian countries.[3]

The diagnosis of Jayaprakash Narayan, one-time militant nationalist, now Gandhian social philosopher, follows a similar pattern:

Indian nationalism grew up as a reaction to aggressive British nationalism. But, unfortunately, it was not strong enough to weld together psychologically all the people of India into one nationality. The result was that almost on the eve of independence there arose a new concept of nationality that challenged the older one . . . A combination of factors conspired and India was partitioned.

Jayaprakash doubts whether a united India would have emerged in the modern world except through the experience of British rule:

Can it be said with any assurance that there would have been today a single national state in India, or at any rate, not more than two? Those who talk

---

[3] C. S. Venkatachar in Edgar McInnis (Ed.) *Democracy and National Development in India*, Toronto, Canada Institute of International Affairs, 1960, p. 11.

sentimentally about undivided India might give serious thought to this question . . . The history of Western Europe has shown that cultural unity does not necessarily lead to a single national state. So, while it is difficult to say with any assurance what would have happened if the British had not brought the whole of India under one government it is a sobering experience to realize that undivided India would have been perhaps one of the lesser possibilities.[4]

Jayaprakash goes on to suggest ways and means for 'building the national community' (in his own phrase). But most Indian intellectuals insist that the nation has already been built: their main concern is to insist upon the pre-eminent role of Indian nationalism among the new nations of the world today. Let us consider, almost at random, an expression of this viewpoint (which happens to be very recent) delivered from among the dreaming spires and ivory towers of Oxbridge and therefore imbued (we may suppose) with more than usual academic detachment:

It is generally conceded that the emergence of India is one of the major factors in the development of Afro-Asian nationalism. India was one of the first nations to gain freedom, the Indian movement for national freedom was one of the oldest and most experienced, and it was used as a model by many other nations of Africa and Asia.

Although the expressions 'nation', 'national', and 'nationalism' are used above so freely, it is difficult to determine in what sense they are employed. One page later some sort of explanation emerges:

The terms 'nation' and 'nationalism' have so much emotive force in them that they defeat any attempt to make a scientific definition. However, it is clear that nationalism is a name given to a movement of a group of people attempting to gain political freedom from the domination of another group of people for a territory which they consider to be their homeland.[5]

Dr. D. N. Mukherjee, the author of these passages, excludes one vital element from his analysis. In the Afro-Asian context the term 'nationalism' is only applied to a group of people attempting to gain political freedom from *white* domination. When those struggling for 'a territory which they consider to be their homeland' are struggling against Asians or Africans, then they are 'rebels' or 'reactionaries' or 'stooges in foreign pay'. This is a point to which we can return later; but even if we accept Dr. Mukherjee's view of what is a nation, this raises more difficulties than it offers solutions. The implication of this view of national-

---

[4] Jayaprakash Narayan, *Three Basic Problems of Free India*, Bombay, 1964, pp. 10–12.
[5] D. N. Mukherjee (Ed.), *South Asian Affairs: Number Two*, St. Antony's Papers. Number 18, London, 1966, pp. 10–11.

ism is that the struggle against colonialism or imperialism is the driving force of national unity; therefore it is necessary to project this struggle into the future in order to preserve unity. Such was the conclusion reached by President Sukarno in his long-drawn-out *Konfrontasi*, first against the Dutch, then against the British. Such, in a less hysterical vein, has been the view of spokesmen for India between the time of Suez and the war of September 1965 and its aftermath. But, as we observed earlier, this is not a positive basis for nation-building. To try to discover what kind of a national community India may become, we must examine the factors making for national unity from the remote past to the present.

India has inherited two elements of unity from the remote past; these are the geographical setting and the Hindu civilization. When Metternich observed that Italy was just a 'geographical expression', he was conceding more than he realized. The geographical unity of encircling mountains, northern plains, and peninsula thrusting down into the ocean created the setting for eventual Italian political unity. India is another Italy on an enormous scale. The northern mountains are not impenetrable; but even the scattered passes are closed except for brief months in summer, and India is effectively separated from the heartland of Asia. The northern plains, with their rivers, provide a great internal corridor of communication from Indus to Brahmaputra. The peninsula gives to India a great trading coastline which makes it possible for Indians under favourable conditions to claim the Indian Ocean as *mare nostrum*. Of course, there are formidable internal barriers within India. The Thar desert seals off the Indus basin from the rest of Northern India. The line of hills which follow the Vindhya and Satpura ranges, and which terminate in the *Maha-kantara*, the great wilderness, represents a no-man's-land between North and South. And the complex river system of Bengal separates the northern plains from the extreme east of India, where South-East Asia begins.[6] All these are significant barriers, but they do not serve to prohibit political, cultural, and economic intercourse.

What geography *does* stamp inevitably upon this setting is the factor of size. The old expression the 'subcontinent' is apt: India is a continental nation. We accept the United States as a continent stretching 'from sea to shining sea'. We ought to recognize China, Brazil, the

---

[6] The geographical divisions of India are analysed in A. Tayyeb, *Pakistan: A Political Geography*, London, Oxford University Press, 1966, Ch. 11, 'The Factors of Indian Unity and Disunity'.

U.S.S.R., and India as the family of continental nations. They are quite distinct and different from all other nations. Even today, distances in India dwarf human activity to insignificance. The writer recalls the incredible train journey between Calcutta and Peshawar. Even by the fastest train, the Frontier Mail, the journey took a night, and a day, and another night. All the time the pattern of human life imperceptibly changed—people, dress, villages, crops, countryside—took on different guises. And yet, until the train plunged north from Lahore and skirted the Salt Range Mountains, the traveller was conscious of passing among similar peoples, separated by enormous spatial intervals.

The second historic feature of Indian unity is the Hindu civilization. Toynbee has treated this as a fossil civilization, but Hinduism shows as great a capacity for evolutionary change as the other great world religions: Judaism, Buddhism, Christianity, and Islam. What specially distinguishes Hinduism from the other world religions—except Judaism —is its exclusive character. Hinduism is not a missionary religion, and its only overseas extension has been to Ceylon and tiny Bali. It may be true that the religion of South-East Asia is permeated with Hindu concepts, but the syncretic Buddhism or Muhammedanism which obtains in that area is as redolent of the spirit of South-East Asia as Hinduism is characteristic of India. In the words of Sir Charles Eliot, a scholar-official, 'Hinduism is not a religion which has moulded the national character, but the national character finding expression in religion'.[7] Rabindranath Tagore put this in more poetic style when he observed that the unity of India is a 'unity of spirit'. Hinduism is unique in being a major religion, in terms of its adherents, and in being virtually confined to the land of its origin. Hinduism has been remarkably successful in continuing to organize the whole life of the subcontinent on its own terms. For a brief while under Aurangzeb, and during the thirty years c. 1830–60, when Evangelical zeal predominated, attempts were made to impose alien creeds upon India. But Hinduism has demonstrated a capacity to liquidate those who would liquidate Hinduism, and to resurrect itself afresh, often with an extra dimension added from the faith of the would-be conqueror. In part this emerges from the philosophy of Hinduism; its emphasis upon consensus or holism which enables any creed to be absorbed into its labyrinthine logic. In part this resilience is due to caste, which appears to be a technique of social organization and communication capable of being adapted to every form of culture from that of the hunter-nomad to that of urban managerial technology. And so Nirad Chaudhuri observes:

[7] Quoted by Venkatachar, op. cit., p. 7.

'When I hear my foreign friends speak of "an Indian" or "Indians" I sometimes interrupt them breezily: "Please, please do not use that word. Say "Hindu" if you have in mind a human type common to the whole continent" . . .'[8]

To these two unifying factors, inherited from the past, the modern age has added three further sets of factors: a common struggle against foreign rule, a reaction against the separatist movement of the Indian Muslims which culminates in a condemnation of all 'communalism', and a commitment to the creation of a new system of government, democracy, and a new social order, introducing justice and 'fair shares' for all.

The struggle against foreign rule (which the quotations from Dr. D. N. Mukherjee emphasized as the basic common denominator of Afro-Asian nationalism) has not been a reliable instrument for creating Afro-Asian nations. In many cases the struggle was too brief and superficial to have any unifying effect. This has been generally true throughout Africa (the Congo being the most disastrous example of the consequences of independence without a struggle): only Egypt and Algeria genuinely fought the West for independence. In a few cases the struggle was too prolonged. Vietnam provides the most appalling example of a national movement which proved inadequate for a long-drawn-out resistance, so that nationalism succumbed to Communism.

India was fortunate in experiencing a national struggle which may be termed creative. The early nationalist leaders, the founding fathers of the Indian National Congress, regarded British rule as a manifestation of Divine Providence and, far from fighting Britain, adopted the techniques of political activity, together with a liberal political philosophy, from the ruling power.[9] When the national movement entered its activist phase, and under Gandhi's inspired leadership mobilized the support of the masses to demonstrate to the British that their time had run out, an important section of the national movement continued to

---

[8] N. C. Chaudhuri, *The Continent of Circe: An Essay on the Peoples of India*, London, Chatto and Windus, 1965, p. 34.

[9] An apt illustration of this attitude occurs in the quotation from the leading Madras newspaper, *The Hindu*, the spearhead of the Congress Movement and of social reform. Writing on 18 April 1887, the editor observed that British rule 'was doing more than any other that preceded it did, to develop the latent feeling of nationality existing among the people. The very fact of the different races of India, the Sikh, the Bengalees, the Mahrattas and the Dravidians being ruled by the same Government and imbibing the spirit of the same civilization, must act as a unifying force. English education has opened the eyes of the people and taught them to feel that they are a common nation, bound together by common interests. The Post, the Telegraph and Railways have done a great deal to give an active effect to this nascent feeling.' This quotation provides a striking contrast to the dictum of Sir John Strachey, voiced at the same time, which was quoted in the first footnote.

co-operate with the British in policy-making (thus ensuring continuity through the transfer of power), while, right to the end, the Indians operating the machinery of the state—the public services and the armed forces—continued to carry out the actual functioning of the British style of administration. The 'Freedom Struggle' was a struggle indeed for a mighty cross-section of the population, and the shared experience of mass demonstrations, police beatings, court proceedings, and jail sentences brought together upper-class barristers, middle-class school-teachers, and peasants in a common brotherhood. Because the move-ment was led by Gandhi, the emphasis upon humanity, upon the attainment of freedom through the inner liberation of men from the thraldom of their own circumstances, gave to participants—whatever their own private motives—a shared sense of a common inspiration. And yet, while the national spirit was kindled by the Freedom Struggle, the essential work of creating what were then called the 'nation-building' departments was going on—under British control, but largely implemented by Indians who saw their patriotic duty in *naukari*, ser-vice to the state, as their forefathers had done under the Mughals and under the East India Company.

The obverse of the forward-looking nationalist movement was the assertion of sectional rights and privileges derived from looking back to the past. Communalism, the derivation of one's political commitment from one's religious background, is a phenomenon encountered in all the continents. Perhaps because in India the inflexible authority of Islam is confronted by the opaque authority of the Hindu caste system, communalism has assumed a frightening intensity. Forward-looking Hindus and forward-looking Muslims seemed able to bridge the gap of religion during the decade 1910–20, and even for some years later. But pressure from Islamic zealots who insisted that the only brother-hood is the brotherhood of believers, combined with pressure from Hindu zealots who insisted that anything foreign, anything not Hindu, must be eliminated from the new India, combined to turn the forward-looking Muslims away from co-operation to a policy of separation. We need not pursue the familiar story of the evolution of the Pakistan demand. One important consequence of this Islamic counter-attack was to discredit religion in politics and to elevate the ideal of the secular state.[10] We shall have to examine how far Hinduism has succeeded in undermining the secular concept in recent years: but certainly the immediate effect was to exclude any overt reference to Hinduism in

[10] See D.E. Smith, *India as a Secular State*, Princeton, N.J., Princeton University Press, 1963, especially Ch. V, 'The Theory of Indian Nationalism'.

the Indian Constitution and to emphasize the importance of freedom of religion.

Finally, Congress governments throughout the states of India have all subscribed to 'the socialist pattern of society', which, in principle, is intended to ensure that 'the benefits of economic development must accrue more and more to the relatively less privileged classes of society'. In order to bring this about 'the state has to take heavy responsibilities as the principal agency speaking for and acting on behalf of the community as a whole'. The goal—a society in which wealth is distributed according to the principle of social justice, irrespective of group or region—and the means to the goal—a centralized state, organized to articulate social and economic functions—are clearly powerful forces towards the consolidation of a national community.

Four factors have been present in India since Independence to assist towards the realization of the goal of democracy and social justice: a venerated national leader, a national political party, a national bureaucracy, and a national army. It is difficult to recall any other new nation which has had the advantage of all these four supports in the task of national consolidation.

Few other statesmen could have supplied as many kinds of leadership as did Nehru. He had the traditional prestige of a Brahmin pandit. He had the glamour of the outstanding 'Freedom Fighter'. To the intellectuals he spoke in tones of Delphic profundity. To the masses he spoke like a prince and a father. Although lacking some of the qualities of an administrator, he apprehended the needs of the planned economy with more prescience than any other contemporary politician. Even his enemies could never accuse him of thinking in any but national terms; caste, creed, town, tongue—none of these loyalties meant anything to him; it was India first and India last.

This leadership was sustained by the backing of the Congress Party: the one party machine in 'free' Asia which is organized to link together the Central Government and the rural district, not merely at times of General Elections, but throughout every day of the year. Its organization, tested by the campaigns against British imperialism, and developed to cope with the largest electorate in the world, is designed to meet the needs of a continent. After the death of Nehru—and, even more, after the sudden death of his successor, Lal Bahadur Shastri— the Congress Party demonstrated the capacity to resolve a situation requiring wide consultation combined with firm decision. No country can rely upon discovering a great national leader more than once in a century: but given this remarkable party political organization, India may expect to carry on through the years when great men are lacking.

The third instrument of national consolidation in India is an elite public service, the heir to the old Indian Civil Service. Small in numbers—the administrative aristocrats still number only some two thousand—selected by open competition, and reflecting no kind of regional or communal quota system, these men are still the 'steel frame' upon which India's nation-wide stability and development chiefly depend. So long as India continues upon the road of a planned economy, these aristocrats will have a fundamental role to play; and all their efforts will be directed towards fostering unity throughout the land.

Under British rule the army was genuinely intercommunal, despite its organization upon the basis of caste and religion, with emphasis upon the *kshatriya* or warrior tradition of the 'martial races' of North India. Before Independence, Congress leaders had termed this an army of mercenaries and insisted that India did not require such a massive military machine for its defence. However, tentative plans for reductions in the armed forces were soon halted as events in Kashmir, Hyderabad, and Goa and on the border with Tibet, demonstrated how vital the army was to India's national interests. The regimental traditions preserved for a hundred years or more assumed a new significance, and the *jawan*, the enlisted man, became an honoured symbol of India's determination to preserve national security. When war with Pakistan came in September 1965, and the armed forces stoutly battled for the nation's cause, enthusiasm for the Sikh, the Rajput, and the Gurkha, as fighters for India, created an emotional bond bringing together the middle classes and the mass, the city and the countryside.

These, then, are the main foundations of an Indian nation. But like all foundations, they must be maintained with care to ensure that they never crumble. The factor of size, as a feature of the geographical unity of India, ought to be candidly examined. Even a country so uniform and conformist as the United States acknowledges the importance of regionalism. India, with its thousands of years of history, ought even more to understand the power of regional loyalties. It ought to be possible to be a Tamil or a Maratha and to give full expression to this loyalty without finding this in any sense incompatible with being a citizen of India. Doubtless the Indian genius can achieve this synthesis, but even more understanding and adjustment will be required in solving the problems posed by the fringe peoples who dwell upon the mountain rim of the subcontinent. Peoples seem to acquire a recognized political personality only when they achieve a literary culture and a religion chronicled in books. Nepal, Bhutan, and Sikkim all have a written culture and each has succeeded in acquiring a status compatible with its overall size. Nepal, a country of 10 million souls, has obtained complete, formal independence. Bhutan, with about a half a million population, has internal autonomy; but accepts a wide measure of Indian control over its external relations. Sikkim's total population numbers less than 200,000 and the state has to accept a good deal of internal supervision by India.

In each case, these Himalayan kingdoms had to resist attempts by India to bring them completely into the Indian orbit, and a considerable degree of bitterness about 'Indian imperialism' exists, to form the basis for a Nepalese, Bhutanese, and Sikkimese sense of individuality. To apply the term 'nationalism' to this feeling may seem to be excessive; but, in effect, this is what it amounts to. Where India has encountered border tribes possessing only an oral tradition and a localized, animist religion—outside the recognized sphere of political personality —these tribes have been not so much enlisted as conscripted into the Indian nation. Some have resisted: the resistance of the Nagas and the Lushai people has reached the point of open war. But the undifferentiated theory of Indian nationalism cannot acknowledge these as national revolts; they must be suppressed as acts of treason.

The unifying power of Hinduism as the expression of the national character has also revealed divisive qualities when asserted in a sectarian manner. Within the philosophy of Hinduism which manifests itself as the spirit of tolerance and of consensus, it was perfectly easy for a secularist agnostic such as Nehru to call himself a Hindu.[11] But the zealots could not be satisfied with such a broad formulation of Hinduism, and they prepared the counter-attack. In the early days, when the murder of Gandhi had discredited the Hindu extremists, they proceeded cautiously. They succeeded in inserting among the directive principles of the Constitution clauses advocating the prohibition of cow slaughter and the use of intoxicating liquor, both practices being repugnant to high-caste Hindus. But the cow-slaughter condition was disguised as a measure for improved animal husbandry, and prohibition of drink as a measure of social reform.[12] Similarly, the contest over the proposed

[11] Sardar Patel, Home Minister after Independence, who was suspicious of the role of the Muslims in the nationalist movement, once said that the only nationalist Muslim he knew was Jawaharlal Nehru.

[12] See Ved Prakash Luthera, *The Concept of the Secular State and India*, London, Oxford University Press, 1964, Ch. XI, 'Cow Protection and Constitutional Provision'.

national language—whether it should be intercommunal Hindustani (as advocated by Gandhi and Nehru) or communal Hindi—had religious overtones. The Hindi fanatics emerged as champions of a Hindi almost unrecognizable because of its total Sanskritization, Sanskrit, of course, being the sacred language of Hinduism. An attempt to substitute the Hindu Nagari numerical symbols for the international or Arabic numerals was only narrowly defeated.[13] Subsequently, legislation was introduced in almost every state of the Union placing a ban on cow slaughter and on the sale of alcohol: measures which affected Muslims and the lowly castes of Hindus respectively.

When the agitation for states representing linguistic boundaries reached its climax in the 1950s, the demand was rapidly conceded in all but two cases. A new pattern of states was drawn in 1956. An attempt was made to maintain Bombay as a bilingual state, but this was abandoned after four years, and Gujarat and Maharashtra came into being. Only one language demand was steadily resisted, being acceded to only in 1966: the demand for a Panjabi-speaking state to be carved out of the bilingual Panjab. The persistent refusal of the Central Government to consider the claims of *Panjabi Suba* was motivated in greater part by a refusal to countenance the emergence of a state with a non-Hindu majority. The agitation was, in effect, a demand for a Sikh state, as Master Tara Singh admitted when he stated: 'We know that a genuinely Panjabi-speaking state will be such that the Sikh religion will be safe in it.' All this was resisted, until the September war with Pakistan highlighted the urgency of satisfying the Sikhs, a key element in the Indian Army.

If the secular state in India becomes a façade for Hindu domination, the minorities may come to feel (as they certainly did not feel in the early years after Independence) that they are second-class citizens. In particular, the condition of the Muslims, always somewhat equivocal, will become one of subjugation or alienation. As Jayaprakash observes, 'the partitition of India would appear to have been a clumsy device that settled nothing and satisfied none'.[14] The 45 million Muslims in India, and the 10 million Hindus in Pakistan, who remain after the mass exchange of populations are communities on probation. Some outstanding Muslims continued firm in their allegiance to the national movement during the critical years 1940–7: they have been honoured and rewarded. Among the rising generation of Muslims a few—a tiny few—have made their way to the front on intellectual merit alone. A larger number

[13] Granville Austin, *The Indian Constitution: Cornerstone of a Nation*, Oxford, Clarendon Press, 1966, p. 294.
[14] Narayan, op. cit., p. 11.

(especially among the commercial families of Muslims on the Bombay side) feel no division of loyalties, and are welcomed into public life as examples (much needed in the Middle East) of the bona fides of India's secular policy. But the great majority of the Muslim community find no place in politics or administration, and penetrate only with difficulty into the outer circle of commerce. A Muslim writer who ardently identifies with Indian nationalism still feels compelled to pose the question: 'All Muslims have to ask themselves whether or not loyalty to the nation is prior to and more important than the loyalty which they owe to religion.'[15]

The modern aspects of Indian nationalism are also not without their dangers. The projection of the 'freedom struggle' against Britain into the present and future may have only minor consequences. India does not appear to set much store by the British connexion; relations with the United States are much more vital. But the nourishment of legendary enmities has had disastrous consequences in the feud with Pakistan. It should be admitted that the war with Pakistan produced a greater sense of national unity in India than at any time after independence. But the strain upon the Indian Muslim community in convincing others of their undivided loyalty to India must have created a trauma which only the years will reveal. Also, the cult of militarism, the cult of the soldier, which the war fostered has opened up again that emphasis upon regimentation and force which in the past led to the successes of Subhas Chandra Bose. It is noticeable that 'Netaji', once a hero only to the Bengalis, is now with Gandhi and Nehru one of the trinity of all-India heroes. All this suggests that if ever again one man succeeds in acquiring all-India leadership he may attain this status through an appeal to chauvinism and violence.

The previous importance of certain 'nation-building' forces in governance and politics—charismatic leadership, the mass party, the all-India bureaucracy, the Indian Army—implies the necessity to maintain the momentum of these forces if nation-building is to develop further. It seems extremely doubtful that an all-India leadership will be seen again, unless the politicians have the vision to choose a leader from beyond the recognized political establishment. Once before, Gandhi was accepted as leader when his early accomplishments had taken place in far-away South Africa. It seems highly unlikely that another such leader will be sought for: even though, in Jayaprakash

---

[15] S. Abid Husain, *The Destiny of Indian Muslims*, London, Asia Publishing House, 1965, p. 195.

Narayan, such a leader can be discerned. How far will the mass party endure? Certainly for many years yet the Congress will dominate the scene, preserving its own methods of articulating politics. But the food crisis during late 1965 and early 1966 has demonstrated that state governments will respond to a national crisis in regional terms when the crisis is internal and not external to India. The work of Paul Brass has indicated how far Congress state politics is now dedicated entirely to 'politicking': to a struggle in which the only question is who will succeed as the fixer, who will find himself fixed?[16] The politics of manipulation may maintain the Congress in power in individual states: but it will certainly lead to a weakening of that nation-wide sense of purpose which was its strength in its great days. Finally, the directing influence exercised by the Indian Administrative Service and the other all-India services cannot long be perpetuated in the new situation in which power and influence passes more every day to those who can command the backing of strategic sections of the electorate. The mandarin concept was well adapted to the old hierarchical society; it coexists most uneasily with today's locally based political power systems. Probably within a decade we shall see the bureaucracy divided between central services, focused upon New Delhi as the stage for their career prospects, and state officials, whose horizon is bounded by a region and a regional language. The old tradition of posting a Madrassi administrator to the U.P. and a Bengali to Bombay has already atrophied. The all-India flavour of Indian higher administration cannot endure much more than a decade.

Then the armed forces will remain the only institution operating upon an India-wide basis. When military rule is such a feature of the newly emergent countries, if the Indian Army becomes the sole guardian of the nation, this may present its own dilemma. Moreover, the army of today is remarkably like the army of yesterday in its heavy emphasis upon the 'martial races' of Northern India. The South, the Central, and the Eastern regions are represented only in small numbers, and mainly in the technical and ancillary services. The Muslims, who formed one-third of the old Indian Army, are sparingly accepted.

An army approaching one million men under arms; an army overwhelmingly recruited from the peasantry of the North. The implications of such an army are mitigated by the composition of the officer corps: middle-class, drawn from almost every state in the Union,

[16] See P. R. Brass, *Factional Politics in an Indian State; the Congress Party in Uttar Pradesh*, Berkeley, University of California Press, 1965, especially Ch. III, 'The Congress Party in Uttar Pradesh: the Growth of Factional Conflict'.

conscious of their role as professional soldiers, not powermakers or breakers. Much depends upon the constancy of this officer corps in the years ahead.

If the nation-building forces are, as this analysis suggests, in the balance—what further development can be envisaged to strengthen the Indian nation? One method might be to carry still further the process of centralization which was the main feature of the Patel-Nehru period of India's post-Independence integration. There is nothing in the Indian Constitution to restrict a steady erosion of state activity, and a takeover by the centre of state functions, in part or in whole. The emergency provisions of the Constitution have already permitted the President to intervene upon seven occasions and impose presidential rule upon the states. Observed an influential member of the Constituent Assembly, K. M. Munshi: 'There is no provincial [state] autonomy, there is no federation by and for itself, these are not sacrosanct words.'[17]

But if, legally and constitutionally, it would be possible to strengthen the centre and reverse the centrifugal trend, in practice it would lead the Union straight into trouble. Immediately after Independence, the Premier of Uttar Pradesh (the state closest to the Congress high command) warned Nehru: 'If it is hoped that the provinces can be made to co-operate against their own will by means of central legislation, that hope is not likely to materialize.'[18] If further centralization would have political reactions, its economic effects are likely to be even more disastrous. Already excessive centralization in planning and development has brought the Indian economy to a condition not far from deadlock.[19]

If centralization is unlikely to provide the answer, perhaps it can be achieved by the introduction of an ethos, an ideology which will emphasize oneness and unity. This, presumably, was the intention of those who tried to foster Hindi as the national language. However, by treating Hindi not as a medium for widening understanding but as a means for bringing back pure Sanskrit—thus actually making communication more difficult—the national-language enthusiasts provoked a countermovement whose consequences still cannot be fully assessed.[20] When the time came for a final decision to be taken on the national language,

[17] Granville Austin, op. cit., p. 216.

[18] Granville Austin, op. cit., p. 201.

[19] See A. H. Hanson, *The Process of Planning: A Study of India's Five Year Plans 1950–1964*, London, Oxford University Press, 1966: 'Regionalization of the planning process is inevitable' (p. 311).

[20] When Nehru received a Hindi translation of the Constitution he wrote to Rajendra Prasad 'that he did not understand a word of it'. Granville Austin, op. cit., p. 282.

after the interim period allowed under the Constitution had elapsed, the then Prime Minister, Lal Bahadur Shastri, sadly underestimated the strength of the opposition to Hindi. Attempting too simple a solution, he unintentionally provoked popular protest movements which, in the South, reached a situation where martyrs were sacrificing their lives to demonstrate the total unacceptability of Hindi. Mr. Shastri was driven to accept as a compromise perhaps the least satisfactory formula put forward, whereby the role of the regional languages gained considerably greater recognition. Once again, it was demonstrated that India's commitment to undertake change by voluntary methods through the choice of the people precludes any form of advancement by imposition of the will of the centre. As a result of the misplaced zeal of the Hindi fanatics, the possibility of the natural growth of a national language has now been put back for decades, and perhaps for ever.

There remains one method, so far untried, whereby India might attain a form of national identity appropriate to the unique character of the Indic civilization. One speaker in the national language debate, S. P. Mookerjee, revealed the essential nature of the situation:

If it is claimed by anyone that by passing an article in the Constitution of India one language is going to be accepted by all by a process of coercion ... that will not be possible to achieve. Unity in diversity is India's keynote and must be achieved by a process of understanding and consent and for that a proper atmosphere has to be created.[21]

One who always understood the implications of 'unity in diversity' was Gandhi. Having a firm faith in the unity of India, he had a vision of a land of 500,000 villages in which dwelt millions of individual souls. Himself a Gujarati, his first political activity was an investigation of a small local grievance a thousand miles away in Champaran District of Bihar. He chose to make his headquarters at Segaon, a village eleven miles from Wardha, right in the centre of India. When he was asked what his purpose was in living in this rural retreat he replied: 'I am here to serve no one but myself; to find my own self-realization through the service of these village folk.' He propounded the equation: 'Real self-government is self-rule or self-control.' The nation is seen as a series of ever-widening circles, beginning with the individual, merging into the village, the district, the region, the country, India. Gandhi expressed his politics in terms of Hinduism, because this was the mode of thinking natural to the peasant masses. But his Hinduism was all-embracing. His prayer meetings were always prefaced by hymn-

21 Granville Austin, op. cit., p. 303.

singing—usually such Christian hymns as 'Lead Kindly Light'—and included among the scripture readings frequent texts from the Quran and the Bible. His greatest mission was the redemption of the untouchables, those excluded for 2,000 years from contact with the caste Hindus.

Gandhi's programme for a free India has often been caricatured as a federation of village republics. But, as his interpreter Jayaprakash Narayan has explained, a Gandhian India would envisage the creation of a network of government by consultation and co-operation at all levels from the village to the nation's capital. The impulse would come from below, but the overall framework would be that of all-India. Almost nothing of the Gandhian idea was incorporated into post-Independence India; as Jayaprakash observes: 'If you consider the political ideologies obtaining in India today, you would find that somehow one who is called the Father of the Nation is completely missing from all of them.'[22]

The Gandhian approach would solve the problem of national loyalty. There would be no conflict between the Muslim, Sikh, or Christian identification and the Indian identification. There would be no confusion between being a Tamil- or a Telugu-speaker, and being an Indian. On a small scale, this dual loyalty has emerged in Britain. With a few exceptions, it is possible to be a Welshman or a Scot and also a loyal subject of the United Kingdom. The two loyalties are different, but not in conflict. If things had turned out differently, it might have been possible to extend this loyalty into a Commonwealth citizenship. The possibility of a nationalism reaching towards internationalism was envisaged by Gandhi:

Just as the cult of patriotism teaches us today that the individual has to die for the family, the family has to die for the village, the village for the district, the district for the province and the province for the country, even so a country has to be free in order that it may die, if necessary, for the benefit of the world. My idea of nationalism, therefore, is that my country may become free, that if need be, the whole country may die, so that the human race may live.[23]

A sober attempt to assess the future of Indian nationalism cannot end with the pious hope that the Gandhian dream will be realized. The history of the world is a record of men's failure to grasp that it is the ideal which is truly practical; the realistic is always inadequate for the reality of tomorrow. Will the Indian nation gradually dissolve, then?

[22] Narayan, op. cit., p. 18.
[23] Quoted by Husain, op. cit., p. 202.

This is certainly not the conclusion which this analysis appears to suggest. India will survive, and a feeling of nationhood will grow. But some will feel alienated in their own land, 'strangers in India', and more will feel frustrated in their desire to identify with the nation and with their own mother-tongue, 'their own folk'. If the Indian genius is to play its full part, then a truly Indian form of nationalism—which we may call 'graduated nationalism'—must evolve.

Note:

These thoughts were composed in the middle of 1966. The general election of February 1967 appears to add urgency to the argument. The Congress Party survives as the only fully articulated national political organization. But its standing is diminished, and a number of its prominent figures have been rejected at the polls. The extreme south of India—Madras and Kerala—have overthrown the Congress and signified their determination to withstand any attempt by the centre to impose its power. The emergence of the Jana Sangha as the main expression of the political feeling of the big cities of the north represents the 'Aryan', Sanskritic voice of the Hindi heartland; in its own way, just as much a regional movement as the Dravidian revolt of the south. These are warning signals to those who have operated the boss-politics of the Congress, preoccupied with securing supreme power at New Delhi, and with securing a big slice of the development funds dispensed from New Delhi. The peoples of India have discovered that they pull back power into their own hands. Dynamic leadership in India now depends upon new forms of political wisdom and flair which are quite distinct from the leadership of the 'Freedom Struggle', or of the supreme command of the Nehru era. A new era requires new leaders who can reconcile regionalism and nationalism, not by manipulation, 'fixing', but through interpreting the will of the people.

Index